Language Variation

Editors: John Nerbonne, Dirk Geeraerts

In this series:

1. Côté, Marie-Hélène, Remco Knooihuizen and John Nerbonne (eds.). The future of dialects.

The future of dialects

Selected papers from
Methods in Dialectology XV

Edited by

Marie-Hélène Côté
Remco Knooihuizen
John Nerbonne

Marie-Hélène Côté, Remco Knooihuizen & John Nerbonne (eds.). 2016. *The future of dialects: Selected papers from Methods in Dialectology XV* (Language Variation 1). Berlin: Language Science Press.

This title can be downloaded at:
http://langsci-press.org/catalog/book/81
© 2016, the authors
Published under the Creative Commons Attribution 4.0 Licence (CC BY 4.0):
http://creativecommons.org/licenses/by/4.0/
ISBN: 978-3-946234-18-0 (Digital)
978-3-946234-19-7 (Hardcover)
978-3-946234-20-3 (Softcover)
978-1-523743-18-6 (Softcover US)
DOI:10.17169/langsci.b81.78

Cover and concept of design: Ulrike Harbort
Typesetting: Remco Knooihuizen, Felix Kopecky, John Nerbonne, Sebastian Nordhoff, Oscar Strik
Illustration: The authors, Adam Liter, Sebastian Nordhoff
Proofreading: Željko Agić, Mario Bisiada, Alireza Dehbozorgi, Carola Fanselow, Martin Haspelmath, Andreas Hölzl, John Judge, Felix Kopecky, Sebastian Nordhoff, Mathias Schenner, Alec Shaw, Debora Siller, Benedikt Singpiel
Fonts: Linux Libertine, Arimo, DejaVu Sans Mono
Typesetting software: X∃LATEX

Language Science Press
Habelschwerdter Allee 45
14195 Berlin, Germany
langsci-press.org
Storage and cataloguing done by FU Berlin

Language Science Press has no responsibility for the persistence or accuracy of URLs for external or third-party Internet websites referred to in this publication, and does not guarantee that any content on such websites is, or will remain, accurate or appropriate.

Contents

1	**Embracing the future of dialects** Marie-Hélène Côté, Remco Knooihuizen & John Nerbonne	1

I The future

2	**Heritage languages as new dialects** Naomi Nagy	15
3	**From diglossia to diaglossia: A West Flemish case-study** Anne-Sophie Ghyselen	35
4	**The future of Catalan dialects' syntax: A case study for a methodological contribution** Ares Llop Naya	63

II Methods

5	**Fuzzy dialect areas and prototype theory: Discovering latent patterns in geolinguistic variation** Simon Pickl	75
6	**On the problem of field worker isoglosses** Andrea Mathussek	99
7	**Tracking linguistic features underlying lexical variation patterns: A case study on Tuscan dialects** Simonetta Montemagni & Martijn Wieling	117
8	**A new dialectometric approach applied to the Breton language** Guylaine Brun-Trigaud, Tanguy Solliec & Jean Le Dû	135

Contents

9   Automatically identifying characteristic features of non-native English accents
Jelke Bloem, Martijn Wieling & John Nerbonne 155

10 Mapping the perception of linguistic form: Dialectometry with perceptual data
Tyler Kendall, Valerie Fridland 173

11 Horizontal and vertical variation in Swiss German morphosyntax
Philipp Stoeckle 195

12 Infrequent forms: Noise or not?
Martijn Wieling & Simonetta Montemagni 215

13 Top-down and bottom-up advances in corpus-based dialectometry
Christoph Wolk & Benedikt Szmrecsanyi 225

14 Imitating closely related varieties
Lea Schäfer, Stephanie Leser & Michael Cysouw 245

15 Spontaneous dubbing as a tool for eliciting linguistic data: The case of second person plural inflections in Andalusian Spanish
Víctor Lara Bermejo 261

16 Dialect levelling and changes in semiotic space
Ivana Škevin 281

17 Code-switching in the Anglophone community in Japan
Keiko Hirano 305

18 Tongue trajectories in North American English /æ/ tensing
Christopher Carignan, Jeff Mielke & Robin Dodsworth 313

19 s-retraction in Italian-Tyrolean bilingual speakers: A preliminary investigation using the ultrasound tongue imaging technique
Lorenzo Spreafico 321

III Japanese dialectology

20 Developing the Linguistic Atlas of Japan Database and advancing analysis of geographical distributions of dialects
Yasuo Kumagai   333

21 Tracing real and apparent time language changes by comparing linguistic maps
Chitsuko Fukushima   363

22 Timespan comparison of dialectal distributions
Takuichiro Onishi   377

23 Tonal variation in Kagoshima Japanese and factors of language change
Ichiro Ota, Hitoshi Nikaido & Akira Utsugi   389

Indexes

Name index   399

Language index   406

Subject index   407

Chapter 1

Embracing the future of dialects

Marie-Hélène Côté
Université Laval

Remco Knooihuizen
University of Groningen

John Nerbonne
University of Groningen, University of Freiburg

> The conference Methods in Dialectology XV was held in Groningen on 11–15 August 2014. In October 2014 we issued a call for a contribution to a volume of proceedings, which led to a gratifying number of excellent reactions. This brief introduction tells a bit more about the conference and provides some orientation to the papers in the volume.

1 The conference

The conference was the fifteenth in the series *Methods in Dialectology*, which started in 1972. It has "generally alternated between Europe and Canada".[1] Following its predecessors, Methods XV issued a broad call for contributions to the conference, emphasizing that areal, social and historical perspectives have all been regarded as tributaries to the discipline of variationist linguistics at least since Chambers and Trudgill's programmatic work (Chambers & Trudgill 1980, Chambers & Trudgill 1998: Chapter 12).[2] Shortly after the conference (in September 2014) we issued a call for papers for this volume among those who presented at Methods XV. We asked for the usual length conference papers, but we also allowed the submission of brief papers (in this volume, papers of six to ten pages).

---

[1] Methods and Methods 14, http://westernlinguistics.ca/methods14/methods_14.html, consulted 20 April 2015.
[2] See Kleiner (2014) for an independent report on Methods XV.

Marie-Hélène Côté, Remco Knooihuizen & John Nerbonne. 2016. Embracing the future of dialects. In Marie-Hélène Côté, Remco Knooihuizen & John Nerbonne (eds.), *The future of dialects*, 1–12. Berlin: Language Science Press. DOI:10.17169/langsci.b81.80

Marie-Hélène Côté, Remco Knooihuizen & John Nerbonne

The conference featured five plenary lectures. Jacob Eisenstein of the Georgia Institute of Technology talked on "Dialectal variation in online social media", and Frans Gregersen of the University of Copenhagen, delivered a lectured entitled "A matter of scale only?" on the different temporal scales analyzed in variationist linguistics on the one hand and historical linguistics on the other. Mark Liberman of the University of Pennsylvania sketched new technical possibilities for collecting and analyzing linguistic data automatically in a lecture entitled "The dialectology of the future", Naomi Nagy of the University of Toronto presented her research on "Heritage languages as new dialects", and Brigitte Pakendorf of the Université Lyon 2 "Lumière" spoke on "Dialectal variation and population genetics in Siberia". A tutorial on Gabmap (Nerbonne et al. 2011) was given by Wilbert Heeringa and Therese Leinonen, while a workshop on integrating perceptual dialectology and sociolinguistics with geographic information systems was organized by Lisa Jeon, Patricia Cukor-Avila, Chris Montgomery and Patricia Rektor. Special sessions on various topics were organized, including one on open access publishing by Martin Haspelmath of Language Science Press. There were 140 single-paper presentations during four-and-a-half days.

The organizers of the conference were especially happy to include – we think for the first time – a poster session consisting of fourteen posters, two of which were awarded prizes named after Lisa Lena Opas-Hänninen, a frequent participant at Methods, and co-organizer of Methods XI in Joensuu, Finland in 2002. These poster prizes for young scholars were generously funded by the Alliance for Digital Humanities Organizations, and papers by both recipients may be found in this volume, "Imitations of closely related varieties" by Lea Schäfer, Stephanie Leser and Michael Cysouw, and "Infrequent Forms: Noise or not?" by Martijn Wieling and Simonetta Montemagni.

Cambridge University Press generously offered to underwrite two prizes for best papers by young scholars. The "Chambers prizes" are named after Jack Chambers, one of the most prominent figures in variationist linguistics of the last half century, and a source of energy, wisdom and inspiration for the *Methods* series. These papers are also included in the volume, namely Anne-Sophie Ghyselen's "Structure of diaglossic language repertoires: Stabilization of Flemish *tussentaal*?" and Simon Pickl's "Fuzzy dialect areas and prototype theory. Discovering latent structures in geolinguistic variation".

2 The papers

2.1 Dialects' Future

Traditional, geographically defined dialects are losing ground, in particular to standard languages in Europe. Naomi Nagy's paper "Heritage languages as new dialects" examines the speech of Cantonese, Faetar, Italian, Korean, Russian and Ukrainian immigrants to Canada from a perspective complementary to the usual European one (Auer, Hinskens & Kerswill 2004), where we see basilectal varieties being eroded under the influence of standard speech, but one which Trudgill (2004) has pursued in depth. In contrast to the "intimate contact" between dialect and standard in Europe, Nagy emphasizes the need to incorporate methods and perspectives from the study of language contact (Hickey 2010). She points to evidence of diversion from varieties in native countries and, true to the focus of *Methods* conferences, devotes the lion's share of her paper to the presentation of methods in use in a large Toronto project.

In fact the erosion of very specific varieties has given rise to the study of "regiolects" (Auer & Hinskens 1996) – forms of speech intermediate between the basilectal varieties of a village or small town and standard languages, typically used in national communications such as radio and television. As Auer (2005: 22) noted, the forms of speech may not be homogeneous and stable enough to deserve the name "variety". Anne-Sophie Ghyselen's prize-winning paper on Belgian Dutch *tussentaal* examines how stable this intermediate form of speech has become, concluding that tussentaal is too heterogeneous and unstable to be regarded as a variety, just as Lenz (2003) concluded for regional forms used in the Eifel.

2.2 Methodological contributions

2.2.1 Dialectometry

Dialect "areas" constituted the standard means of presentation of dialectological wisdom about the influence of geography of variation for many decades even if it was recognized that continua were also to be found in the data, and that areas, when found, were often delimited by vague borders. Simon Pickl's prize-winning paper "Fuzzy dialect areas and prototype theory. Discovering latent structures in geolinguistic variation" suggests that it is time to eschew dialectometric techniques such as clustering, which always yields sharp partitions among data collection sites, in favor of techniques such as factor analysis, which give rises to areas with "fuzzy" borders. He links these ideas to prototype theory in cognitive science and Berruto's notion of "condensation areas".

Andrea Mathussek examines "the problem of field worker isoglosses" as she encounters these in the *Sprachatlas von Mittelfranken* ('Dialect Atlas of Middle Franconia', SMF, Munske & Mathussek 2013). Mathussek emphasizes that the field workers were aware of the potential problems and actively took measures to try to avoid idiosyncrasies in transcription, e.g. transcribing the same data as an exercise and then comparing the results, but differences remained. Mathussek used the web application Gabmap (Nerbonne et al. 2011), which is based on dialectometric techniques, to show that the field worker effects persisted even into aggregate levels of comparison. It was crucial for tracking the effects that Gabmap supports the identification of characteristic elements of clusters (Prokić, Çöltekin & Nerbonne 2012).

Simonetta Montemagni and Martijn Wieling focus on lexical dialectology and apply an alternative calculation for identifying characteristic features in "Tracking linguistic features underlying lexical variation patterns: A case study on Tuscan dialects", namely one based on graph theory (Wieling & Nerbonne 2011). They note that dialectometry identifies groups similar to those in traditional Tuscan dialectology, but go on to identify which words are most characteristic, introducing *en passant* the innovation in combining the measures of how representative and how distinctive features are. They combine not additively, as earlier work had, but multiplicatively, effectively ensuring that only features that score highly on both components are regarded as characteristic. Montemagni and Wieling also attend to age differences in their analyses.

Jelke Bloem, Martijn Wieling and John Nerbonne apply a technique developed in dialectometry, namely a quantitative measure of how characteristic a speech trait is, to a non-dialectological problem, namely automatically identifying characteristic features of non-native English accents, in their paper of the same title. It has long been recognized that there are parallels between traditional dialects and socially delimited varieties on the one hand and contact varieties on the other (Trudgill 1986), but the authors likewise claim that the introduction of dialectometric techniques into the study of foreign accents may improve the latter by providing aggregate perspectives in an area that has largely relied on the study of a small number of phenomena.

Tyler Kendall and Valerie Fridland's "Mapping the perception of linguistic form: Dialectometry with perceptual data" proposes a collaboration between two of the most innovative strands within modern variationist linguistics, namely perceptual phonetics and dialectometry. They focus on the varying boundaries of vowel perception within the US and examine inter alia the relation between perception and production boundaries. Given perceptual dialectology's standard attention to social factors (Niedzielski 1999), their collaboration also entails understanding how dialectometry and sociolinguistics might join forces, an areas which has received too little attention thus far (Nerbonne et al. 2013). On the dialectometric side they make extensive use of the geo-statistical techniques Grieve, Speelman & Geeraerts (2011) have championed.

While Philipp Stoeckle does not identify his contribution "Two dimensional variation in Swiss German morpho-syntax" as dialectometrical, he makes use of the Delaunay-Voronoi techniques made popular by Goebl (2006, and references there) and he aggregates over 57 different syntactic items to obtain an index of variation, effectively the degree to which forms at a given site agree with the most frequent one. This provides insight into a second dimension in his study of variation in addition to the geographic "one". The paper is also notable for its quantitative attention to syntax, an area where Spruit (2008) still stands as one of the few more substantial works. Given the syntactic focus, there are not lots of alternatives to Stoeckle's measure of local variability, but Kretzschmar, Kretzschmar & Brockman's work (2013) on the Gini coefficient would be an interesting alternative.

As Martijn Wieling and Simonetta Montemagni note in their note "Infrequent forms: Noise or not?" opinions differ as to the value of including infrequent forms. Goebl (1984) introduced an inverse frequency measure to count infrequent items as stronger indications of dialectal similarity, and Nerbonne & Kleiweg (2007) provide empirical confirmation of the wisdom of this step. But corpus-based approaches often insist on the opposite, effectively ignoring infrequent items due to their inherent unreliability. It may turn out that some differences are due to the different data collection techniques. After all, since there's no guarantee of having exactly commensurable items in corpus-based work, some "trimming" is inevitable, while the use of questionnaires and check lists ensures that information on even infrequent items normally will be elicited.

Christoph Wolk and Benedikt Szmrecsanyi provide a very useful overview and comparison of approaches in "Top-down and bottom-up advances in corpus-based dialectometry". The earliest work was done by Szmrecsanyi, who collected frequencies of 57 morphosyntactic features, specifying the features ahead of time in a "top-down" manner, converted these to relative frequencies and applied a logarithmic transformation to prevent frequent elements from dominating the measure. In a probabilistic variant, generalized additive models are used to predict the values, and the predicted values are used, effectively smoothing the log relative frequencies. The third, bottom-up technique uses bigrams of part-of-speech tags (POS tags) in the entire corpus, obviating the need to select features ahead of time. The reliability of the POS bigrams is assayed using a resampling procedure, yielding features for analysis. Wolk (2014) promises all the details!

2.2.2 Other methods

Lea Schäfer, Stephanie Leser and Michael Cysouw report on two interesting data sets collected to investigate the mechanisms of imitating closely related language varieties in "Mechanisms of dialect imitation". The poster presentation won one of the "best poster" awards at the conference. Purschke (2011) was one of the earliest works on dialect imitation, but Schäfer and colleagues build on Myers-Scotton's (1993) model of code-switching between different languages, and their goal is to learn not only about the language being imitated (the "target"), but also about the imitator's usual speech (the "matrix"), acknowledging that other varieties may also be influential in how the imitation is realized. 600 subjects participated in an internet survey in which they imitated dialect speech, and the researchers quantified imitation features in an effort to understand what is imitated.

In "Spontaneous dubbing as a tool for eliciting linguistic data: The case of second person plural inflections in Andalusian Spanish", Victor Lara Bermejo introduces a new methodology for eliciting linguistic data, whereby informants dub short scenes shown on videos and accompanied by a description and a lead sentence designed to trigger specific syntactic structures. This technique appears particularly useful for eliciting linguistic features that prove too rare in traditional sociolinguistic interviews, while maintaining a level of spontaneity that is not compatible with pre-established questionnaires. The methodology is successfully applied to the case of the second person plural pronoun in Andalusian Spanish, which neutralizes the standard distinction between the formal *ustedes* and the informal *vosotros*. The Andalusian usage is shown to be doubly variable, in the choice of pronoun and in the agreement patterns of *ustedes* between 2nd and 3rd person. The standard variants appear to be spreading hierarchically, typically conditioned by age and educational background.

Ivana Škevin's paper "Dialect levelling and changes in semiotic space" introduces Lotman's (1985 [2015]) concept of semiotic space as an additional explanatory factor in dialect levelling. Drawing on fieldwork in Betina, Croatia, she shows that much of the traditional Romance-based vocabulary in Dalmatian dialects is being lost. In many cases, this is not due to accommodation to or influence from Standard Croatian, but simply because the concepts these lexical items signify have lost importance in the speakers' daily lives. The effect of this change in semiotic space is similar to that of dialect levelling: the traditional dialect loses many of its salient characteristics.

A multi-method approach to the study of variation is presented in Ares Llop Naya's "The future of Catalan dialects' syntax: A case study for a methodological contribution". Llop combines a revision of existing linguistic studies on Catalan with data from speaker recordings, popular dialect literature, grammaticality judgments and even folk linguistics to arrive at a refined analysis of the constraints on the use of the dialectal negative marker *cap*. Although this work is in its early stages, it clearly shows that methodological innovation can also lie in the combination of existing methods.

Keiko Hirano investigated the use of Japanese vocabulary in the native English speech of English teachers in Japan for her paper "Code-switching in the Anglophone community in Japan". Her corpus of conversations between 39 native English-speaking teachers in the Fukuoka area contained over 1200 of such code-switches. Analysis of the data shows that the use of Japanese lexicon increases the longer a speaker has lived in Japan, and that it correlates positively with the strength of a speaker's social network with other English teachers, both native speakers and Japanese. Hirano suggests many code-switches involve group phraseology and proposes a community-of-practice explanation for this trend.

Two papers take advantage of the ultrasound tongue imaging technique and illustrate its relevance in dialectological studies. In "Tongue trajectories in North American English short-a tensing", Christopher Carignan, Jeff Mielke and Robin Dodsworth take a new look at the classic /æ/ variable. While the different regional realizations of /æ/ and their segmental conditioning are relatively well known, the phonetic motivations for the patterns observed remain unclear. The authors compare the articulatory trajectories of /æ/ before different coda consonants, with speakers from regions known to exhibit different patterns of /æ/ tensing. The results suggest in particular that different North American dialects have phonologized patterns of vowel-consonant coarticulation to different degrees. More generally, the authors emphasize the attractiveness of the ultrasound imaging technique in dialectology, due to its low cost and transportability.

Lorenzo Spreafico applies the same technique to another variable in "/s/-retraction in Italian-Tyrolean bilingual speakers: A preliminary investigation using the ultrasound tongue imaging technique". The author investigates the of /s/ by Tyrolean speakers in the Italian region of South Tyrol, as opposed to the apical articulation characteristic of Italian. He compares tongue shapes during the production of /s/ in /sV/ vs. /sCV/ contexts in Italian and Tyrolean words by Italian-dominant, Tyrolean-dominant and balanced bilingual speakers. Differences are observed across contexts, languages and speakers, suggesting that the articulation of /s/ is influenced by the degree of contact with Italian, even with minimal or no perceptual effects. Further studies are required to clarify the sociophonetic relevance of such results.

2.3 Japanese dialectology

Four papers report on current developments in Japanese dialectology. The first of these, "Developing the Linguistic Atlas of Japan Database and advancing analysis of geographical distributions of dialects" by Yasuo Kumagai details ongoing work on the digitization of the materials collected for the Linguistic Atlas of Japan between 1966 and 1974. Over half a million data cards are being digitized, including multiple responses, comments, and additional material that did not make it into the initial publication of the LAJ. Kumagai showcases some of the work that this updated material allows, such as investigating the geographical distributions of standard forms or the degree of linguistic similarity between locations; the emerging patterns are related to extralinguistic factors like transport networks.

Two papers make use of longitudinal data derived from a comparison of LAJ material with more recent linguistic surveys. In her paper "Tracing real and apparent time language changes by comparing linguistic maps", Chitsuko Fukushima overlays linguistic maps from four surveys in the Niigata area to investigate diachronic change. The superimposition of the maps shows isoglosses moving in real time, with Western Japanese dialect forms first spreading to Niigata from Kyoto, and then retreating again. The maps also show transitional stages of changes in progress.

Takuichiro Onishi's "Timespan comparison of dialectal distributions" investigates the wave theory of linguistic change by comparing LAJ data with two more recent surveys. He finds that, firstly, the spread of a change occurs in a rapid burst, rather than gradually and continually, and that secondly, dialect change need not spread from a central area to the periphery, but may also show an inverse pattern. These three papers on Japanese dialectology together show a wealth of data in the process of being unlocked for advanced analysis.

The final paper in this section is Ichiro Ota, Hitoshi Nikaido and Akira Utsugi's "Tonal variation in Kagoshima Japanese and factors of language change". The authors discuss the effect of various phonological and social factors in an ongoing change in the tonal system of Kagoshima Japanese (KJ). The traditional KJ system differs in important respects from that of Standard Japanese, both varieties sharing a basic contrast between accented and unaccented words. The accented and unaccented patterns appear to be associated with different social meanings, as an asymmetry is observed between change toward the accented pattern of SJ and change toward the unaccented pattern, interpreted respectively as 'de-dialectization' and 'de-standardization'. The paper also points to the role of mass media in language change (see Sayers 2014 and the ensuing debate).

Acknowledgments

The conference was organized by Charlotte Gooskens, Nanna Haug Hilton, Bob de Jonge, John Nerbonne and Martijn Wieling, who were very capably assisted especially throughout the final months by Alexandra Ntelifilippidi and Mara van der Ploeg. We were able to call on Joan Beal, the chair of the standing committee for the Methods conference series, whenever an element of tradition seemed obscure.

We received generous financial support from The Royal Netherlands Academy of Arts and Sciences; the University of Groningen in collaboration with the City of Groningen; the Netherlands Organization for Scientific Research; the Center for Language and Cognition, Groningen; CLARIN-NL, the Dutch branch of the European Common Language and Technology Infrastructure program, John Benjamins Publishing company, and Brill Publishers. The Alliance of Digital Humanities Organizations sponsored prizes for the two best posters by young scholars, and Cambridge University Press underwrote two Chambers prizes, which were awarded for the two best papers by young scholars.

We thank Oscar Strik, Groningen, and Sebastian Nordhoff, Language Science Press, for technical assistance with this first volume in the series *Language Variation*[3] of Language Science Press. We are especially grateful to the many colleagues who volunteered their time to review submissions, judge their quality with respect to publication, and provide authors with notes on how to improve their work. These were Birgit Alber, Will Barras, Charles Boberg, Miriam Bouzouita, Silvia Brandao, David Britain, Marc Brunelle, Paul de Dekker, Vittorio Dell'Aquila, Veronique De Tier, Jacob Eisenstein, Hans Goebl, Charlotte Gooskens, Jack Grieve, Lauren Hall-Lew, David Heap, Wilbert Heeringa, Steve Hewitt, Kris Heylen, Daniel Ezra Johnson, Roland Kehrein, Tyler Kendall, Brett Kessler, Nicolai Khakimov, Stefan Kleiner, Bill Kretzschmar, Haruo Kubozono, Laurence Labrune, Therese Leinonen, Andreas Lötscher, Andrea Mathussek, Jeff Mielke,

---

[3] http://langsci-press.org/catalog/series/lv

Simonetta Montemagni, Chris Montgomery, Naomi Nagy, Enrique Pato, Simon Pickl, Jelena Prokić, Simon Pröll, Christoph Purschke, Stefan Rabanus, Daniel Recasens, Lori Repetti, Andrés Salanova, Lea Schäfer, Oliver Schallert, Yves Scherrer, Koen Sebregts, James Stanford, Femke Swarte, Erik Tjong Kim Sang, Kristel Uiboaed, Hans Van der Velde, Øystein A. Vangsnes, Helmut Weiß, Martijn Wieling and Heike Wiese. They have improved the volume immensely!

References

Auer, Peter. 2005. Europe's sociolinguistic unity, or: A typology of European dialect/standard constellations. In Nicole Delbecque, Johan van der Auwera & Dirk Geeraerts (eds.), *Perspectives on variation: Sociolinguistic, historical, comparative*, 7–42. Berlin / New York: Mouton de Gruyter.

Auer, Peter & Frans Hinskens. 1996. The convergence and divergence of dialects in Europe. New and not so new developments in an old area. *Sociolinguistica (1996)* 10. 1–30.

Auer, Peter, Frans Hinskens & Paul Kerswill (eds.). 2004. *Dialect change: Convergence and divergence in European languages*. Cambridge, New York: Cambridge University Press.

Chambers, J. K. & Peter Trudgill. 1980. *Dialectology*. Cambridge, New York: Cambridge University Press.

Chambers, J. K. & Peter Trudgill. 1998. *Dialectology*. 2nd edn. Cambridge, New York: Cambridge University Press.

Goebl, Hans. 1984. *Dialektometrische Studien: Anhand italoromanischer, rätoromanischer und galloromanischer Sprachmaterialien aus AIS und ALF*. Tübingen: Niemeyer.

Goebl, Hans. 2006. Recent advances in Salzburg dialectometry. *Literary and Linguistic Computing* 21(4). 411–435.

Grieve, Jack, Dirk Speelman & Dirk Geeraerts. 2011. A statistical method for the identification and aggregation of regional linguistic variation. *Language Variation and Change* 23(2). 193–221.

Hickey, Raymond (ed.). 2010. *The handbook of language contact*. Hoboken, NJ: Wiley.

Kleiner, Stefan. 2014. Bericht. Methods in Dialectology XV 11.-15. August 2014, Groningen. *Zeitschrift für Dialektologie und Linguistik* 81(1). 61–66.

Kretzschmar, William A., Brendan A. Kretzschmar & Irene M. Brockman. 2013. Scaled measurement of geographic and social speech data. *LLC: Journal of Digital Scholarship in the Humanities* 28(1). 173–187.

Lenz, Alexandra N. 2003. *Struktur und Dynamik des Substandards: Eine Studie zum Westmitteldeutschen (Wittlich/Eifel)*. Stuttgart, Wiesbaden: F. Steiner.

Lotman, Juri. 1985 [2015]. On the semiosphere. *Sign Systems Studies* 33(1). 215–239.

Munske, Horst Haider & Andrea Mathussek. 2013. *Handbuch zum Sprachatlas von Mittelfranken: Dokumentation und Auswertung*. Heidelberg: Universitätsverlag Winter.

Myers-Scotton, Carol. 1993. *Duelling languages: Grammatical structure in code-switching*. Oxford: Oxford University Press.

Nerbonne, John & Peter Kleiweg. 2007. Toward a dialectological yardstick. *Journal of Quantitative Linguistics* 14(2). 148–166.

Nerbonne, John, Rinke Colen, Charlotte Gooskens, Peter Kleiweg & Therese Leinonen. 2011. Gabmap – a web application for dialectology. *Dialectologia* Special Issue II. 65–89.

Nerbonne, John, Sandrien van Ommen, Charlotte Gooskens & Martijn Wieling. 2013. Measuring socially motivated pronunciation differences. In Lars Borin & Anju Sacena (eds.), *Approaches to measuring linguistic differences*, 107–140. Berlin: De Gruyter.

Niedzielski, Nancy. 1999. The effect of social information on the perception of sociolinguistic variables. *Journal of Language and Social Psychology* 18(1). 62–85.

Prokić, Jelena, Çağri Çöltekin & John Nerbonne. 2012. Detecting shibboleths. In *Proceedings of the EACL 2012 Joint Workshop of LINGVIS & UNCLH*, 72–80. Association for Computational Linguistics.

Purschke, Christoph. 2011. *Regionalsprache und Hörerurteil. Grundzüge einer perzeptiven Variationslinguistik* (ZDL-Beihefte 149). Stuttgart: Franz Steiner.

Sayers, Dave. 2014. The mediated innovation model: A framework for researching media influence in language change. *Journal of Sociolinguistics* 18(2). 185–212.

Spruit, Marco René. 2008. *Quantitative perspectives on syntactic variation in Dutch dialects*. University of Amsterdam PhD thesis.

Trudgill, Peter. 1986. *Dialects in contact*. Oxford: Blackwell.

Trudgill, Peter. 2004. *New-dialect formation. the inevitability of colonial Englishes*. Edinburgh: Edinburgh University Press.

Wieling, Martijn & John Nerbonne. 2011. Bipartite spectral graph partitioning for clustering dialect varieties and detecting their linguistic features. *Computer Speech & Language* 25(3). 700–715.

Wolk, Christoph. 2014. *Integrating aggregational and probabilistic approaches to language variation*. Freiburg: University of Freiburg PhD thesis.

Part I

The future

Chapter 2

Heritage languages as new dialects

Naomi Nagy
University of Toronto, Department of Linguistics

> In order to compare heritage and homeland varieties, to determine whether the heritage varieties constitute new and distinctive dialects, we need innovative methods and a cohesive definition of "new dialect." Toronto's Heritage Language Variation and Change Project provides testing grounds for both: it is designed for intergenerational, cross-linguistic, and diatopic (heritage vs. homeland varieties) analysis of spoken Cantonese, Faetar, Italian, Korean, Russian and Ukrainian. With reference to the heritage varieties examined in this project, I contrast ways of defining new dialects. I then describe methodological innovations that permit variationist analysis of linguistic patterns and the involvement of large numbers of student-researchers who are speakers of the putative new dialects, two elements critical to the success of the project.

1 Introduction

The XVth meeting of *Methods in Dialectology* sought to "bring traditional approaches to dialectology together with the latest advances in data collection technologies, new analysis instruments, and new interpretations of the concept of dialect".[1]

This paper compares interpretations of the concept of 'dialect', and particularly of dialect divergence, contrasting the outcomes of linguistically- and socially-oriented approaches. It then describes some advances in methods applied in a multilingual speech corpus project whose goal is to understand the process of divergence of heritage varieties from their homeland counterparts.

The study of dialect convergence [dc] and divergence [dd] therefore needs to be informed by both subdisciplines [historical linguistics and sociolinguistics]… Research into dc and dd lies at the crossroads between contact linguistics and variationist linguistics, i.e. between the study of language change as a result of

---

[1] http://methodsxv.webhosting.rug.nl/

language contact and the study of language variation as a synchronic manifestation of language change..." (Auer, Hinskens & Kerswill 2004b: 16).

The Heritage Language Variation and Change Project (HLVC, Nagy 2011) is, in fact, motivated by the complications of intersecting contact linguistics and variationist linguistics, as in the above quotation. We develop and use a multilingual corpus for inter-generational, cross-linguistic, and diatopic (heritage vs. homeland varieties) comparisons in order to develop generalizations about the types of variable features, structures or rules that are borrowed earlier and more often in contact contexts.

The ultimate goal is to better understand what happens in contact situations and what the best predictors are of different linguistic outcomes. For this purpose, a set of consistent methods are applied to a set of linguistic variables that are found in a set of HERITAGE LANGUAGES (HLs) spoken in Toronto, Canada. HLs are defined, in the Canadian context, as mother tongues other than Canada's two official languages (French and English), cf. Cummins & Danesi (1990).[2] I will first discuss whether such varieties may be considered new dialects, contrasting definitions based on linguistic factors and attitudes, and then describe some innovations developed in this inquiry.

1.1 When do new varieties constitute new dialects?

While we are all familiar with the maxim that "a language is a dialect with an army and a navy," it is surprisingly difficult to find viable definitions of what constitutes a dialect. From my admittedly outsider's perspective, dialectologists' definitions may be based on structural features and/or community orientation toward the language. Trudgill (1986; 2004) focuses on linguistic effects, that is, types of features or changes in the language, denying the relevance of attitudinal factors to the concept of new dialect formation (see Meyerhoff 2006: 186 for further discussion). Schneider (2003; 2007), in contrast, focuses more on orientation of the community toward the language, while also including linguistic features, in a model designed to describe the trajectory of post-colonial varieties of English. I have also found Auer, Hinskens & Kerswill's (2004) edited book (hereafter AHK) thought-provoking as I consider how HLs may fit into the discussion of new dialect formation. In order to focus on convergence and divergence as particular

---

[2] Mother tongue is "the first language learned at home in childhood and still understood by the person at the time the data was collected. If the person no longer understands the first language learned, the mother tongue is the second language learned. For a person who learned two languages at the same time in early childhood, the mother tongue is the language this person spoke most often at home before starting school..." (Statistics Canada 2014).

aspects of dialect change, they must grapple with the question of what a dialect is. Their basic definition excludes HLs outright:

> We will use the notion of 'dialect' to refer to a language variety which is used in a geographically limited part of a language area in which it is 'roofed' by a structurally related standard variety (Auer, Hinskens & Kerswill 2004b: 1).

This would exclude heritage varieties from being considered dialects of their parent language. Indeed, any diasporic variety cannot be considered a dialect of its homeland language, unless the emigrés land in a country where the same language is spoken. Other aspects of their definitions would seem to be hospitable to the inclusion of HLs as new dialects (discussed in §2).

1.2 How are heritage languages like new dialects?

We begin by situating this study in the Canadian context. Few would question whether Canadian English and Canadian French constitute different dialects from their European counterparts. The varieties of French and English spoken in Canada have been explicitly labeled as distinct varieties for longer than Canada has been a nation. Canadian English has been labeled as a distinct dialect of English since at least 1857, when The Rev. A. Constable Geikie titled a speech he read before the Canadian Institute "*Canadian English*." Bouchard (1998 [2002]) proposed that a grammatical debate in 1840–41 between Abbé Maguire, Jérôme Demers and Michel Bibaud marked the transition from considering "French spoken in Canada" to the development of the concept of Canadian French. A few years later, in an epistolary novel, Coursen (1846) referred to "the French Canadian dialect," extending the label beyond academic discourse. It is thus possible for people to label as new dialects the varieties of national languages spoken by immigrant groups.

But what of languages that do not enjoy official recognition in Canada? Languages without official status are not named in government documents. I am not aware of academic recognition of these varieties. For example, there is no Cantonese parallel to *The Canadian Oxford Dictionary* or the university course *Canadian English*. To check for less formalized references to HLs as new dialects, I collected online citations paralleling "Canadian French" and "Canadian English" for HLs spoken in Toronto. This is an effort to capture early evidence of the emergence of named status for these varieties, looking for the modern equivalents of Geikie's speech or Coursen's novel. Dialects can be arrayed on a continuum from least to most recognized, as listed in the top of Table 1.

In the first row of Table 1, check marks indicate the existence of this status of recognition, i.e., Named variety, for each language, while blank cells indicate that no such evidence has been found. The next rows of part (a) indicate additional levels of recognition (outside the HLVC project) enjoyed by some of Toronto's HLs. These constitute evidence of new dialects on normative or attitudinal grounds and will be discussed in §2. Table 1 (b) summarizes the linguistic status of differentiation of these varieties from their homeland counterparts. "S" indicates that variationist analysis has found the same pattern of variable usage in homeland and heritage varieties of that language, while "D" marks documented differences between homeland and heritage varieties, that is, evidence of (partial) formation of a new dialect, based on linguistic criteria. Blank cells remain to be filled in by future work, which will also include additional variables. Table 1 (c) shows each community's average Ethnic Orientation score (explained below). A cursory comparison of the top two parts of the table indicates a lack of relationship between these two ways of considering whether a new dialect has emerged. We also see no connection with the community's degree of attitudinal separation from their homeland. These incongruities point up a problem with deterministic approaches to new dialect formation where we might expect similar outcomes across all languages, if social factors weren't relevant.

At this point, we can conduct the same comparative exercise with Schneider's five phases of new dialect formation, with the same unsatisfying lack of convergence in outcome. For this discussion, I refer numerically to the four types of markers laid out in Schneider's (2003: 255) Table 1: (1) History and politics, (2) Identity construction, (3) Use/attitudes, and (4) Linguistic developments/structural effects.

All HLs included in the HLVC project have undoubtedly made it to Phase 1 on all counts. They exhibit Phase 2 markers for (3) Use/attitudes (acceptance of original norm) and (4) Linguistic developments (lexical borrowing, cf. Danesi (1983) for Italian, but not for (1) or (2). (2)has been explicitly probed by the HLVC project, with the results shown in Table 1 (c). Speakers are asked, "Do you think of yourself as Italian, Canadian or Italian-Canadian?" (*mutatis mutandis* for each language). Open-ended responses are quantified on a scale in which a homeland-oriented response (e.g., "Italian") scores two points while "Canadian" scores 0, with mixed responses scoring 1. In the first generation, all language groups average near 1.5, quite homeland oriented. Differences emerge in the second generation, painting the picture in Table 1 (c). Thus the HL communities straddle the IDENTITY construction definitions for Schneider's Phases 1-4.

Toronto's HLs have reached Phase 3 in terms of (2) (3) markers though, against expectation, not (4): our project has uncovered very little structural spreading

2 Heritage languages as new dialects

Table 1: Comparison of (a) status-related, (b)structural-related, and (c) attitudinal indicators of new dialect formation for a sample of Toronto's heritage languages. Faetar is omitted from section (c) of this table. The trilingual nature of the community eludes my quantification.

	Faetar	Korean	Cantonese	Russian	Italian	Ukrainian
(a) Status of recognition						
Named varieties		√		√	√	
Social or demographic attributes ascribed to the variety						√
Linguistic features of variety described			√	√	√	
Systematic quantitative analysis of linguistic variation						√
(b) Heritage – Homeland comparison of linguistic features						
Basic vocabulary (Nagy 2011)	S					
Voice Onset Time (Nagy & Kochetov 2013; Kang & Nagy 2013)		D		D	S	
Null vs. pronoun subjects (Nagy 2015; Nagy & Iannozzi 2014)	D			D	S	
(c) Orientation toward heritage nation *vs.* Canada						
0 = "I am Canadian," 1 = mixed, 2 = "I am Korean/etc."	n/a	1.3	1.0	1.6	1.4	1.1

from English to the HLs (see references in Table 1). We find scattered evidence of the "complaint tradition" that constitutes an ATTITUDE marker of Phase 3: e.g., Struk (2000) anticipates the "total extinction" of Ukrainian in (Alberta) Canada due to massive English influence and the negative views of Canadian Cantonese cited in §2.2.

Schneider's model unravels a bit more at Phase 4, where HL speakers in Toronto exhibit markers for (2), as noted above, but none of the other markers of endonormative stabilization. A return to this question when more linguistic features of the HLs have been analyzed will be critical.

2 A little more about Toronto's HLs as new dialects

The following sections describe the status of Toronto's HLs in greater detail, grouping information according to the recognition characteristics in Table 1 (b). Relevant suggestions in AHK are evaluated as they apply to the status of Toronto's HLs. A lack of correspondence between the rankings in Table 1 (b) by linguistic features, à la Trudgill, and by orientation, à la Schneider, in Table 1 (a, c), will be evident. This underscores the inappropriateness of equating one language to one culture, or monolithic descriptions of either (cf. Foley 2005).

2.1 No status as dialects

Searching the web, including academic resources, yielded no hits for "Canadian Korean" or "Canadian Faetar". We are aware of no published descriptions of these varieties, or claims of them as dialects distinct from their homeland varieties. Both have been spoken in Toronto since about the middle of the twentieth century, but have never had large numbers of speakers.

2.2 Named varieties

Speakers of Cantonese outnumber speakers of Korean by more than 10:1 in Toronto (Statistics Canada 2011a), although the Cantonese arrived in the city only about one decade earlier. In the five years between the 2006 and 2011 census, there was an increase of almost 10% in the number of people of Chinese ethnic origin living in Toronto (Statistics Canada 2011b), the majority of whom likely speak Cantonese.[3] While not recognized at the institutional level, "Canadian

---

[3] Imprecise because many respondents indicating that they speak "Chinese" without specifying their variety.

Cantonese" has gained the status of a distinct dialect among (some) community members. The variety is named, as in posts such as these, at http://www.gamefaqs.com/boards/981401-sleeping-dogs/63775307:

> what bothers me, is that it's not authentic cantonese, but *canadian cantonese*. huge difference (#2BloodyBooger, Posted 8/18/2012, emphasis mine)

> Some of the accents are terrible, you can tell they're *Canadian cantonese* speakers. On the other hand, I personally know a lot of people who have both English and Cantonese as their mother tongues, Queen's English accents and all (myself being one of them), and sometimes when we speak, we tend to mix in English words or vice versa to get our point across (ZeroHiei, Posted 8/18/2012, emphasis mine).

Struk (2000: 71) describes Ukish, "a mixture of Ukrainian and English." Italian also exists as a named variety, cf. the article *"Canadian Italian* as a marker of Ethnicity" (Danesi 1983; 1984). Giovanardi, Gualdo & Coco (2003) label the variety as *Italiese*. The varieties that have been named are distinguished by larger numbers of speakers, tentatively a necessary, but not sufficient condition for dialect identification.

2.3 Social or demographic attributions ascribed

Kerswill & Trudgill (2004) propose a characteristic not directly related to linguistic structure: a new dialect is a variety which lacks a "local stable model" and thus cannot be transmitted. This definition does not seem to apply to the HL context because transmission is certainly attested in our corpus of HL speakers of up to five generations since immigration. Many heritage community institutions offer language classes which adhere to what is considered a stable homeland model. Because of, or perhaps in spite of these courses, the heritage variety is transmitted.

Canadian Ukrainian, however, is well-enough established to have a Wikipedia (2014) entry:

> *Canadian Ukrainian* [...] is a dialect [...] specific to the Ukrainian Canadian community descended from the first two waves of historical Ukrainian emigration to Western Canada. [...] Canadian Ukrainian was widely spoken from the beginning of Ukrainian settlement in Canada in 1892 until the mid-20th century. [...] cut off from their co-linguists by wars and social changes,

and half the globe [...] exposed to speakers of many other languages in Canada, especially English. [...] introduced to many new technologies and concepts, for which they had no words. Consequently Canadian Ukrainian began to develop in new directions from the language in the "Old Country."

Here demographic information is presented to bolster the status of the new variety: when, where and why the language emerged, and the circumstances that encouraged its divergence.

2.4 Linguistic features described

Although not all have achieved the status of being named varieties, the heritage versions of Russian, Italian and Ukrainian are recognized as valid objects of linguistic study, having been spoken in Toronto for over a century (about twice as long as the others in Table 1). They are the object of descriptions with less negative connotations than are found in the above descriptions of Canadian Cantonese. For example, in a website called "Canadian dialects of European languages," a Canadian Russian dialect is described, but not named (Language Factory 2013):

> Canada's Doukhobor community, especially in Grand Forks and Castlegar, British Columbia, has kept its *distinct dialect of Russian*. It has a lot in common with South Russian dialects, showing some common features with Ukrainian.

This site also mentions Heritage Ukrainian, but no other languages in the HLVC project. The Wikipedia extract about Ukrainian (§2.3) also includes linguistic description. It explicitly mentions linguistic features that distinguish the Canadian dialect from the European dialect of Ukrainian. This variety is well-enough established that there are also published descriptions of phonetic and syntactic variation in the heritage variety, cf. Hudyma (2011), Struk (2000). Danesi (1983; 1984) describes lexical features of Canadian Italian, but claims that it is not grammatically or phonologically distinct from its homeland counterpart:

> From all structural points of view it is essentially Peninsular Italian, *i.e.*, in its phonology [...], morphology [...] and Syntax [...], it is identical to Peninsular Italian, or to any of its regional and dialectal variants. In its lexical repertoire, however, it contains many new words ...

In addition to ascribing specific linguistic features, we could also seek *types* of features in our quest for testable means of identifying new dialects. For example, Auer, Hinskens & Kerswill (2004b: 1), cite Chambers & Trudgill (1998: 5): "a dialect typically displays structural peculiarities in several language components." It goes without saying that "peculiarities" are subjectively defined and that this will be tautologically true if a minority variety is compared to a mainstream variety. This definition is at odds with others offered in AHK. For example, Berruto (1995, cited in Auer, Hinskens & Kerswill 2004b: 11) notes that dialects lose their "oddest features," e.g., loss of certain word order options or prodrop optionality. Similarly, Kerswill & Trudgill (2004: 198) suggest that the leveling process which contributes to new dialect features includes simplification. For example, "invariable word forms, as well as the loss of categories such as gender, the loss of case marking, simplified morphophonemics (paradigmatic leveling), and a decrease in the number of phonemes," stipulating that

> Mixing, leveling, and simplification are the necessary precursors of new-dialect formation. Together, they can be said to constitute *koineisation* (Auer, Hinskens & Kerswill 2004b: 199).

These contradictory definitions may have led to Auer & Hinskens' (2004: 356) summary statement that the connection between variation and change is still unknown. The HLVC project has not yet documented any examples of these types of changes.

2.5 Quantitative analysis of linguistic variation

Establishing the existence of distinct linguistic features of a variety is not sufficient for understanding the diachronic process of new dialect formation. Auer, Hinskens & Kerswill (2004b: 6) suggest, rather, that the patterns of use such features, or the use of "different features more often," is what constitutes dialect distinctions. This is at the heart of the comparative variationist methods (cf. Cacoullos & Travis 2010) applied in the H eritage Language Variation and Change (HLVC) Project. It requires a focus on distributional patterns and conditioning effects, rather than a simpler test of presence vs. absence of certain structures or forms. In a similar vein, Kerswill & Trudgill (2004: 215) note, as part of a series of steps that define new dialect formation, that children of immigrants will have lots of variation. These promising approaches require further quantification – comparing across varieties used by different groups, what does it mean for a group to have "more variation"? Is it simply a larger number of surface forms? How is that compatible with the processes of simplification that are reported to accompany diffusion of linguistic patterns discussed in §2.4? Can we develop metrics to compare the degree of variation at lexical, phonetic, structural and discourse levels? Until such methods are in place, these definitions also cannot serve as diagnostics of whether a variety constitutes a new dialect. Furthermore, appropriate data will be needed. Beyond the HLVC output,[4] I am aware of no quantified descriptions of variation in Toronto's HLs except Ukrainian (Budzhak-Jones 1994; Chumak-Horbatsch 1987).

2.6 Summary: identifying HLs as new dialects

This survey has illustrated possibilities for recognition of HLs as "diverged" dialects of their homeland variety, ranging from a complete lack of recognition of a distinct dialect (Faetar, Korean) to naming of the transported variety ("Canadian Cantonese," "Italiese," "Ukish"), to attribution of social and linguistic features of the distinct variety (Italian, Russian), and finally to systematic data analysis to substantiate claims of distinct grammars (Ukrainian). As comparable homeland data become available, the HLVC project will be able to investigate both linguistic and attitudinal features for the difference in degrees of recognition of Toronto's heritage varieties as distinct "new Canadian" dialects. The remainder of the paper introduces the project's methods designed to achieve these goals.

3 The HLVC Project

The HLVC project intertwines descriptive and theoretical goals – so that we can answer the question of whether a variety has achieved "new dialect" status on both *linguistic* and *attitudinal* grounds. We document HLs as spoken by immigrants and two generations of their descendants living in the Toronto area. The three-generation model allows for direct application of models such as Trudgill's (1986) model which offer different roles for speakers of each generation. We are building a corpus of transcribed conversational speech, accompanied by relevant information about the speakers' linguistic habits, attitudes, and experiences, available to interested researchers. Our theoretical goals include better understanding of the relationship between language variation and change, to be achieved by pushing variationist research beyond its monolingually-oriented core. A variety of new tools and techniques have been developed to integrate lesser-documented varieties into the variationist tradition.

---

[4] http://projects.chass.utoronto.ca/ngn/HLVC/1_5_publications.php

These developments have stemmed from my being trained in sociolinguistics by a graduate program with a focus on methods useful for investigating well-documented languages (such as English, French and Spanish)[5] by native-speaker, or at least, very fluent fieldworkers and analysts. This approach was at odds with other aspects of my training in formal linguistics which featured data and examples from many lesser-documented languages. This contradiction came to the fore when these two streams of training merged in a dissertation documenting and theorizing variation in Faetar (Nagy 1996), a language that had been subject to little previous description, none quantified or theorized. I was a non-speaker of the variety at the outset of fieldwork. So, some twenty years later, what have I done to modify tools and approaches as I continue in this vein of applying quantitative variationist methods to lesser-studied varieties? How can we best test whether the sociolinguistic generalizations that have emerged from the study of well-documented languages apply more universally?

An important component of the HLVC project is to use the same methods to describe the variable patterns of both homeland and heritage varieties before trying to answer the question of whether the heritage varieties constitute new dialects or not. Innovations developed to allow for parallel analyses of more- and less-documented varieties include:

- integrating transcription, coding and extraction of sociolinguistic variables in ELAN;
- automated forced alignment and formant extraction for languages beyond English;
- a web map with voice clips as examples of the varieties, accessible to non-linguists;
- integration of research and teaching in courses for undergraduate and graduate students, by paid and volunteer research assistants, and by students and professors in nine countries (so far);
- sharing and training for methods, tools, instruments developed in this project and controlled sharing of data.

It is hoped that this project may help predict the future of (these) dialects and advance the study of dialects more generally and that the following brief descriptions of these innovation may prove useful in that endeavor.

---

[5] Nagy & Meyerhoff (2008) found that studies of these three languages constituted some 98% of variationist studies published in two leading sociolinguistic journals.

3.1 HLVC methods of data collection and organization

While generational differences are unquestionably an aspect of new dialect formation, sociolinguists have established that other factors are also necessary for the accurate description of linguistic variation. This necessitates a socially-stratified sample and quantitative analysis that considers the effects of multiple conditioning factors. Addressing this first need, the HLVC project has developed a sampling protocol that uses convenience sampling to recruit and record participants as follows.

For each language, a particular geographic region or city of origin is specified and all speakers in the corpus trace their ancestry to that one locale. This is meant to reduce one parameter of variation in the data, though it allows for variation in both the founder population and successive generations. For Italian, for example, all speakers in the corpus are (descendants of) Calabrese, selected because it is one of the two largest regionally defined groups of Italians in Toronto. Calabria is a region in the south of Italy where 25% of the population currently report speaking either in Italian or in Calabrese (an Italian dialect) and an additional 10% report speaking in Calabrese (ISTAT (Istituto Nazionale di Statistica) 2007: Tavola 10).

Within each language, speakers are selected to fill cells representing all combinations of generation, age, and sex criteria, defined as follows.

Generation:

- GENERATION 1 speakers are born in the home country and moved to Toronto after age 18. They have subsequently been in Toronto 20+ years.
- GENERATION 2 speakers are born in Toronto or came from the home country before age 6. Their parents are in Generation 1.
- GENERATION 3 speakers are born in Toronto. Their parents are in Generation 2.

Age: Four age groups per generation: 60+, 39-59, 21-39, <21.[6]

Sex: Two males and two females represent each age by generation cell.

Our target sample for each language comprises 40 speakers (two speakers of each sex per age group per generation). However, we have only two generations

---

[6] The two youngest groups do not exist for Generation 1, who are older than 38 by definition. Otherwise, age and generation are orthogonal in the design.

for Korean (too recently arrived) and Faetar (population too small to produce a third generation). Additionally, we have representation of Generations 4 and 5 for Ukrainian, and pilot samples for Hungarian and Polish. Currently the corpus includes transcribed recordings for 190 Heritage speakers, across eight languages.

Sociolinguistic research in the variationist paradigm has found that changes in progress are frequently linked to certain patterns of variation, allowing us to use synchronic variation as a tool for understanding change (Bailey et al. 1991; Labov 2001; 2007). In addition to the factors Generation, Age and Sex, we collect Ethnic Orientation information via an oral, open-ended questionnaire which allows us to consider the effects of (self-reports of) speakers' language practices, attitudes and experiences.[7]

The effects of these factors, and, in turn, their ability to help us understand ongoing changes in the variety, are best interpreted through the Comparative Variationist Analysis approach (cf. Labov 1972; Tagliamonte 2006; Walker 2010). Thomason & Kaufman (1988: 111) point out the vexing issue that once contact has occurred, it may not be easy to access the pre-contact variety, yet contrasting these is crucial. Cross-group comparison, an essential component of the approach, allows us to address issues that would ideally be resolved by comparing the pre-contact variety to its post-contact variety. This method involves comparison of rates of forms, as is typical in experimental approaches, but also compares conditioning effects. This approach, with its accumulated knowledge of synchronic patterns that often signal change, augmented by contrasting speakers with greater and lesser contact with English, provides a fast-track view of language change. Rather than contrasting elusive "pure" contact and non-contact varieties, the HLVC project seeks gradually increasing effects on HLs correlating to gradually increasing contact with English, to address these questions sequentially:

1. What aspects of the language vary?

2. How does the variation differ by community? Can we point to specific demographic or attitudinal differences as predictors?

3. Do the patterns of variation suggest that there is change away from the homeland variety? As Thomason (2001) notes, this requires fieldwork and parallel methods in the home countries as well.

---

[7] http://projects.chass.utoronto.ca/ngn/pdf/HLVC/short_questionnaire_English.pdf

Responses to these questions are, so far, based on small samples (see details in publications at http://projects.chass.utoronto.ca/ngn/HLVC/1_5_publications.php). Once the corpus is complete, we will return to the question of whether the quality and/or quantity of change is sufficient to meet a definition of a "new dialect."

To prepare data for this approach, we collect samples of about one hour of conversational speech from each participant, using sociolinguistic interview methodology (Labov 1984). We transcribe the recordings and then code many instances of each variant of phonetic, lexical and structural variables. We have developed an integrated approach for time-aligned orthographic transcribing and coding tokens (instances) of dependent variables as well as the predictors or independent variables in a single file (detailed in Nagy & Meyerhoff 2015). This provides seamless connections between recording, transcript, and coding of the dependent variable (response) and independent variables (predictors), facilitating revision and intercoder reliability testing. In a project that relies on a large and changing team of student researchers, this tight connection between representations of the data at various stages of analysis is imperative. It also allows for the reuse of contextual factor coding (e.g., style, topic, interlocutor) as well as some structural (morphological, syntactic) tags in successive projects. An additional advantage is the archivability of all mark-up related to each data file in a consistent manner in small files, again particularly useful in a large project where different researchers conduct different stages of the work.

Time-aligned transcription also allows us to test the feasibility of using various automated processes which have been developed for better-documented languages, such as forced alignment (of transcription to sound at a segmental level), vowel formant extraction, speech rate calculators which consider amplitude variation, and VOT measures. Preliminary results are promising and suggest that these will be immensely time-saving approaches for analysis of large data sets (Tse & Nagy 2014).

3.2 Integrating research and teaching in HLVC

The inclusion of student-researchers who are speakers of these HLs make it possible to investigate this range of languages. No one researcher can be a native-speaker, let alone expert, in this range of HLs, making the integration of research and teaching an essential and productive component of the HLVC project.⁸ Class-based activities that work with HLVC data encourage the development of critical thinking, writing skills, oral presentation and research methods, affording a more unified focus on research. In turn, the project benefits from insights and innovations from students with differing degrees of familiarity with the communities. I have structured a successful first-year undergraduate course around the premise that the students, as a group, will prepare an article for the journal *Heritage Languages*, about the ethnolinguistic vitality of heritage languages spoken in the Greater Toronto Area and the way the languages are spoken. For this purpose, the course introduces them to definitions of "heritage language"; the concepts of ethnolinguistic vitality, the status of heritage languages, and methods of measuring them; principles of academic writing; field methods and methods for conducting a sociolinguistic analysis. The assignments for this course are posted at http://individual.utoronto.ca/ngn/LIN/courses/TBB199/TBB199.14W_syll.htm. One assignment, collecting and describing resources for heritage language speakers and learners, has developed into an important section of the project's website.⁹

Students' responses to the integration of research in their course were positive, as indicated by their enthusiasm for continued involvement with the project after the course and these excerpts from their course blogs:

> I had never thought before that linguists and researchers might be interested in learning more about heritage languages, but I think it is wonderful that they are doing work related to this area. – Lesia
>
> Because of this course, I began to realize how you can learn so much about your roots just through language and the importance of heritage languages. It is another thing pushing me to improve my Chinese and hopefully begin to learn Vietnamese. – Ashley
>
> I decided to take this course because I feel that a heritage language is an integral part of a person, and a part that cannot be ignored, and instead should be embraced. Learning more about other's experiences seem to be very interesting, as is sharing my own encounters and perceptions on heritage languages. I believe I will come out of this class every week with many new ideas and information. – Seiwon

---

⁸ Van Herk, De Decker & Thorburn (2015) note the financial benefit that many universities have resources available for developing pedagogical tools, particularly to enable inquiry-based learning and independent research by undergraduates.
⁹ http://projects.chass.utoronto.ca/ngn/HLVC/2_1_speakers.php

> After yesterday's class, I'm more interested than ever to learn about heritages languages and how it has been for those who have immigrated to Canada many generations ago! –Siquian
>
> I am happy to know that Russian is one of the languages that we will be studying, and i am honoured to be able to help with the program/research. Through this course, I am looking forward to learning new academic skills, alongside expanding my knowledge about not only my language but other heritage languages in Toronto. – Evgeny
>
> My analytical skills have continuously gotten better as has my research and observation skills, which was developed through the multiple assignments that we've had throughout the semester – Claudia

Use of an online data server has made it easier to integrate students into the project. We encourage students to use the audio recordings and time-aligned transcriptions for empirical research as part of their studies, and have integrated a consent process where students acknowledge that they understand the ethical requirements for using the data prior to viewing it. Details are available at https://corpora.chass.utoronto.ca/, a site supported by curriculum development grants. Transcripts and recordings are available for use by scholars at other institutions, through a similar, but offline, consent-granting process.

It is immensely rewarding to tap into the abilities and enthusiasm of students who are members of the communities under investigation. The HLVC project has benefitted from hours of volunteer efforts from students.[10] Students are invaluable for recruiting participants, noticing innovations as potential variables for investigation, transcribing, and keeping channels of communication open between communities and researchers. One example of the latter benefit is the interactive speaker map.[11] A team of students compiled voice clips with time-aligned transcriptions and translations, representing the speech of several members of each generation of the HLs in the project. Speech samples are (roughly) geo-located on a map of Toronto, by residence of the speaker and labeled by language, age, sex and generation. This allows exploration of the possibility that varieties develop differently in different neighborhoods, related to settlement patterns of more and less recent immigration.

---

[10] Recognized at http://projects.chass.utoronto.ca/ngn/HLVC/3_2_active_ra.php and http://projects.chass.utoronto.ca/ngn/HLVC/3_3_former_ra.php.

[11] http://projects.chass.utoronto.ca/ngn/HLVC/4_1_map.php

4 Conclusion

A survey of different ways of describing and defining dialects, presented in the first half of the paper, shows the diversity of approaches, but also suggests a continuum along which varieties progress as they diverge from their parent variety. Dialects may be defined by social and/or linguistic attributes. Using the admittedly limited HLVC data available to date, we are not able to show congruence of outcomes from these different approaches to defining new dialects. However, patterns of relationships between the social and linguistic features may be documented, producing descriptions of the grammars of these varieties which may diverge from their parent varieties. Comparisons of the homeland and heritage (putatively "new") dialects can be made when appropriately organized data is available. The second half of the paper reviewed the methods of the HLVC project, suggesting a productive process for making headway on understanding the relationships between linguistic variation and change in order to answer such questions. I thank the organizers of *Methods XV* for giving me a place to integrate these thoughts.

Acknowledgements

I thank SSHRC and my collaborators in the HLVC project[12] and research assistants [13][14] for their valuable support, without which I would not be writing this paper. I also thank Beau Brock, Jack Chambers, Rick Grimm and Anne-José Villeneuve for assistance in locating early labeling of Canadian English and Canadian French. I thank the reviewers and editors for helpful direction in better integrating my interests with literature on dialect formation.

References

Auer, Peter & Frans Hinskens. 2004. The role of interpersonal accommodation in a theory of language change. In Peter Auer, Frans Hinskens & Paul Kerswill (eds.), *Dialect change: Convergence and divergence in European languages*, 335–357. Cambridge, New York: Cambridge University Press.

---

[12] Recognized at http://projects.chass.utoronto.ca/ngn/HLVC/3_1_investigators.php
[13] http://projects.chass.utoronto.ca/ngn/HLVC/3_2_active_ra.php
[14] http://projects.chass.utoronto.ca/ngn/HLVC/3_3_former_ra.php

Auer, Peter, Frans Hinskens & Paul Kerswill (eds.). 2004a. *Dialect change: Convergence and divergence in European languages.* Cambridge, New York: Cambridge University Press.

Auer, Peter, Frans Hinskens & Paul Kerswill. 2004b. The study of dialect convergence and divergence: Conceptual and methodological considerations. In Peter Auer, Frans Hinskens & Paul Kerswill (eds.), *Dialect change: Convergence and divergence in European languages*, 1–51. Cambridge, New York: Cambridge University Press.

Bailey, Guy, Tom Wikle, Jan Tillery & Lori Sand. 1991. The apparent time construct. *Language Variation and Change* 3(3). 241–264.

Berruto, Gaetano. 1995. *Fondamenti di sociolinguistica.* Roma / Bari: Laterza.

Bouchard, Chantal. 1998 [2002]. *La langue et le nombril: Histoire d'une obsession québécoise.* 2nd edn. (Nouvelles études québecoises). Montréal: Fides.

Budzhak-Jones, Svitlana. 1994. Variable rule analysis of V/U alternation constraints in Canadian Ukrainian. *Journal of Quantitative Linguistics* 1(3). 202–211.

Cacoullos, Rena & Catherine Travis. 2010. Testing convergence via code-switching: Priming and the structure of variable subject expression. *International Journal of Bilingualism* 15(3). 241–267.

Chambers, J. K. & Peter Trudgill. 1998. *Dialectology.* 2nd edn. Cambridge, New York: Cambridge University Press.

Chumak-Horbatsch, Roma. 1987. Language use in the Ukrainian home: A Toronto sample. *International Journal of the Sociology of Language* 63. 99–118.

Coursen, Charlotte. 1846. *It blows, it snows: A winter's rambles through Canada.* Dublin: Brady.

Cummins, James & Marcel Danesi. 1990. Lifting the multicultural veil. *Our Schools/Our Selves* Special Issue: Heritage Languages(Heritage Languages). 13.

Danesi, Marcel. 1983. Canadian Italian as a marker of ethnicity. *NEMLA Italian Studies* 7(8). 99–105.

Danesi, Marcel. 1984. Canadian Italian: A case in point of how language adapts to environment. *Polyphony* 7. 110–113.

Foley, W. 2005. Personhood and linguistic identity, purism and variation. In Peter K. Austin (ed.), *Language documentation and description*, vol. 3, 157–180. London: SOAS.

Giovanardi, Claudio, Riccardo Gualdo & Alessandra Coco. 2003. *Inglese - italiano 1 a 1: Tradurre o non tradurre le parole inglesi?* San Cesario di Lecce (Lecce): Manni.

Hudyma, Khrystyna. 2011. Ukrainian language in Canada: From prosperity to extinction? *Working Papers of the Linguistics Circle of the University of Victoria* 21(1). 181–189.

Kang, Yoonjung & Naomi Nagy. 2013. VOT merger in Heritage Korean in Toronto. *Proceedings of the Canadian Linguistics Association* 2012. 1–13.

Kerswill, Paul & Peter Trudgill. 2004. The birth of new dialects. In Peter Auer, Frans Hinskens & Paul Kerswill (eds.), *Dialect change: Convergence and divergence in European languages*, 196–220. Cambridge, UK; New York: Cambridge University Press.

Labov, William. 1972. *Sociolinguistic patterns*. Philadelphia: University of Philadelphia Press.

Labov, William. 1984. Field methods of the project on linguistic change and variation. In J. Baugh & J. Scherzer (eds.), *Language in use: Readings in sociolinguistics*, 28–53. Englewood Cliffs, NJ: Prentice Hall.

Labov, William. 2001. *Principles of linguistic change Vol. 2: Social factors*. Vol. 2. Oxford [etc.]: Blackwell.

Labov, William. 2007. Transmission and diffusion. *Language* 83(2). 344–387.

Language Factory. 2013. *Canadian dialects of European languages*.

Meyerhoff, Miriam. 2006. Linguistic change, sociohistorical context, and theory-building in variationist linguistics: New-dialect formation in New Zealand. *English Language and Linguistics* 10(1). 173–194.

Nagy, Naomi. 1996. *Language contact and language change in the Faetar speech community*. University of Pennsylvania PhD dissertation.

Nagy, Naomi. 2011. A multilingual corpus to explore geographic variation. *Rassegna Italiana di Linguistica Applicata* 43(1-2). 65–84.

Nagy, Naomi. 2015. A sociolinguistic view of null subjects and VOT in Toronto heritage languages. *Lingua* 164(2). 309–327.

Nagy, Naomi & Michael Iannozzi. 2014. *Older speakers use more null subjects, but is the variable stable? Accounting for contrasting reports of contact effects*. NWAV44 Chicago.

Nagy, Naomi & Alexei Kochetov. 2013. VOT across the generations: A cross-linguistic study of contact-induced change. In Peter Siemund, Ingrid Gogolin, Monika Schulz & Julia Davydova (eds.), *Multilingualism and language contact in urban areas: Acquisition - Development - Teaching - Communication*, 19–38. Amsterdam: John Benjamins.

Nagy, Naomi & Miriam Meyerhoff. 2008. *The love that dare not speak its name– The fascination with monolingual speech communities in sociolinguistics*. Poster. Houston.

Nagy, Naomi & Miriam Meyerhoff. 2015. Extending ELAN into Variationist Sociolinguistics (description and tutorial).

Schneider, Edgar W. 2003. The dynamics of New Englishes: From identity construction to dialect birth. *Language* 79(2). 233–281.

Schneider, Edgar W. 2007. *Postcolonial English: Varieties around the world.* New York: Cambridge Press.

Struk, Danylo. 2000. Between Ukish and oblivion: The Ukrainian language in Canada today. First wave emigrants: The first fifty years of Ukrainian settlement in Australia. In H. Koscharsky (ed.), *Proceedings of the Third Conference of the Ukrainian Studies Association of Australia, in association with the Shevchenko Scientific Society in Australia, Macquarie University, 3–5 July 1998,* 67–74. Huntington, NY: Nova Science Publishers.

Tagliamonte, Sali. 2006. *Analysing sociolinguistic variation.* Cambridge etc.: Cambridge University Press.

Thomason, Sarah Grey. 2001. *Language contact.* Washington D.C.: Georgetown University Press.

Thomason, Sarah Grey & Terrence Kaufman. 1988. *Language contact, creolization, and genetic linguistics.* Berkeley: University of California Press.

Trudgill, Peter. 1986. *Dialects in contact.* Oxford: Blackwell.

Trudgill, Peter. 2004. *New-dialect formation. the inevitability of colonial Englishes.* Edinburgh: Edinburgh University Press.

Tse, Holman & Naomi Nagy. 2014. *Exploring automated formant analysis for variationist study of Heritage Cantonese.* CRC Summer Phonetics/Phonology Workshop, Toronto, June 19, 2014.

Van Herk, Gerard, Paul De Decker & Jennifer Thorburn. 2015. *Undergraduate-conducted surveys: Balancing learning and data collection.* Methods in Dialectology XV, Groningen, August 12, 2015.

Walker, James A. 2010. *Variation in linguistic systems.* New York [etc.]: Routledge.

Statistics Canada. 2014. *Mother tongue of person.*

Statistics Canada. 2011a. *Census profile.*

Statistics Canada. 2011b. *2011 Census Highlights: Factsheet 6.*

Wikipedia. 2014. *Canadian Ukranian.*

ISTAT (Istituto Nazionale di Statistica). 2007. *La lingua italiana, i dialetti e le lingue straniere (2006).*

Chapter 3

From diglossia to diaglossia: A West Flemish case-study

Anne-Sophie Ghyselen
Ghent University

> Auer (2005; 2011) distinguishes five types of dialect/standard constellations in Europe, which stand in a diachronic relationship and of which the diaglossic repertoire, marked by intermediate forms between standard and dialect, would be the most widespread in Europe today. While a lot of current research focuses on contemporary shifts in diaglossic situations towards dialect loss (cf. Vandekerckhove 2009), shifts from diglossia to diaglossia remain relatively understudied (cf. Auer 2005: 23). The present paper reports on the West Flemish area, where the language is said to be evolving from a diglossic to a diaglossic situation (De Caluwe 2009, Willemyns 2007: 272). In order to tap into the structure of this West Flemish repertoire, the language use of 10 speakers from Ypres is analysed systematically by means of a correspondence analysis of 26 phonological and morphosyntactic variables in five speech settings. These analyses show that in West Flanders, the emerging intermediate variations are mainly used in supraregional informal settings, illustrating the need to focus on this at present understudied speech setting when studying changing repertoires. The data clearly indicate that in the incipient transition from diglossia to diaglossia, both dialect and (an intended form of) standard language are still vital as means of regional informal and supraregional formal communication respectively. Structurally, the intermediate variations mainly result from dialect-to-standard convergence, but some speakers also show horizontal dialect convergence.

1 Introduction

All over Europe factors such as geographical and social mobility, a high level of education, the growing impact of mass media and a general decreasing level of formality in public life have caused various types of language change (Taeldeman 2009: 355). Heeringa & Hinskens (2014) for instance find convergence between dialect varieties and dialect groups in the Dutch language area, Cheshire et al.

Anne-Sophie Ghyselen. 2016. From diglossia to diaglossia: A West Flemish case-study. In Marie-Hélène Côté, Remco Knooihuizen & John Nerbonne (eds.), *The future of dialects*, 35–63. Berlin: Language Science Press. DOI:10.17169/langsci.b81.82

(2011) report on the emergence of Multicultural London English, Auer & Spiekermann (2011) find homogenisation of the spoken standard across Germany, and according to Kristiansen (2001) a double standard norm is emerging in Denmark. These are only some examples of the many studies reporting contemporary language change in Europe. The described changes at first sight appear very diverse and language-specific, but as Auer (2005: 7) argues, "on a sufficient level of generalization there is a systematicity behind the superficial heterogeneity". He distinguishes five types of dialect/standard constellations, which stand in a diachronic relationship and of which the diaglossic repertoire, marked by intermediate forms between standard and dialect, would be the most widespread in Europe today. While a lot of current research focuses on contemporary shifts in diaglossic situations towards dialect loss (cf. Ghyselen & De Vogelaer 2013; Grondelaers & van Hout 2011a; Vandekerckhove 2009), "the exact nature of the transition from diglossia to diaglossia is not yet clear" (Auer 2005: 23). Which pragmatic functions are initially allocated to the newly emerged intermediate variations? To what degree does the change from diglossia to diaglossia imply dialect loss, either structural or functional (Auer & Hinskens 1996)? What impact do the new intermediate variations have on the structure and function of the standard language? How do new intermediate variations structurally take shape? To gain insight into these issues, the present paper reports on the West Flemish dialect area, where the repertoire is said to be evolving from a diglossic one into a diaglossic one (De Caluwe 2009, Willemyns 2007: 272). To tap into the structure of this West Flemish repertoire and the functionality of its components, the language use of 10 speakers from Ypres is analysed systematically. A correspondence analysis of 26 phonological and morphosyntactic variables in five speech settings shows that in Ypres, some speakers still have diglossic repertoires, whereas others have diaglossic ones. The latter speakers use intermediate variations in supraregional informal settings, but speak dialect and standard language in informal regional and formal supraregional settings respectively. This variation between repertoire structures indicates that in the West Flemish incipient transition from diglossia to diaglossia, both dialect and (an intended form of) standard language are still vital as means of respectively regional informal and supraregional formal communication. Structurally, the intermediate variations mainly result from dialect-to-standard convergence; some speakers however also show horizontal dialect convergence.

2 Language variation and change in Flanders

In this study, the term *Flanders* is used in its political sense to refer to the northern, Dutch speaking part of Belgium.[1] This area shares a standard language with the Netherlands, although it has developed its own national variety, i.e. Belgian Dutch (cf. Grondelaers & van Hout 2011a). The Belgian Dutch standard language is in its spoken form often referred to as 'VRT-Dutch', as it is the variety used by official broadcasters on the Vlaamse Radio- en Televisieomroep (VRT), the Flemish public broadcaster. This VRT-Dutch is often said to be a mainly virtual colloquial variety, as it is desired by the authorities, but rarely spoken in practice (De Caluwe 2009: 19). Instead, in daily life, non-standard language is ubiquitous. A wide variety of dialects can for instance be heard when travelling through Flanders. These dialects are traditionally classified into four main dialect groups (cf. figure fig:ghys:Flanders): the West Flemish, East-Flemish, Brabantic and Limburgian dialects (cf. Vandekerckhove 2009). Moreover, intermediate language use between dialect and standard language (the so-called *"tussentaal"*[2]) is increasingly prevalent (De Caluwe 2006), turning the Flemish language repertoire into a largely diaglossic repertoire (cf. §3).

Since the Nineties, the status of both dialects and standard language in Flanders has changed significantly, just as in many other European language communities. Dialect studies have shown that the dialects in Flanders are suffering from both functional (Ghyselen & Van Keymeulen 2014) and structural (Heeringa & Hinskens 2014; Vandekerckhove 2000) loss:[3] increasingly fewer people are speaking dialect in increasingly fewer situations, and those who still speak their local dialect are using fewer and fewer local dialect features. In this process of dialect loss clear regional differences can be distinguished: whereas dialect loss has progressed furthest in East Flanders, Brabant and Limburg, West Flanders (and especially the south-western part of this area) still shows considerable dialect vitality (cf. Ghyselen & Van Keymeulen 2014). The observed functional dialect loss mainly benefits the use of intermediate language (De Caluwe 2006), although *tussentaal* does not seem to be the mere result of dialect loss. *Tussentaal* would also function as a 'lingua franca' in informal settings where dialect speakers from different areas meet (cf. Gabel 2010).

---

[1] In its dialectological sense, the notion *Flanders* refers to the area where the West, East, French, and Zeeuws Flemish dialects are spoken. This area coincides with the old county of Flanders and comprises the western part of northern Belgium, northern France, and the southwest of the Netherlands.

[2] See Ghyselen (2015) on the way in which dialect can be distinguished from *tussentaal*.

[3] See Ghyselen & Van Keymeulen (2014) for an in-depth discussion of the distinction between functional and structural dialect loss.

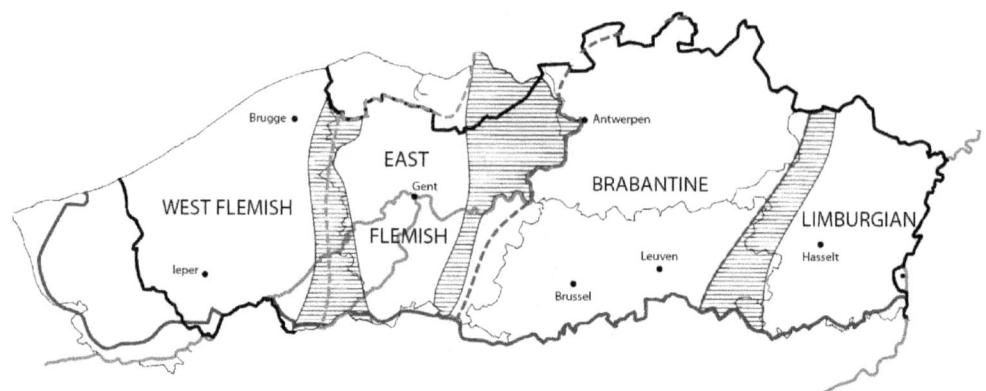

Figure 1: Dialect areas in Flanders; based on Taeldeman (2009: 359).

At the standard end of the language repertoire, several processes of language change have been observed as well. Plevoets (2008) concludes on the basis of an extensive corpus study that speakers born in the 50s and 60s of the previous century frequently use Standard Dutch, whereas those from the 70s and 80s are more prone to speak *tussentaal*. Delarue (2013) observes in the same vein that several teachers aged 50 or older speak exclusively Standard Dutch in their classes, whereas younger teachers tend to use non-standard variants more frequently while teaching. These observations point towards "standard loss" in Flanders, although it has to be borne in mind that this loss pertains mainly to the spoken standard: as Grondelaers & van Hout (2011b: 9) and Vandekerckhove (2005) emphasise, the written standard in Flanders is fairly resistant to change. While increasing numbers of empirical studies focus on the changing position of the standard language in Flanders (see e.g. Plevoets 2008), a number of issues continue to be highly controversial. One of these is the shape of the change process, namely whether the "standard loss" in Flanders should be thought of as an instance of destandardisation "whereby the established standard language loses its position as the one and only 'best language'" (Coupland & Kristiansen 2011: 28), or rather as demotisation, i.e. the process whereby the "'standard ideology' as such stays intact while the valorisation of ways of speaking changes" (Coupland & Kristiansen 2011: 28). Related to this question is the debate on the potential 'stabilisation of *tussentaal*', that is whether one more or less homogeneous *tussentaal* is emerging, as suggested in Willemyns (2005) for instance. For a discussion of the relationship between the homogeneisation of *tussentaal* on the one hand and demotisation and destandardisation on the other, see Ghyselen (2015).

3 From diglossic to diaglossic repertoires

Auer (2005; 2011) distinguishes five macrotypes of dialect/standard constellations. The first two types, the exoglossic diglossia and the medial diglossia, will not be elaborated on here, as these are rare in Europe and do not occur in Flanders. The types which are of interest in this chapter, are the third, fourth and fifth repertoire types, respectively the spoken diglossia, the diaglossic repertoire, and the dialect loss repertoire. Spoken diglossia are generally defined as repertoires in which the spoken standard is strictly separated, both structurally and functionally, from the local dialects. These varieties each have specific pragmatic functions, which force speakers to code-switch depending on the situation they are in. The diaglossic repertoire, however, is marked by intermediate variants between standard and dialect. In this repertoire type, there are not only code-switches between dialect and the standard, but speakers can also make subtler shifts from a more dialectal variant to a more standard one. These shifts have been accounted for in relation to the attention a speaker devotes to his or her speech (Labov 1972: 208) and to several situational parameters, such as the (language use of) the speech partners (Bell 1984), the conversational topic or the medium (Giles & Powesland 1975). Recent approaches to style-shifting, however, argue that style shifts are not merely triggered by external parameters, but that speakers can also actively use them to construct social meaning and to act out identities which may for instance not be symbolised through the base dialect (Auer 2005: 23, Schilling-Estes 2002: 378). The precise mechanisms by which diaglossia evolve out of diglossia are at present not clear and many questions remain. For example, what pragmatic functions are initially allocated to the newly emerging intermediate variations in diaglossic repertoires? What is the impact on the functionality of both dialect and standard language? From a more structural perspective, how do the intermediate variations take shape? Auer (2005: 25) suggests dialect change targeted towards the standard language as one of the main driving forces in the emergence of intermediate variations, but also highlights that this process may co-occur with destandardisation, implying that regional features are increasingly tolerated in the standard variety. In dialect loss situations, the fifth repertoire type discussed by Auer (2005; 2011), destandardisation would occur even more frequently. It appears that the disappearance of the linguistic forms with the most restricted geographical reach stimulates processes of divergence from the national standard (Auer 2005: 30). According to Auer (2005: 30), this divergence is steered by speakers' "need to sound different from the codified standard".

Auer's distinction between diglossia and diaglossia seems quite straightforward. However, in empirical studies, different approaches towards these concepts can be distinguished. Rys & Taeldeman (2007) for instance label the Flemish language repertoire as diaglossic because production data from Flanders show frequent non-dialectal, non-standard language. Willemyns & Vandenbussche (2008), however, seem to take speaker intention as a central criterion: though they recognise that in West Flanders intermediate language use can be heard, they nonetheless argue that the repertoire in the western peripheral region is of a diglossic nature, as speakers would intend to speak either dialect or standard and perceive the language repertoire in a bipolar way. This distinction between production- and perception-oriented approaches is closely intertwined with a distinction between studies at the level of the individual speaker and those at the level of the speech community. Repertoire studies at these different levels can yield very different results; where individual speakers may have diglossic repertoires with a clear structural distance between dialect and some form of intended standard, a combination of all those individual repertoires may yield a diaglossic overall picture. In this study, I adopt a production-oriented approach focusing on the language use of individual speakers. If speakers code-switch between two structurally and functionally separate systems, their repertoire is labelled diglossic; if they dispose of more than two types of language use and make more subtle style-shifts, their repertoire is classified as diaglossic. On the level of the speech community, the shift from a diglossic to a diaglossic repertoire can therefore be characterised as a shift from a community in which most speakers show a diglossic individual repertoire to one in which most speakers have diaglossic individual repertoires.

While the Flemish language area is generally said to be diaglossic and evolving towards dialect loss, the language repertoire in West Flanders is still usually classed as largely diglossic (De Caluwe 2009, Willemyns & Vandenbussche 2008), with individual speakers making clear code-switches between dialect and some form of standard language. Recently, however, Gabel (2010) found that West Flemish adolescents have more than two codes at their disposal; her study shows how adolescents switch to non-standard, non-dialectal language use in supraregional informal settings. This observation points towards changing repertoire structures in West Flanders, but as the supraregional informal language use of older speakers has not been studied so far – supraregional informal language as such has remained largely out of the picture in most variationist research – straightforward conclusions concerning ongoing changes are difficult to draw.

4 Methodology

In order to study the potentially changing repertoires in West Flanders, this research analyses the linguistic repertoires of ten highly educated women[4] from Ypres systematically by studying their language in several speech settings. This practice has a considerable tradition in German dialectology and variationist linguistics (cf. Kehrein 2012, Lenz 2003, Stellmacher 1977) but is fairly novel in Dutch sociolinguistics. The studied women were born between 1981 and 1986 (n=5) or between 1955 and 1961 (n=5)[5], and were recorded in five speech settings: (1) a dialect test, (2) a standard language test, (3) a conversation with a friend[6] from the same city, (4) a conversation with a friend from a different dialect area and (5) a sociolinguistic interview with an unknown interviewer from a different dialect area. During the sociolinguistic interviews, data were gathered about the linguistic background of the informants and their perceptions of their own language use. In the dialect and standard tests, the informants heard stimuli sentences spoken in either standard Dutch or in the local dialect, which they had to translate into respectively the dialect of the oldest people of their town and standard Dutch "as heard during news broadcasts". These tests were used to determine the informant's proficiency in the most acrolectal versus basilectal speech styles available in a relevant location.[7] The gathered recordings were transcribed orthographically using Praat (Boersma & Weenink 2011)[8] and a searchable corpus was built using the software package EXMARaLDA (Schmidt & Worner 2009).

---

[4] They all have a university degree, but they do not practice a language-oriented profession (no linguists, interpreters, journalists, speech therapists, actors or teachers).
[5] Speakers from the younger age group have the letter 'a' in the speaker code (e.g. wvla1), whereas the older speakers have the letter 'b' (e.g. wvlb1). I compared the language use of younger and older women, not of younger women and older men (contrary to Heeringa & Hinskens 2014), as I did not want age effects to be confounded by gender effects.
[6] Gender was not controlled for in these conversations, as it was already difficult finding suitable informants without making demands on the gender of the speech partners. 6 of the 20 conversations with friends (of the same or of a different dialect area) were mixed-sex conversations, so the majority were same-sex conversations. This potentially confounding factor will be taken into account when discussing the results.
[7] The data obtained in the test settings are of a very different nature than the spontaneous speech data (cf. Lenz 2003: 57–62). This difference will be taken into account when analyzing the results.
[8] Of each conversation with a friend 30 minutes were transcribed; the interviews and dialect and standard tests were transcribed entirely.

The built corpus was analysed using a correlative sociolinguistic approach: the distributions of 26 phonological and morphosyntactic features were studied in the five types of data. In total, 22495 tokens were auditorily categorised into 60 variant categories by one linguist. To judge the objectiveness of these categorisations, a random sample of about 190 tokens was taken for each phonological variable, which was subsequently rated by a second linguist. If the inter-rater agreement proved to be too low (Cohen's kappa <0.61, cf. Landis & Koch 1977: 165), the variable was excluded from the study. A list of the selected variables and their attested variants is given in Tables 1 and 2, where information is also given on the frequency of the variants and the variant type:[9]

1. [-st,+ypr]-variants, i.e. non-standard variants endogenous in the dialect of Ypres;

2. [+st,+ypr]-variants, i.e. standard variants which also occur in the dialect of Ypres

3. [-st,-ypr]-variants, i.e. variants which do not occur in the standard, nor in the dialect of Ypres.

4. [+st,-ypr]-variants, i.e. standard variants which do not occur in the dialect of Ypres;

The second column of Table 1 gives information on the regional spread of the [-st, +ypr]-variants: (a) a region smaller than West Flanders, (b) West Flanders, (c) West and East Flanders or (d) an area larger than West and East Flanders. A last category of variables (category e) contains variables of which the [-ypr, -st]-variant occurs in almost all dialects in Flanders, except in the Ypres area. This information on the regional spread of the [-st] variants is highly relevant, as the regional spread of dialect features is known to strongly influence the dynamics of those features (cf. Schirmunski 1930, Taeldeman 2009). Since it would involve going too far afield to discuss all of the 23 variables in detail, I refer to SAND

---

[9] In order to make this distinction, benchmarks for both the standard and dialect were necessary. As benchmark for standardness, the pronunciation dictionary of Heemskerk & Zonneveld (2000) and the *Algemeen Nederlandse Spraakkunst* (Haeseryn 1997) were used. The Ypres dialect norm was determined using SAND (Barbiers 2005, Barbiers & Devos 2008), FAND (De Wulf, Goossens & Taeldeman 2005, Goossens, Taeldeman & Verleyen 2000, Goossens et al. 1998) and MAND (De Schutter et al. 2005, Goeman 2008). For a number of variables, specialised dialectological descriptions were consulted (Cornips & De Vogelaer 2009 on gender in Dutch, De Vogelaer 2008 on subject marking, De Vogelaer & Vandenberghe 2006 on indefinite pronouns and adverbs).

(Barbiers 2005, Barbiers & Devos 2008), FAND (De Wulf, Goossens & Taeldeman 2005, Goossens, Taeldeman & Verleyen 2000, Goossens et al. 1998), MAND (De Schutter et al. 2005, Goeman 2008), De Vogelaer (2008), Cornips & De Vogelaer (2009) and De Vogelaer & Vandenberghe (2006) for detailed information. Ghyselen (2015) describes how the variables were selected.

To study how the attested variants correlate to each other and to the independent variables (age and speech setting), profile-based Multiple Correspondence Analysis was performed (cf. De Sutter, Delaere & Plevoets 2012, Plevoets 2008) with age, speech setting and speaker as independent variables. Multiple Correspondence Analysis (MCA) is a descriptive data analysis technique which studies correspondences or associations between rows and columns of a frequency table and "provides a detailed description of the data, yielding a simple, yet exhaustive analysis" (Costa et al. 2013: 1). The technique allows for the detection of potential clusters of linguistic features which behave alike, for instance clusters of dialect features or clusters of Standard Dutch features, and to visualise the structural distance (or the lack of a structural gap) between those clusters. As such, it is the ideal technique to study whether speakers have diglossic or diaglossic repertoires. The first step in correspondence analysis is to calculate two matrices with distances,[10] one for the distances between columns (for instance the association between the speech setting dialect test and the situation interview for the 60 studied variants) and one for the distances between rows (for instance the association between the *ke*-diminutives and the *ge*-pronomina for the different speech settings and ages). The second step is plotting the calculated distances in a two-dimensional space. For this purpose, the originally multidimensional matrices are reduced to two-dimensional matrices using singular value decomposition, a dimension reduction technique which aims at preserving as much relevant information as possible. The distances from these two low-dimensional matrices are subsequently plotted in a biplot, in which the relative positions of the data points are indicative of their associations: variants plotted far away from each other are marked by low degrees of association; variants plotted close to each other show high associations. The distances between data points and the way in which these cluster is therefore important in the interpretation of correspondence plots; the x- and y-axes do not have predetermined interpretations (cf. Geeraerts 2010).

---

[10] Given that the input data are frequency tables, the distances are calculated using chi-square metrics.

Table 1: Overview of the analysed variables and attested variants ([-st,+ypr] , [+st,+ypr] , [-st,-ypr] , and [+st,-ypr]) for phonology.

Region	Variable	Attested variants (variant number, variant frequency)
a	Realisation verbal prefix <ge> in past participles	• [-st,+ypr] Deletion first consonant (1, n=107): [æ]daan, [ə]daan ('done') • [+st,-ypr] Realisation first consonant (2, n=969): [ɣə]daan
	Representation Standard Dutch [sχ] in anlaut	• [-st,+ypr] [ʃχ] (3, n=122): [ʃχoːlə] ('school') • [+st,-ypr] [sχ] (4, n =154): [sχoːl]
b	Representation Standard Dutch [ɛ.i] (not before r or in auslautposition)	• [-st,+ypr] Short monophthong (5, n=978): [mɪn] ('mine') • [+st,-ypr] Long monophthong or diphthong[a] (6, n=1183): [mɛːn], m[ɛ.i]n
	Representation Standard Dutch [œ.y] (> wgm. û)	• [-st,+ypr] Short monophthong (7, n=370): [hys] ('house') • [-st,-ypr] Long monophthong (8, n=340): [hœ.s] • [+st,-ypr] Diphthong[b] (9, n=227): [hœ.ys]
	Representation Standard Dutch [ɔ.u] before [t] of [d]	• [-st,+ypr] Short monophthong (10, n=116): [kut] ('cold') • [-st,-ypr] Long monophthong (11, n=44): [kɔːt] • [+st,-ypr] Diphthong (12, n=95): [kɔ.ut]
	Representation Standard Dutch [oː](> ogm. au) before dental consonant	• [-st,+ypr] Diphthong[c] (13, n=87): [ɣruət] ('big') • [+st,-ypr] Long monophthong (14, n=135): [ɣroːt]

[a] No distinction was made between the long monophthong [ɛː] and the dipthong [ɛ.i], nor between closed and open variants of the diphthongs. Without acoustic analyses, those distinctions proved too difficult to make objectively (Cohen's kappa <0.61).

[b] For this variable and also for the realisation of Standard Dutch [ɔ.u] the distinction between long monophthongs and diphthongs proved objectively analysable without acoustic analysis (Cohens's kappa >0.61); no distinction was however made between different degrees of openness in the realisation of these vowels, as these were too difficult to make without acoustic analyses.

[c] In some areas of the research area, the diphthong is a typical feature of the dialect; in the city centre of Ypres, however, the basilectal form is the long monophthong which also characterises the standard language.

3 From diglossia to diaglossia: A West Flemish case-study

Region	Variable	Attested variants (variant number, variant frequency)
c	Representation Standard Dutch [ɣ]	• [-st,+ypr] Laryngalisation (15, n=4533): [h]oed [h]edaan ('well done') • [+st,-ypr] [ɣ] (16, n=1109): [ɣ]oed [ɣ]edaan
	Preservation of non-suffixal final schwa	• [-st,+ypr] Variant with schwa (17, n=105): *bedde* ('bed') • [+st,-ypr] Variant without schwa (18, n=168): *bed*
	Representation Standard Dutch [o:] (> wgm û in open syllables)	• [-st,+ypr] Palatalised form (19, n=95): [zønə] ('son') • [+st,-ypr] [o:] (20, n=115): [zo:n]
d	Representation of Standard Dutch initial [h] in a selection of words	• [-st,+ypr] H-procope (21, n=1461): *oed* ('hat') • [+st,-ypr] Realisation [h] (22, n=258): *hoed*
	t-deletion in *niet* ('not') or in *dat* ('that') + C	• [-st,+ypr] T-apocope (23, n=3608): *je moet da nie doen.* ('you do not have to do that') • [+st,-ypr] Realisation final consonant (24, n=262): *je moet dat niet doen.*
e	t-deletion in *dat* ('that') + V	• [-st,-ypr] T-apocope (25, n=104): *da ook* ('that too') • [+st,+ypr] Realisation final consonant[a] (26, n=879): *dat ook*

[a] No distinction is made between the variants *da[t]* and *da[d]*, since that distinctions is often difficult to make without acoustic analyses.

Table 2: Overview of the analysed variables and attested variants ([-st,+ypr] , [+st,+ypr] , [-st,-ypr] , and [+st,-ypr]) for morphosyntax.

Region	Variable	Attested variants (variant number, variant frequency)
a	Male singular indefinite article	• [-st,+ypr] *e* (27, n=426): *e vent* ('a guy') • [-st,-ypr] *ne* (28, n=120): *ne vent* • [+st,-ypr] *een* (29, n=109): *een vent*
	Verb form present simple 1st singular (in sentences without inversion)	• [-st,+ypr] Infinitive[a] (30, n=493): *ik spelen* ('I play') • [-st,-ypr] root +e (31, n=34): *ik spele* • [+st,-ypr] root (32, n=266): *ik speel*
	Possessive pronoun 1st plural form of pronoun	• [-st,+ypr] *(n)us/(n)uze* (33, n=77): *(n)us kind, (n)uze moeder* ('our child', 'our mother') • [+st,-ypr] *ons/onze* (34, n=145): *ons kind, onze moeder*
	Personal pronoun 'he' - weak form in postverbal position or after conjunctions	• [-st,+ypr] *'n/ne* (35, n=95): *Komt 'n ook?* ('is he coming too?') • [-st,+ypr] *'n em* (36, n=28): *Komt 'n em ook?* • [-st,-ypr] *em* (37, n=39): *Komt em ook?* • [+st,-ypr] *ie* (38, n=86): *Komtie ook?* • [+st,-ypr] *hij* (39, n=66): *Komt hij ook?*
	Indefinite pronoun/adverb of person, matter or place	• [-st,+ypr] *etwien, etwat/etwuk, etwaarschen* (40, n=113): *Is er etwat?* ('is something going on?') • [+st,-ypr] *iemand, iets, ergens* (41, n=246): *Is er iets?*

[a] This infinitive form is widespread in Flanders in a few historically athematic monosyllabic verbs (a.o. *doen* 'do' and *gaan* 'go'), but the occurrence of the infinitive form in thematic verbs is confined to a small area in West Flanders. The variable was studied in all thematic verbs occurring in the first person singular.

3 From diglossia to diaglossia: A West Flemish case-study

Region	Variable	Attested variants (variant number, variant frequency)
c	Subject doubling: 3rd singular mascular/feminine, 1st plural, 3rd plural in sentences with inversion and dependent clauses, with a full subject[a]	• [-st,+ypr] Subject doubling (42, n=80): *A me wider komen...* (Lit: 'if we come') • [+st,-ypr] No subject doubling (43, n=204): *Als wij komen...* (Lit: 'if we come')
	Auxiliary in present perfect with *zijn* ('to be'), *tegenkomen* ('meet') and *vallen* ('fall') as main verbs	• [-st,+ypr] *hebben* (44, n=27): *Ik heb ziek geweest.* (Lit: 'I have ill been') • [+st,-ypr] *zijn* (45, n=113): *Ik ben ziek geweest* (Lit: 'I am ill been')
d	Subject doubling 2nd singular/plural and 1st singular in sentences with inversion and dependent clauses, with a full subject	• [-st,+ypr] Subject doubling (46, n=260): *Morgen kom ek ik ook* (Lit: 'tomorrow come I I too') • [+st,-ypr] No subject doubling (47, n=403): *Morgen kom ik ook.* (Lit: 'tomorrow come I too')
	Preposition in subclauses with to-infinitives	• [-st,+ypr] Preposition *voor*[b] (48, n=99): *Dat kost veel voor te wassen.* (Lit: 'that costs much for wash') • [+st,-ypr] Preposition *om* (49, n=109): *Dat kost veel om te wassen.* (Lit: 'that costs much to wash')
	Expletive *dat* ('that') after the conjunctions *wie, wat, waar, hoe, wanneer* and *of*	• [-st,+ypr] With expletive *dat* (50, n=312): *Ik weet niet wie dat er komt* (Lit: 'I know not who that is coming') • [+st,-ypr] Without expletive *dat* (51, n=47): *Ik weet niet wie er komt.* (Lit: 'I know not who is coming')

[a] In these cases subject doubling with a weak pronoun is obligatory in the local dialect (cf. De Vogelaer 2008: 326).
[b] It can be debated whether the construction with the *voor*-preposition is endogenous in the dialect of Ypres. See Ryckeboer (1983) for more information.

Region	Variable	Attested variants (variant number, variant frequency)
e	Personal pronoun 2nd singular, weak form in preverbal position	• [-st,-ypr] ge (52, n=153): *Ge komt.* ('you are coming') • [+st,+ypr] je (53, n=321): *Je komt.* • [-st,+ypr] je...gie (54, n=15): *Je komt gie.*
	Diminutives with nouns of which the root does not end in [t]	• [-st,-ypr] *ke*-diminutive (55, n=55): *bloemke/bloemeke* ('little flower') • [+st,+ypr] *je*-diminutive[a] (56, n=169): *bloempje*
	Negation in sentences with *nooit* ('never'), *niemand* ('no one'), *nergens* ('nowhere')	• [-st,-ypr] Double negation (57, n=3): *Ik ga dat nooit nie doen.* (Lit: 'I go that never never do') • [+st,+ypr] Single negation (58, n=103): *Ik ga dat nooit doen.* (Lit: 'I go that never do')
	Possessive pronoun 1st plural inflection before female singular nouns, male singular nouns referring to a family relationship, or before plural nouns	• [-st,-ypr] No inflection (59, n=18): *ons moeder* ('our mother') • [+st,+ypr] With inflection (60, n=37): *onze moeder*

[a] The allomorphy within the *je*-suffix was not taken into account as this complicates the calculation of distance measures: some of the *je*-suffixes in the Ypres dialect coincide for instance with Standard Dutch *je*-suffixes (*bloemetje*, 'little flower'), whereas others have a different allomorph (*boeksje* versus *boekje*, 'little book').

In this study, a profile-based variant of MCA was used. This profile-based approach differs from "traditional" correspondence analysis in that the different variants are not treated as autonomous data points, but as sublevels of a main variable. In the case of this study, *ke*-diminutives and *je*-diminutives were for instance treated as sublevels of the variable 'diminutive', and not as two autonomous variables. For more information on (the advantages of) this profile-based approach, see De Sutter, Delaere & Plevoets (2012) and Speelman, Grondelaers & Geeraerts (2003). Another aspect in which the correspondence analyses performed in this article differ from traditional MCA is that hypothesis-testing statistics were added; the technique was therefore not purely descriptive. More specifically, confidence ellipses were drawn using bootstrap confidence interval construction (for more information, see Plevoets 2013). These ellipses are interpreted in the same way as traditional confidence intervals (cf. Plevoets 2013): if ellipses of two categories (e.g. two age groups) do not overlap, the distance between those two categories is significant; if they do overlap, there is no evidence of statistical significance.

Correspondence analysis is closely related to cluster analysis, a descriptive multivariate technique which aims to identify clusters in multivariate data in such a way that "the members of one group are very similar to each other and at the same time very dissimilar to members of other groups" (Gries 2013: 337). As Lebart & Mirkin (1993) describe, the process involved (grouping of similar categories by measuring co-variation) is distinct from correspondence analysis (projection onto a principal subspace), but the results are usually fairly similar; both methods are descriptive techniques which group variables based on their degree of correspondence. In this paper, correspondence analysis is used as the main analysis technique for the principal reason that it goes a step further than cluster analysis: whereas cluster analysis shows whether different variables are related to each other, correspondence analysis can also explain how these variables are related by showing associations with main effects such as age and speech setting. Moreover, at present no profile-based variants of cluster analysis are available, while this profile-based approach has proven advantageous in usage-based studies of language varieties (cf. Speelman, Grondelaers & Geeraerts 2003). However, cluster analysis also has advantages over correspondence analysis. Lebart & Mirkin (1993: 15) highlight the practical advantage that "it is much easier to describe a set of clusters than a continuous space". Moreover, where correspondence plots usually only plot two dimensions for reasons of feasibility, a cluster dendrogram can take more dimensions into account. For these reasons it can be useful to combine the two approaches. In this study the output of the correspondence analysis is used as input for cluster analysis. By means of a screeplot, it is first determined how many dimensions of the correspondence analysis are ideally maintained after the singular value decomposition. Only two of those dimensions can be plotted in the correspondence plot, but a multidimensional dataset can serve as input for the cluster analysis. By combining the results of the cluster analysis (i.e. the multidimensional dendrogram) with that of the correspondence analysis (i.e. the two-dimensional correspondence plot), a thorough insight can be achieved in the data structure. In the cluster analysis the Ward-method, often also called 'the minimum variance' method, is used. This method, which has proven relevant in several linguistic studies, aims at minimizing the variance within each cluster (Gries 2013: 317).

5 Results

5.1 The repertoire at community level

Figure 2 shows the biplot of the data obtained by profile-based correspondence analysis. All attested variants are plotted against the main effects for age and speech setting.[11] Variants plotted close to each other show strong associations; if variants are plotted far away from each other, the association is weak. The same goes for the main effects: if two main effects (e.g. the dialect test 'DIA' and the conversations with friends of the same region 'REG') are close to each other, it means the language use in these speech settings or of these age groups is very similar. The small black ellipses, drawn in full black lines in Figure 2, represent the 95% confidence intervals of the main effects (cf. §4); if these overlap, there is no significant difference between the plotted categories.

A study of the plotted variants shows a horizontal continuum, stretching from [+ypr] in the left to [+st] in the right. In the upper right corner, several [-st, -ypr] variants cluster together. When looking for structure in this overall repertoire, there do seem to be clusters of co-occurring features. In the left of the graph for instance several dialect features, such as the possessive pronoun *(n)us* (33) and the realisation of Standard Dutch [sχ] as [ʃχ] (3), cluster together; elsewhere the image is less clear. A cluster analysis, using four dimensions of the correspondence analysis as input,[12] confirms that the biggest distinction in the data is one between the dialectal variants in the left and all other features, but also shows different subclusters within the non-dialectal space.[13] In total, roughly five clusters can be distinguished in the Ypres repertoire (marked with dotted lines and the letters a-b in Figure 2):

---

[11] The main effects for the variable 'speaker' were not plotted for reasons of surveyability. This variable was however added to the analyses; the plotted age and situation effects are hence controlled for speaker.

[12] The two dimensions plotted in Figure 2 only account for 59.26% of the original variance (eigenvalue dimension 1=47.17%, eigenvalue dimension 2=12.10%). This is a fairly low percentage; in dimension reduction the aim is usually to account for 70 to 80% of the original variance (cf. Di Franco & Marradi 2014: 83–84). A study of all dimensions of the correspondence analysis shows that an analysis with 4 dimensions would be ideal for the studied data, as 4 dimensions account for 73.28% of the original variance. Moreover, a screeplot of the eigenvalues for the different dimensions, shows an "elbow" at the fourth dimension (cf. Di Franco & Marradi 2014: 83–84). This elbow shows that the dimensions following the fourth dimension do not have much explanatory power. Plotting four dimensions is not feasible, but these dimensions can be used as input for cluster analysis.

[13] The dendrogram of this cluster analysis can be consulted via [14].

3 From diglossia to diaglossia: A West Flemish case-study

(a) a 'dialect' cluster, containing only [+ypr]-features;

(b) a 'cleaned up dialect' cluster, which mainly consists of [+ypr]-features, such as the indefinite article *e* (27) and *h*-deletion (21), but also has some [+st, -ypr]-features, such as the auxiliary *zijn* in the present perfect of *zijn, tegenkomen* and *vallen* (45);

(c) a [-st, -ypr]-cluster, which only contains [-st, -ypr]-features, such as the personal pronoun *ge* (52) or *ke*-diminutives (55). Interestingly enough, most of these features have been labelled "colloquial Belgian Dutch markers" by a.o. Geeraerts & Van de Velde (2013: 534–5). These variants, which occur in almost all Flemish dialects, except in our research area, seem to be so firmly embedded in the Flemish intermediate language use, that even speakers who do not have the variants in their local dialects use them.

(d) a 'near standard' cluster, which mainly contains standard Dutch features, such as the preposition *om* introducing subclauses with to-infinitives (49).

(e) A 'VRT-Dutch' cluster, which only contains standard Dutch features, such as the realisation of final *t* in the words *niet* and *dat* (24) or the lack of expletive *dat* (51).

It is up for debate to what degree clusters (c) and (d) should be seen as separate clusters, as the cluster analysis shows they are very close to each other. I have chosen to analyse them separately, as cluster (c) contains several features which according to Taeldeman (2008) are part of the homogeneising *tussentaal* in Flanders, making it interesting to analyse them separately.

On the basis of Figure 2, it is possible to suggest that the language repertoire in Ypres is of a diaglossic nature, stretching from dialect to standard language, with a range of intermediate variations. However, as argued in §3, the personal repertoires of the individual speakers need to be studied first, as the overall diaglossic image might result from a combination of mainly diglossic personal repertoires, each comprising slightly different language codes.

5.2 The individual repertoires

To gain insight in the individual repertoires of the recorded speakers, the interactions between speaker effects and speech setting effects were studied. In this way it is possible to investigate which of the above described clusters the individual

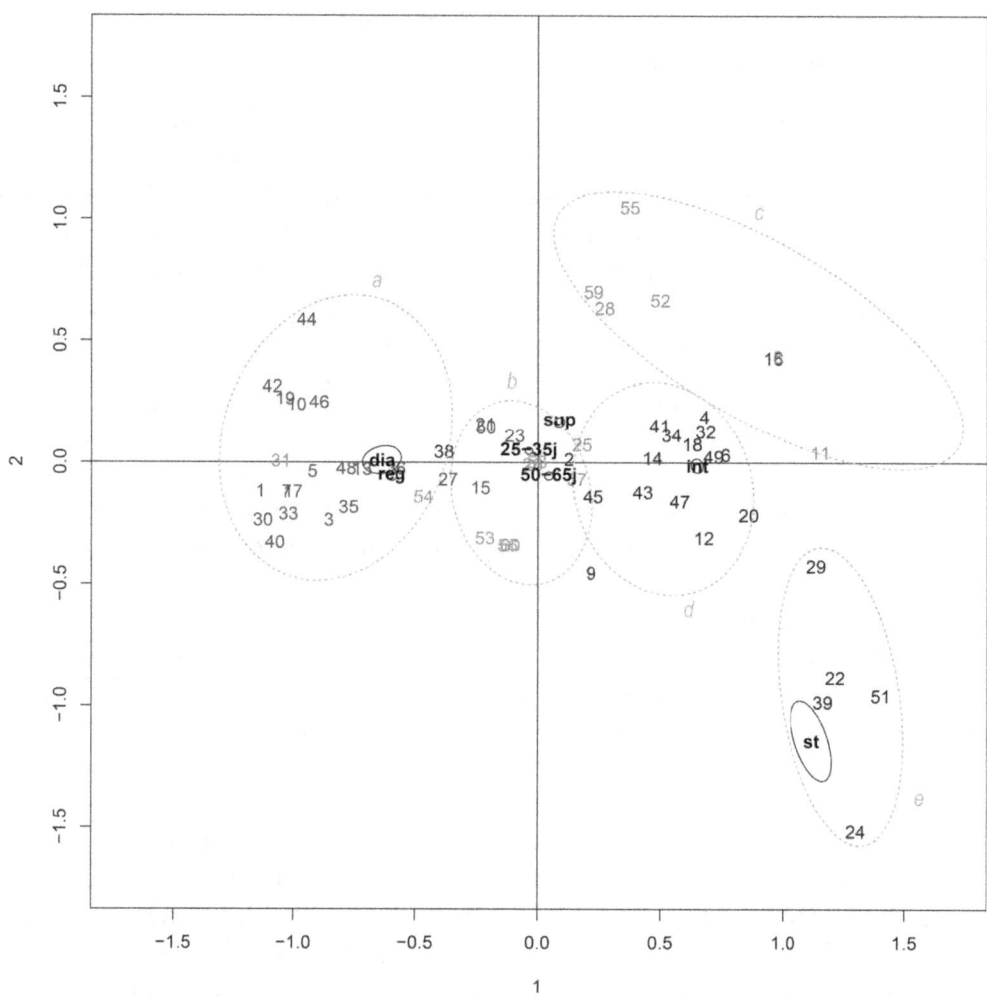

Figure 2: Correspondence biplot with speech setting, age and speaker as main effects. Dark red: [-st, +ypr]-variants; Light red: [+st, +ypr]-variant; Light blue: [-st, -ypr]-variants; Dark blue: [+st, -ypr]-variants; Black: Main effects and their 95% CI ellipses; Encircled areas (a-e): Clusters shown by cluster analysis.

Table 3: (Strong) associations found between clusters and speakers. In the 'Speaker' column, ** indicates that for this speaker, the conversation with a friend from a different dialect area was a mixed-sex conversation, whereas * indicates that the conversation with a friend from the same region was a mixed-sex conversation. No speaker had more than one mixed-sex conversation.

Age	Speaker	a) Dialect	b) "Cleaned up dialect"	c) [-st, -ypr] -cluster	d) "Standard Dutch with an accent"	e) VRT-Dutch
25–35y	Wvla1	X	X		X	X
	Wvla2	X	X		X	X
	Wvla3**	X		X		X
	Wvla4*	X		X	X	X
	Wvla5*	X			X	X
50–65y	Wvlb1**	X	X		X	X
	Wvlb2	X			X	X
	Wvlb3	X			X	X
	Wvlb4**	X	X		X	X
	Wvlb5*	X		X		X

speakers show associations with in which speech settings[15]. Table 3 illustrates how all speakers show strong associations with cluster (a), the dialect cluster, and cluster (e), the VRT-Dutch cluster, but that only a selected number of speakers shows associations with clusters (b), (c) and (d). The dialectal cluster belongs to the repertoire of every speaker, and is used in both the dialect test and the conversations with friends from the same area (cf. the very small distance between the dialect test, 'DIA', and the regional informal conversations, 'REG', in Figure 2). In the same vein, VRT-Dutch occurs in the language repertoire of all speakers, but as this cluster only shows associations with the fairly artificial standard language test ('ST'), it could be argued that the cluster represents a mainly virtual colloquial norm which is not realised in real life speech settings. To confirm this hypothesis, however, research with more speech settings (e.g. also studying the speakers when giving presentations or during job interviews) is necessary. The interview setting ('INT' in Figure 2) shows strong associations with cluster (d) for all speakers. It is interesting that some speakers (wvla5, wvlb4, wvlb3) use this "Standard Dutch with an accent" in both the interview setting and the conversa-

---

[15] See https://zenodo.org/record/33588 for the ten correspondence plots showing the interactions between speaker and speech setting effects.

tions with friends from a different dialect area ('SUP'), whereas other speakers make a clear difference between the interview setting and the supraregional informal conversations. Speakers wvla1, wvla2, wvlb1 and wvlb4 for instance use 'cleaned up dialect' (cluster b), rather than Standard Dutch with an accent in conversations with friends from a different region. This type of language is not realised in an attempt to speak Standard Dutch; the mentioned speakers indicate themselves during the interview that they merely 'clean up' their dialect for reasons of comprehensibility. The cleaned up dialect structurally results from dialect-to-standard convergence (cf. Auer 2005: 25) – the cluster is characterised by [+st, +ypr]- and [+st, -ypr]-features – confirming that dialect-to-standard convergence plays a pivotal role in the transition from diglossia to diaglossia (Auer & Hinskens 1996). Speaker wvla5, however, does not use cleaned up dialect in her conversation with a colleague of a different region, but rather a language characterised by several [-st, -ypr]-features (cluster c), which she does not use in the interview setting. It can therefore be said that in Ypres, there is also a kind of *tussentaal* which does not merely result from dialect-to-standard convergence, but is also influenced by 'horizontal' dialect convergence (Auer & Hinskens 1996). One could argue that the observed [-st, -ypr]-features are merely the result of accommodation at the interactual level - the speech partner of wvla5 was observed to use the forms too - but the behaviour of speakers wvla3 and wvlb5 seems to indicate that the forms are anchored more deeply in the language repertoires of a group of Ypres speakers. Speakers wvla3 and wvlb5 were observed to use the [-st, -ypr]-variants in both the supraregional informal conversations and the more formal interview setting, even though the interviewer never used the forms herself. This observation demonstrates that the [-st, -ypr]-variants do not solely result from interpersonal accommodation.[16]

When ignoring the fairly artificial VRT-Dutch code, which was not realised by the speakers in spontaneous speech settings, the conclusion can be drawn that some speakers seem to have diaglossic repertoires (e.g. wvla1, wvla2, wvla4, wvlb1, wvlb4), consciously realising intermediate language use in supraregional informal settings, whereas others have a rather diglossic repertoire, switching between dialect and either Standard Dutch with an accent (wvla5, wvlb2, wvlb3) or a form of Standard Dutch marked by several [-st, -ypr]-features (wvla5, wvlb5). It is important to note here that research with more speech settings might reveal more clusters and that the results are strongly determined by the speech partners involved. All informants were asked to record conversations with friends of about the same age, but of course, there are different kinds of friendship. Speaker

---

[16] See Auer & Hinskens (1996) on different levels of accommodation.

wvla2 was for instance observed to speak cleaned up dialect with her sister-in-law, who is from the East Flemish dialect area, but she might speak 'Standard Dutch with an accent' with close colleagues from the same East Flemish region. Potentially, the sex of the speech partner (see asterisks in Table 3) also has an influence, though no straightforward patterns could however be detected in this respect. Even when taking these caveats into account, the results seem to clearly indicate that there is variation between diglossic and diaglossic repertoire types in Ypres, hinting at a transition from diglossia to diaglossia.

5.3 Changing repertoires

Ongoing language change is often mirrored in age-related variation patterns (cf. Bailey et al. 1991). In this research, however, no clear age effects could be found. Table 3, for instance, shows diaglossic repertoires among both younger and older speakers. When looking at the interactions between age and speech setting[17], the only significant difference that could be found was that younger speakers ('2535') show slightly stronger associations with cluster (c) in the interview setting and in conversations with friends from a different dialect area than the older speakers ('5065'), a difference which can also be seen in the main effects in Figure 2. This significant difference could point towards some form of destandardisation in Ypres, with younger speakers allowing more [-st]-variants in their intended standard language. The hypothesis is however debatable, as the observed differences are very small, not to say negligible (cf. Figure 2). In the standard language test, the dialect test and the regional informal conversations, no significant age differences can be found. This firstly illustrates the dialect vitality in the Ypres area; both younger and older speakers still use the same local dialect in regional informal settings. Of course, this observation is based on a study of phonological and morphosyntactic variables; it is very likely that lexically, there is structural dialect loss. Secondly, the lack of age differences in the standard language test shows that highly educated young and older women have a comparable knowledge of the standard language norm. The general lack of age effects should however not be interpreted as showing a lack of language change in Ypres; age differences would probably be observed when studying younger informants (cf. Soete 2012) or more traditional NORM-speakers. This was not done in this research as the aim was to study supraregional informal conversations, which

---

[17] See https://zenodo.org/record/33588 for the biplot. Overlapping 'confidence ellipses', i.e. the small ellipses drawn in full black lines, indicate that the distance between the plotted effects is not significant.

requires mobile speakers with a network of supraregional contacts. The variation between repertoire structures among the studied speakers is indicative of a variation phase in the change from a society in which all speakers have diglossic repertoires to one in which all speakers have diaglossic repertoires. The observed patterns moreover show how intermediate variations in this change process are firstly used for supraregional informal communication and that dialect and (an intended form of) standard language are still vital as means of respectively regional informal and supraregional formal communication.

6 Conclusion

Which pragmatic functions are initially allocated to the newly emerged intermediate variations in diaglossic repertoires? To what degree does the change from diglossia to diaglossia imply dialect loss, either structural or functional? What impact do the new intermediate variations have on the structure and functionality of the standard language? How do new intermediate variations take shape structurally? These were the questions raised at the beginning of this chapter. A systematic analysis of the language use of 10 highly educated West Flemish women in five speech settings shows that in Ypres, some speakers have a diaglossic repertoire, using intermediate variations in supraregional informal conversations, whereas other personal repertoires have a diglossic structure with speakers switching between dialect and some form of intended standard language. No clear age patterns could be recognised, but it was argued that the variation in personal repertoire structures indicates a change from an overall diglossic to an overall diaglossic repertoire. That shift seems in its incipient phase not to have a significant impact on the function and structure of the local dialect: all speakers, both young and old, with a diglossic or a diaglossic repertoire, speak dialect in regional informal settings. What does vary, however, is the language used in supraregional informal settings: whereas speakers with a diglossic repertoire mostly speak some kind of 'Standard Dutch with an accent' in all supraregional settings, speakers with a diaglossic repertoire distinguish between supraregional informal and formal settings, only speaking Standard Dutch in more formal speech settings. In informal speech settings, these speakers use either a 'cleaned-up' dialect or a form of standard language with many [-st, -ypr]-features. The standard language hence seems to lose some functionality in diaglossic repertoires, which of course should also be linked to the increasing degree of supraregional informal contact in contemporary society. Concerning the structure of the standard language, the observation was made that younger speakers are a bit more inclined to use [-st, -ypr]-features, which might point to some form of destandardisation. This hypothesis however has to be treated cautiously, as the observed age effects were very small. The results do show how in West Flanders intermediate language use does not only arise via dialect-to-standard convergence, but also via horizontal dialect convergence (Auer & Hinskens 1996). More research, with more age groups and more speech settings is necessary to map the ongoing change in detail. An in-depth qualitative analysis of the 'intermediate language' conversations would moreover be interesting to study lower-level style-shifts and to investigate how speakers construct social meaning and diverse identities when shifting in the dialect-to-standard continuum. Clearly, a lot of work remains to be done, but I hope I have been able to show that if one wants to gain understanding of the change from diglossia to diaglossia, it is essential to focus on supraregional informal speech settings.

References

Auer, Peter. 2005. Europe's sociolinguistic unity, or: A typology of European dialect/standard constellations. In Nicole Delbecque, Johan van der Auwera & Dirk Geeraerts (eds.), *Perspectives on variation: Sociolinguistic, historical, comparative*, 7–42. Berlin / New York: Mouton de Gruyter.

Auer, Peter. 2011. Dialect vs. standard: A typology of scenarios in Europe. In Bernd Kortmann & Johan van der Auwera (eds.), *The languages and linguistics of Europe. A comprehensive guide*, 485–500. Berlin / New York: De Gruyter Mouton.

Auer, Peter & Frans Hinskens. 1996. The convergence and divergence of dialects in Europe. New and not so new developments in an old area. *Sociolinguistica (1996)* 10. 1–30.

Auer, Peter & Helmut Spiekermann. 2011. Demotisation of the standard variety or destandardisation? The changing status of German in late modernity (with special reference to south-western Germany). In Tore Kristiansen & Nikolas Coupland (eds.), *Standard languages and language standards in a changing Europe*, 161–176. Oslo: Novus.

Bailey, Guy, Tom Wikle, Jan Tillery & Lori Sand. 1991. The apparent time construct. *Language Variation and Change* 3(3). 241–264.

Barbiers, Sjef. 2005. *Syntactische atlas van de Nederlandse dialecten. Deel I: Pronomina, congruentie en vooropplaatsing*. Vol. I. Amsterdam: Amsterdam University Press.

Barbiers, Sjef & Magda Devos. 2008. *Syntactische atlas van de Nederlandse dialecten. Deel II.* Amsterdam: Amsterdam University Press.

Bell, Allan. 1984. Language style as audience design. *Language in Society* 13(02). 145–204.

Boersma, Paul & David Weenink. 2011. *Praat: Doing phonetics by computer.*

Cheshire, Jenny, Paul Kerswill, Sue Fox & Eivind Torgersen. 2011. Contact, the feature pool and the speech community: The emergence of Multicultural London English. *JOSL Journal of Sociolinguistics* 15(2). 151–196.

Cornips, Leonie & Gunther De Vogelaer. 2009. Variatie en verandering in het Nederlandse genus: Een multidisciplinair perspectief. *Taal en tongval* 61(1). 1–12.

Costa, Patrício Soares, Nadine Correia Santos, Pedro Cunha, Jorge Cotter & Nuno Sousa. 2013. The use of multiple correspondence analysis to explore associations between categories of qualitative variables in healthy ageing. *Journal of Aging Research* 2013. 1–12.

Coupland, Nikolas & Tore Kristiansen. 2011. SLICE: Critical perspectives on language (de)standardisation. In Tore Kristiansen & Nikolas Coupland (eds.), *Standard languages and language standards in a changing Europe*, 11–35. Oslo: Novus.

De Caluwe, Johan. 2006. Tussentaal als natuurlijke omgangstaal in Vlaanderen. In Johan De Caluwe & Magda Devos (eds.), *Structuren in talige variatie in Vlaanderen*, 19–34. Gent: Academia Press.

De Caluwe, Johan. 2009. Tussentaal wordt omgangstaal in Vlaanderen. *Nederlandse Taalkunde* 14(1). 8–25.

De Schutter, Georges, Boudewijn Van den Berg, Ton Goeman & Thera De Jong. 2005. *Morfologische atlas van de Nederlandse dialecten.* Amsterdam: Amsterdam University Press.

De Sutter, Gert, Isabelle Delaere & Koen Plevoets. 2012. Lexical lectometry in corpus-based translation studies: Combining profile-based correspondence analysis and logistic regression modeling. In Michael P. Oakes & Meng Ji (eds.), *Quantitative methods in corpus-based translation studies: A practical guide to descriptive translation research*, 325–345. Amsterdam: John Benjamins.

De Vogelaer, Gunther. 2008. *De Nederlandse en Friese subjectsmarkeerders: Geografie, typologie en diachronie.* Gent: Koninklijke Academie voor Nederlandse Taal- en Letterkunde.

De Vogelaer, Gunther & Roxanne Vandenberghe. 2006. Iemand of entwie, ergens of ieveranst. Een taaltypologisch perspectief op onbepaalde voornaamwoorden en bijwoorden in de Zuid-Nederlandse dialecten. In Johan De Caluwe &

Magda Devos (eds.), *Structuren in talige variatie in Vlaanderen*, 91–113. Gent: Academia Press.

De Wulf, Chris, Jan Goossens & Johan Taeldeman. 2005. *Fonologische atlas van de Nederlandse dialecten. Deel IV, Deel IV,* Gent: Koninklijke academie voor Nederlandse taal- en letterkunde.

Delarue, Steven. 2013. 'Teachers' Dutch in Flanders: The last guardians of the standard? In Tore Kristiansen & Stefan Grondelaers (eds.), *Language (de)standardisation in late modern Europe: Experimental studies*, 193–226. Oslo: Novus.

Di Franco, Giovanni & Alberto Marradi. 2014. *Factor analysis and principal component analysis.* Milano: FrancoAngeli.

Gabel, Heidi. 2010. Taalaccommodatie in Vlaanderen. Een onderzoek naar het taalgebruik van jongeren binnen de peer group en in contact met niet-streekgenoten. *Taal en tongval* 62(2). 163–203.

Geeraerts, Dirk. 2010. Schmidt redux: How systematic is the linguistic system if variation is rampant? In Kasper Boye & Elisabeth Engberg-Pedersen (eds.), *Language usage and language structure*, 237–262. Berlin / New York: De Gruyter Mouton.

Geeraerts, Dirk & Hans Van de Velde. 2013. Supra-regional characteristics of colloquial Dutch. In Frans Hinskens & Johan Taeldeman (eds.), *Language and space. An international handbook of linguistic variation. Volume 3: Dutch*, 532–556. Berlin / Boston: De Gruyter.

Ghyselen, Anne-Sophie. 2015. Stabilisering van tussentaal? Het taalrepertorium in de Westhoek als casus. *Taal en Tongval* 67. 43–95.

Ghyselen, Anne-Sophie & Gunther De Vogelaer. 2013. The impact of dialect loss on the acceptance of Tussentaal: The special case of West-Flanders in Belgium. In Stefan Grondelaers & Tore Kristiansen (eds.), *Experimental studies of changing language standards in contemporary Europe*, 153–170. Olso: Novus.

Ghyselen, Anne-Sophie & Jacques Van Keymeulen. 2014. Dialectcompetentie en functionaliteit van het dialect in Vlaanderen anno 2013. *Tijdschrift Voor Nederlandse Taal-en Letterkunde* 130(2). 801–816.

Giles, Howard & Peter Francis Powesland. 1975. *Speech style and social evaluation.* London: Academic Press.

Goeman, Ton. 2008. *MAND Morfologische atlas van de Nederlandse dialecten. Volume II.* Amsterdam: Amsterdam University Press.

Goossens, Jan, Johan Taeldeman & Geert Verleyen. 2000. *Fonologische atlas van de Nederlandse dialecten II - III. Deel II: De Westgermaanse korte vocalen in open syllaben. Deel III: De Westgermaanse lange vocalen en diftongen.* Gent: Koninklijke academie voor Nederlandse taal- en letterkunde.

Goossens, Jan, Johan Taeldeman, Geert Verleyen & Chris De Wulf. 1998. *Fonologische atlas van de Nederlandse dialecten. Deel I: Het korte vocalisme*. Gent: Koninklijke academie voor Nederlandse taal- en letterkunde.

Gries, Stefan Thomas. 2013. *Statistics for linguistics with R: A practical introduction*. Berlin: De Gruyter.

Grondelaers, Stefan & Roeland van Hout. 2011a. The standard language situation in the Low Countries: Top-down and bottom-up variations on a diaglossic theme. *Journal of Germanic Linguistics* 23(03). 199–243.

Grondelaers, Stefan & Roeland van Hout. 2011b. The standard language situation in The Netherlands. In Tore Kristiansen & Nikolas Coupland (eds.), *Standard languages and language standards in a changing Europe*, 113–118. Oslo: Novus.

Haeseryn, Walter (ed.). 1997. *Algemene Nederlandse spraakkunst*. Groningen, Deurne: Martinus Nijhoff/Wolters Plantyn.

Heemskerk, Josée S & Wim Zonneveld. 2000. *Uitspraakwoordenboek*. Utrecht: Het Spectrum.

Heeringa, Wilbert & Frans Hinskens. 2014. Convergence between dialect varieties and dialect groups in the Dutch language area. In Benedikt Szmrecsanyi & Bernhard Wälchli (eds.), *Aggregating dialectology, typology, and register analysis linguistic variation in text and speech*, 26–52. Berlin / Boston: Walter de Gruyter.

Kehrein, Roland. 2012. *Regionalsprachliche Spektren im Raum. Zur linguistischen Struktur der Vertikale*. Stuttgart: Franz Steiner Verlag.

Kristiansen, Tore. 2001. Two standards: One for the media and one for the school. *Language Awareness* 10(1). 9–24.

Labov, William. 1972. *Sociolinguistic patterns*. Philadelphia: University of Philadelphia Press.

Landis, J. R. & G. G. Koch. 1977. The measurement of observer agreement for categorical data. *Biometrics* 33(1). 159–74.

Lebart, L. & B. G. Mirkin. 1993. Correspondence analysis and classification. In Carlos María Cuadras & Calyampudi Radhakrishna Rao (eds.), *Multivariate analysis: Future directions*, 341–357. Amsterdam: North-Holland.

Lenz, Alexandra N. 2003. *Struktur und Dynamik des Substandards: Eine Studie zum Westmitteldeutschen (Wittlich/Eifel)*. Stuttgart, Wiesbaden: F. Steiner.

Plevoets, Koen. 2008. *Tussen spreek- en standaardtaal: Een corpusgebaseerd onderzoek naar de situationele, regionale en sociale verspreiding van enkele morfosyntactische verschijnselen uit het gesproken Belgisch-Nederlands*. Katholieke Universiteit Leuven PhD dissertation.

Plevoets, Koen. 2013. De status van de Vlaamse tussentaal: Een analyse van enkele socio-economische determinanten. *Tijdschrift voor Nederlandse Taal- en Letterkunde* 129(3). 26–44.

Ryckeboer, Hugo. 1983. Voor te + infinitief. Verkenning naar de dynamiek van een dialectisme. *Taal en Tongval* 35. 39–89.

Rys, Kathy & Johan Taeldeman. 2007. Fonologische ingrediënten van Vlaamse tussentaal. In Dominiek Sandra, R. Rymenans, P. Cuvelier & P. Van Petegem (eds.), *Tussen taal, spelling en onderwijs: Essays bij het emeritaat van Frans Daems*, 1–8. Gent: Academia Press.

Schilling-Estes, Natalie. 2002. Investigating stylistic variation. In J. K. Chambers, Peter Trudgill & Natalie Schilling-Estes (eds.), *The handbook of language variation and change*, 375–401. Malden / Oxford: Blackwell.

Schmidt, Tanja & K. Worner. 2009. EXMARaLDA - Creating, analysing and sharing spoken language corpora for pragmatic research. *Pragmatics* 19(4). 565–582.

Soete, Nel. 2012. *Morfologische, fonologische en lexicale dialectkennis in Ieper. Een sociolinguïstisch onderzoek naar de dialectkennis van drie generaties Ieperlingen.* Gent: Universiteit Gent BA dissertation.

Speelman, Dirk, Stefan Grondelaers & Dirk Geeraerts. 2003. Profile-based linguistic uniformity as a generic method for comparing language varieties. *Computers and the Humanities* 37(3). 317–337.

Stellmacher, Dieter. 1977. *Studien zur gesprochenen Sprache in Niedersachsen: Eine soziolinguistische Untersuchung.* Marburg: Elwert.

Taeldeman, Johan. 2008. Zich stabiliserende grammaticale kenmerken in Vlaamse tussentaal. *Taal en Tongval* 60. 26–50.

Taeldeman, Johan. 2009. Linguistic stability in a language space. In Peter Auer & Jürgen Erich Schmidt (eds.), *Language and space: An international handbook of linguistic variation*, 355–374. Berlin: De Gruyter Mouton.

Vandekerckhove, Reinhild. 2000. *Structurele en sociale aspecten van dialectverandering: De dynamiek van het Deerlijkse dialect.* Gent: Koninklijke Academie voor Nederlandse Taal- en Letterkunde.

Vandekerckhove, Reinhild. 2005. Belgian Dutch versus Netherlandic Dutch: New patterns of divergence? On pronouns of address and diminutives. *Multilingua - Journal of Cross-Cultural and Interlanguage Communication* 24(4). 379–397.

Vandekerckhove, Reinhild. 2009. Dialect loss and dialect vitality in Flanders. *International Journal of the Sociology of Language* 2009(196-197). 196–197.

Willemyns, Roland. 2005. Verkavelingsbrabants. Werkt het integratiemodel ook voor tussentalen? *Neerlandica Extra Muros* 43. 27–40.

Willemyns, Roland. 2007. De-standardization in the Dutch Language Territory at Large. In C. Fandryc & Reinier Salverda (eds.), *Standard, variation and language change in Germanic languages*, 265–279. Tübingen: Gunter Narr.

Willemyns, Roland & Wim Vandenbussche. 2008. Diglossie versus Kontinuum? Der Einfluss von Dialektverlust. *Sociolinguistica Jahrbuch* 22. 48–65.

Chapter 4

The future of Catalan dialects' syntax: A case study for a methodological contribution

Ares Llop Naya
Universitat Autònoma de Barcelona

> Given that Catalan micro-syntactic studies are still at a preliminary stage, this contribution aims to present an already-tested methodological roadmap for the study and the analysis of a particular dialect syntax variable. Specifically, we present the different data compilation methods used to obtain fine-grained data to characterise morpho-syntactically the expression of negation in Pallarese Catalan, expressed by the post-verbal negative minimiser *cap* ('head'). In order to obtain robust evidence, the appearance of each linguistic structure is matched to one of the following data compilation strategies: exhaustive revision of Catalan dialect literature; recorded speech conversation and participant observation in speakers' daily routines; scan reading of literature written by 'dialect aware' authors; grammatical judgments and 'meta-corpus'. Data obtained is interesting both from an intra-linguistic and a cross-linguistic point of view, regarding: the relation of the marker *cap* with the sentential marker *no* and other negative elements (n-words, NPIs, etc.); and regarding its position and mobility in the sentence and in verbal complexes. To sum up, with this brief case study, we exemplify the idea that the survey of micro-syntactic phenomena in Catalan is a promising challenge. In effect: linguistic research may play an important role in the social acknowledgement and valuation of dialectal phenomena that are neither present in the normative language, nor in the standard variety of the media and schools.

1 Introduction and background

1.1 General remarks

Even if Catalan has a long tradition of dialectal studies on phonology, morphology and lexicology, micro-syntactic studies still are at a preliminary stage. General properties of the language have been investigated; descriptive generalisa-

Ares Llop Naya. 2016. The future of Catalan dialects' syntax: A case study for a methodological contribution. In Marie-Hélène Côté, Remco Knooihuizen & John Nerbonne (eds.), *The future of dialects*, 63–72. Berlin: Language Science Press. DOI:10.17169/langsci.b81.83

tions have been stated and some syntactic variants have been noted, but dialectal syntax phenomena are still rather unexplored –data is sparse and unsystematic and there is no dialectal syntax-oriented annotated corpus. In this sense, this contribution aims to present the methodological roadmap and strategies used for the study and the analysis of a particular dialect syntax variable.

Such kind of research looks forward to the promotion of Catalan in the well-stablished net of European dialect syntax studies and projects. Furthermore, developing an exhaustive survey on how to approach Catalan syntax variation can lead to the acknowledgement, use and attachment to dialect structures used by speakers –but reflected neither in the normative language, nor in the standard variety of the media and schools. As stated by Trudgill (2002: 30): "If we wish to maintain linguistic diversity and oppose linguistic homogenisation, we have to consider speakers' attitudes to their own dialects. [...] There is often a direct relationship between the degree of hostility to dialects, the amount of denigration of vernacular varieties, and the rate at which they disappear". Therefore, the fruitful period of standardisation of the Catalan language developed after years of prohibition has to be followed by an attempt to preserve the richness and status of the dialects, especially peripheral and minority ones, such as Pallarese Catalan, the one we study here.

1.2 Aim

The aim of our research was to design, apply and test data compilation methods to obtain fine-grained data to characterise morphosyntactically negative emphatic constructions in Catalan and other Pyrenean IberoRomance dialects (cf. Berns & van Marle 2002 for a detailed description of the interests of studying dialectal variation regarding negation). Specifically, we studied the expression of negation in Pallarese Catalan (the North-western Pyrenean Catalan dialect: one of the most conservative Catalan dialects, in contact with Aranese Gascon, Aragonese and French), expressed by the negative marker element *cap* ('head') (cf. section 1.4. for further information about the element).

1.3 Methodological framework

Micro-comparative syntax projects have designed a 'layered methodology' (Cornips & Poletto 2007) to approach dialect syntax and data collection progressively and rigorously; to clearly understand the general properties of the area investigated by carrying out detailed analysis of single phenomena. This method has been chosen wisely as: on the one hand it is used in well-established dialect syntax projects in Europe, and on the other hand it updates and adjusts traditional data compilation methods to syntax-oriented investigations; it starts with a broad survey, and progressively narrows the target to find something interesting for micro-comparative linguistic research".

The strong point of our proposal, in accordance with this framework, has been to develop a rigorous morphosyntactic analysis by matching each of the strategies used to compile data related to a specific variable or context. Fine-grained data can also be determinant to stablish not only cross-linguistic differences but also intra-linguistic variation.

1.4 Case study

As in other Romance languages, in the Pyrenean dialects of Catalan (mainly Pallarese), emphatic negation is constructed by adding a post-verbal particle originating from a minimiser to a sentence containing the sentential negative marker equivalent to 'no'. The singularity of this kind of reinforcement is that, originally, it was a minimiser (noun denoting a minimal amount of something). Cross-linguistically, these elements were reanalysed in negative contexts and lost their nominal value. After different stages of reanalysis they became negative polarity items, emphatic polarity particles or even markers of sentential negation, e.g. *pas* 'step', *goutte* 'drop', *point* 'point' (French), *mica* 'crumb' (Italian), etc. (see Schwegler 1988; Detges & Waltereit 2002).

According to Rigau (2012), it is worth studying these kinds of particles not only as an instantiation of lexical variation, but as micro-syntactic phenomena. In this case, after a preliminary survey –and following Cornips & Poletto (2007) studies on micro-syntax and negation– we detected that in the north-western Pyrenean dialects of Catalan the behaviour of *cap* was interesting cross-linguistically (cf. French and Occitan examples) and intra-linguistically (cf. standard Catalan, Central Catalan, Roussillonais Catalan examples) regarding: (1) its relation with the sentential marker *no* and other negative markers; and (2) its position and mobility in the sentence and in verbal complexes.

1. From a semantico-syntactic point of view, *cap* can be legitimated by the sentential negative marker *no* (like in standard Catalan). It can also appear without *no* (like the marker *pas* in colloquial negative sentences in French, and the sentential negative marker *pas* in Occitan and Roussillonais Catalan). This might be an indication of an ongoing process of change from *cap* carrying an emphatic value to expressing sentential negation by itself (cf. *Jespersen's Cycle*, Jespersen 1917; revisited in theoretical terms by Roberts

2007; Schwenter 2006). In this sense it is worth studying the relationship of negative concord with different negative quantifiers so as to determine its formal features and conditions of legitimisation.

(1) (Jo) (no) vindré **cap.** (Pall. Cat.)
    (Jo) no vindré pas. (Stand. Cat.)
    (Jo) vindré pas. (Rouss. Cat.)

    (Ieu) vendrai pas. (Occ. Leng.)
    Je (ne) viendrai pas. (French)

    1.sg. NEG 1.come.FUT. EMPH/NEG.
    'I will not come (at all).'

(2) (Jo) (no) tornaré **cap** mai. (Pall. Cat.)
    (Jo) no tornaré pas mai. (Stand. Cat.)
    (Jo) tornaré pas mai. (Rouss. Cat.)

    (Ieu) tornarai pas jamai. (Occ. Leng.)
    Je (ne) viendrai (*pas) jamais. (French)

    1.sg. NEG 1.come.FUT. EMPH/NEG. never
    'I will never come back.'

2. We also decided to investigate the position of the negative marker in relation to the verb and other elements in the same syntactic position (i.e. the low IP focus position, à la Belletti 2004). Keeping in mind that the equivalent particle in standard Catalan *pas* allows mobility in certain contexts, we also analyzed the position of the particle in verbal complexes, embedded clauses, raising clauses and restructuring predicates so as to determine the degree of mobility or rigidity of the particle.

1.5 Strategies used

The five strategies used to compile data were conceived to match with a specific variable or context of interest to our research. The methods used were:

- **Exhaustive revision of Catalan dialect literature**; i.e. dialect monographs, dictionaries, articles and books where the topic is touched on briefly, to compile preliminary data and prescriptive rules about the use of the element.

- **Recorded speech conversation and participant observation in speakers' daily routine**: semi-structured interviews (à la Lebo, about anthropological topics) to find more complex examples and to explore variation depending on the register. We also recorded 'casual speech' contexts (outside the interview format) and we obtained data from 'participant observation' in daily-routine contexts, as well as from 'out of the blue' examples –collected unexpectedly in colloquial contexts. The main aim of this strategy was to instantiate how language change takes place earlier in more colloquial registers and in specific grammatical contexts and later spreads to other more complex constructions, cf. Roberts (2007: §3.4).

- **Scan reading of literature written by "dialect aware" authors**: to find natural and real emphatic constructions in literary works written by native Catalan Pallarese speakers, who compiled oral stories and transcribed recorded conversations. We expected to attest find more complex and less common structures than the ones obtained from the previous methods in oral speech (such as periphrasis, raising, passive and factitive constructions).

- **Grammatical judgments**: to elicit constructions that hardly ever occur in informal speech for a fine-grained characterisation of all possible contexts and interactions of *cap* (periphrasis, subordinate clauses, raising constructions and clitic climbing phenomena, answers to a *yes-no* question, imperative and interrogative sentences, biased questions, as a marker of constituent negation and as an expletive); and to examine negative data. The questionnaires of grammatical judgements (designed following Espinal's works and with specially designed statements, cf. Espinal 1993; 2002), were written in Pallarese Catalan and presented to native speakers with a high degree of dialect awareness. The participants were advised that this was a study of dialectal forms and not standard forms of Catalan.

- **'Metacorpus'**: following Silverstein's works, we compiled a corpus of sociolinguistic and metalinguistic comments stated by native informants during the process of data collection. This kind of data constitutes additional information about what Niedzielski & Preston (1999) call *folk-linguistic facts* (linguistic objects as viewed by nonlinguists).

2 Results and discussion

Our study explored the strong points of five different strategies to obtain the most fine-grained qualitative data to characterise morphosyntactically the unexplored negative marker *cap*, and to determine the range of variation and the variables of changes. We came across more than 260 occurrences from almost 30 different contexts and types of sentences (cf. Llop 2013). The main results obtained per strategy were the following:

- **Exhaustive revision of Catalan dialect literature**: the results were restrictive, and examples were insufficient for a rigorous characterisation of the whole picture. The variable studied was mainly considered from a lexical point of view and the most recurrent structure was the one with the preverbal marker *no*, simple tense and postverbal negative marker *cap*. Prescriptive grammars didn't mention the marker studied at all and all references to emphatic negation were to comment on the standard variant *pas*.

- **Recorded speech conversation and participant observation in speakers' daily routine**: the number of examples stated was not really high (17%), but it was interesting that in more colloquial contexts and with simple tenses, the presence of the variable without the preverbal *no* licensing the emphatic marker *cap* increased significantly; it was systematic with certain verbs such as *saber* 'know'. We could compile evidence in favour of an ongoing (and uncertain) process of change towards a further stage of grammaticalisation of *cap*, already given for *pas* in French and Occitan, languages in contact with this northern Catalan dialect

- **Scan reading of literature written by "dialect aware" authors**: this strategy was the most productive in terms of quantity –the examples found represent the 72% of the corpus–, and in terms of richness of constructions (periphrasis, embedded clauses, raising constructions, idioms, factitive construction, etc.). In regards to speakers, the use of complex syntactic structures with *cap* can be an interesting way to emphasise its productivity and to show up and diffuse the constraints of use. We discovered, for example, that Pallarese *cap* is sensitive to the "embedded negation constraint" stated for French by Horn (1978: 193), i.e.: differently to *pas* in Central Catalan, Pallarese doesn't allow the movement of the negative marker from the main clause to the embedded clause –even if blocking effects of the embedded clause boundary are neutralised by using modal constituents (cf. Espinal 1993; Llop 2013).

- **Grammatical judgments**: the answers to the grammatical judgements and the degree of acceptation or rejection were very regular and uniform in all informants. Initial written questionnaires for grammatical judgements, were changed into oral ones to avoid informants being disturbed by unfamiliar written forms of dialectal variants. The most interesting discovery was the fixed position of *cap* in restructuring predicates (in contrast to *pas* in Central and North-western Catalan, where it is much more mobile).

    (1) (3) (Jo) No **ho** puc (✓cap / pas) fer (*cap / ✓pas).
        1.sg. NEG CL.it 1.PRES.MOD.can EMPH/NEG. INF.do EMPH/NEG.
        'I can't do it.'

- **Metacorpus**: we collected general comments about the structure studied, about: attitudes and sociolinguistic variables (generation divergences, comments related to the pressure of the standard language, etc.); linguistic variables (presence and absence of *no*, with NPI and N-words); and further examples.

3 Conclusions

Our contribution is an already tested methodological backbone for innovation and optimisation in Catalan dialect syntax variation research. Catalan syntax variation is almost an unexplored territory which benefits from every humble initiative that promotes its launch into the European net of syntactic studies. With the research we have briefly summarised here, we have worked on a very specific phenomenon. We have obtained evidence about: the morphosyntactic value of the negative marker *cap*, its structural position from a theoretical point of view (cf. Llop 2013; 2014), its features and the necessity of legitimation by a negative element, etc. With this data we have looked very briefly –due to space constraints– at descriptive, historic, theoretical and micro-comparative insights.

Developing further approaches as the one presented here we can revitalise and make visible an important amount of focalisation or emphatic dialectal particles and its semantic and pragmatic properties within the framework of the expression of negation in natural languages.

Concerning the future of our dialects, the presence of dialectal structures in standard language taught at school and in the media and creative literature can be, by far, the most influential agents for the reinforcement of dialect speakers' awareness and self-confidence. Nevertheless, linguistic research may also play an important role in the acknowledgement and valuation of the richness of dialectal phenomena and unstudied structures such as the one presented here. In that sense, Rigau (1998: 80) postulated that "the clearer we know the terms and limits of variation, the better the knowledge and use of our language will be." Following up, Trudgill (2002: 31) stated that "linguists are in a particularly strong position to oppose this discrimination and consequent homogenisation because they, as experts on language, have the knowledge and ability to engender positive attitudes and to counter the denigration". The survey of a wider range of micro-syntactic phenomena in Catalan is a promising challenge to be followed up.

References

Belletti, Adriana. 2004. Aspects of the Low IP Area. In Luigi Rizzi (ed.), *The structure of CP and IP. The cartography of syntactic structures*, vol. 2, 16–51. Oxford: Oxford University Press.
Berns, J. B & Jaap van Marle. 2002. *Present-day dialectology problems and findings*. Berlin: Walter de Gruyter.
Cornips, Leonie & Cecilia Poletto. 2007. *Field linguistics meets formal research: How a microparametric view can deepen our theoretical investigation (sentential negation)*. Paper presented at ICLaVE 4, University of Cyprus, Nicosia 18-06-2007.
Detges, Ulrich & Richard Waltereit. 2002. Grammaticalization vs. reanalysis: A semantic-pragmatic account of functional change in grammar. *Zeitschrift für Sprachwissenschaft* 21(2). 151–195.
Espinal, Maria Teresa. 1993. Two squibs on modality and negation. *Catalan Working Papers in Linguistics* 3. 113–138.
Espinal, Maria Teresa. 2002. La negació. In Joan Solà & Gemma Rigau i Oliver (eds.), *Gramàtica del català contemporani*, vol. 3, 2729–2793. Barcelona: Editorial Empúries.
Horn, Laurence R. 1978. Remarks on neg-raising. In Peter Cole (ed.), *Syntax and semantics. 9: Pragmatics*, 129–220. New York: Academic Press.
Jespersen, Otto. 1917. *Negation in English and other languages*. København: Luno.
Llop, Ares. 2013. *La negació en pallarès. Sintaxi de l'adverbi cap*. Barcelona: Universitat Autònoma de Barcelona MA thesis.
Llop, Ares. 2014. *Cap, molla, got. Syntactic characterization of three Pyrenean Catalan minimizers*. Poster. Madrid.

Niedzielski, Nancy & Dennis Preston. 1999. *Folk linguistics*. Berlin, New York: Mouton de Gruyter.

Rigau, Gemma. 1998. La variació sintàctica: Uniformitat en la diversitat. *Caplletra* 25. 63–82.

Rigau, Gemma. 2012. Mirative and focusing uses of the Catalan particle *pla*. In Laura Brugé, Anna Cardinaletti, Giuliana Giusti, Nicola Munaro & Cecilia Poletto (eds.), *Functional heads. The cartography of syntactic structures*, vol. 7, 92–102. Oxford, New York: Oxford University Press.

Roberts, Ian G. 2007. *Diachronic syntax*. Oxford; New York: Oxford University Press.

Schwegler, Armin. 1988. Word-order changes in predicate negation strategies in romance languages. *DIA Diachronica* 5(1-2). 21–58.

Schwenter, Scott. 2006. Fine tuning Jespersen's Cycle. In Laurence R. Horn, Betty J. Birner & Gregory L. Ward (eds.), *Drawing the boundaries of meaning. Neo-Gricean studies in pragmatics and semantics in honor of Laurence R. Horn*, 327–344. Amsterdam: John Benjamins.

Trudgill, Peter. 2002. *Sociolinguistic variation and change*. Edinburgh: Edinburgh University Press.

Part II

Methods

Chapter 5

Fuzzy dialect areas and prototype theory: Discovering latent patterns in geolinguistic variation

Simon Pickl
University of Salzburg

> In this article, a threefold link is established between the concept of dialect areas as scientific constructs, prototype theory as a descriptive model and factor analysis as an operationalisation of the former two. While the idea of using prototype theory to model emic, folk concepts of dialect areas is not new, it is here for the first time used to establish a scholarly, etic model of dialect areas, which will make it easier to compare emically and etically defined dialect areas in the future. Dialect areas can be conceived of as being crisp or fuzzy, but in most cases, they are best conceptualised as being fuzzy. Following work by Gaetano Berruto, fuzzy dialect areas are defined on the basis of sets of similarly distributed variants. In a second, more practical step, an operationalisation of this model is presented that uses factor analysis to extract spatial patterns from geolinguistic data that satisfy the model's definition of dialect area. This methodology is illustrated by applying it to dialect data from Bavarian Swabia (Southern Germany). The geolinguistic structures revealed demonstrate the utility of factor analysis as a tool both for a detailed, in-depth differentiation of fuzzy dialect areas and for the detection of hitherto unknown, even very weak spatial patterns.

1 Conceptualising dialect areas as fuzzy categories

A priori, there is no such thing as a dialect area within a language space, i.e. the division of space in such areas is not a linguistic fact but an abstract concept that can differ depending on which definition is preferred and what criteria are chosen. Instead, language space can be conceived of as a dynamic arrangement of more or less mobile speakers, whose language behaviour allows linguistic forms to be attributed to certain places or regions. The distributions of these forms in the dimension of space do not normally constitute distinct dialect areas; more

Simon Pickl. 2016. Fuzzy dialect areas and prototype theory: Discovering latent patterns in geolinguistic variation. In Marie-Hélène Côté, Remco Knooihuizen & John Nerbonne (eds.), *The future of dialects*, 75–98. Berlin: Language Science Press. DOI:10.17169/langsci.b81.84

often, they form a spatial continuum. Any efforts to divide space into dialect areas are therefore acts of deliberation, and they will inevitably lead to different results depending on who performs them and on the approach taken. In that sense, dialect areas are constructions.

Being ideational rather than factual entities, they have a very long tradition as conceptual realities. In the history of dialectology, the existence of dialect areas has been a permanent presupposition since its very beginnings. The cognitive organisation of dialectal variation in terms of areas or varieties seems to be virtually inevitable, or at any rate very compelling, when dealing with language in space. This can be illustrated with a passage from Chambers & Trudgill (1998), who state that they use such categories because they are handy, although they convey a strictly inaccurate picture of how language varieties are organised (in space or otherwise):

> We shall [...] be using labels for linguistic varieties that may suggest that we regard them as discrete entities. It will be as well, nevertheless, to bear in mind that this will in most cases be simply an ad hoc device and that the use of labels such as 'language', 'dialect' and 'variety' does not imply that continua are not involved.
> (Chambers & Trudgill 1998: 12)

Also Peter Wiesinger (1983: 807) sees a general need or propensity to group similar ways of speaking together, which pertains to both linguists and non-linguists. Such groupings can be used, together with some salient linguistic features that are regarded as typical of them, to allocate speakers to a certain region. He stresses the practicality of regarding varieties as "discrete entities", as doing so makes it easier for speakers and for linguists alike to deal with the complexity of dialectal differences. Put more generally, dialect areas or varieties can be regarded as the expression of a mental requirement for categories, the result of a conscious or unconscious attempt to cognitively organise a large number of disparate but interrelated ways of speaking. Dialect areas are, like all kinds of categories, groupings of elements that are defined by certain traits.

There are different kinds of categories; one basic distinction often made is between crisp and fuzzy categories. Crisp categories are defined by certain traits or features that are either necessary or sufficient conditions. These categories make it very easy to decide whether a given element belongs to them or not: if the element has all the necessary or at least one of the sufficient features, then it is a member of the category. However, the definition of categories and their conditions might be regarded as arbitrary in the first place. Fuzzy categories, on

5 Fuzzy dialect areas and prototype theory

the other hand, are defined by a number of traits or features that serve as cues for that category, which are, however, neither necessary nor sufficient. If an element has many of the features associated with that category, then it is very likely that it belongs to it. Also the features themselves can have different degrees of importance for the category. Thus, no definitive answer is given as to whether an element belongs to a category or not; instead, membership is expressed as a gradual value or a probability.

Dialect areas, like other kinds of categories, can be modelled as crisp or fuzzy categories. The classical dialect area with sharp boundaries is a crisp category of local dialects; Girard & Larmouth (1993: 108–113), on the other hand, explicitly conceptualise dialect areas as "fuzzy sets", assigning local membership values between 0 and 1 to individual dialects. To obtain crisp dialect areas, specific defining features have to be selected. In this way, it is almost inevitable to pick those features that will reconstruct and thereby justify preconceived notions of areas. Therefore it is preferable not to preselect defining features, but to look at a large set of variables which may or may not be relevant. Dialect areas can then be delimited by looking for sets of bundling isoglosses. Depending on whether they coincide exactly or bundle together loosely, they delimit crisp or fuzzy dialect areas. This method is well-established in dialectology (cf. e.g. Hans Kurath 1972) and can be traced back to August Bielenstein (1892). Craig M. Carver (1987) used a similar approach for constructing dialect "layers" by combining features with similar geographic distribution. Also cluster analysis can be used to construct crisp or fuzzy dialect areas, depending on the method used (e.g. bootstrap clustering or noisy clustering; cf. Nerbonne et al. 2011: 83), without having to preselect defining features. Generally, it seems advisable to use tools that allow for fuzzy structures to emerge from the data and do not restrict the form of the outcomes to crisp structures. Later on in this paper, I will argue that factor analysis is a statistical tool particularly suited for identifying fuzzy dialect areas.

From a more theoretical perspective, viewing dialects against the background of fuzzy set theory (cf. Zadeh 1965) seems to provide a useful formalism for dealing with fuzzy dialect areas (cf. Girard & Larmouth 1993). Treating local dialects as elements that can have different degrees of belonging to an area implies that there are more and less TYPICAL examples of a dialect variety, which we could also call a DIALECT TYPE. This way of treating dialects has also been used for describing how dialects are organised cognitively by members of the speech community.

> Lectal categories, in short, constitute prototype categories. If lectal varieties constitute prototype categories, some realizations will be more 'typical' or

'central' or 'better examples' of a given variety than others. (Kristiansen 2008: 59)

This is one example of a number of attempts to apply prototype theory (Rosch 1973; Lakoff 1987) to dialect geography, all of which are, as far as I see, folk linguistic approaches (Christen 1998; 2010; Berthele 2006; Kristiansen 2008; Pustka 2009) in the sense that they deal with how speakers conceptualise language in space. Perceptual dialectology has produced many new insights in the cognitive perspective of language geography in the past decades, spearheaded by Dennis Preston (cf. e.g. Preston 1989; 1999; Anders, Hundt & Lasch 2010). It appears that prototype theory is a useful framework to describe how dialects are organised cognitively, and it is compatible with fuzzy set theory (see, however, Kretzschmar 2009: 218–250, who is critical of using prototype theory and favours schema theory). Prototype theory assumes that cognitive concepts are fundamentally fuzzy: examples for a concept can be more or less typical, depending on their traits or features (cf. also Labov 1973). Consequently, a specific way of speaking can be a more or less typical example of a dialect type. Folk linguistic dialect types are EMIC categories; they are cognitive concepts of the speakers whose speech is at the same time the object of linguistic investigation.

There is no reason why the fundamental linguistic concept of a dialect variety should differ from the folk linguistic concept. In other words, scholarly or ETIC ideas about geolinguistic entities can and should have the same principal structure as lay persons' implicit ideas about dialects in space while being based on transparent – and, as far as possible, objective – criteria that are not derived from the speakers' ideas, but from scientific reasoning. Only in this way, the question of to what extent emic and etic dialect types coincide and why (not) can be tackled: In what way do some folk linguistic ideas of space diverge from linguistic ones, and why? It appears worthwhile to use a linguistic (etic) notion of dialect types that is similar to the folk linguistic (emic) one, but based on intersubjective criteria. This way, it becomes possible to compare emic and etic dialect types directly and identify how and why they differ.

If dialect varieties – emic or etic ones – take the shape of fuzzy categories, then they have no clear-cut boundaries or distinct features; instead, their spatial distributions are fuzzy, and local dialects are typical of them to varying degrees. Also, linguistic features are not simply features of one variety or the other, but they have different degrees of relevance for them. Thus, individual dialects can be better or worse examples of a variety, i.e. they have different values of TYPICALITY for a dialect type. Typicality is a measure for the graded membership of dialects, thus providing the structure of a fuzzy set. If typicality or membership values of a dialect type are projected into space, the result is a graded or fuzzy dialect area; being fuzzy, it can overlap with other dialect areas. Linguistic features, on the other hand, can be better or worse cues for a dialect type, i.e. they have varying degrees of cue validity or FEATURE VALIDITY. Consequently, the way in which dialect types are arranged in space takes the form of concretions with broad transition areas (cf. Figure 1). Note that there is no requirement for dialect types to have a core area in the sense that there must be locations that belong a hundred percent to them; instead, the core area of a dialect type can be defined as the area where it is DOMINANT, i.e. the area where it is the dialect type with the highest local typicalities. There may even be dialect types that are dominant nowhere. Because dialect types overlap in space, they appear layered; the individual layers consist of congruent distribution areas of co-occurring linguistic forms.

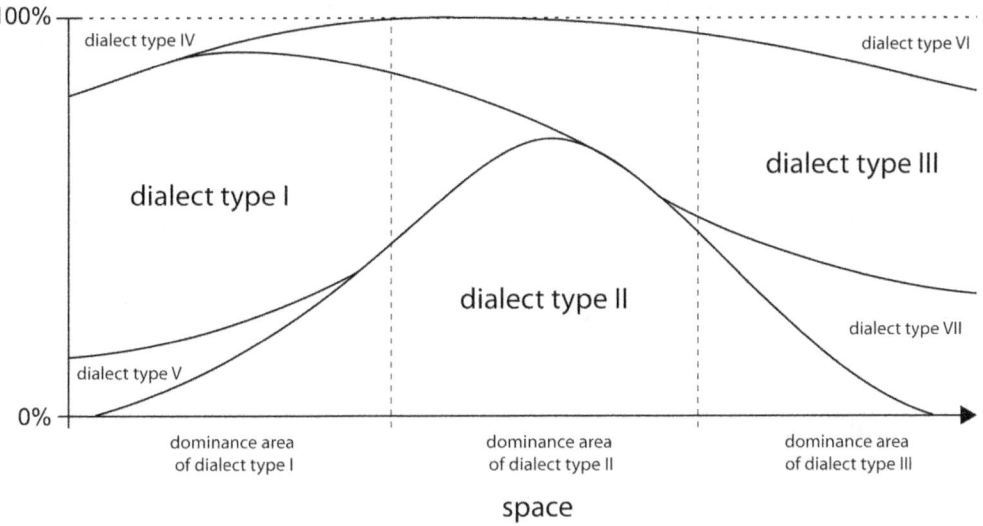

Figure 1: Layer model of dialect types in space (adapted from Pickl 2013a: 70).

This is in line with Gaetano Berruto's definition of varieties, which is based on the simple assumption that when a number of linguistic variants tend to occur together, then these variants constitute a variety:

> The tendential co-occurrence of variants gives rise to linguistic varieties. Therefore, a linguistic variety is conceivable as a set of co-occurring variants; it is identified simultaneously by both such a co-occurrence of variants, from the linguistic viewpoint, and the co-occurrence of these variants with extralinguistic, social features, from the external, societal viewpoint. (Berruto 2010: 229)

This notion captures several of the usual requirements for varieties: their relative internal homogeneity and their relative mutual dissimilarity, and also their association with language-external factors.[1] Varieties are thus condensations of co-occurring variants that can be pinned to a certain geographical expanse only to some extent – they are fuzzy and they overlap. Their arrangement in space is similar to the one depicted in Figure 1. According to Berruto, a variety as a condensation area is defined by certain co-occurring linguistic variants (its features). Depending on how many of these features are present in a given dialect, this dialect has a specific degree of membership between 0 (none of the features are present) and 1 (all of the features are present).

How are dialect types to be determined? Any method that is intended to identify linguistic varieties in the sense of Berruto's condensations will have to identify co-occurrences among linguistic variants. Craig M. Carver's (1987) approach did something similar in using lexical congruencies to establish 'layers' in American dialects,[2] "essentially speech areas characterised by sets of words with a similar geographic distribution" (Boberg 2005: 24). The resulting structure is quite similar to what is illustrated in Figure 1.

The remaining part of this paper is dedicated to demonstrating how the theoretical idea of fuzzy dialect types can be implemented methodologically and practically. It is to be shown that taking such an approach does not only reproduce well-established geolinguistic structures in a more nuanced way, but also that it yields new insights, e.g. regarding weaker, non-dominant structures.

2 A tool for identifying dialect types

There are various methods available for the identification of dialect areas (see Grieve 2014 for a more detailed comparison of popular statistical methods). Some of them, like fuzzy clustering, are suitable for identifying dialect types as fuzzy categories. However, I will argue that most of them are not suited for the identification of dialect types conceived of as layers of linguistic co-occurrence, either because of the structure of their outcomes or because of their internal working mechanisms, and that there are two options that are similarly well suited for this goal.

---

[1] It does not capture, however, their emic status, as required by Auer (1986: 99) and Lenz (2003: 389–390). As I treat emic and etic varieties separately, focussing on etic varieties, this is consistent and does not pose a problem.

[2] I would like to thank an anonymous referee for making me aware of this connection.

cluster analysis, the quantitative method that is to date the most popular tool to identify dialect areas (see e.g. Goebl 1983; Prokić & Nerbonne 2008; Prokić 2010: 17–29), analyses the aggregated similarities between local dialects to establish groups of local dialects that are relatively homogeneous internally and at the same time relatively distinct from each other. These groups or clusters are based on a measure of similarity between sites but not between distribution areas; it does not take into account the distribution patterns of individual variants and *their* mutual similarities, which would be a requirement for identifying condensations in Berruto's sense. cluster analysis does not identify types and their features, but clusters. For this reason, it is also impossible for a cluster analysis to come up with anything more subtle than global, exclusively dominant areas; subordinate, non-dominant areas that are determined by smaller numbers of features cannot be identified by cluster analysis. So, even though there are 'fuzzy' implementations of cluster analysis that yield overlapping clusters (e.g. bootstrap clustering or noisy clustering; cf. Nerbonne et al. 2011: 83), it is not a candidate for the operationalisation of dialect types. Bipartite spectral graph partitioning, which can also determine clusters of local dialects, simultaneously identifies the linguistic variants associated with these clusters (cf. Wieling & Nerbonne 2011) and is therefore in theory suitable for identifying areas together with their features. However, for our purpose this method has the disadvantage that it does not yield fuzzy areas but crisp clusters, at least as implemented by Wieling & Nerbonne (2011) or Wieling, Shackleton & Nerbonne (2013).

Multi-dimensional scaling (MDS) (see Wieling & Nerbonne 2015: 245 for an overview), "the de facto standard in dialectometry" according to an anonymous referee, arranges local dialects in a coordinate system of two or more dimensions, thus summarising the multiple similarities between local dialects. Again, the basis for the analysis are the linguistic similarities between sites, not the similarities between distribution areas. "MDS takes a site × site distance table as input and tries to assign the sites in the table to coordinates in a small-dimensional space, typically consisting of two or three dimensions" (Wieling & Nerbonne 2015: 245). Thus, it does not actually yield dialect areas but rather a dialect continuum without distinguishing condensations. Even if we took the axes as representing some sort of types, there would still be the problem, as with cluster analysis, that the results are based on global similarities between sites only, while similarities or differences between linguistic variants' spatial distributions are not taken into account. Therefore, the results of MDS cannot be interpreted as dialect types as discussed in the preceding section.

Two methods that are similar in the form of their results, but not in their internal functioning, are promising candidates for identifying fuzzy dialect areas as dialect types. Both Principal Component Analysis (PCA) and Factor Analysis (FA)[3] take feature × site matrices as data input and express recurring patterns in the data as principal components or FACTORS, usually producing a principal component/factor × site matrix as output. Additionally, a principal component/factor × linguistic feature matrix can be calculated. One of the earliest applications of PCA/FA in linguistics comes from Douglas Biber, who used it to analyse stylistic variation in written texts.

> In a factor analysis, a large number of original variables, in this case the frequencies of linguistic features, are reduced to a small set of derived variables, the 'factors'. Each factor represents some area in the original data that can be summarised or generalised. That is, each factor represents an area of high shared variance in the data, a grouping of linguistic features that co-occur with a high frequency. (Biber 1988: 79)

As a method for the reduction of high-dimensionality data, FA condenses the variation in a large data collection to a smaller number of underlying tendencies or factors. PCA does something very similar. By summarising large numbers of variants that have similar distributions, the variation in a data collection is condensed, providing a summary of predominant patterns in the data. Thus factors – "grouping[s] of linguistic features that co-occur with a high frequency" – or principal components are exactly what an operationalised method for identifying dialect types as condensations of co-occurring variants in the geographical dimension should output. The principal components or factors can be seen as condensations or layers because they are summaries of the distributions of co-occurring variants. Since co-occurrence is mathematically determined in terms of correlations, it is a technical requirement that the variant occurrences are given in the form of something like frequencies. Thus both PCA and FA meet the requirements of identifying linguistic layers as condensations of co-occurring variants and of yielding fuzzy areas as results. Hence, applying FA or PCA to geolinguistic data to find spatial patterns that qualify as varieties seems promising.

PCA and FA work quite similarly as far as their outcomes are concerned, but they function differently "under the hood". Both methods have been used several times before in dialectology.[4] For the present purpose, FA is favoured over PCA because FA is less susceptible to random variation and therefore "a more

---

[3] For a general introduction to both methods, see Tabachnick & Fidell (2012).

[4] See, among others, Shackleton (2005); Hyvönen, Leino & Salmenkivi (2007); Szmrecsanyi &

suitable method for identifying co-occurring linguistic features" (Leinonen 2010: 106). Leino & Hyvönen, comparing different component models including FA and PCA in an application to Finnish data, found that FA "gave solid and easily interpretable results" (2008: 186) and could be used as a default method.

The implementation of FA for dialectometric analyses presented in the following section was developed in the DFG-funded research project *New Dialectometry Using Methods of Stochastic Image Analysis*[5] (Department of German Linguistics, University of Augsburg, and Institute of Stochastics, Ulm University). It is included in *GeoLing – a software package for geolinguistic data*, which was developed in the project and is available as open source software (GPLv3) at www.geoling.net. The results reported in this article were obtained using this software.

3 Dialect types in Bavarian Swabia

In this section, the approach outlined in the previous sections will be exemplified with data from the *Sprachatlas von Bayerisch-Schwaben* (SBS, König 1996–2009), a dialect atlas that covers an area in the south of Germany. The area of investigation is delimited by the administrative region of Swabia in the south-west of Bavaria plus some adjoining stretches in the north and east, minus a part in the south that is already covered by the *Vorarlberger Sprachatlas* (VALTS). The data were collected under the direction of Werner König in the form of dialect interviews that were conducted at 272 record locations. The published version of the SBS contains approx. 2,700 maps covering lexical, morphological and phonetic variables in 14 volumes. Per location and map, up to three different variants are documented.

In previous research from the project that reported results from FA (Pickl 2013a,b; 2014; Pröll 2015), the individual subsets (lexicon, morphology, phonetics) were analysed either separately or all combined. In this article, the morphological and phonetic subsets will be analysed together, excluding the lexical subset to provide an additional angle. The rationale behind this is that morphology and

---

Wolk (2011); Wieling, Shackleton & Nerbonne (2013) for PCA and e.g. Clopper & Paolillo (2006); Nerbonne (2006); Grieve, Speelman & Geeraerts (2011) for FA. Grieve (2009) and Leinonen (2010) use both, while Leino & Hyvönen (2008) compare PCA and FA with other component models. The approach and data used in this paper are based on previous research by Pickl (2013a,b; 2014); Pröll, Pickl & Spettl (2015) and Pröll (2015).

[5] *Neue Dialektometrie mit Methoden der stochastischen Bildanalyse*
(http://www.philhist.uni-augsburg.de/de/lehrstuehle/germanistik/sprachwissenschaft/projekte/dialektometrie/)

phonetics are usually seen to be more systematically organised and thus more relevant for geolinguistic abstractions (cf. Francis 1983: 20; Labov, Ash & Boberg 2006: 41, 119).[6] For a more detailed comparison for FA based on different subsets, see Pröll (2015: 84–132); generally, he finds that morphological and phonetic variation can be slightly better summarised (61% and 64% explained variance, respectively) than lexical variation (57% explained variance).

The data for this study consist of 831 phonetic and 541 morphological maps (1,372 in total) containing data from 272 locations. There are a total of 14,825 linguistic variants in the data,[7] i.e. each of the maps, representing an individual linguistic variable, contains on average 10.8 variants. In order to be workable for FA, these data have to be pre-processed. This is done by converting their occurrences at each location into 'weights' ranging between 0 and 1; the weight is the fraction of times a variant has been recorded at a location in relation to all records of variants at that location. Thus 0 means that a variant is not recorded at a location, 1 means that it is the only variant recorded there, 0.5 means that the variant has been recorded there together with 1 other variant, and so on, so that the values of all variants at a location add up to 1 for each variable. This seems to be the easiest and most straightforward way to deal with the non-frequency data while at the same time providing something that can be used by FA and interpreted as relative frequencies (even though as record frequencies and not necessarily as usage frequencies).

The local variant weights are filled into a location × variant matrix, which forms the basis for the analysis. Usually FA in dialectology is performed as an R-type FA, which means that spatial correlations among linguistic variants are identified. In order to perform an R-type FA, the number of cases (= sites) has to be larger than the number of items (= variants), which is clearly not the case with our data. The alternative, Q-type FA, looks for correlations among cases across items, identifying linguistic patterning of sites. The difference between Q-type FA and R-type FA is that the matrix is transposed prior to analysis, and that consequently the results are agglomerations of cases, not of items. While this is conceptually different, the outcome is very similar. "The choice of R or its transpose […] is […] not a matter of end goal but of convenience and of the ease of

---

[6] For a complementary analysis, looking at the lexicon alone, see Pickl (2013a,b); for an integrated analysis, looking at all linguistic subsets together, see Pröll (2015).

[7] The exact number of variants depends, of course, on the granularity of the classification of the records. For the SBS data, three levels of granularity have been defined, each being more general than the one before, thus aggregating more records together (cf. Pickl 2013a: 75–78; Pröll 2015: 47–48). For the analysis, I use Level 1 with the finest granularity, which means most of the differences between records are rendered as different variants.

5 Fuzzy dialect areas and prototype theory

meeting statistical requirements" (Cattell 1978: 326). As FA requires the number of cases to be larger than the number of items, Q-type FA has to be applied for the data used in this study to identify types of local dialects. In consequence, the FACTOR LOADINGS matrix contains the values specifying the relations between factors and locations. Varimax rotation is applied to optimise the results. Additionally, a FACTOR SCORES matrix is calculated using Bartlett's method to specify the relations between factors and variants. Both factor loadings and factor scores can take on positive and negative values.

A further parameter to be specified is the number of factors to be extracted. This choice is much less crucial as the number of clusters for cluster analysis, since from a certain number onwards, the preceding larger factors change only very little when more factors are added. This is because each additional factor explains less variance than the ones preceding it. A popular guideline is the Kaiser criterion, which admits only factors with eigenvalues greater than or equal to 1. In this case, this means that it explains the equivalent of the variance of one location.

In the present application, the Kaiser criterion leads to a total of 16 factors. These factors account for 62.21% of the variance in the data, i.e. 62.21% of the data can be explained with recurring patterns, which is in line with Pröll's (2015) findings regarding phonetics and morphology separately. The remaining 37.79% cannot be summarised by the FA. While the number of factors may seem surprisingly high, it should be borne in mind that the number of items is also very high (14,825 variants). Even the smallest factors, with well below 1% of explained variance, still contain the same amount of variation as about a hundred variants. The amount of variance accounted for has to be seen in relation to the absolute numbers; even one of the dominant factors (Factor 11) has an explained variance of less than 1%, which illustrates that even factors this small can be indispensable for getting a complete picture.

Figure 2 shows the first factor, i.e. the factor with the highest explained variance. Each location is coloured depending on its factor loading (the darker the colour, the higher the loading). The total variance explained by this factor is 15.68%. The maximal local explained variance (which is the square of the local factor loading) is 62.41% at location 163 (Olgishofen). This factor's expanse coincides roughly with an area that is traditionally identified as the Middle East Swabian dialect area (cf. e.g. Nübling 1988: 118). As a number of variants with high scores for Factor 1 are associated with this area, Middle East Swabian can be seen as a dialect type constituted by these variants. Therefore, a variant's relevance as feature, its feature validity, is specified by its factor score from FA.

Simon Pickl

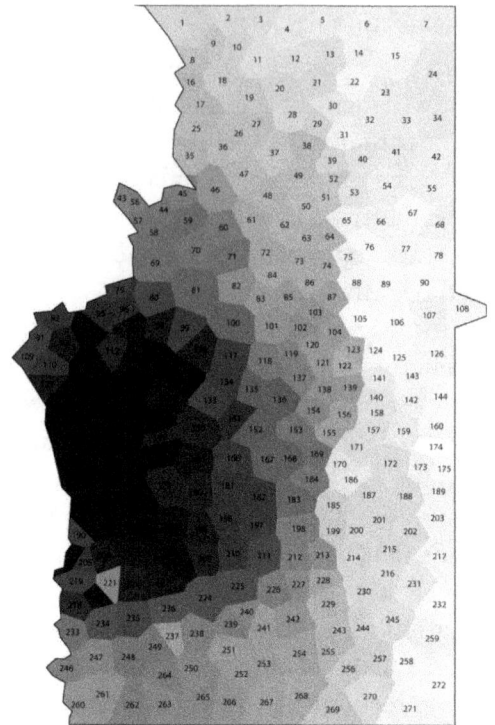

Figure 2: Factor 1 (15.68%).

Table 1 shows the 20 variants with the highest factor score for factor 1, or the top 20 of the features of Middle East Swabian. Even though these are only the top 20 out of 2,557 variants with positive factor scores (most of them have scores close to zero), some linguistic phenomena can be ascribed to this factor: the loss of *h*, *ch* and *g* in certain positions (5, 8, 9, 14, 17, 19), the realisation of MHG *ou* as *ao* (3, 4, 7, 10, 11), and the preservation of vowel length (8, 12, 14). A deeper look at the variants with high factor scores can lead to additional insights in the linguistic make-up of this dialect type and in the alignment between variants and their distributions, but is skipped here for reasons of brevity.

Figures 3–10 show the geographic distributions of all the other dominant factors (Factors 2–7, 10–11), i.e. of all the factors that are strongest at one location at least. The explained variances are given in brackets. Divergent colours in the individual maps represent negative loadings.

Most of these factors can be associated with traditional dialect areas: Factor 2 with North East Swabian, Factor 3 with East Algovian, Factor 4 with Central Bavarian, Factor 5 with Lechrainian, Factor 6 with Northern Bavarian, Factor 7

Table 1: Top 20 features of Factor 1. MHG: Middle High German. OHG: Old High German.

	Variable (map)	Variant	Score
1	*man* (before stress) (9.275)	*mɑ/mə*	6.226463
2	MHG *ʒ* (germ. **t*) in *heraußen* (7.143)	fricative, lenis	6.112138
3	MHG *ou* in *auch* (5.118)	*ao*	6.045917
4	MHG *ou* in *(ein)kaufen* (5.124)	*ao*	5.823385
5	OHG Strong verbs, Class V (*siehst*, 2nd sg.) (6.58)	*sīš* (*h* not realised)	5.800744
6	MHG *ë* in *Besen* (4.57)	*ēə*	5.787916
7	MHG *ou* in *laufen* (5.125)	*ao*	5.748020
8	MHG *h* in *siehst* (7.201)	*h* not realised (long vowel)	5.721860
9	MHG *h* (germ. **h*) in *hoh-* (7.193)	*h* not realised	5.715720
10	MHG *ou* in *Auge(n)* (5.121)	*ao*	5.677732
11	MHG *ou* in *glauben/Glaube(n)* (5.119)	*ao*	5.645496
12	MHG *b* in *geglaubt* (7.14)	*b* (long vowel)	5.631118
13	*(voll)er* (*deine Hose ist ... Dreck*) (9.310)	*ə*	5.576183
14	MHG *ch* in *Furche* (7.190)	*ch* not realised (long vowel)	5.575329
15	OHG Strong verbs, class Ib (*geschneit*, participle) (6.36)	*gšnīə̯*	5.570381
16	OHG Strong verbs, class VI (*trägst*, 2nd sg.) (6.75)	*drâeš*	5.562552
17	MHG *h* in *(ich) sehe, (er) sieht* (7.197)	*h* not realised	5.534073
18	MHG *û* (*iu*) before *l* in *Säulen* (5.K3)	*ẹi* (first element closed)	5.521782
19	*sagst/sagt* (6.K23)	*sē(š)(d)/sâe(š)(d)* (*g* not realised)	5.508044
20	MHG *k* in *Onkel* (7.93c)	unaspirated, fortis	5.423593

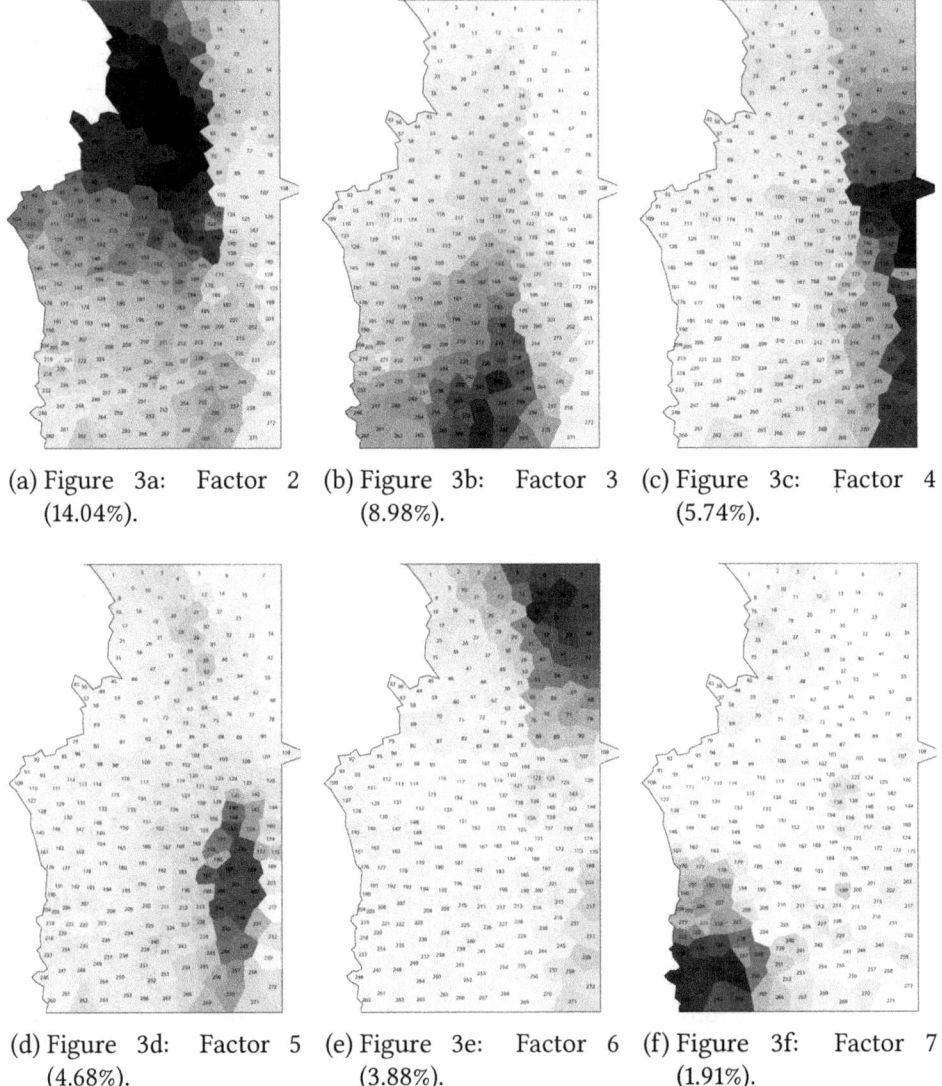

(a) Figure 3a: Factor 2 (14.04%).
(b) Figure 3b: Factor 3 (8.98%).
(c) Figure 3c: Factor 4 (5.74%).
(d) Figure 3d: Factor 5 (4.68%).
(e) Figure 3e: Factor 6 (3.88%).
(f) Figure 3f: Factor 7 (1.91%).

5 *Fuzzy dialect areas and prototype theory*

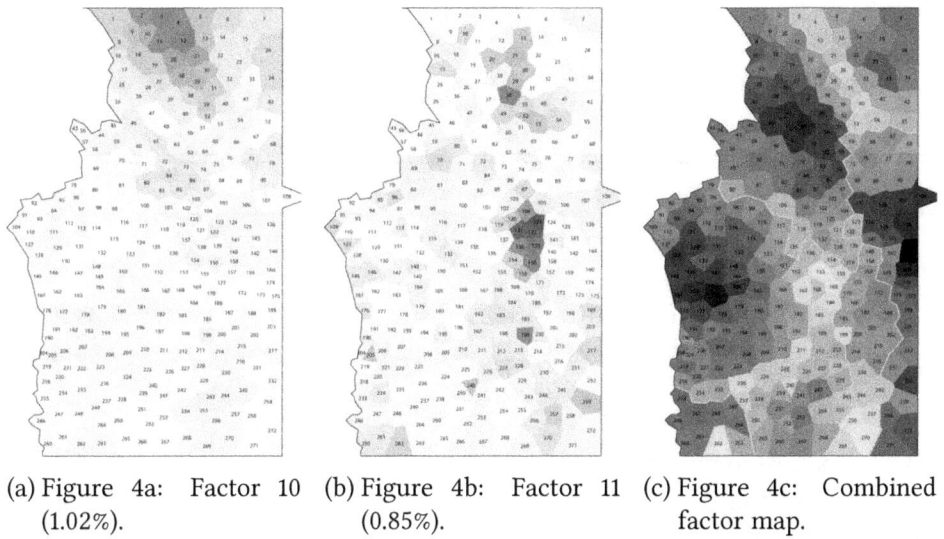

(a) Figure 4a: Factor 10 (1.02%). (b) Figure 4b: Factor 11 (0.85%). (c) Figure 4c: Combined factor map.

with West Algovian, Factor 10 with East Franconian. Factor 11 appears to capture variants that are characteristic for towns and cities: The agglomeration around location 122 is the metropolitan area of Augsburg, and most of the other locations with high loadings are larger towns: Landsberg am Lech (199), Memmingen (205), Kaufbeuren (240), Weilheim (Oberbayern) (259), Neu-Ulm (109), Günzburg (96), Dillingen (70), Kaisheim (38), Rain am Lech (53), Donauwörth (49), Nördlingen (17), Oettingen (10), Monheim (30) with its boroghs Itzing (29) and Weilheim (21), Wemding (20), Möhren (13) (borough of Treuchtlingen). The correlation between Factor 11's loadings and the populations[8] of all 272 locations is 0.45, which corresponds to an explained variance of $R^2 = 20\%$; the logarithmic relation is somewhat stronger ($R^2 = 28\%$). Factor 11, therefore, can be interpreted as a geographically discontinuous urban variety; it captures variants that are used predominantly and typically in larger towns and cities. Table 2 lists the top 20 features for this type. The preservation of vowel shortness (2, 3, 4, 5, 6, 8, 12, 15, 16, 17, 18, 20) seems to be especially characteristic of this factor. It does not come as a surprise that almost all of the variants are identical with the respective standard variants. The lenition of plosives and fricatives (1, 10, 19, 20) seems to be an exception (except for 10, where lenition occurs also in the standard), which would qualify it as a unique feature of regional urbanity that is distinct from the standard.

---

[8] Figures for 1971 are taken from: Bayerisches Statistisches Landesamt (1972).

Table 2: Top 20 features of Factor 11.

	Variable (map)	Variant	Score
1	MHG *pf* after *m*, word-final (*Dampf, Strumpf*) (7.215)	lenis affricate	8.066857
2	*i* before *ch* (*Stich(e)*) (sg./pl.) (3.2)	short vowel	7.848610
3	Vowel quantity in *Stich(e)* (sg./pl.) (9.30)	short vowel in singular and plural	7.548978
4	*o* before fortis fricative (*Frosch*) (3.8)	short vowel	7.436807
5	Vowel quantity in *Darm* (3.66)	short vowel	7.253476
6	MHG *i/u* in *Zinken* (4.47)	short open *i* (monophthong)	7.102994
7	MHG *u/o* in *donnern* (4.49)	neutral/closed *o*	7.009078
8	Vowel quantity in *First* (3.42)	short vowel	6.999477
9	Gender of *Teller* (9.165)	masculine	6.919323
10	MHG *t* after nasal, word-final (*tausend*) (7.K68c)	lenis plosive	6.914453
11	*im* (*Bett*) (9.373)	i̯m	6.901412
12	*a/o* before *ch* (*Bach/Dach/Loch*) (3.1)	short vowel	6.759506
13	MHG *â* in *Salat* (5.55)	neutral *ā*	6.635629
14	*-ig* in *König* (9.26)	*-ig*	6.581771
15	MHG *o* before *pf* in *Kopf* (4.100a)	short closed *o* (monophthong)	6.542050
16	Vowel quantity in *Stall* (3.26)	short vowel	6.491926
17	MHG *o* before *pf* in *Zopf* (4.100c)	short closed *o* (monophthong)	6.490776
18	unorganic *r* in *waten* and *Schatten* (7.254)	no *r*, short vowel	6.323896
19	MHG *t* in *Feiertag* (7.74)	lenis plosive (*r* realised)	6.303051
20	MHG *pf* in *Kopf* (7.216)	lenis affricate, short vowel	6.246637

5 Fuzzy dialect areas and prototype theory

In Figure 11, all dominant factors are combined into one map, with each location assigned to the locally dominant factor. Consequently, only information about the locally dominant factors is depicted, which means that only the surface of the dialectal landscape is visible. The resulting division into areas is in principle comparable to classifications obtained using cluster analysis or similar methods. A distinction of the present map lies in the colour shades of the individual locations, which represent the different degrees of dialect area membership. Another benefit of these results is that they retain variation 'below' the threshold of dominance, which is not visible in Figure 11 but latently present. This variation belongs firstly to the locally non-dominant parts of the globally dominant factors: each factor has loadings other than zero outside of its dominance area, but these proportions are hidden. However, they can be viewed by regarding one factor at a time (Figures 2–10).

There are also factors that are dominant nowhere in the area under investigation. They do not show up in Figure 11 at all, but again, they are latently present and can be viewed individually (Figures 12–18). Summarising small fractions of the data, they contribute to a more complete picture of overall variation and the dialectal landscape, even though they represent non-dominant dialect types, dialect areas without a core area. Many of the factors can be interpreted in a meaningful way. Several of the factors shown in Figures 12–18 seem to be related to (former) market towns: their central areas (and in some cases also their counter-centres with negative values, in red) coincide with the respective market towns' catchment areas (as documented in Volume 1 of the SBS). For Factor 12, the blue centre correlates with the catchment area of (Neu-)Ulm (109), the red centre with the catchment area of Mindelheim (195); for Factor 13, the blue centre correlates with the catchment area of Lauingen (without number); for Factor 14, the blue centre correlates with the catchment area of Nördlingen (17), the red centre with that of Wertingen (72); for Factor 15, the blue centre correlates with the catchment area of Jettingen (without number), the red centre with the catchment area of Memmingen (205), for Factor 16, the blue centre correlates with the catchment areas of Schongau and Weilheim (Oberbayern) (259), the red centre with the catchment area of Mering (158).[9] These effects are relatively weak – the factors have between 0.51% and 0.85% of explained variance, which is, however, still the equivalent of 76 to 126 variants and their distributions, and they are clearly associated with their respective counterparts. Hence it is justified to speak of non-dominant dialect types that are constituted by features character-

---

[9] For similar findings for lexically-based factors and a more in-depth discussion, see Pickl (2013a: 170–196); Pickl (2014).

istic of these towns' surrounding areas. With these findings, a level of detail and depth is reached that goes beyond what has been attainable with previous methods of dialect classification.

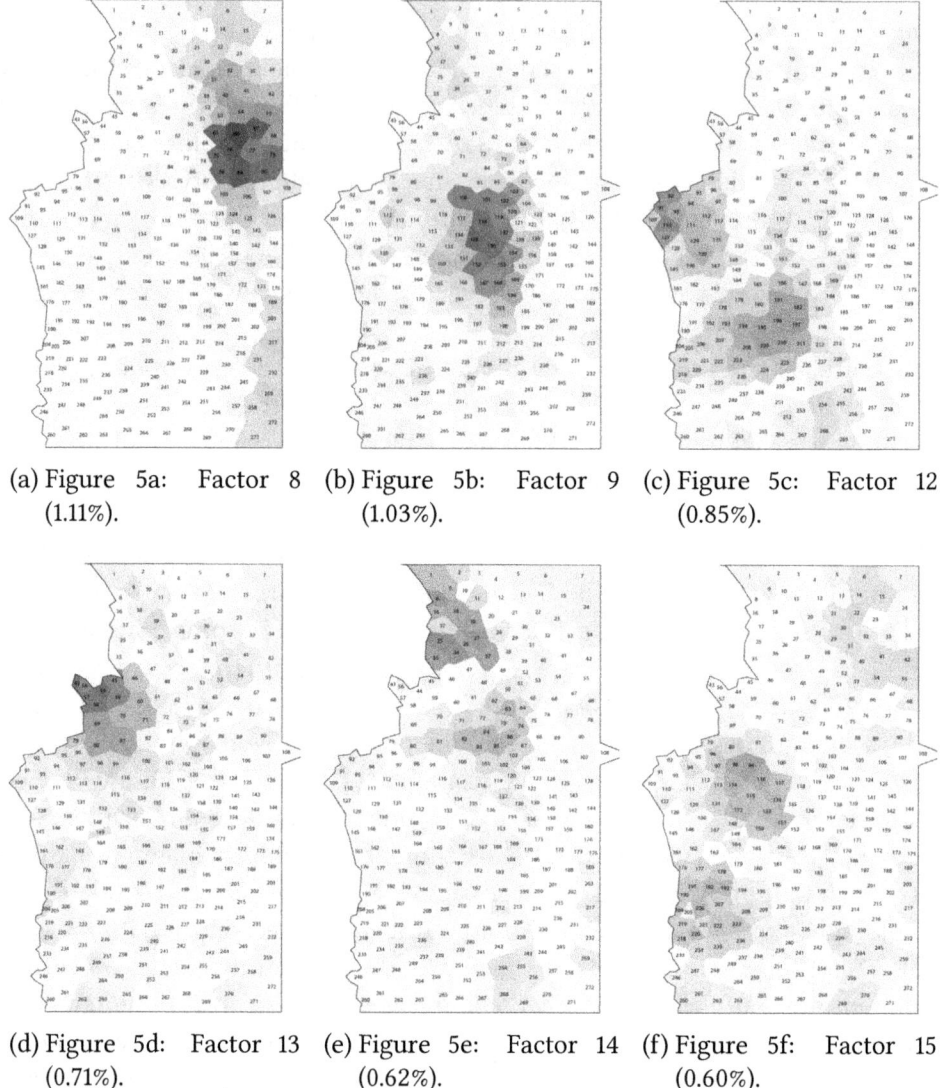

(a) Figure 5a: Factor 8 (1.11%).

(b) Figure 5b: Factor 9 (1.03%).

(c) Figure 5c: Factor 12 (0.85%).

(d) Figure 5d: Factor 13 (0.71%).

(e) Figure 5e: Factor 14 (0.62%).

(f) Figure 5f: Factor 15 (0.60%).

5 *Fuzzy dialect areas and prototype theory*

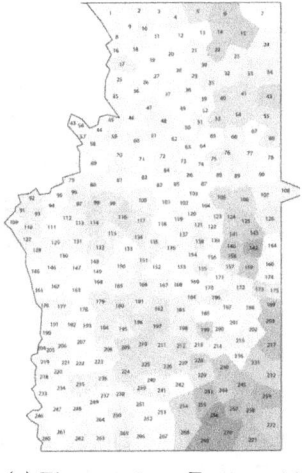

(a) Figure 6a: Factor 16 (0.51%).

4 Conclusion

It has been demonstrated how prototype theory can be used not only to describe emic, folk ideas of dialects, but also to establish a scholarly, etic notion of dialect areas. Since the two are conceptually similar, they can be compared in a straightforward way in the future to gain insights in the relative importance of individual variants and their evaluation and assessment, e.g. based on their salience.

In this paper, it was argued that emic and etic dialect areas alike are best viewed as fuzzy dialect types, which can be described in terms of prototype theory. Dialect types have an unsharp spatial expanse, individual locations exhibiting differential membership values, and are characterised by linguistic features that have individual degrees of relevance for a type.

Following this approach, dialect areas or types are constituted by sets of co-occurring features. It was argued that factor analysis, which has been used before in dialectology, is a suitable method for the identification of such sets and thus of dialect types. Its expedience was demonstrated using data from the *Sprachatlas von Bayerisch-Schwaben* (SBS), yielding 16 factors representing dialect types. Nine of them are locally dominant within the area of investigation and lead to a classification into fuzzy dialect areas, with broad spans of overlap. Seven are non-dominant, because everywhere other factors are stronger; they, too, represent meaningful patterns and can be interpreted, as was illustrated using cities' and towns' catchment areas.

Acknowledgments

This work has been supported by the *Deutsche Forschungsgemeinschaft* (DFG), which funded the joint research project *Neue Dialektometrie mit Methoden der stochastischen Bildanalyse* of the Department of German Linguistics (University of Augsburg) and the Institute of Stochastics (Ulm University). My cordial thanks go to all of my colleagues who have contributed to this work, as well as to the editors and referees of this volume.

References

Anders, Christina Ada, Markus Hundt & Alexander Lasch (eds.). 2010. *Perceptual dialectology. Neue Wege der Dialektologie*. Berlin; New York: De Gruyter.

Auer, Peter. 1986. Konversationelle Standard-Dialekt-Kontinua (Code-Shifting). *Deutsche Sprache* 14. 97–124.

Berruto, Gaetano. 2010. Identifying dimensions of linguistic variation in a language space. In Peter Auer & Jürgen Erich Schmidt (eds.), *Language and space an international handbook of linguistic variation. Vol. 1*, vol. 1, 226–241. Berlin; New York: De Gruyter Mouton.

Berthele, Raphael. 2006. Wie sieht das Berndeutsche so ungefähr aus? über den Nutzen von Visualisierungen für die kognitive Laienlinguistik. In Hubert Klausmann (ed.), *Raumstrukturen im Alemannischen: Beiträge der 15. Arbeitstagung zur alemannischen Dialektologie*, 163–175. Graz: Neugebauer.

Biber, Douglas. 1988. *Variation across speech and writing*. Cambridge: Cambridge University Press.

Bielenstein, August Johann Gottfried. 1892. *Die Grenzen des lettischen Volksstammes und der lettischen Sprache: In der Gegenwart und im 13. Jahrhundert : Ein Beitrag zur ethnologischen Geographie und Geschichte Russlands*. St. Petersburg: Eggers & Co.

Boberg, Charles. 2005. The North American regional vocabulary survey: New variables and methods in the study of North American English. *American Speech* 80(1). 22–60.

Cattell, Raymond Bernard. 1978. *The scientific use of factor analysis in behavioral and life sciences*. New York, N.Y., [etc.]: Plenum Press.

Chambers, J. K. & Peter Trudgill. 1998. *Dialectology*. 2nd edn. Cambridge, New York: Cambridge University Press.

Christen, Helen. 1998. *Dialekt im Alltag: Eine empirische Untersuchung zur lokalen Komponente heutiger schweizerdeutscher Varietäten*. Tübingen: Niemeyer.

Christen, Helen. 2010. Was Dialektbezeichnungen und Dialektattribuierungen über alltagsweltliche Konzeptualisierungen sprachlicher Heterogenität verraten. In Christina Ada Anders, Markus Hundt & Alexander Lasch (eds.), *Perceptual dialectology: Neue Wege der Dialektologie*, 269–290. Berlin; New York: De Gruyter.

Clopper, Cynthia & John C. Paolillo. 2006. North American English vowels: A factoranalytic perspective. *Literary and Linguistic Computing* 21(4). 445–462.

Girard, Dennis & Donald Larmouth. 1993. Some applications of mathematical and statistical models in dialect geography. In Dennis Preston (ed.), *American dialect research celebrating the 100th anniversary of the American Dialect Society, 1889-1989*, 107–131. Amsterdam/Philadelphia: John Benjamins Pub. Co.

Goebl, Hans. 1983. Stammbaum und Welle. *Zeitschrift für Sprachwissenschaft* 2. 3–44.

Grieve, Jack. 2009. *A corpus-based regional dialect survey of grammatical variation in written Standard American English*. Flagstaff: Northern Arizona University PhD dissertation.

Grieve, Jack. 2014. A comparison of statistical methods for the aggregation of regional linguistic variation. In Benedikt Szmrecsanyi & Bernhard Wälchli (eds.), *Aggregating dialectology, typology, and register analysis: Linguistic variation in text and speech* (Lingua & Litterae 28), 53–88. Berlin, New York: Walter de Gruyter.

Grieve, Jack, Dirk Speelman & Dirk Geeraerts. 2011. A statistical method for the identification and aggregation of regional linguistic variation. *Language Variation and Change* 23(2). 193–221.

Hyvönen, Saara, Antti Leino & Marko Salmenkivi. 2007. Multivariate analysis of Finnish dialect data — An overview of lexical variation. *Literary and Linguistic Computing* 22(3). 271–290.

Kretzschmar, William A. 2009. *The linguistics of speech*. New York: Cambridge University Press.

Kristiansen, Gitte. 2008. Style-shifting and shifting styles: A socio-cognitive approach to lectal variation. In René Dirven & Gitte Kristiansen (eds.), *Cognitive sociolinguistics language variation, cultural models, social systems*, 45–88. Berlin; New York: Mouton de Gruyter.

Kurath, Hans. 1972. *Studies in area linguistics*. Bloomington/London: Indiana University Press.

König, Werner (ed.). 1996–2009. *Sprachatlas von Bayerisch-Schwaben*. Heidelberg: Winter.

Labov, William. 1973. The boundaries of words and their meanings. In Charles James Nice Bailey & Roger W Shuy (eds.), *New ways of analyzing variation in English*, 340–373. Washington: Georgetown University Press.

Labov, William, Sharon Ash & Charles Boberg. 2006. *The atlas of North American English: Phonetics, phonology and sound change*. Berlin, New York: Mouton de Gruyter.

Lakoff, George. 1987. *Women, fire, and dangerous things: What categories reveal about the mind*. Chicago, Ill., [etc.]: The University of Chicago Press.

Leino, Antti & Saara Hyvönen. 2008. Comparison of component models in analysing the distribution of dialectal features. *International Journal of Humanities and Arts Computing* 2(1–2). 173–187.

Leinonen, Therese Nanette. 2010. *An acoustic analysis of vowel pronunciation in Swedish dialects*. Groningen: Rijksuniversiteit Groningen Ph.D. dissertation.

Lenz, Alexandra N. 2003. *Struktur und Dynamik des Substandards: Eine Studie zum Westmitteldeutschen (Wittlich/Eifel)*. Stuttgart, Wiesbaden: F. Steiner.

Nerbonne, John. 2006. Identifying linguistic structure in aggregate comparison. *Literary and Linguistic Computing* 21(4). 463–475.

Nerbonne, John, Rinke Colen, Charlotte Gooskens, Peter Kleiweg & Therese Leinonen. 2011. Gabmap – a web application for dialectology. *Dialectologia* Special Issue II. 65–89.

Nübling, Eduard. 1988. *Studien und Berichte zur Geschichts-, Mundart- und Namenforschung Bayerisch-Schwabens: Festgabe zum 80. Geburtstag des Verfassers*. Augsburg; Weissenhorn: Schwäbische Forschungsgemeinschaft ; In Kommission bei A.H. Konrad.

Pickl, Simon. 2013a. *Probabilistische Geolinguistik: Geostatistische Analysen lexikalischer Variation in Bayerisch-Schwaben*. Stuttgart: Steiner.

Pickl, Simon. 2013b. Verdichtungen im sprachgeografischen Kontinuum. *Zeitschrift fur Dialektologie und Linguistik* 80(1). 1–35.

Pickl, Simon. 2014. Dialekträume 'unter der Oberfläche'. Nicht-dominante wortgeographische Strukturen in Bayerisch-Schwaben. In Rudolf Bühler, Rebekka Bürkle & Nina Kim Leonhardt (eds.), *Sprachkultur, Regionalkultur: Neue Felder kulturwissenschaftlicher Dialektforschung*, 198–217. Tübingen: Tübinger Vereinigung für Volkskunde e. V.

Preston, Dennis. 1989. *Perceptual dialectology nonlinguists' views of areal linguistics*. Dordrecht: Foris Publications.

Preston, Dennis. 1999. *Handbook of perceptual dialectology*. Vol. 1. Amsterdam; Philadelphia: J. Benjamins.

Prokić, Jelena. 2010. *Families and resemblances.* Groningen: Rijksuniversiteit Groningen Ph.D. dissertation.

Prokić, Jelena & John Nerbonne. 2008. Recognizing groups among dialects. *International Journal of Humanities and Arts Computing* 2. 153–171.

Pröll, Simon. 2015. *Raumvariation zwischen Muster und Zufall. Geostatistische Analysen am Beispiel des Sprachatlas von Bayerisch-Schwaben.* Stuttgart: Steiner.

Pröll, Simon, Simon Pickl & Aaron Spettl. 2015. Latente Strukturen in geolinguistischen Korpora. In Michael Elmentaler, Markus Hundt & Jürgen Erich Schmidt (eds.), *Deutsche Dialekte - Konzepte, Probleme, Handlungsfelder: Akten des 4. Kongresses der Internationalen Gesellschaft für Dialektologie des Deutschen (IGDD)*, 247–258. Stuttgart: Steiner.

Pustka, Elissa. 2009. A prototype-theoretic model of Southern French. In Kate Beeching, Nigel R. Armstrong & Françoise Gadet (eds.), *Sociolinguistic variation in contemporary French*, 77–94. Amsterdam; Philadelphia: John Benjamins Pub. Co.

Rosch, Eleanor. 1973. Natural categories. *Cognitive Psychology* 4. 328–350.

Shackleton, Robert. 2005. English-American speech relationships. *Journal of English Linguistics* 33(2). 99–160.

Szmrecsanyi, Benedikt & Christoph Wolk. 2011. Holistic corpus-based dialectology. *Revista Brasileira de Linguística Aplicada* 11(2). 561–592.

Tabachnick, Barbara G & Linda S. Fidell. 2012. *Using multivariate statistics.* Boston, Munich: Pearson.

Wieling, Martijn & John Nerbonne. 2011. Bipartite spectral graph partitioning for clustering dialect varieties and detecting their linguistic features. *Computer Speech & Language* 25(3). 700–715.

Wieling, Martijn & John Nerbonne. 2015. Advances in dialectometry. *Annual Review of Linguistics* 1. 243–264.

Wieling, Martijn, Robert Shackleton & John Nerbonne. 2013. Analyzing phonetic variation in the traditional English dialects: Simultaneously clustering dialects and phonetic features. *Literary and Linguistic Computing* 28(1). 31–41.

Wiesinger, Peter. 1983. Die Einteilung der deutschen Dialekte. In Werner Besch, Ulrich Knoop, Wolfgang Putschke & Herbert Ernst Wiegand (eds.), *Dialektologie. Ein Handbuch zur deutschen und allgemeinen Dialektforschung. Zweiter Halbband*, 807–900. Berlin/New York: de Gruyter.

Zadeh, Lotfi A. 1965. Fuzzy Sets. *Information and Control* 8. 338–353.

Bayerisches Statistisches Landesamt (ed.). 1972. *Einwohnerzahlen am 31. Dezember 1971. Jährliches Ergänzungsheft zum Amtlichen Gemeindeverzeichnis für Bayern.*

Chapter 6

On the problem of field worker isoglosses

Andrea Mathussek
University of Freiburg

> As a number of authors have shown, the traditional approach of collecting and transcribing speech material in direct investigations may lead to differences in the data that do not represent real diatopic variation but are based on the individual transcription habits of the different field workers involved. If such differences result in isoglosses separating not speech areas but different field workers' investigation areas ("field worker isoglosses"), researchers run the risk of mapping the organizational structure of projects instead of true linguistic similarities or differences. The following article shows how dialectometric analysis can be used to visualize field worker phenomena in speech data using the example of the *Sprachatlas von Mittelfranken* (SMF), which is part of the *Bavarian Speech Atlas*.

1 Definition: field worker isogloss (FWI)

To define the concept of 'field worker isogloss' (FWI) one has to start by explaining the term "isogloss". Isoglosses are usually characterized as boundary lines between two dialect realizations of a linguistic phenomenon (cf. Glück 2005: 296–297). An isogloss – or sometimes a bundle of more than one isogloss – then forms the border of a speech area in traditional dialect geography. The phenomenon is illustrated in Figure 1. Here, the different colors of the speech bubbles symbolize the different realizations of the linguistic variable under investigation and the blue line stands for the isogloss.

Based on this concept, FWIs can be defined as boundary lines between two different realizations in phonetic transcription, given that there is no variation in the audio data under investigation. Field worker isoglosses are thus boundary lines between two field worker areas. The illustration on the right in Figure 1 exemplifies this.

A (fictitious) example might be the realization of the vowel in *Frosch* ('frog'), which may be pronounced [uː] by the informants from both villages. This is

Andrea Mathussek. 2016. On the problem of field worker isoglosses. In Marie-Hélène Côté, Remco Knooihuizen & John Nerbonne (eds.), *The future of dialects*, 99–116. Berlin: Language Science Press. DOI:10.17169/langsci.b81.145

Figure 1: Schematic layout of the concepts "isogloss" and "fieldworker isogloss"

symbolized by the usage of red color for both speech bubbles. The particularity now lies in the fact that despite the consistency of the informants' speech the field workers write down two different phonetic symbols and thus differ in their phonetic transcription of the speech, which is illustrated by the use of different colors for the note pads.[1]

It might be expected that field worker phenomena only occur rarely – especially because the problem has been well known in dialectology for quite a while (cf. Hotzenköcherle 1962: 59–73). Unfortunately, it appears that the problem occurs more often than expected.

In this paper I will explain – based on the example of the *Middle Franconian Speech Atlas* (SMF) – how field worker effects find their way into linguistic data and analysis. While there are a number of established practices used by project members to avoid this problem, even atlases published in the last 10 years betray traces of the individual field workers' influence. I will then show how dialectometry can be useful to discover fieldworker phenomena in the transcribed corpora of linguistic data surveyed by different people in different places.

2 The potential risk in traditional dialect atlas data

2.1 Example data

The data serving as an example in this article comes from the *Sprachatlas von Mittelfranken* (Dialect Atlas of Middle Franconia, SMF). This project started in 1989 and was supervised by Horst Haider Munske in Erlangen (cf. Munske 2013: 11). The map in Figure 2 shows the position of the administrative district Middle Franconia in Germany marked in red. It is located in Southern Germany and adjoins Bavaria in the west. The region is interesting from a dialectological point of view

---

[1] Phonetic transcription is always only a model for reality. Versions A and B may also differ in their degree of detail. This may lead e.g. to one field worker marking nasalization or lenition while another leaves them unmarked. Differing transcriptions do not always mean that somebody made a mistake (cf. Mathussek 2014: 41–69).

because three High German dialects meet here: Eastern Franconian, Swabian and Northern Bavarian (cf. SMF 1: 7).

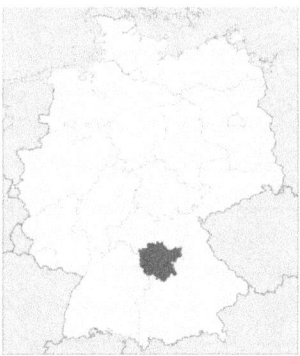

Figure 2: Position of Middle Franconia in Germany (GFDL. Orginal source: http://commons.wikimedia.org/wiki/File:Locator_map_Mittelfranken_in_Germany.svg)

It is worth emphasis that the *Middle Franconian Atlas* is only one example where such phenomena occur — other atlases using similar traditional methods may be expected to reflect transcriber-specific phenomena as well.

2.2 Reasons for FWIs

As Kerswill and Wright summarize: "Transcription is a messy thing" (Kerswill & Wright 1990: 273). I will illustrate this with reference to the SMF in the following pages.

The Middle Franconian Atlas – like most of the regional dialect atlases of the 20th century – is an atlas of the so-called 2nd generation. That means that direct investigation was used as a method to collect data.[2] Typically, atlases of this type are mono-dimensional atlases[3] with a few exceptions. The interviews took place in the informants' living rooms and were usually recorded on cassettes. However, the audio material was used as a reference source in problematic cases

---

[2] For the direct method, a "trained fieldworker makes on-location recordings and works through a comprehensive questionnaire with the informant. [...] The investigator and the informant are united in the attempt to unearth the oldest accessible form at a particular location [...]." (König 2010: 502)

[3] Mono-dimensional atlases, in contrast to two-dimensional atlases, do not take pragmatic or social variation into account. (cf. *Mittelrheinischer Sprachatlas* Institut für Geschichtliche Landeskunde an der Universität Mainz (ed.): *Mittelrheinischer Sprachatlas*; http://www.igl.uni-mainz.de/service/impressum.html, 2015/05/20)

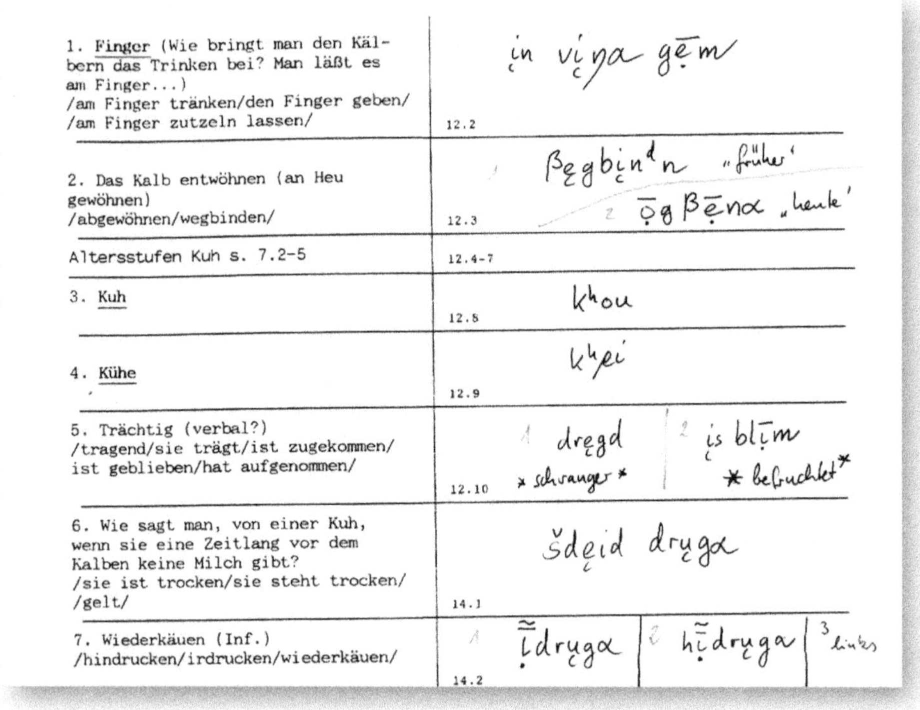

1. Finger (Wie bringt man den Kälbern das Trinken bei? Man läßt es am Finger...) /am Finger tränken/den Finger geben/ /am Finger zutzeln lassen/	12.2	in viŋa gēm
2. Das Kalb entwöhnen (an Heu gewöhnen) /abgewöhnen/wegbinden/	12.3	1 βegbindn „früher' 2 ōgβēnα „heute'
Altersstufen Kuh s. 7.2-5	12.4-7	
3. Kuh	12.8	khou
4. Kühe	12.9	khei
5. Trächtig (verbal?) /tragend/sie trägt/ist zugekommen/ ist geblieben/hat aufgenommen/	12.10	1 dregd *schwanger* 2 is blīm *befruchtet*
6. Wie sagt man, von einer Kuh, wenn sie eine Zeitlang vor dem Kalben keine Milch gibt? /sie ist trocken/sie steht trocken/ /gelt/	14.1	šdeid druga
7. Wiederkäuen (Inf.) /hindrucken/irdrucken/wiederkäuen/	14.2	1 īdruga 2 hīdruga 3 links

Figure 3: Original page of a SMF-questionnaire

rather than as the basis for analysis. Instead, the basis for analysis consisted of the questionnaire and the handwritten phonetic transcriptions the field worker noted immediately after the informant answered a question.

Figure 3 shows a part of one page from the Middle Franconian questionnaire. The "questions" are printed in the left column. They are sometimes real questions as in number 6 "what do you call it when a cow does not give any milk for some time before she calves?" The answer here can be translated literally as "stands dry" and is written down in Theutonista in the right column by the field worker. This happens "on line", while the informant is waiting for the next question. It is evident that such time pressure can lead to imprecision or even mistakes. This becomes even clearer when we have a closer look at the transcription system here.

Figure 4 shows part of the vowel diagram as it was used for the Bavarian Speech atlases. The enlarged part lists some of the possibilities to record open

6 On the problem of field worker isoglosses

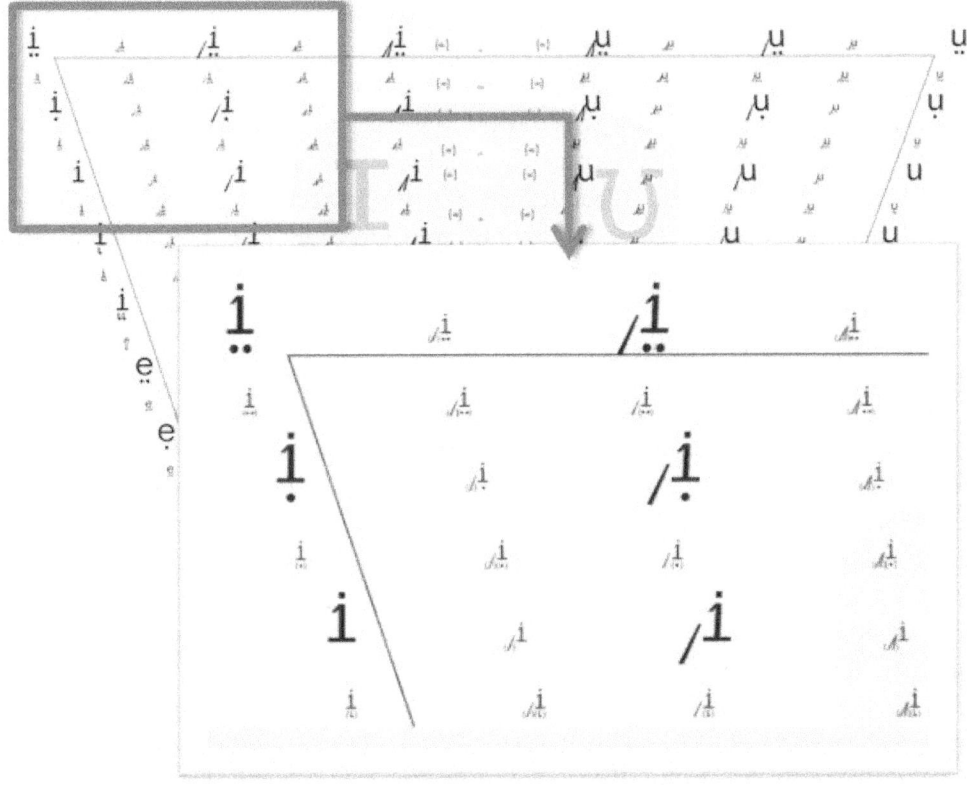

Figure 4: Part of the Theutonista vowel diagram (cf. SMF 1: 82)

fronted vowels. It becomes obvious that it is nearly impossible for two persons to write down the same symbol with exactly the same diacritics when this degree of detail is used. This is at least one source of possible interpersonal differences in the transcriptions.

Such interpersonal variation, of course, becomes a problem, especially when more than one person is working in the field.[4] But a division of labor is often necessary, even in comparatively small areas of investigation such as the administrative district of Middle Franconia, if a high density of locations is to be surveyed.

For the *Atlas of Middle Franconia*, investigations were carried out in 167 mainly rural villages in an area of 7.000 square kilometers. In every village, about six people (men and women) served as informants – which makes a total of around 1.000

---

[4] Even with one transcriber, there may be intrapersonal inconsistencies.

interviews with an average duration of 10 hours. The questionnaire contained 2.808 questions (cf. SMF 1: 29 ff.). It is quite clear that it would be impossible for one person to manage 10.000 hours of interviews. The easiest and most economical way to split the work was to divide the area of investigation into areas assigned to different field workers. The field workers at the *Middle Franconian Atlas*, for example, lived in different areas of the administrative district or had family there – it was therefore an obvious solution to divide the area according to the field workers' locations.

2.3 Arrangements to avoid FWIs

It is interesting to see what measures the project members undertook to avoid the appearance of field worker phenomena. First of all, the members of the project were aware of the fact that such effects can occur in the data, as previous and neighboring projects had also alluded to the problem and suggested solutions.[5] In the introductory volume, the text near the map showing the field workers' areas (see Figure 5) says: "Map 11 shows which investigations were carried out by which field worker. The field workers' individual background and the specifics of their phonetic transcriptions are given below" (Klepsch 2013a: 47). The authors even identify and describe individual transcribing habits,[6] which is an indication of transparency. A closer look at the description of those individual "specifics of phonetic transcriptions" as they are described in the introductory volume will make this point even clearer. The following text is a translation of Alfred Klepsch's characterization as a field worker:

> Alfred Klepsch was born in Schwabach in 1954 and lived there from 1954 to 1961. From 1961 to 1974 he lived in Spalt, from 1974 to 1986 in Schwabach again, from 1986 to 1995 in Baiersdorf, from 1995 to 2000 in Erlangen and since then he has been living in Nuremberg. He speaks the regional dialect of the Nuremberg area. [...] His transcription shows indetermination especially in the area of half-closed short vowels. From 1989 to 1992, he nearly always recorded open e-sounds [corresponds closest to æ in IPA] and o-sounds. After the coordinator M. Renn told Klepsch that the dialect variant of the Middle High German primary umlaut e has a more closed quality [...] the field worker tried to close that "hearing gap". The transcriptions of 1993, then, certainly contain some hypercorrections [...]
> (Klepsch 2013a: 47 [translated and slightly adapted])

---

[5] Cf. e. g. Hotzenköcherle (1962: 59) and König (1997: 45).
[6] The SDS again serves as a model here (cf. Hotzenköcherle 1962: 61–73).

6 On the problem of field worker isoglosses

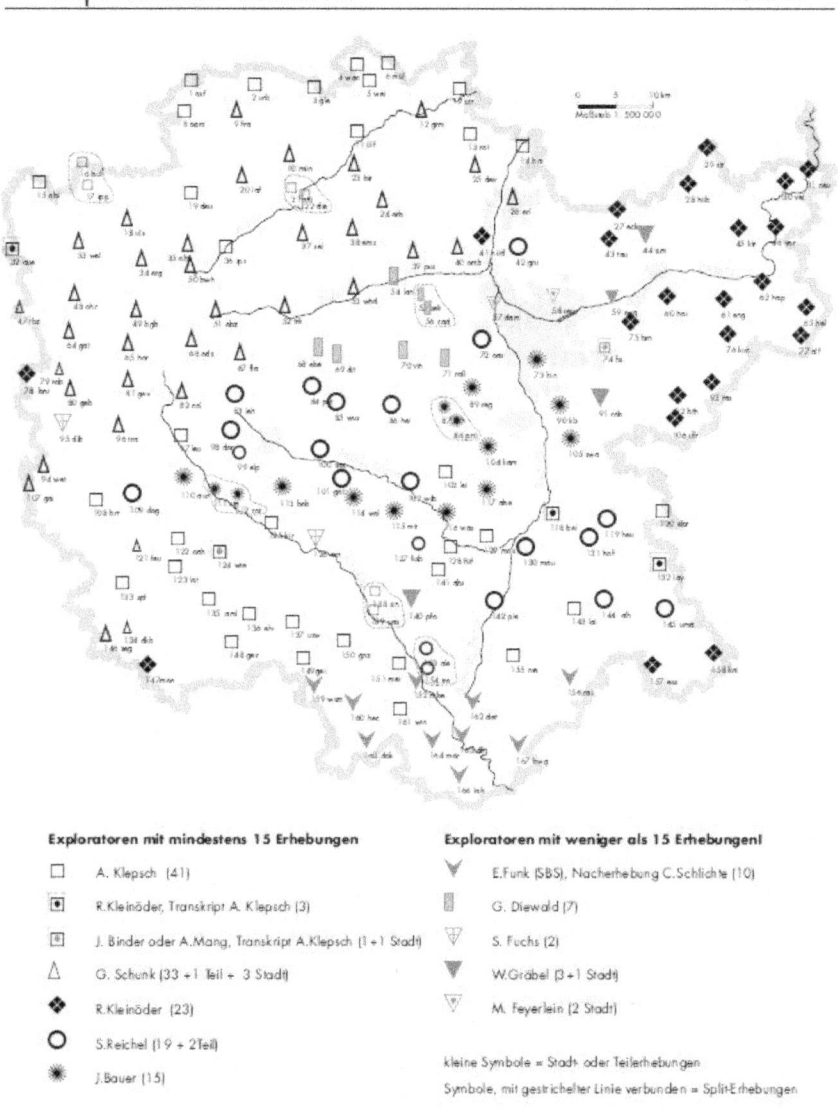

Figure 5: The field workers' working sections in the SMF project (SMF 1: 48)

The text deals with the background and the individual transcribing habits of Alfred Klepsch, who was the coordinator of the project. In the first paragraph it provides the reader with information about the villages in Middle Franconia Alfred Klepsch lived in and information on his speech and transcribing habits. Further on, the text honestly names a number of Klepsch's habits, which shows a really high degree of transparency. The question is: How often does a reader not only notice such texts in introductory volumes, but also use them for his or her interpretation of the data or the maps?

The members of the project did not leave it up to the reader to work out the problem of FWI, but rather applied various methods to address this issue.

First of all, there was a lot of discussion and comparison among the sister projects (cf. Klepsch 2013b: 25 ff.). The Middle Franconian Atlas is only one part of a big project comprising the whole federal state of Bavaria. Moreover, the field workers within the project always made great efforts to adjust their transcriptions. They used methods such as co-transcribing and attending each other's test investigations, while also organizing meetings and workshops. In addition there was one interview which was transcribed by all field workers. This transcription served as a reference point from then on (cf. Klepsch 2013b: 26).

Klepsch writes about the beginnings of the project in retrospective: "The comparison of the transcripts and the audio data completely puzzled the field workers. The differences between the [...] transcripts were immense" (Klepsch 2013b: 25). Despite all the efforts he concludes: "None of the field workers achieved a level of perfection in the course of his or her career" (Klepsch 2013b: 27).[7]

3 Dialectometry as a means to discover FWI

Field worker effects are often considered something you have to expect in the data – but also something that can be addressed and dealt with when it comes to interpretation.[8] Because of this common opinion field worker isoglosses were not really on my mind when I was attempting to detect speech areas and speech

---

[7] As Kerswill and Wright (1990: 226) point out, a reason for this may be that transcribers use different strategies for "rationalizing and reducing to symbols the differences they have heard" (cf. Kerswill & Wright 1990: 269).

[8] Ogura and Wang proposed a statistical "method for clarifying fieldworker isoglosses" using the Spearman rank order correlation. They correlate the frequencies of reflexes of different ME vowels inside and outside individual investigation areas of the SED. This method sounds very promising to me. For reasons of simplicity with respect to implementing the method, I will describe another procedure to detect field worker phenomena (cf. Ogura & Wang 1992).

6 On the problem of field worker isoglosses

borders in the investigation area of Middle Franconia – using the data and material of the SMF-project (cf. Mathussek 2014).

The dialectometric analysis of the realization types of 517 lexemes/phrases showed that the individual variants formed cohesive areas, irrespective of the specific statistical method used. The colored regions in Figure 8 (not the symbols) are the result of a clustering technique (Ward's method, 8 clusters) carried out by Gabmap.[9] Figure 6 shows a small part of the table that was used as a basis for the analysis with Gabmap.

	A	B	C	D	E
1		Kuh	Stroh	Höhe	die alten Häuser
2	1	KH&U2.-	S7DRO5-	HE5$.-X7	DI2-2H,A5.L;DNHO5E2SA,
3	2	KH&U2.-	S7DRO5.-	HE5-X7	DI5A6L9DNHA2E2S%A,
4	3	KH&U2.-	S7DRO5-	HE5-X7	DI2A6.L;DNHA2E2SA,
5	4	KH&U6.-	S7DRO2-	HE2$-	DI5O6L;DNHO5E2SA,
6	5	KH&U2.-	S7DRO2-	HE5.$-	DI5O6L;DNHA2.ESA,
7	6	KH&U5-	S7DRO2-	HE5.$-	DI5O6L;DNHO5E2SA,
8	7	KH&U2-	S7DRO2-	HE2-	DI5A5L;&DNHO5E2S%A,
9	8	KH&U2-	S7DRO5-	HE5-	DI5O6.L;9DNHO5E2SA,
10	9	KHU2.-	S7DRA5$.-	HE2-	DI5A6LDNHO5$.-2E1SE,5
11	10	KHU-	S7DRA6$-	HE5-X6	DI5A5LDNHA2-2E2SE,5
12	11	KH&U2-	S7DRO5-	HE2-	DI5A6L;9DNHA2E2SA,
13	12	KHU-	S7DRO-	HE2.-N7	DI5A6LDNHO5E1$SEE:,

figure 6: Part of the data table prepared for the analysis with Gabmap ('cow', 'straw', 'height', 'the old houses'; locations 1 to 12). The table does not show IPA or Theutonista but the so called "Kodate" – a code that translates the basic signs and diacritics of Theutonista into ASCII (American Standard Code for Information Interchange) (cf. Reichel 2013: 38–40).

The comparison of this analysis with maps developed with traditional methods then revealed some discrepancies. Figure 7 visualizes some results of the traditional approach. I picked out about 40 Middle High German speech sounds in different sound environments and looked for different realizations in the 167 villages. The resulting isoglosses in the area of consonants are shown in black; the isoglosses for vowel phenomena are marked in red.

What attracts one's attention here is that besides some obvious similarities between the isoglosses in Figure 7 and the areas in Figure 8 – such as the bundle

---

[9] Gabmap is a free "web application that visualizes dialect variation", which was developed in Groningen. (cf. Nerbonne et al. 2011.) For a description of how cluster analysis works see http://www.gabmap.nl/~app/doc/manual/clustering.html, accessed 2015/5/21.

Figure 7: Traditional approach: consonantal and vocalic isoglosses (Mathussek 2014: 107).

of isoglosses along the western border of the area of investigation and the area in light orange and pink taken together – there are areas on the map in Figure 8 that do not coincide with the results of the traditional analysis.

The explanation for the apparently new borders problem is revealed when one considers the striking match between the dialectometric analysis and the investigation areas of the individual field workers. What the dialectometric analyses showed were, without much doubt, not really speech areas, but rather field worker effects in the data!

The map in Figure 8 is a blend of a Gabmap cluster map and the map in the introductory volume of the Middle Franconian Atlas showing which field worker collected data in which village (SMF 1: 48, see Figure 5 above). There is a noticeable coincidence of symbols and clusters on the map. In particular, the dark green and the light blue section match the symbols one-to-one, which means that exactly one field worker worked in all the villages Gabmap clustered together here as one. It was also exactly one person who was responsible for both the light green and the light orange areas, taken together.

The next task was to find out which properties of the data were responsible for the clustering – or in other words: whether different transcription habits were so

6 *On the problem of field worker isoglosses*

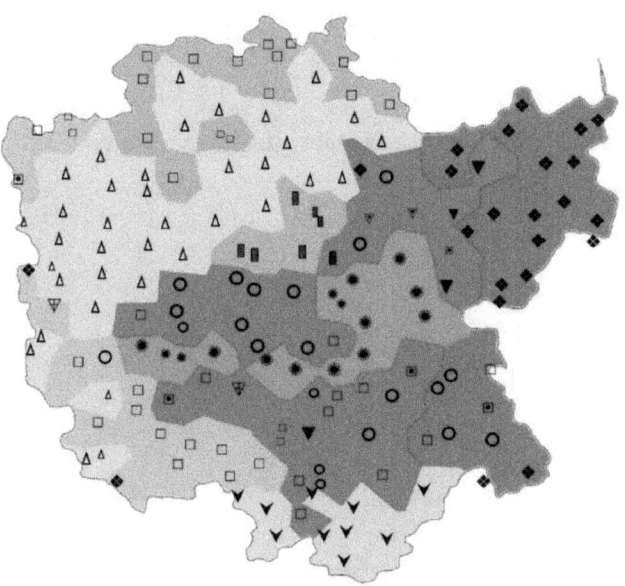

Figure 8: Clusters and field worker's collection areas (Mathussek 2014: 216).

influential that they marginalized the real linguistic differences. Gabmap offers a very useful tool named cluster determinants. The tool helps to identify those lexemes that are the most relevant for a cluster. That means the realization types are very similar or identical within the cluster and they rarely or never appear in other clusters.[10]

I will only give a few examples here, but more are to be found. The analysis of the cluster determinants for the light green cluster (cf. figure 8) showed that in the villages in this area, words like [oːʃdən][11] *Ostern* ('Easter') and [dsɪxəd] (*er*) *zöge* ('he would pull') often have the highest values in the cluster determinants' analysis. Moreover, this field worker noted aspirated voiceless dental plosives, whereas the others didn't. One example here is [gvidətʰ] *gefüttert* ('fed'). Thirdly, the field worker in this area transcribed clusters of vowels and used many diacritics, as in *heiraten* ('marry'), which may look like Figure 9 in Theutonista. This was a peculiarity that very rarely occurred in other regions.

In case of the light blue cluster in the south of Middle Franconia we find a very clear example of a field worker phenomenon. Figure Figure 10 shows the

---

[10] Cf. Nerbonne et al. (2011).
[11] IPA is used here to make the presentation more generally accessible. As I pointed out above, SMF and the other Bavarian speech atlases used Theutonista.

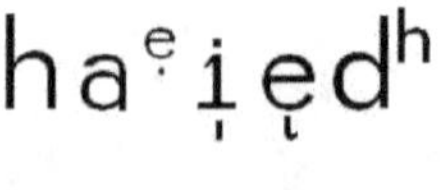

$$ha^e\underset{\textstyle\raise1pt\hbox{,}}{i}\underset{\textstyle\raise1pt\hbox{,}}{e}d^h$$

Figure 9: Theutonista transcription of *heiraten* ('marry').

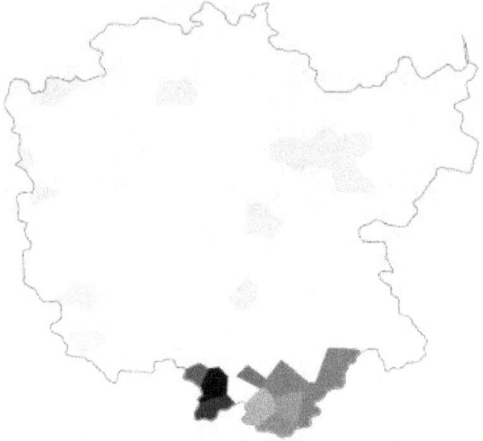

Figure 10: Distribution of <w> (Mathussek 2014: 226).

distribution of the phonetic symbol <w>, which stands for the bilabial fricative in Theutonista. As one can see, the area corresponds perfectly with the cluster in light blue in the south of the investigation area (cf. Figure 7). A closer look into the data shows that <w> only appears in transcripts from this area where two neighboring projects made investigations. The *Middle Franconian Atlas* got data here from the *Atlas of Bavarian Swabia* (SBS) and they had slightly different transcription conventions there (cf. SMF 1: 30). In the rest of the investigation area the field workers used the sign <ß> in all of the cases where the Swabians used <w>. This shows a very clear case of field worker influence indirectly reflecting phenomena in a neighboring project. However, those cases are not the dangerous ones because they can easily be recognized in the data:[12]

Figure 10 is an example for a distribution map made with Gabmap. This feature allows the mapping of the distribution of individual items or strings of items in the data. In this case the map shows that the symbol <w> only occurs in those locations that were examined by members of the SBS project (light blue cluster in Figure 8).

---

[12] At least when the editor takes a closer look into the data.

All in all, the data analysis showed a clear correlation between the Gabmap clusters and the field workers' individual areas of investigation. In the corpus, individual transcription habits were much more relevant for initial analysis than the real linguistic differences.

The last step was then to check the linguistic features which the cluster determinants analysis had shown were especially relevant for the structure of the data in the audio material. Of course, only a random sample could be tested here. The check confirmed the results of the dialectometric analysis: in most cases under suspicion, the differences in the transcriptions were not a matter of real linguistic variance.

To sum up, I recommend a dialectometric analysis of dialect geographical data in six steps:[13] Firstly, the whole corpus is mapped using a cluster technique with approximately the number of clusters that would be expected from traditional approaches. Secondly, the results should be compared (if possible) to the results of traditional approaches. In a third step, the results should be compared to the information about investigation areas and field workers that is accessible. If there are inconsistencies, or if the areas seem to correspond more to the investigation areas than to the areas noted in traditional approaches (or if there is no accessible information on one of the aspects) the analysis of cluster determinants should be conducted to find out about the lexemes or phrases that are mostly "responsible" for the clusters in a fourth step. The results of this analysis can be checked with distribution maps (fifth step), before in a sixth step relevant features should be examined in the audio data.

4 FWIs on actual maps in the printed atlases?

Subsequently, an important question to ask was to what extent this had influenced the maps and results in the printed volumes of the atlases. The following two short examples show that field worker phenomena even made it into the printed volumes.[14]

The first example can be found in map 45 in volume 4 of the *Middle Franconian Atlas*. It deals with the realizations of Middle High German t in the position

---

[13] Of course, this analysis can be done with different software, too.

[14] It's easier to discover field worker phenomena in the volumes of the SBS, where the members decided to print investigation areas on every base map. This enables a quick check whether feature isoglosses correlate or not with boundaries of fieldworker areas (cf. SBS 1: 45). Due to the fact that 13 people worked as field workers for the SMF (SMF 1: 48) project (but only 3 for SBS, SBS 1: 45), the investigation areas are not printed on the base map in the Middle Franconian Atlas.

Figure 11: Field worker effects in SMF 1, map 45: MHG t in the position between -s- and -en and one individual field worker's working area (in green) (cf. Mathussek 2014: 240).

between -s- and -en as in the lexemes *Bürste* ('brush'), *Fenster* ('window'), *Gerste* ('barley') and *Husten* ('cough'). The green line around the investigation area of the field worker Johannes Bauer in Figure 11 corresponds perfectly to the area where reduced plosives were plotted on the map. Nowhere else in the area of investigation had field workers noted reduced plosives. The unique shape of the area makes it hard to believe that the coincidence is only accidental.

The second example (see Figure 12) is taken from the second volume of the *Middle Franconian Atlas* and refers to the realizations of the vowel in the demonstrative pronoun *die* (meaning 'this' or 'these'). This part of map 100 is intended to illustrate the border between a realization type "closed vowel" and a realization type "neutral or open vowel". I drew an isogloss between the two types and compared it to the border between Alfred Klepsch's (orange) and Gunter Schunk's (light green) investigation area. There is a one-to-one match between the two borders – despite the fact that its course is quite unique.

Those are only two examples, but it is quite certain that there are more – and not only in the *Middle Franconian Atlas*. In both cases mentioned above, audio

6 On the problem of field worker isoglosses

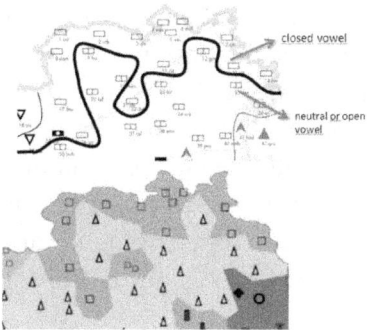

Figure 12: Field worker effects in SMF 2, map 100: Realization of the vowel in the demonstrative pronoun *die* (Mathussek 2014: 241).

data was checked for reference. It was not possible to identify any differences between the dialect realizations inside and outside the clusters.

Field worker isoglosses, then, are present in speech atlases and are presented as real isoglosses separating speech variants.

5 Implications

The findings of this analysis lead to a few implications.

First of all, it is important for anyone working with speech atlases in which different field workers were responsible for collecting the data to pay attention to the field workers' individual areas of investigation. That, of course, may not always be possible or easy because the degree of transparency varies a lot from atlas to atlas.

Despite that fact, the search for field worker phenomena has to be carried out systematically and needs to be expanded to other atlas projects and their maps and data. Dialectometric approaches can be used to explore the data and to identify the relevant features in the data.

Furthermore, the findings show that the analysis of large amounts of data does not make traditional approaches redundant. That does not mean that dialect geographers have to lean over hand-drawn maps again – Gabmap offers tools for "traditional" methods, too – but a close examination of the data is absolutely necessary.

A last point concerns the question of the degree of detail in phonetic transcription. Do we really want all those diacritics if it is seemingly impossible for two people to use them in the same way?

Here, more modern approaches and methods of investigation seem to provide help. For the project "Effects of the national border on the linguistic situation in the Upper Rhine Area" (*Frontière linguistique au Rhin Supérieur*, FLARS) for example, there were no transcripts made in the actual investigation situation, but the researchers only transcribed relevant parts later with the help of the audio data (cf. Auer et al. 2015).[15] This leads to a closer relation between audio data and analysis; the process of (phonetic) transcribing is carried out by one person[16] in a relatively short time, and the focus is on the aspect that will be the object of analysis.

References

Auer, Peter, Julia Breuninger, Dominique Huck & Martin Pfeiffer. 2015. Auswirkungen der Staatsgrenze auf die Sprachsituation im Oberrheingebiet (Frontière linguistique au Rhin Supérieur, FLARS). In Roland Kehrein, Alfred Lameli & Stefan Rabanus (eds.), *Regionale variation des deutschen*, 323–348. Berlin, New York: De Gruyter.

Bellmann, Günter, Joachim Herrgen & Jürgen Erich Schmidt. *Mittelrheinischer Sprachatlas*.

Glück, Helmut. 2005. *Metzler Lexikon Sprache*. Stuttgart; Weimar: Metzler.

Hotzenköcherle, Rudolf. 1962. *Einführung in den Sprachatlas der Deutschen Schweiz. A: Zur Methodologie der Kleinraumatlanten*. Bern: Franke.

Kerswill, Paul & Susan Wright. 1990. On the limits of auditory description: A sociophonetic perpective. *Language Variation and Change* 2. 255–275.

Klepsch, Alfred. 2013a. *Sprachatlas von Mittelfranken. Bd. 1: Einführung*. Vol. 1. Heidelberg: Winter.

Klepsch, Alfred. 2013b. Wie entstand der Sprachatlas von Mittelfranken? Planung, Exploration und Publikation. In Horst Haider Munske & Andrea Mathussek (eds.), *Handbuch zum Sprachatlas von Mittelfranken: Dokumentation und Auswertung*, 19–38. Heidelberg: Universitätsverlag Winter.

König, Werner. 1997. *Sprachatlas von Bayerisch-Schwaben. Band 1: Einführung*. Heidelberg: Winter.

---

[15] Cf. also the note on Hammarström's method of *transcription phonétique indirecte* ('subsequent transcription of audio material under laboratory conditions') in Hotzenköcherle (1962: 73).

[16] This method, of course, does not solve the problem of "within-transcriber variability" (Kerswill & Wright 1990: 258).

König, Werner. 2010. Investigating language in space: Methods and empirical standards. In Peter Auer & Jürgen Erich Schmidt (eds.), *Language and space. An international handbook of linguistic variation. Vol. 1: Theories and methods*, vol. 1, 494–511. Berlin / New York: De Gruyter.

Mathussek, Andrea. 2014. *Sprachräume und Sprachgrenzen im Untersuchungsgebiet des Sprachatlas von Mittelfranken: Traditionelle Dialektgeographie – Wahrnehmungsdialektologie – Dialektometrie*. Heidelberg: Winter.

Munske, Horst Haider. 2013. Zur Geschichte des Sprachatlas von Mittelfranken. In Horst Haider Munske & Andrea Mathussek (eds.), *Handbuch zum Sprachatlas von Mittelfranken: Dokumentation und Auswertung*, 11–19. Heidelberg: Universitätsverlag Winter.

Nerbonne, John, Rinke Colen, Charlotte Gooskens, Peter Kleiweg & Therese Leinonen. 2011. Gabmap – a web application for dialectology. *Dialectologia* Special Issue II. 65–89.

Ogura, Mieko & W. S.-Y. Wang. 1992. Isoglosses – Artificial or real? In Bela Brogyanyi (ed.), *Prehistory, history and histography of language, speech, and linguistic theory*, 153–181. Amsterdam / Philadelphia: John Benjamins.

Reichel, Sibylle. 2013. Die elektronische Datenverarbeitung im Sprachatlas von Mittelfranken. Von den Daten zur Sprachkarte. In Horst Haider Munske & Andrea Mathussek (eds.), *Handbuch zum Sprachatlas von Mittelfranken: Dokumentation und Auswertung*, 38–51. Heidelberg: Universitätsverlag Winter.

Chapter 7

Tracking linguistic features underlying lexical variation patterns: A case study on Tuscan dialects

Simonetta Montemagni
Istituto di Linguistica Computazionale "Antonio Zampolli", ILC-CNR

Martijn Wieling
University of Groningen, CLCG

> In this paper, we illustrate the application of hierarchical spectral partitioning of bipartite graphs in the study of lexical variation in Tuscany based on the data from a regional linguistic atlas. This method makes it possible not only to identify existing patterns of lexical variation in Tuscany, but also to uncover the underlying lexical features in terms of the most characteristic concept-lexicalization pairs. The results are promising, demonstrating the potential of the method for tracking the linguistic features underlying identified patterns of lexical variation and change across generations.

1 Introduction

In dialectometry (Séguy 1971) the focus lies on the aggregate analysis of dialect variation. In contrast to "cherry-picking" a few linguistic items confirming the analysis one wishes to settle on (Nerbonne 2009), the advantage of the aggregate approach is that it offers a more objective view of dialect variation. Unfortunately, many studies focusing on the aggregate pattern of dialect variation have disregarded the underlying linguistic basis. As a consequence, linguists have remained critical of the dialectometric approach (Schneider 1988; Woolhiser 2005; Loporcaro 2009).

To counter this criticism, various new dialectometric methods have been developed aimed at identifying the linguistic basis of dialectal variation (as reviewed in Wieling & Nerbonne 2015). For example, Nerbonne (2006) and Pröll, Pickl

& Spettl (in press) use an approach based on factor analysis, whereas Shackleton (2005) uses principal component analysis. Grieve, Speelman & Geeraerts (2011) follow the workflow of traditional dialectology (i.e. identifying isoglosses, bundling isoglosses and cluster analysis) by using multivariate spatial analysis.

The method we will apply here, Hierarchical Bipartite Spectral Graph Partitioning (HBSGP), has been developed by Wieling & Nerbonne (2009; 2010; 2011), who adopted it from information retrieval (Dhillon 2001) and applied it to dialectology. HBSGP results in a clustering of geographical varieties while *simultaneously* providing a linguistic basis for each of the identified clusters. The approach of Wieling & Nerbonne (2011) has been successfully applied to study phonetic variation in Dutch dialects (Wieling & Nerbonne 2011), English dialects (Wieling, Shackleton & Nerbonne 2013) and Tuscan dialects (Montemagni et al. 2012; 2013). More recently, the method has also been applied to investigate lexical variation in contemporary English dialects on the basis of the BBC *Voices* data (Wieling et al. 2014).

In this study, we focus on lexical variation. Our dataset, a regional lexical atlas of Tuscan dialects whose data have a diatopic and diachronic characterization, allows us to explore the potential of the HBSGP method in the study of lexical variation. In particular, it enables us to identify lexical features and their relationships on the one hand and to reconstruct the dynamics of lexical change across generations on the other hand. Technically, a new measure is proposed for determining the most important lexical features associated with the identified dialectal areas.

2 Data

We investigate Tuscan lexical variation on the basis of a linguistic atlas of Tuscany, the *Atlante Lessicale Toscano* (ALT, Giacomelli et al. 2000), now available as an online resource (http://serverdbt.ilc.cnr.it/ALTWEB). ALT is a regional Italian lexical atlas focusing on dialectal variation throughout Tuscany, where both Tuscan and non-Tuscan dialects are spoken. In this paper we focus on Tuscan dialects only, recorded in 213 localities by a total of 2060 informants who were selected with respect to various socio-demographic parameters (such as age, education and gender).

ALT interviews were carried out on the basis of a questionnaire of 745 target items, designed to elicit mainly lexical, but also semantic and phonetic variation. This study is based on the results of onomasiological questions, i.e. starting from concepts and looking for their lexicalizations. A typical onomasiological question asks how a given concept is designated or named, e.g. "what is the name for flat and crispy bread, seasoned with salt and oil?". To avoid interference with non-lexicalized answers, we excluded questions prompting 50 or more distinct lexical items. Furthermore, we only considered nouns (the large majority of items of ALT questionnaire) in this study. The resulting subset consists of 170 questionnaire items for which a total of 5,174 distinct normalized answers were given (on average 30 lexical variants per concept) distributed into 61,496 geo-referenced responses (i.e. associated with locations). The total number of speaker-responses was 384,454.

To abstract away from phonetic variation, we used the most abstract representation level present in ALT (Cucurullo et al. 2006). This normalized representation was meant to abstract from phonetic variation (caused by productive phonetic processes), but did not remove morphological variation or variation caused by unproductive phonetic processes. In this study we used the normalized lexical answers to the selected subset of 170 onomasiological questions. The same set of questions has also been used by Wieling, Upton & Thompson (2014) in a study of lexical differences between Tuscan dialects and standard Italian.

The representativeness of the selected sample with respect to the whole set of ALT onomasiological questions (i.e. a total of 460 questionnaire items) was assayed using the correlation between overall lexical distances and lexical distances obtained from the selected sample (Wieling, Upton & Thompson 2014). The Pearson's correlation coefficient was r = 0.94, showing the representativeness of the selected sample with respect to the whole set of onomasiological questions.

3 Methods

In this study, we use hierarchical bipartite spectral graph partitioning as our method of choice (Wieling & Nerbonne (2011)). As mentioned before, this approach simultaneously clusters the geographic locations together with the linguistic features characterizing them. In this case, a cluster of locations is characterized by a linguistic basis expressed in terms of the most salient lexical features. These lexical features can be seen as a proxy of the traditional notion of lexical isoglosses, establishing the boundaries of dialectal areas.

Every variety attested in a given location is described in terms of Concept-Lexicalization (CL) pairs linking each of the 170 selected concepts with its lexicalization(s) (reported in the normalized form) in the specific location. CL frequencies are normalized by dividing the number of recorded answers by the number of informants in a given location, with their value ranging between 0 and 1. Since there was a socio-demographically differentiated group of informants potentially giving rise to multiple responses to denote the same concept for each location, the sum of normalized frequencies of lexical variants associated with the same concept in a certain location can be greater than 1.

The input for the HBSGP method is a bipartite graph which contains two sets of vertices, locations and CL pairs, connected by lines. There exists a line between a location and a CL pair whenever at least one of the speakers in the location uses the lexical variant. The lines are weighted between 0 and 1. A value of 0 indicates that no speakers in the location use the lexical variant (and thus equals the absence of a line), whereas a value of 1 indicates that all speakers in the location use the lexical variant to denote the concept being investigated. Table 1 gives an example of (a tabular representation of) the bipartite graph, with the rows corresponding to the locations and the columns to the CL pairs. About 80% of the speakers in Caprese Michelangelo use the form *aràncio* to denote an ORANGE (henceforth, concept denominations are represented by small caps). A similar number of speakers also uses *melàngola* to denote the same (speakers frequently provided multiple lexicalizations to denote a certain concept).

The input matrix is then subjected to Singular Value Decomposition (SVD), and the k-means clustering algorithm (with k equals 2) is applied to the results of the SVD resulting in a two-way clustering. The k-means clustering was repeated 1000 times for robustness. As the output of the SVD combines the locations with the CL pairs, the clustering likewise groups locations and CL pairs. Consequently, lexical variants grouped with locations can be seen as characteristic elements of those locations. For more mathematical details, we refer the interested reader to Wieling & Nerbonne (2011).

In order to identify the most characteristic linguistic features for a group of locations, Wieling & Nerbonne (2011) combined two different criteria which were implemented in two different and complementary measures: representativeness and distinctiveness. Representativeness measures the relative frequency of the lexicalization of a given concept in the locations in the cluster. For example, if the cluster contains ten locations and all speakers in seven locations use the lexical variant, the representativeness is 0.7. Distinctiveness measures how frequently the lexical variant occurs within as opposed to outside of the cluster (corrected for the relative size of the cluster, which is calculated by dividing the number of locations in the cluster by the total number of locations in the dataset). A distinctiveness of 1 indicates that the lexical variant is only used inside the cluster. The distinctiveness equals 0 when the relative frequency of the lexical variant in the cluster is equal to the relative size of the cluster (i.e. it is not distinctive). Inter-

7 Tracking linguistic features underlying lexical variation patterns

Table 1: Tabular representation of a bipartite graph. The numbers represent the normalized frequency (obtained by dividing by the number of speakers) of the lexical variant associated with a given concept in the different locations which ranges between 0 and 1. As the speakers may use multiple variants to denote a concept, the normalized frequencies associated with a concept in a certain location do not have to sum to 1.

Location	ORANGE-*arància*	ORANGE-*aràncio*	ORANGE-*melàngola*
Caprese Michelangelo	0.1379	0.7931	0.7931
Pieve Santo Stefano	0.4000	0.7333	0.2000
Anghiari	0.0000	0.7059	1.0000
Sansepolcro	0.0000	1.0000	1.0000

estingly, the measures of representativeness and distinctiveness are reminiscent of the "consistency" and "homogeneity" measures introduced by Labov and colleagues for the construction of isoglosses in the *Atlas of North American English* (Labov, Ash & Boberg 2006). Homogeneity measures how much variation exists within the region defined by the isogloss (i.e. corresponding to a non-chance corrected variant of distinctiveness) and consistency (i.e. corresponding to representativeness) measures how strongly the variable is concentrated within a given region.

The two measures capture two different equally important desiderata of isoglosses: to put it in the words of Labov, Ash & Boberg (2006), "First, we want the area defined to be as uniform as possible [...]. Second, we want as high a proportion of hits as possible to be located within the isogloss". For this reason they need to be combined. Wieling & Nerbonne (2011) combined representativeness and distinctiveness measures by averaging them, yielding the importance score. Here, we propose that to determine the relevance of CL pairs in the characterization of identified lexical areas it is better to multiply the two values. The advantage of this approach is that it is not possible to assign high importance values to lexical variants which score high on a single measure only. For example, lexical variants occurring in all locations are highly representative, but not distinctive. Similarly, a lexical variant only occurring in a single location is highly distinctive, but not representative (unless the cluster contains a single location). Note that constraints on isogloss construction were also foreseen by Labov, Ash & Boberg (2006) by enforcing frequency thresholds. However, the advantage of the approach proposed by Wieling & Nerbonne (2011) and its evolution presented here consists in the fact that no *a priori* constraints on the values of individual measures are defined.

4 Results

In this section, we report the results of applying the HBSGP method to the selected ALT dataset. The results obtained are based on 5,174 CL pairs and 213 locations, which correspond to all lexical data gathered through fieldwork (as opposed to a dataset in which infrequent lexical variants are filtered out) for the 170 selected concepts. See Wieling & Montemagni (2015) for a discussion of the advantages connected with this dataset.

The map in Figure 1 shows the geographic visualization of the clustering of Tuscan varieties into seven groups designated as follows: the Florence area (A), the western Tuscan area (C) and the dialects from Arezzo, Siena, Grosseto and

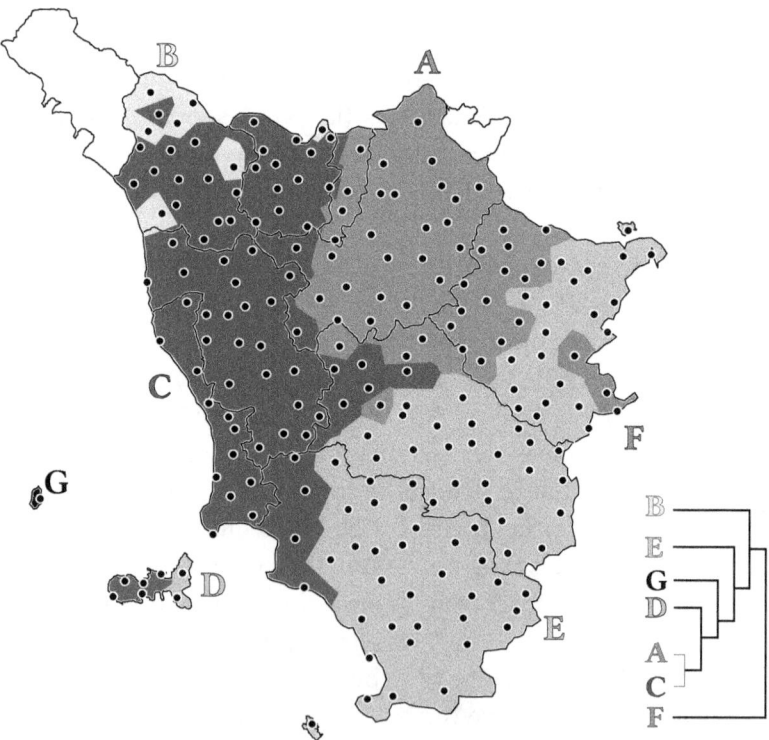

Figure 1: Geographic visualization of the clustering of Tuscan varieties into seven groups.

7 Tracking linguistic features underlying lexical variation patterns

Mount Amiata (E) which represent the three main groupings, together with the dialects from Elba island (D), Chiana Valley (F), Capraia Island (G) and Apuan Alps (B) which are minor but clearly distinct dialectal areas.

It is interesting to note that this result is in line with the classifications of Tuscan dialects proposed by Giacomelli (1975) for what concerns the lexicon, and by Giannelli (1976 [2010]) which is based instead on phonetic, phonemic, morpho-syntactic and lexical features. It is also in line with the subdivision of Tuscan dialects by Pellegrini (1977), in spite of it being mainly based on the distribution of phonetic phenomena.

4.1 Linguistic features underlying identified lexical areas

For what concerns the underlying lexical features, we first focus on the three main dialectal clusters (A, C and E). Table 2 reports for each cluster the five most important CL pairs with associated values of representativeness, distinctiveness and importance.

The relevance of the lexical features with respect to the dialectal subdivision emerges clearly from the value maps in Figure 2, which show the geographic distribution of the first and second topmost lexical features of each of the three

Table 2: The five topmost lexical variants for the three main clusters of Tuscan dialects.

Cluster	Concept-Lexicalization pair	Representativeness	Distinctiveness	Importance
E	TURKEY-*bìllo*	0.863	0.700	0.604
	CORNER OF TISSUE-*pìnzo*	0.724	0.795	0.576
	EYE GUM-*cipìcchia*	0.624	0.920	0.574
	OIL JAR-*zìro*	0.879	0.609	0.535
	VAT-*bigónzo*	0.649	0.821	0.533
A	ORANGE-*arància*	0.779	0.675	0.526
	LADLE-*romaiòlo*	0.788	0.536	0.423
	OIL JAR-*órcio*	0.671	0.590	0.396
	TURKEY-*tàcco*	0.390	1.000	0.390
	BRAWN-*capofréddo*	0.432	0.900	0.389
C	OIL JAR-*cóppo*	0.749	0.696	0.522
	EYE GUM-*cìspia*	0.702	0.676	0.474
	BREAST-*pùppa*	0.649	0.717	0.466
	FLEA-*pùce*	0.602	0.686	0.413
	CLUSTER OF GRAPES-*pìgna*	0.570	0.701	0.400

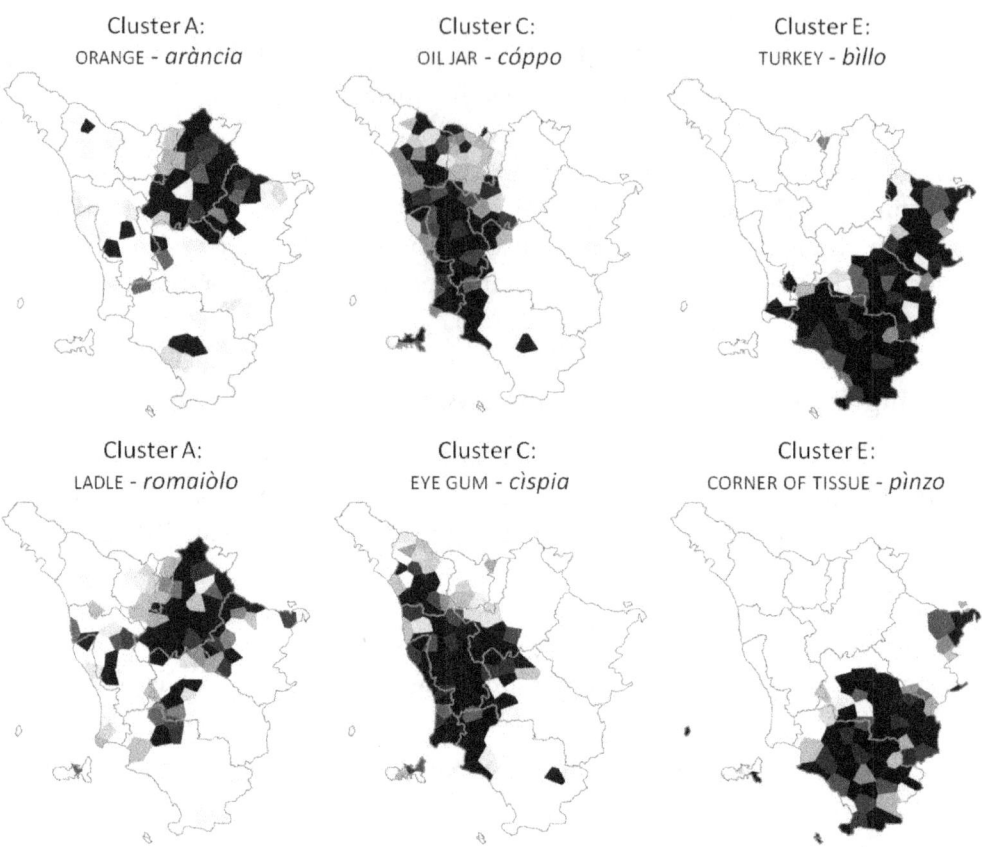

Figure 2: Value maps of the first (row 1) and second (row 2) topmost CL pairs for the A, C and E dialectal clusters. Areas with darker (blue) color denote a greater frequency of occurrence of the selected lexical variant; lighter colors denote a lower frequency, while no coloring (white) denotes the absence of the variant.

main identified clusters (A, C and E). The topmost lexical features associated with each identified cluster can be assimilated with the traditional notion of bundle of isoglosses, which have long been considered a major criterion for the definition of dialect areas: as Chambers & Trudgill (1998) put it, "the significance of a dialect area increases as more and more isoglosses are found which separate it from adjoining areas".

By comparing the maps of Figure 2, we can observe that the geographic distribution of the topmost CL pairs of the E, A and C clusters does not cover all and

7 Tracking linguistic features underlying lexical variation patterns

only the locations in the cluster. Each of them can be seen as a quantitative visualization of individual isoglosses, where darkness of color denotes the frequency of occurrence of the represented lexical variant (dark colors denote a greater frequency, lighter colors lower frequency, and no coloring indicates the absence of the variant). As can be observed, lexical variants shown in Table 2 may occur beyond the border of the cluster area, thus lowering the distinctiveness value of the CL pair, or they may not occur in the whole cluster area resulting in a lower representativeness. For instance, in cluster A comparable representativeness values are observed for the two topmost CL pairs (0.77-0.78), whereas the CL ranked in second place, i.e. LADLE-*romaiòlo*, has a lower distinctiveness value (0.53) than the topmost CL (i.e. whose distinctiveness value is 0.67). Different patterns can be observed in clusters E and C, with decreasing representativeness and increasing distinctiveness in the former case, and with both of them decreasing in the latter case. Despite these slight differences, in all cases representativeness and distinctiveness show relatively high values which never reach the value of 1 (with the only exception of the CL pair TURKEY-*tàcco* in cluster A whose distinctiveness is equal to 1). The average values of the five topmost lexical features for representativeness and distinctiveness range between 0.61 and 0.74, and 0.69 and 0.77 respectively, demonstrating that the corresponding dialect areas are not marked by very clear and strong dialect borders.

Different distinctiveness-representativeness patterns are observed in the case of the smaller peripheral areas B, D, F and G (see Table 3). Here, the most salient CL pairs are highly distinctive (their average values ranges from 0.84 to 1), with the average representativeness ranging from 0.49 to 1. Thus smaller dialect areas are characterized by much more distinctive features than the larger areas.

Besides the strength of dialectal borders, granularity of the identified dialectal areas is another open issue in the study of dialectal variation. Consider, for instance, the traditional dialectal subdivision of Tuscan dialects by Pellegrini (1977) and Giannelli (1976 [2010]). In his *Carta dei Dialetti d'Italia,* Pellegrini (1977) identifies a western variety of Tuscan which is further subdivided into Pisano-Livornese-Elbano, and Pistoiese and Lucchese. On the other hand, Giannelli (1976 [2010]) identifies Pisano-Livornese, Lucchese, Elbano and Pistoiese as independent dialectal varieties in his seminal work *Toscana.* The two subdivisions are compatible with each other but adopt different levels of granularity, i.e. they are seen through lenses differing in their magnifying power. Depending on the specific goals of a study, different levels of granularity of the dialectal landscape may be appropriate. By exploiting the hierarchical clustering results, the HBSGP method can also be used to identify increasingly smaller dialectal areas associ-

Table 3: The five topmost lexical variants for the smaller peripheral areas F, B, D and G.

Cluster	Concept-Lexicalization pair	Representativeness	Distinctiveness	Importance
F	FINCH-*frenguéllo*	1.000	1.000	1.000
	CUCUMBER-*citróne*	1.000	0.973	0.973
	HAIL-*granìschia*	0.667	1.000	0.667
	GOOSE-*ciucióne*	0.667	1.000	0.667
	LIZARD-*racanàccio*	0.667	1.000	0.667
B	SNOW-*gnéva*	0.429	1.000	0.429
	ROLLING PIN-*canèlla*	0.429	1.000	0.429
	STYE-*orzaiolo*	0.653	0.633	0.414
	GARBAGE-*rùsco*	0.531	0.734	0.389
	LIZARD-*ciortellóne*	0.430	0.853	0.367
D	HORNET-*buffóne*	0.950	1.000	0.950
	KHAKIS-*cicàchi*	0.500	1.000	0.500
	KHAKIS-*cicàco*	0.500	1.000	0.500
	PINE CONE-*pignòcca*	0.500	1.000	0.500
	TROUGH-*tròlego*	0.500	1.000	0.500
G	WATERMELON-*patècca*	1.000	1.000	1.000
	MELON-*melóne*	1.000	1.000	1.000
	CLUSTER-*raspòllo*	1.000	1.000	1.000
	SQUIRREL-*miseràngolo*	1.000	1.000	1.000
	LIZARD-*bìscia*	1.000	1.000	1.000

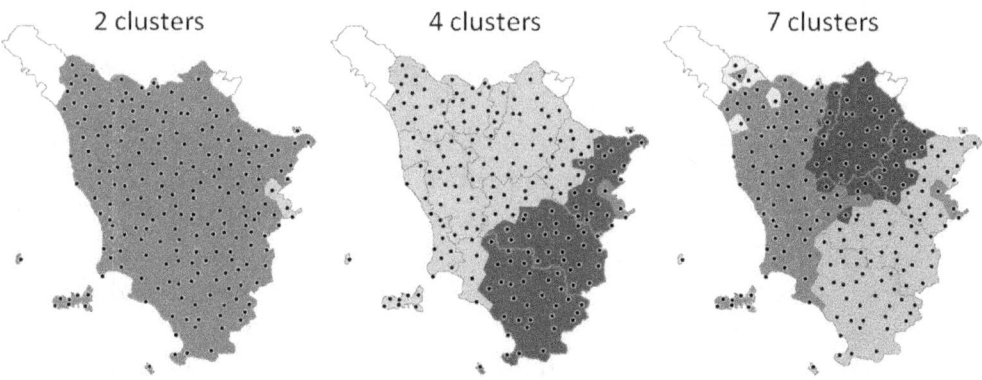

Figure 3: Geographic visualization of the clustering of Tuscan varieties into two, four and seven groups.

Table 4: The five topmost lexical variants of the red, cyan and pink areas in the two, four and seven-cluster maps of Tuscan dialects.

Cluster	Concept-Lexicalization pair	Representativeness	Distinctiveness	Importance
Two-cluster map: Red	SINK-*acquàio*	0.909	1.000	0.909
	CELERY-*sèdano*	0.853	1.000	0.853
	MELON-*popóne*	0.844	1.000	0.844
	LAUREL-*allòro*	0.801	1.000	0.801
	WATERMELON-*cocómero*	0.794	1.000	0.794
Four-cluster map: Cyan	THIMBLE-*anèllo*	0.495	0.857	0.424
	OIL JAR-*cóppo*	0.525	0.808	0.424
	CATERPILLAR-*brùcio*	0.448	0.928	0.416
	EYE GUM-*cìspia*	0.498	0.798	0.397
	TURKEY-*lùcio*	0.445	0.872	0.388
Seven-cluster map: Pink	OIL JAR-*cóppo*	0.749	0.696	0.522
	EYE GUM-*cìspia*	0.702	0.676	0.474
	BREAST-*pùppa*	0.649	0.717	0.466
	FLEA-*pùce*	0.602	0.686	0.413
	CLUSTER OF GRAPES-*pìgna*	0.570	0.701	0.400

ated with progressively more specific lexical features. These nested dialect areas are characterized by nested isoglosses (i.e. the spatial distribution of one feature is entirely contained within that of another). To assess these nested isoglosses, we compare the geographical and linguistic results obtained by clustering the selected dataset into two, four and seven groups (with the latter representing the clustering discussed so far).

Figure 3 reports the geographic visualization of clustering the Tuscan varieties into two, four and seven groups. In the map with two clusters (Figure 3, left), the large red cluster corresponds to the composite set of Tuscan dialects, excluding only the Chiana Valley dialects (cyan cluster). The map with four clusters (Figure 3, middle) shows the main subdivision of Tuscan dialects between Northern dialects (cyan and green clusters), covering (from east to west) Fiorentino, Pistoiese, Lucchese and Pisano-Livornese, and Southern dialects (violet and red clusters), i.e. (from east to west) the dialect from Arezzo, Siena and Grosseto (violet cluster) and from the Chiana valley (red cluster). The map containing seven clusters (Figure 3, right) has already been discussed above.

Table 4 shows the lexical features characterizing the red, cyan and pink clusters in the first, second and third map, respectively. These clusters cover a progressively restricted area. Table 4 reports, for each of these clusters, the five topmost lexical variants with their associated scores. The most salient CL pairs characterizing the red cluster of the two-clusters map coincide with pan-Tuscan words well known from the literature (Giacomelli & Poggi Salani 1984): they show a distinctiveness value equal to 1 and very high representativeness values (≥ 0.79). Similar observations hold for the cluster corresponding to the set of Northern Tuscan dialects (the cyan cluster in Figure 3, middle) with one main difference: all values are considerably lower, with a general reduction observed at the level of representativeness. This illustrates that the cyan cluster is a heterogeneous area. However, by comparing the CL pairs underlying the cyan cluster in the second map and the pink cluster in the third map, we can also see there are two shared lexical variants, namely OIL JAR-*cóppo* and EYE GUM-*cìspia*, which appear among the topmost features whose importance values in the smaller pink cluster are higher (determining a higher ranking), despite their unavoidably lower distinctiveness. In this case, these CL pairs are more characteristic of the smaller cluster, whereas a word such as THIMBLE-*anèllo* is more characteristic of the larger cluster (in the pink cluster it appears in a lower position with much lower values). This suggests that whenever the same features appear to qualify nested clusters, they should be taken as relevant features for the cluster in which they play a more prominent role (i.e. having a higher importance value). Consequently, OIL JAR-*cóppo* and EYE GUM-*cìspia* should be removed from the most salient features of the cyan cluster due to the lower importance (0.424 against 0.522 for the former, and 0.397 against 0.474 for the latter) with respect to the nested pink cluster.

In sum, these results show that hierarchical spectral partitioning can be usefully exploited to identify dialectal areas at different levels of granularity with their associated lexical features. In particular, the method may help in the selection of the most appropriate isoglosses for each dialectal area and in the reconstruction of nested isoglosses.

4.2 Reconstructing the dynamics of lexical change

The hierarchical spectral partitioning method can also be used for studying the dynamics of lexical change across generations. For this purpose, ALT speakers were grouped in an old age group (born in 1930 or earlier – 1930 was the median year of birth) and a young age group (born after 1930). To guarantee comparability of results, we focused on two maps each having four clusters. As Figure 4 shows, the analysis of the two datasets results in slightly different, partially overlapping lexical areas, with the area corresponding to the southeastern (cyan) cluster being more restricted for the older speakers. Major differences, however, are

7 Tracking linguistic features underlying lexical variation patterns

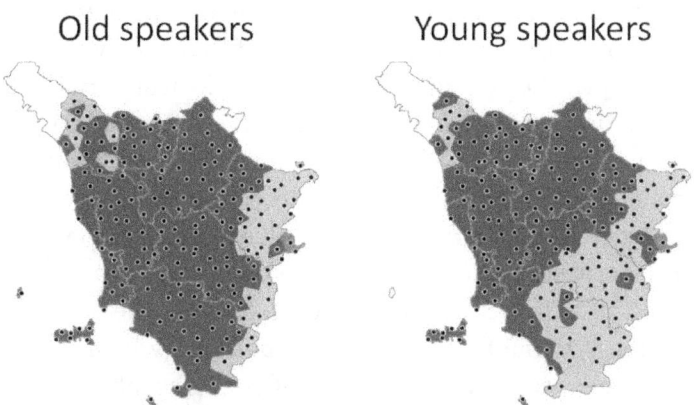

Figure 4: Geographic visualization of a four-way clustering of Tuscan varieties on the basis of data from young vs. old speakers.

explicitly clear at the level of the underlying lexical features. In particular, the central blue area is more restricted (and also linked with fewer CL pairs: 881 vs. 1193) in the map built on the basis of the answers by the young speakers.

Besides the different size of the set of associated linguistic features (i.e. more reduced in the case of young speakers), it is interesting to note that 424 salient lexical features underlying the old speakers map do not appear among the features underlying the young speakers map. These CL pairs emerging from old speakers correspond typically to old-fashioned and traditional notions as well as less common plants and animals. Examples include STRUCTURE FOR BED WARMER-*prète*, POPPY-*ròsolo*, MUTTON-*bìrro*, SET OF POPLARS-*alborellàia*. These CL pairs can be seen as lexical variants which are no longer being used by younger speakers, and these are likely to disappear altogether.

The number of CL pairs restricted to young speakers is much lower (112) than the number of CL pairs restricted to the old speakers. In this case, the CL pairs correspond to standard Italian words (e.g., CLOSET-*ripostìglio*, WEEPING WILLOW-*sàlice piangènte*, HARVEST-*mietitùra*), generic terms (e.g., AFTERNOON-*dópo mangiàto*, SLUG-*lumàca ignùda*) or "distorted" (i.e. deviant with respect to traditional pronunciation) variants of dialectal terms (e.g., TUSCAN COLD CUT FROM PORK SHOULDER-*capricòllo*). The typology of these lexical variants shows the dynamics of lexical change ongoing in younger Tuscan generations, characterized by the loss of local features in favor of generic or standard terms, and by the creative distortion of dialectal words.

In both cases, however, these CL pairs are not highly ranked (i.e. not the most important) for the associated old and young clusters. Instead, the CL pairs underlying both maps (a total of 769) show clear differences with respect to their ranking. For example, the 1st, 10th, 20th and 50th lexical variants in the ranked list of CL pairs underlying the old speakers map correspond to the 60th, 809th, 59th and 818th position in the young CL pairs list, respectively. Similarly, the 1st, 10th, 20th and 50th ranked lexical variants of the young speakers are ranked (respectively) in the 100th, 13th, 17th and 69th position in the old speakers list. The asymmetry between the old-young vs. young-old correspondences can be seen as the result of a dialect leveling process, causing the lower importance of old-fashioned lexical variants for the young speakers (which are top-ranked for the old speaker). Seen from the perspective of young speakers, the disalignment of the ranking is more reduced, reflecting an additional shared set of dialectal lexical items.

Table 5 reports the five topmost CL pairs underlying the blue cluster in the two maps. Clearly, the importance values associated with the blue cluster of the old speakers are higher than those associated with the blue cluster of the young speakers. This pattern is confirmed by comparing the average importance scores of the top-10 and top-100 CL pairs in the two lists, which are much higher for the old speakers (0.42 vs. 0.34 for the top-10 and 0.26 vs. 0.17 for the top-100). This may also be seen as evidence in support of dialect leveling: lexical areas inferred from young speakers data are characterized by less distinctive and/or representative features.

Table 5: The five topmost lexical variants of the blue cluster in the young vs. old speakers maps of Tuscan dialects.

Cluster	Concept-Lexicalization pair	Representativeness	Distinctiveness	Importance
Old speakers: Blue cluster	GRAPE-*chìcco*	0.721	0.828	0.597
	CHESTNUT HUSK-*rìccio*	0.706	0.661	0.467
	EMBERS-*bràce*	0.673	0.632	0.425
	BRAZIER-*bracière*	0.596	0.680	0.405
	HAZELNUT-*nocciòla*	0.794	0.507	0.403
Young speakers: Blue cluster	BAT-*pipistrèllo*	0.736	0.538	0.396
	BREAST-*pùppa*	0.428	0.900	0.385
	THIMBLE-*anèllo*	0.394	0.893	0.352
	OIL JAR-*cóppo*	0.437	0.772	0.337
	EYE GUM-*cìspia*	0.431	0.779	0.335

5 Conclusion

In this paper, we illustrated the application of hierarchical spectral partitioning of bipartite graphs in the study of lexical variation in Tuscany based on the dialectal corpus of the *Atlante Lessicale Toscano*. Our results demonstrate the potential of the method in bridging the gap between models of linguistic variation based on aggregate analyses and more traditional analyses based on individual linguistic features.

By using the HBSGP method, we not only identified existing patterns of lexical variation in Tuscany on the basis of the whole dialectal corpus, but also uncovered the underlying lexical features in terms of the characterizing concept-lexicalization pairs. The most relevant CL pairs represent the features used to classify and define each identified lexical area. To put it in more traditional terms, they can be seen as a proxy of lexical isoglosses marking both the qualitative and quantitative distribution of the lexical variants identified as discriminating features of a given lexical dialect area. This entails that the set of the topmost CL pairs associated with each identified lexical dialect area acts as a proxy of bundles of isoglosses, where the grading of individual isoglosses within the bundle is determined on the basis of the combination of representativeness and distinctiveness. If the representativeness score associated with identified isoglosses (CL pairs) can help to shed light on how much variation exists within the area defined by a given isogloss, the distinctiveness score reflects how strongly the lexical variant is concentrated within that area. By comparing the results obtained for different dialect areas, we have seen that different stages of the process of dialect differentiation can be inferred from the different values of these two measures: dialectal subdivisions range from clearly defined areas to areas characterized by fuzzy borders.

We also investigated whether and to what extent patterns of lexical variation and their associated features varied with respect to the granularity of the identified dialectal areas and with the age of informants, revealing interesting results. The possibility of exploring linguistic variation at different levels of granularity makes it possible to customize the analysis with respect to the user's needs. The linguistic features associated with increasingly smaller areas can be seen as nested isoglosses, occurring when the spatial distribution of one feature is contained entirely within that of another and establishing an implicational relationship between the two.

The analysis and comparison of lexical variation patterns and associated features across generations showed that the method can also be usefully exploited to track the change in the typology of features in young vs. old informants and to monitor the vitality of a dialect in a given area. In particular, the HBSGP method turned out to effectively capture the dynamics of lexical change in Tuscany, by highlighting the emergence of lexical innovations and the obsolescence of old-fashioned traditional dialectal words.

Current directions of research include testing the robustness of these results by noisy clustering and the analysis of lexical variation patterns across semantic domains.

Acknowledgements

The research reported in this article was carried out in the framework of a Short Term Mobility program of international exchanges funded by the National Council of Research (CNR, Italy). The authors thank the anonymous reviewers for their comments, which have helped to improve this article.

References

Chambers, J. K. & Peter Trudgill. 1998. *Dialectology*. 2nd edn. Cambridge, New York: Cambridge University Press.

Cucurullo, Nella, Simonetta Montemagni, Matilde Paoli, Eugenio Picchi & Eva Sassolini. 2006. Dialectal resources on-line: The ALT-Web experience. In *Proceedings of the 5th International Conference on Language Resources and Evaluation (LREC-2006)*, 1846–1851. Genova.

Dhillon, Inderjit S. 2001. Co-clustering documents and words using bipartite spectral graph partitioning. In *Proceedings of the Seventh ACM SIGKDD International Conference on Knowledge Discovery and Data Mining* (KDD '01), 269–274. New York, NY, USA: ACM. DOI:10.1145/502512.502550

Giacomelli, Gabriella. 1975. Aree lessicali toscane. *La ricerca dialettale* 1. 115–152.

Giacomelli, Gabriella & Teresa Poggi Salani. 1984. Parole toscane. *Quaderni dell'Atlante Lessicale Toscano* 2(3). 123–229.

Giacomelli, Gabriella, Luciano Agostiniani, Patrizia Bellucci, Luciano Giannelli, Simonetta Montemagni, Annalisa Nesi, Matilde Paoli, Eugenio Picchi & Teresa Poggi Salani. 2000. *Atlante lessicale toscano*. Roma: Lexis Progetti.

Giannelli, Luciano. 1976 [2010]. *Toscana*. Pisa: Pacini Editore.

Grieve, Jack, Dirk Speelman & Dirk Geeraerts. 2011. A statistical method for the identification and aggregation of regional linguistic variation. *Language Variation and Change* 23(2). 193–221.

Labov, William, Sharon Ash & Charles Boberg. 2006. *The atlas of North American English: Phonetics, phonology and sound change*. Berlin, New York: Mouton de Gruyter.

Loporcaro, Michele. 2009. *Profilo linguistico dei dialetti italiani*. Roma, Bari: Laterza.

Montemagni, Simonetta, Martijn Wieling, Bob De Jonge & John Nerbonne. 2012. Patterns of language variation and underlying linguistic features: A new dialectometric approach. In Patricia Bianchi, Nicola De Blasi, Chiara De Caprio & Francesco Montuori (eds.), *La variazione nell'italiano e nella sua storia. Varietà e varianti linguistiche e testuali. Atti dell'XI congresso SILFI (Società Internazionale di Linguistica e Filologia Italiana)*, 879–889. Firenze: Franco Cesati.

Montemagni, Simonetta, Martijn Wieling, Bob De Jonge & John Nerbonne. 2013. Synchronic patterns of Tuscan phonetic variation and diachronic change: Evidence from a dialectometric study. *Literary and Linguistic Computing* 28(1). 157–172.

Nerbonne, John. 2006. Identifying linguistic structure in aggregate comparison. *Literary and Linguistic Computing* 21(4). 463–475.

Nerbonne, John. 2009. Data-driven dialectology. *Language and Linguistics Compass* 3(1). 175–198.

Pellegrini, Giovanni Battista. 1977. *Carta dei dialetti d'Italia*. Pisa: Pacini.

Pröll, Simon, Simon Pickl & Aaron Spettl. in press. Latente Strukturen in geolinguistischen Korpora. In Michael Elmentaler, Markus Hundt & Jürgen Erich Schmidt (eds.), *Deutsche Dialekte - Konzepte, Probleme, Handlungsfelder*. Stuttgart: Steiner.

Schneider, Edgar W. 1988. Qualitative vs. quantitative methods of area delimitation in dialectology: A comparison based on lexical data from Georgia and Alabama. *Journal of English Linguistics* 21. 175–212.

Shackleton, Robert. 2005. English-American speech relationships. *Journal of English Linguistics* 33(2). 99–160.

Séguy, Jean. 1971. La relation entre la distance spatiale et la distance lexicale. *Revue de Linguistique Romane* 35(138). 335–357.

Wieling, Martijn & Simonetta Montemagni. 2015. Infrequent forms: Noise or not? In Marie-Hélène Côte, Remco Knooihuizen & John Nerbonne (eds.), *The Future of Dialects*. Berlin: Language Science Press.

Wieling, Martijn & John Nerbonne. 2009. Bipartite spectral graph partitioning for clustering dialect varieties and detecting their linguistic features. In *Proceedings of the 2009 Workshop on Graph-Based Methods for Natural Language Processes*, 14–22. Stroudsburg, PA: ACL.

Wieling, Martijn & John Nerbonne. 2010. Hierarchical spectral partitioning of bipartite graphs to cluster dialects and identify distinguishing features. In *Proceedings of the 2010 workshop on graph-based methods for natural language processing*, 33–41. Stroudsburg, PA: ACL.

Wieling, Martijn & John Nerbonne. 2011. Bipartite spectral graph partitioning for clustering dialect varieties and detecting their linguistic features. *Computer Speech & Language* 25(3). 700–715.

Wieling, Martijn & John Nerbonne. 2015. Advances in dialectometry. *Annual Review of Linguistics* 1. 243–264.

Wieling, Martijn, Robert Shackleton & John Nerbonne. 2013. Analyzing phonetic variation in the traditional English dialects: Simultaneously clustering dialects and phonetic features. *Literary and Linguistic Computing* 28(1). 31–41.

Wieling, Martijn, Clive Upton & Ann Thompson. 2014. Analyzing the BBC Voices data: Contemporary English dialect areas and their characteristic lexical variants. *Literary and Linguistic Computing* 29(1). 107–117.

Wieling, Martijn, Simonetta Montemagni, John Nerbonne & R. Harald Baayen. 2014. Lexical differences between Tuscan dialects and Standard Italian: A sociolinguistic analysis using generalized additive mixed modeling. *Language* 90(3). 669–692.

Woolhiser, Curt. 2005. Political borders and dialect divergence/convergence in europe. In Peter Auer, Frans Hinskens & Paul Kerswill (eds.), *A handbook of varieties of English*, 236–262. New York: Cambridge University Press.

Chapter 8

A new dialectometric approach applied to the Breton language

Guylaine Brun-Trigaud
CNRS & Université de Nice-Sophia-Antipolis, France

Tanguy Solliec
Université de Paris Descartes, France

Jean Le Dû
Université de Bretagne Occidentale, France

> This paper presents a new dialectometric approach applied to the Breton language in the heart of Breton-speaking Brittany. It is based on data from the Nouvel Atlas Linguistique de la Basse-Bretagne Le Dû (2001). We process qualitative data using the Levenshtein algorithm which allows us to accurately measure and take into account the discrepancies or similarities between different pronunciations of a given word. This contribution aims to determine whether linguistic distance is caused by a frequent repetition of the same phenomenon or whether it is the outcome of multiple changes. Our first results suggest new ways of analysing Breton data.

1 Introduction

At a time when the number of languages in use is bound to reduce drastically in the next decades, documenting endangered languages is a major challenge for linguists, as is the urgency to study and analyse their internal variation. Nowadays, Breton is considered to be an endangered language, according to the definition proposed by UNESCO (Moseley 2010). The intergenerational transmission of the language ceased during the 60's. Most of its speakers are now over 70 years of age and, at present, the language is disappearing quickly. We propose to present a dialectometric approach applied to the Breton language based on Le Dû's (2001)

Guylaine Brun-Trigaud, Tanguy Solliec & Jean Le Dû. 2016. A new dialectometric approach applied to the Breton language. In Marie-Hélène Côté, Remco Knooihuizen & John Nerbonne (eds.), *The future of dialects*, 135–154. Berlin: Language Science Press. DOI:10.17169/langsci.b81.147

Guylaine Brun-Trigaud, Tanguy Solliec & Jean Le Dû

Nouvel Atlas Linguistique de la Basse-Bretagne (henceforth NALBB) (Le Dû 2001) so as to re-examine the geolinguistic landscape of Lower Brittany.

Little dialectometric work has been done on the Breton language (German 1984, German 1991, Costaouec 2012). Our approach is based on a new methodology: we have applied the principles of edit distance (i.e., the Levenshtein Distance, henceforth LD), which allows us to measure the linguistic distance between two strings of characters (phonetic transcriptions). This distance is defined as the minimal number of characters that need to be deleted, inserted or replaced, in order to transform one string of characters to another. We have introduced modifications in processing the data.

Our work aims to test this new approach and to observe its advantages and disadvantages when applied to Breton. It was tested for the first time on dialects in the Occitan area. This research constitutes the very first step of a PhD thesis by Solliec (2014), whose goal is to process the data available in the NALBB in order to sketch the geolinguistic configuration of the area based on a dialectometric approach. This first study focuses on the phonetics of Breton because the data contained in the NALBB are richer in phonetics than in the lexicon.

2 Preliminary research

2.1 A first test on Occitan dialects

Dialectometry was initiated by Séguy (1971; 1973), and Guiter (1973). Its aim is to quantify linguistic variation with the help of mathematical tools. This approach allows us not only to account for the differences or similarities between the dialects studied, but also to display them with the help of maps and tables. Nowadays, many research groups work with various methods. One of them, the Groningen School, led by Nerbonne and Heeringa (Nerbonne & Heeringa 2001; 2010, Heeringa 2004), uses the Levenshtein algorithm. This methodology allows for the accurate measurements of the number of operations (replacement, deletion or insertion) necessary to transform one string of characters to another and displays the results as a number or a percentage of similarity.

As this method is intended to provide an overall characterization, it accounts most of the time for dialectal distance from a quantitative point of view. However, it does not describe the results qualitatively in a direct way. In others words, it does not indicate the exact proportion of each difference involved in dissimilarity. Does the dissimilarity result from one sole phoneme correspondence (replacement) which occurs frequently while other kinds of variations remain very

Table 1: An example of a quantitative measurement between 2 locations of enquiry for the word 'a day (long)' in the Occitan language.

Clermont (pt 22)	ʒ	u	r		'	n	a	ð	ɔ
Fauillet (pt 20)	ʒ	u	ʀ		'	n	a	d	œ
			1					1	1	3

3 differences = 63% of similarity / 37% of dissimilarity

minor or, on the contrary, does the dissimilarity result from an important array of different correspondences which are more or less of equal importance? In the first case, mutual comprehension between the speakers is not really affected, while in the second case, it is likely to be jeopardized. In order to contrast the two kinds of variation, Brun-Trigaud decided to modify the algorithm. To accomplish this, she implemented it as a function in Visual Basic for Applications (VBA) in an Excel spreadsheet so as to obtain, not a percentage or a number of characters, but rather a record of the phonemes undergoing the operations and their frequency. She then treated them statistically. She carried out a first experiment (Brun-Trigaud 2014) using data taken from the *Atlas Linguistique et Ethnographique du Languedoc Occidental*, gathered in a region located in the Occitan area in southern France. This language area is distinguished by both a large and relatively homogeneous central zone around the city of Toulouse and by two mixed zones, one to the North in contact with Limousin and the other to the South, bordering the Catalan-speaking area.

Table 2: An example of a qualitative measurement between 2 locations of enquiry for Occitan

segments	concept	answ (22)	answ (20)	LD1	LD2	LD3
22 > 20	day	ʒur'naðɔ	ʒuʀ'nadœ	repl. r by ʀ	repl. ð by d	repl. ɔ by œ
22 > 20	he snores	'r:ũŋkɔ	'ʀũŋklœ	repl. r: by ʀ	ins. of l	repl. ɔ by œ
22 > 20	fair	'fjɛrɔ	'fjɛʀɔ	repl. r: by ʀ	repl. ɔ by œ	

When all the data taken from two different locations were compared, as in Table 2, she obtained: replacing r by ʀ (= 36%) and replacing ɔ by œ (= 22%). Brun-Trigaud demonstrated that, for the area studied, from East to West, divergences were caused by the preponderance of a single phonetic correspondence, appearing very frequently, whereas in the North of the area differences in numerous phonetic variables appear, which affects mutual understanding between speakers of different areas.

In order to validate these initial results, she invited her fellow Breton dialectologists, Solliec and Le Dû, the author of the NALBB, to test the new version of the algorithm on Breton data.

3 Earlier dialectometric works on Breton

Studies by Falc'hun (1981) based on the *Atlas Linguistique de la Basse-Bretagne* (Le Roux 1924–1963, henceforth ALBB) have deepened the geolinguistic understanding of the Breton language. They constitute an important reference on the issue.

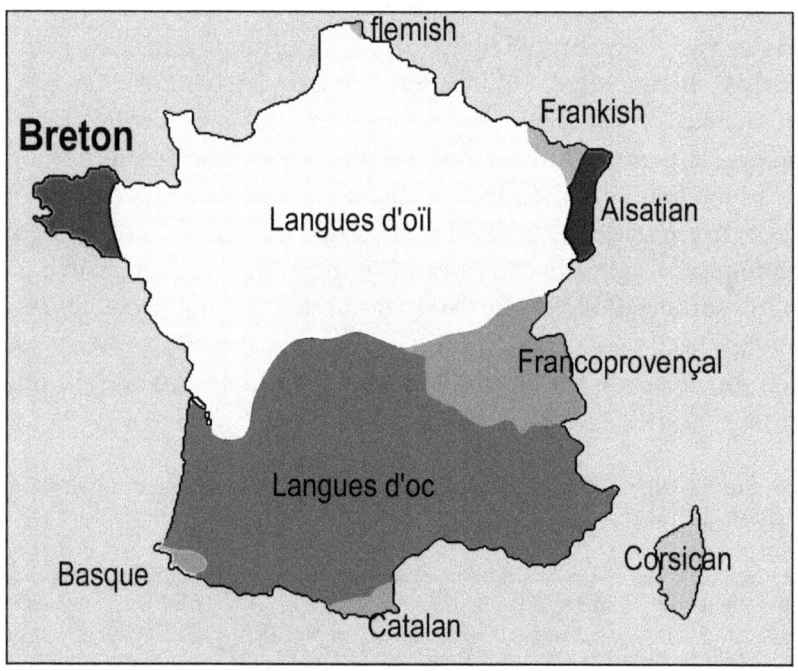

Figure 1: Situation of the Breton language.

Until now very little quantitative work has been done on the Breton language. German (1984; 1991) is the very first to have applied a dialectometric approach to Breton data. A cluster analysis using the Lerman algorithm allowed him to classify the dialect areas according to their linguistic similarities and differences with the Breton of Saint-Yvi he described in his PhD thesis (1984). More recently

Costaouec (2012) correlated the internal dialect borders inside a small area of the Breton speaking region with other aspects of social, cultural or economical factors around the village of La Forêt-Fouesnant, whose speech he described in his thesis (Costaouec 1998). These two studies are based on Le Roux's ALBB, where the data were collected between 1913 and 1920 for a range of 87 sites of enquiry published in 600 maps. Le Dû began working on his NALBB (2001) in 1968 (187 sites and 601 maps). He himself transcribed all the data in order to avoid transcription biases. Since no recent study has tackled the Breton language as a whole, as we mentioned before, further works by Solliec will aim to fill this gap. In order to accomplish this, he will take into account the NALBB data. This article constitutes the first step in this process.

4 The area investigated

We have deliberately chosen to investigate a restricted and quite homogeneous area for the following reasons: on the one hand, we do not want to confront this modified version of the LD algorithm, from a technical point of view, with an area where linguistic variation is very intense, as in the case of the *Vannetais* dialect (South-East of Lower-Brittany). Moreover, as was shown by Falc'hun (1981), innovations have been spreading across this region for centuries. It would then be interesting to compare them with sites from more conservative peripheral areas. Over the past few years, Solliec has been carrying out a project to describe and document local varieties in this area and is therefore aware of the local variation phenomena.

On the methodological side, we have decided to use an inter-site approach: to do so, each location of the area is linked to its closest geographical neighbours in order to establish a comparison we called the "segment". Doing so allows the researcher to detect spatial continuities and discontinuities (breaches) on the phonetic level (Goebl 2012: 137). In this view we selected 23 investigation sites for 165 phonetic maps (i.e. using only one lexeme and its phonetic variations for each concept). We had not beforehand determined which variables to observe in our corpus: our objective was to consider the data as a whole and to observe which phenomena produce linguistic distance and at which frequencies.

It led us to divide the area into a net of 53 "segments", each of which connect a site in the atlas with its neighbours on all sides. This brings us to a total of 8745 comparisons between strings of characters.

Our aim has been on the one hand to gather quantitative indicators and, on the other hand, to identify qualitatively the most common correspondences involved

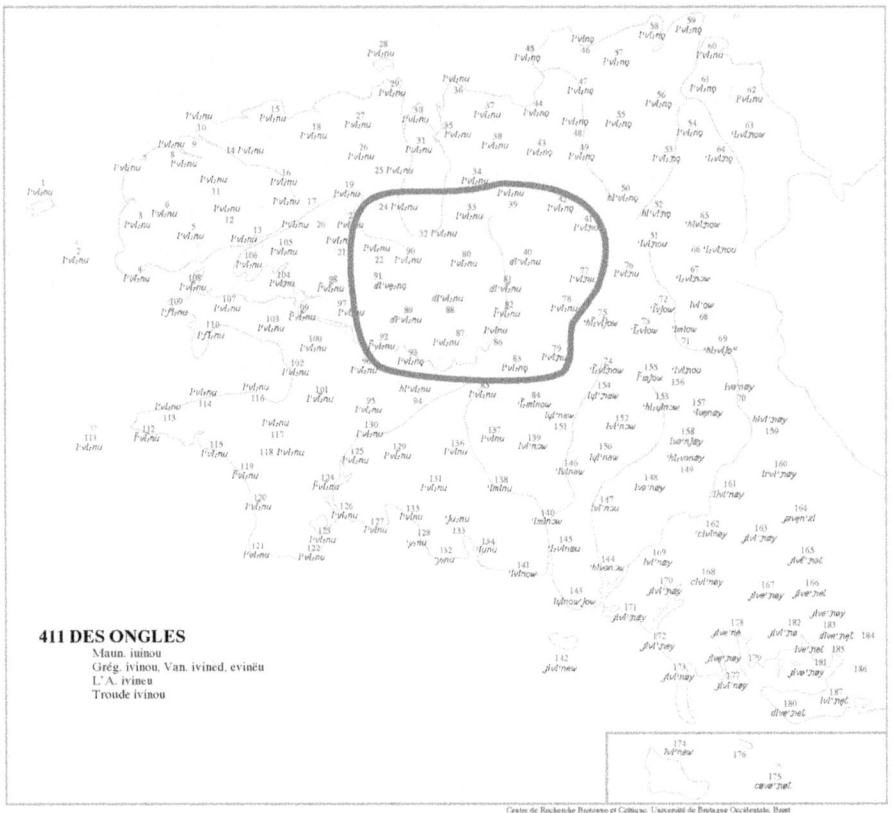

Figure 2: NALBB Map 411 'Fingernails'. The area investigated is delimited in black.

in phonetic variation. Even though the latter are well known (Falc'hun 1981; Jackson 1967), we do not know how frequently they occur.

5 The problems LD meets with Breton

In confronting LD with Breton language data, we noticed difficulties: Table 3 shows an excerpt of the data where the algorithm repeatedly failed to analyze the data, while at the same time the FuzzyMatch function did not work as we can see in Table 3. This last function returns a percentage reflecting the probability of correspondences (and differences) between two words.[1]

---

[1] See https://x443.wordpress.com/2012/06/25/fuzzymatch-in-vbavbscript/

Table 3: Examples of the difficulties encountered by LD for the concept 'that one (masc.)'

segments	answ1	answ2	test Exact	FuzzyMatch	Levenshtein1	Levenshtein2	Levenshtein3	Levenshtein4
40 > 41	hẽːs	hẽːs	TRUE	Not a match				
32 > 80	'ẹnes	'ẹnnəs	FALSE	50% (2)	Rep. n by nn	Rep. e by ə		
32 > 33	'ẹnes	'hẹnnəs	FALSE	25% (3)	#VALUE! (Ins. of h)	#VALUE! (Rep. n by nn)	#VALUE! (Rep. e by ə)	
33 > 39	'hẹnnəs	hẽː	FALSE	Not a match	Del. of s	Del. of ə	Del. of nn	Rep. ẹ by ẽː

Although we were careful to use a unique character for each phonetic segment and its diacritics (including diphthongs and geminates), it appears that our implementation of the Levenshtein algorithm experiences difficulties when treating languages like Breton for which variation in the number of syllables is frequent (e.g., site 80 Berrien ['parọs] vs. site 81 Poullaouen [paːʀs] 'parish' (NALBB map 7)).

Nevertheless, after checking and adjusting the function, we ended by incorporating most observations. On the one hand, the raw results obtained from the FuzzyMatch function produces the following distribution (see map in Figure 3):

The map shows several areas involving significant degrees of similarity, particularly in the North around sites 24 on the one hand and 39 on the other, and in the South around site 88. It is clear that the geographic distance between the surveyed localities often correlates with phonetic similarity; for example, there is high phonetic similarity between nearby sites 87 and 88 and low similarity between distant sites 83 and 93. However, there are some exceptions, for instance, between sites 22 and 24 or, vice versa, between 91 and 89. We will later see why they occurred.

On the other hand, the results returned by the new function of the algorithm bring us to the following conclusions: first of all, amongst the 11,949 non-identical phonetic correspondences, "alternations" or "differences" according to our terminology, we had to manage an important dispersion of the distinctive correspondences (nearly 450). They were generated by the narrow phonetic transcription. With the consent of Le Dû, the author of the atlas, we grouped some alternations in order to have to deal with fewer details. This limited the number of the different kinds of alternations to 200. The most frequent ones are listed in Table 4.

These alternations are distributed as follows on the map (Figure 4): for each segment (i.e. a pair of enquiry sites) we calculated the most frequent alternation proportional to its frequency (identical correspondences are excluded).

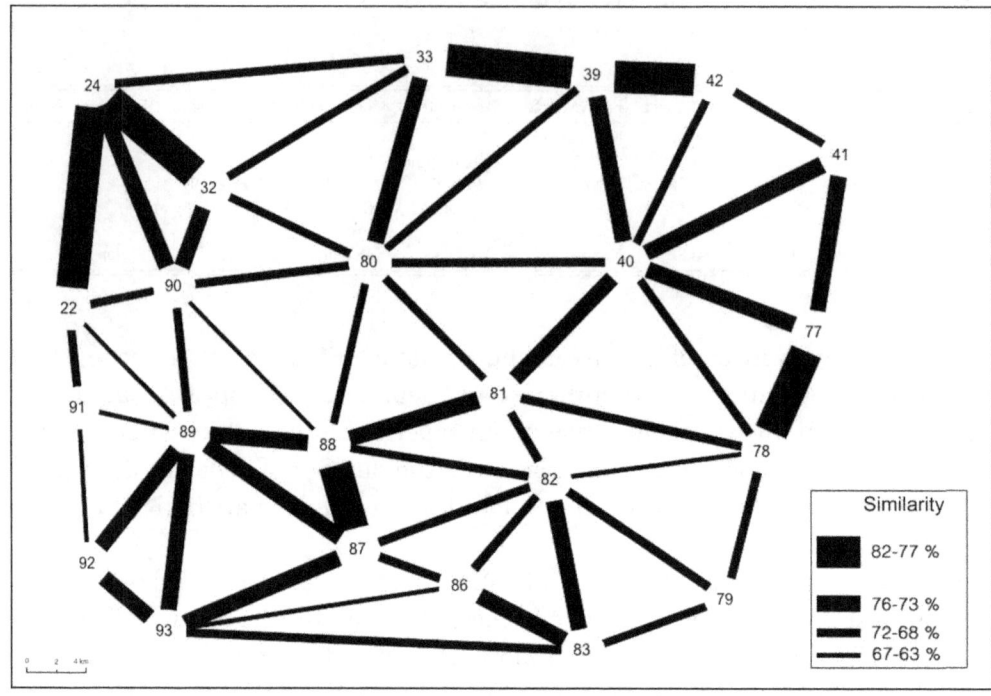

Figure 3: FuzzyMatch results for the area on a schematic map

Table 4: List of the most frequent alternations

1	r/ʀ/ʁ	14.70%	
2	e (ẹ/e/e:)	6%	25%
3	a/ə	4.5%	
4	r (+/-)	4.3%	
5	e/ə	4%	
6	ə (+/-)	3.5%	50%
7	e/ɛ	3%	
8	o (ọ/o/o:)	3%	25%
9	e/i	2%	
10	n (n/nn/ṇ)	2%	
11	æ/a	1.7%	
12	i (i/i:)	1.6%	

8 A new dialectometric approach applied to the Breton language

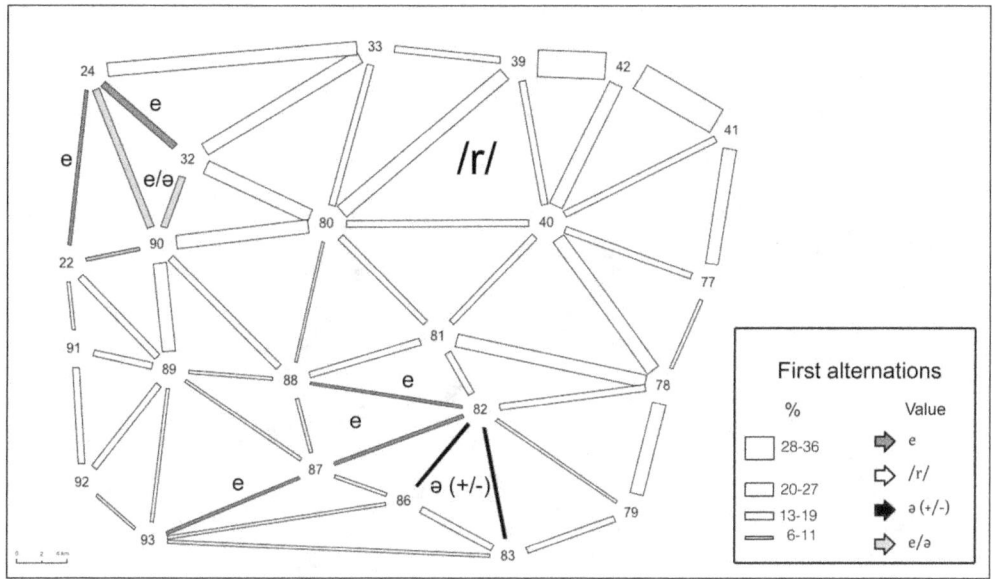

Figure 4: Distribution of the most frequent alternations across the area

Apart from the [r] variations, the proportions of changes are relatively small, but they are quite similar to the results found in the Occitan region, with one notable difference: there were far more changes in the consonants Brun-Trigaud (2014: 135). In addition, as noted by Le Dû, [r] variations are probably idiolectal, so that we consequently decided to concentrate on other more relevant changes with his agreement.

The nature of the differences is more varied in the second most frequent alternation (map in Figure 5).

Taking into account the fact that the proportions of changes are relatively low – 3 to 13% at most – the map in Figure 5 shows that the south-eastern area is marked by the presence or absence of schwa (dark colour), the central area by alternations between [a] and [ə] (white colour), and, finally, that the north-west is characterized by an alternation between [e] and [ə] (dark grey).

6 Analysing the first results

The values the algorithm returned provided a considerable amount of data. They had to be explored carefully. The following analyses are instances of what can be done when scrutinizing geolinguistic data from a statistical perspective when

143

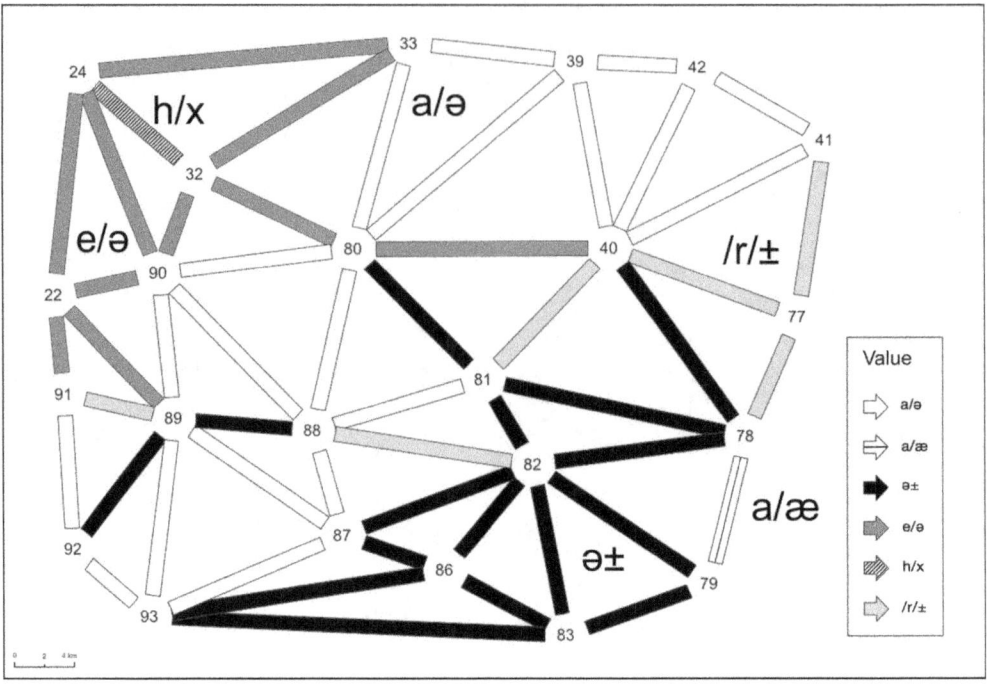

Figure 5: Distribution of the second most frequent alternation across the area

associated with a qualitative approach. First, we will observe how one specific alternation occurs across the area, involving [a] and [ə]. Secondly, we will study the results for one locality, Collorec, site 88 of the NALBB.

6.1 Examining only one kind of difference across the area

The most important kind of change from a numerical point of view, apart from the variation of the rhotics, is the one which affects the vowels [a] and [ə]. In our corpus, this alternation ([a]/[ə])[2] constitutes 9% of the non-identical phonetic correspondences we have gathered and appears in 54 of the 165 maps we selected.

The realizations [a] or [ə] occur in the following phonetic contexts. Each one can interplay with another:

Eighteen of the 165 maps we used included a definite article and 11 had infinitive word forms. These are instances of the alternations under study (see examples a. and e. in Table 5).

---

[2] The alternation is indicated by the brackets ( ) in order to distinguish it from the specific sounds [a] and [ə]

Table 5: Phonetic contexts for the alternations ([a]/[ə])

Type of context	Map number & concept	Examples
a. Definite article's initial vowel	263 'the stable'	(81) Poullaouen [ə hʀow] vs. (80) Berrien [a hʀow]
b. Final unstressed syllables	464 'clothes'	(93) Lennon [ˈdiʎət] vs. (89) Lannédern [ˈdiʎat]
c. Cluster of phones /-uwar/ or /-uarn/	196 'blackberries'	(87) Landeleau [ˈmuːwəʀ] vs. (93) Lennon [ˈmuwaʁ]
	170 'iron'	(32) Plounéour-Ménez [ˈuːaʁn] vs. (33) Plougonven [ˈuːʀən]
d. Epenthesis vowel	301 '(a) scythe' (literary form: [falx])	(78) Locarn [ˈvalax] vs. (82) Plounévézel [ˈvʰaləx]
e. Infinitive mark	50 'to count'	(90) Botmeur [ˈkǫntə] vs. (32) Plounéour-Ménez [ˈkǫnta]

This strong presence may result from our selection of maps but, on the other hand, these alternations are very frequent in this language. On a more general level, ([a]/[ə]) alternation is interesting because it offers a perspective on the degree of centralization of vowels by Breton speakers. Breton final-syllable vowels tend to be centralized when unstressed, especially in the central dialect area (Wmffre 1998: 8–10). The occasional appearance of a clear [a] in post-stress context goes against the general economy of the language (Martinet 1955).

The ([a]/[ə]) alternation occurs regularly but with only a slight number of occurrences across the area. The data for this alternation can be classified according to their frequency of appearance in each location under enquiry. Three zones can be spotted according to the spatial distribution of the difference under examination (see Table 6 and Figure 6).

This kind of difference occurs the most intensely in the central area in dark grey. In the two other areas located on the fringes, the frequency is less important. At present, it is still difficult to draw a conclusion because we do not understand how this small area is connected to the rest of the Breton-speaking region, continuously or discontinuously.

Finally, a closer look at these results led us to identify a particular realization of the kind that occurs recurrently. Some words may end with an [a] and a final consonant (a+Cons.) in post-stressed contexts when a more common realization with a schwa and a final consonant (ə+Cons.) would have been expected as in the

Table 6: Values for the alternation ([a]/[ə])

N° of the location	Name of the location	Number of occurrences for the alternation ([a]/[ə])	Proportion amongst these category of alternation (%)	Proportion of the [ə] words involved in the alternation (%)
080	Berrien	93	8.80	65.60
090	Botmeur	80	7.57	46.25
040	Plourac'h	79	7.48	65.80
089	Lannédern	78	7.38	66.60
093	Lennon	66	6.25	13.60
088	Collorec	60	5.68	55.00
082	Plounévézel	52	4.92	61.50
039	Guerlesquin	49	4.64	20.40
033	Plougonven	48	4.54	37.50
022	Saint-Cadou	42	3.97	38.00
087	Landeleau	41	3.88	58.50
081	Poullaouen	40	3.78	67.50
092	Pleyben	40	3.78	67.50
042	Loguivy-Plougras	35	3.31	51.42
091	Saint-Rivoal	34	3.21	52.90
032	Plounéour-Menez	33.00	3.12	27.27
041	Plougonver	32	3.03	34.37
024	Guimiliau	31	2.93	12.90
078	Locarn	30	2.84	40.00
086	Cléden-Poher	26	2.46	8.70
083	Motreff	24	2.27	62.50
077	Saint-Servais	22	2.08	77.27
079	Paule	21	1.98	19.04
		1056	99.9	

8 A new dialectometric approach applied to the Breton language

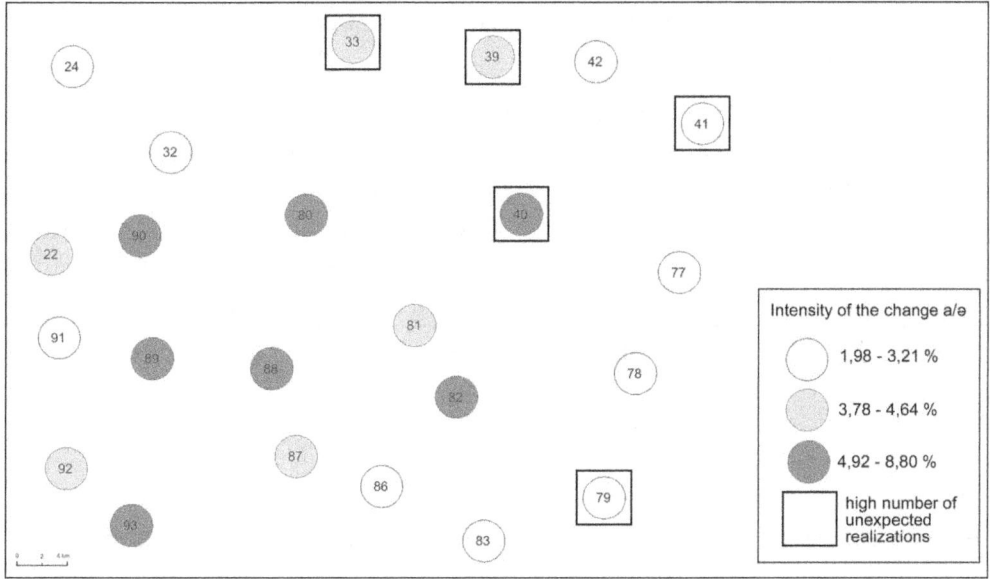

Figure 6: Intensity of the alternation ([a]/[ə]) across the area & locations with a high number of specific realizations

following example: NALBB map 109 'a day (long)' site (33) Plougonven [ˈdẹ:vas] vs. site. (80) Berrien [ˈdẹ:vəs].

This specific realization operates in a quite clear context especially in nouns and in the past participle forms of the verbs. This alternation cannot be explained by etymology.

The realization of [a] for [ə] in final unstressed syllables occurs only in 45 cases in this category that is, 4.26% of the total of the alternations ([a]/[ə]) and only 15 different lexemes in our corpus were affected by this specific realization. But it occurs in one little area and this specific realization is distributed as Table 7 shows.

This appears to be simply anecdotal on the surface but this specific realization regularly occurs in our corpus. Interestingly, the phenomenon is concentrated in the same micro-area around Plougonven (site 33). This means that this specific and not so common realization of a final unstressed (a+Cons.) could be salient from a sociolinguistic perspective as a sign of local identity and explain why an additional unneeded articulatory effort after the stressed syllable is produced for some words. Nevertheless, only a deeper scale study on these issues could help us to better understand the centralization of vowels in Breton.

Table 7: Distribution of the different occurrences of (a+Cons.) according to the location investigated

Number of the point of enquiry	Location	Number of comparisons displaying the realization (a+Cons.)	Number of lexemes affected by the realization (a+Cons.)
33	Plougonven	15	9
40	Plourac'h	10	2
41	Plougonver	4	2
79	Paule	3	1
88	Collorec	5	2

6.2 The differences around one locality

Another approach is a close examination of the data for one location in order to determine the phonetic similarity between neighbouring sites. We decided to do this for Collorec (site 88), which is worth analysing because of its centrality and on account of the large number of results gathered for this place: 1354 alternations. They account for nearly 11% of all the non-identical correspondences we observed in our corpus. This number is far higher than the average of changes for each locality (519) of the area. The following figures display the linguistic distance between Collorec and its closest neighbouring locations from a phonetic point of view.

Table 8 shows how the differences observed between Collorec and its neighbouring sites are represented spatially. For each segment the number of alternations we noticed corresponds to the average observed for all the other segments across the area (225 on average).

Figure 7 shows that the level of intensity with respect to the differences varies according to the site-pair involved: three locations (80, 82, 90) are phonetically more distant from Collorec than the others. The distance we have noticed for sites 80 and 90 could be explained by a geographic factor: a bog named *Yeun Ellez* spreads out between these sites and Collorec. These findings about phonetic traits match Solliec's own research in the area. This marshy bog, which is an obstacle to travel, seems to promote linguistic differences more than the hills

8 A new dialectometric approach applied to the Breton language

Table 8: Number of differences to neighbouring sites around Collorec (site 88)

Site Comparison	Number of differences	Percentage compared to the number of differences
88>90	293	21.63
82>88	256	18.90
80>88	246	18.17
88>89	206	15.21
81>88	191	14.10
87>88	162	11.96
	1354	99.97

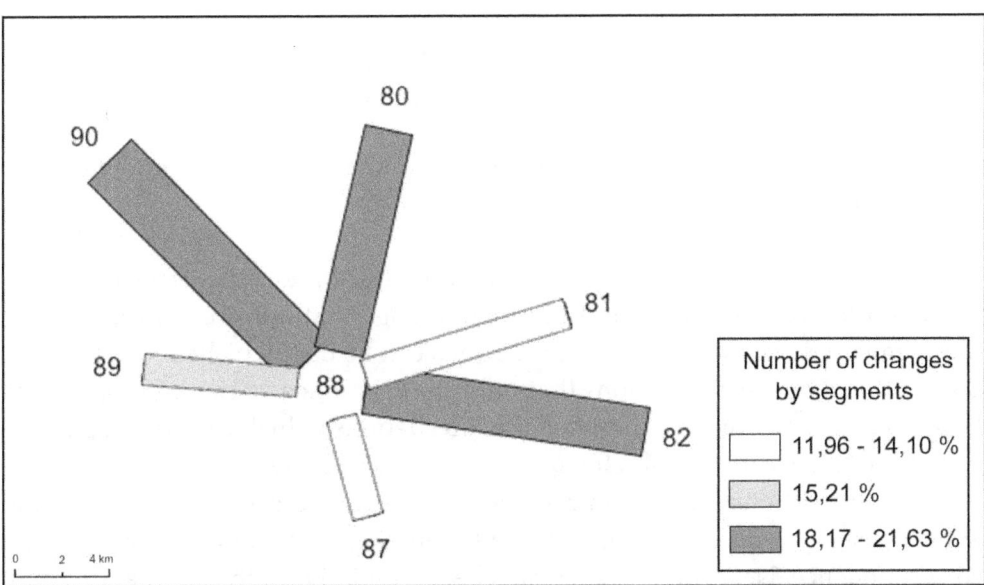

Figure 7: Number of differences to neighbouring sites around Collorec (point 88)

149

(named *Monts d'Arrée*), on the North-Western edge of the area, which are easy to get over (see Figure 3: FuzzyMatch map).

Moreover, through the statistical use of the data returned by the LD algorithm, the features of the linguistic variation in Collorec can be examined. The alternations observed for Collorec are detailed in the following figures.

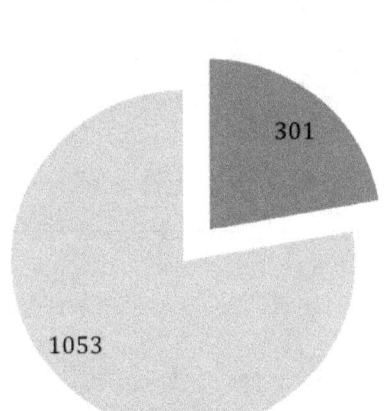

Figure 8: Nature of the alternations between Collorec and its surrounding neighbours

The diagrams 8 and 9 show how the non-identical phonetic correspondences we found between Collorec and its surrounding locations are distributed. As these figures show, two types of alternations can be distinguished. The first one groups together the alternations that only show up once or twice in the results. In the second category are gathered the alternations, which can be clearly individualized (Figure 9) and which happen on a quite frequent basis.

These alternations are the same as those occurring across the whole area and with the same frequency, such as the different kinds of rhotics or the ([a]/[ə]) correspondence. Nevertheless, one must keep in mind that the number of occurrences for each alternation is low. For instance, 20 occurrences out of 1354 only account for 1.5% of them. We did not find any alternation unique to Collorec in spite of the large amount of data we have at our disposal for this specific location,

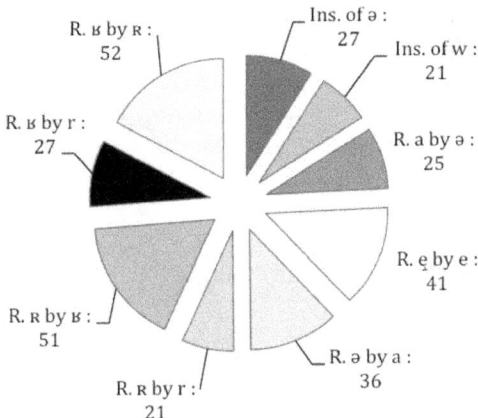

Figure 9: Nature of the alternations between Collorec and its surrounding neighbours

whose features thus share in the general tendencies of the area, which is quite uniform in phonetic terms.

These two different approaches, the first about a specific alternation and the second dealing with the phonetic features of one location are the type of investigation opportunities this new usage of the LD algorithm offers for geolinguistic research.

7 Conclusion

To conclude, we want to stress that the sample of data used for this investigation was small because we deliberately restricted the size of the area under investigation as well as the amount of data. This paper reflects the first step of a more ambitious research to present a dialectometric analysis covering the whole Breton-speaking area. Our specific use of the LD algorithm allows us to treat qualitative data statistically. Linguistic variation can be described from a quantitative viewpoint while taking into account the specific features at stake so as to present a more comprehensive view of the data under analysis.

Furthermore, this new method allows us to divide the results obtained into 3 main categories: vowels, consonants and rhotics. These categories will have to be analysed individually while keeping in mind they can interact. A further step to this research will be to elaborate a dialectometric analysis on a larger scale, based on the data of the NALBB, being conducted by Solliec as part of his PhD at the University of Brest in France. For this purpose, he will compare different dialectrometric techniques. The Breton-speaking area is interesting as it constitutes a real linguistic laboratory thanks to its important inner variations and to its distinctiveness from the neighbouring Romance varieties.

Acknowledgement

We would like to thank Professor Gary German (UBO Brest) for his precious help in rereading and revising this paper.

References

Brun-Trigaud, Guylaine. 2014. Un usage particulier de l'algorithme de Damerau-Levenshtein dans le domaine occitan. In F. Diémoz & D. Aquino-Weber (eds.), *Toujours langue varie ... Mélanges de linguistique historique du français et de dialectologie galloromane offerts à M. Le Professeur Andres Kristol par ses collègues et anciens élèves*, 127–147. Geneva: Droz.

Costaouec, Denis. 1998. *Le breton parlé à La Forêt-Fouesnant (Finistère). Pratique actuelle, problèmes de phonologie et de syntaxe.* Paris: Université Paris 5 PhD Thesis.

Costaouec, Denis. 2012. Linguistic geography of Breton and sociocultural motivations. *STUF - Sprachtypologie und Universalienforschung* 65(1). 47–64.

Falc'hun, François. 1981. *Perspectives nouvelles sur l'histoire de la langue bretonne.* Paris: UGE.

German, Gary. 1984. *Une étude linguistique sur le breton de Saint-Yvi.* Brest: Université de Bretagne Occidentale PhD Thesis.

German, Gary. 1991. Une méthode dialectométrique (assistée par ordinateur) pour l'analyse des atlas linguistiques. *La Bretagne linguistique* 7. 177–213.

Goebl, Hans. 2012. Introduction aux problèmes et méthodes de l'« école dialectométrique de Salzbourg » (avec des exemples gallo-, italo- et ibéroromans). In X. A. Álvarez Pérez, E. Carrilho & C. Magro (eds.), *Proceedings of the international symposium on limits and areas in dialectology (LimiAr). Lisbon 2011*, 117–166. Lisbon: Centro de Linguística da Universidade de Lisboa.

Guiter, Henri. 1973. Atlas et frontières linguistiques. In G. Straka & P. Gardette (eds.), *Les dialectes romans de la France à la lumière des atlas régionaux*, 61–109. Paris: Éditions du CNRS.

Heeringa, Wilbert. 2004. *Measuring dialect pronunciation differences using Levenshtein distance*. Groningen: University of Groningen PhD Thesis.

Jackson, Kenneth Hurlstone. 1967. *A historical phonology of Breton*. Dublin: Dublin Institute for advanced studies.

Le Dû, Jean. 2001. *Nouvel atlas linguistique de la Basse-Bretagne*. Brest: Centre de recherche bretonne et celtique, Université de Bretagne occidentale.

Le Roux, Pierre. 1924–1963. *Atlas linguistique de la Basse-Bretagne*. 77 sites of investigation. 600 maps. Rennes; Paris: Plihon et Hommay.

Martinet, André. 1955. *Économie des changements phonétiques. Traité de phonologie diachronique*. Bern: Éditions A. Francke S. A.

Moseley, Chris (ed.). 2010. *Atlas of the world's languages in danger*. 3rd edn. Paris: UNESCO Publishing.

Nerbonne, John & Wilbert Heeringa. 2001. Computational comparison and classification of dialects. *Dialectologia et Geolinguistica* 2001(9). 69–83.

Nerbonne, John & Wilbert Heeringa. 2010. Measuring dialect differences. In Jürgen Erich Schmidt & Peter Auer (eds.), *Language and space: Theories and methods* (Handbooks of Linguistics and Communication Science), 550–567. Berlin: Mouton de Gruyter.

Solliec, Tanguy. 2014. *Dialectométrie de la Basse-Bretagne : Enjeux, méthodologie et applications. Quantifier et qualifier la variation linguistique, vision symbolique de l'espace et écho du dynamisme synchronique en breton*. Brest: Université de Bretagne Occidentale PhD Thesis.

Séguy, Jean. 1971. La relation entre la distance spatiale et la distance lexicale. *Revue de Linguistique Romane* 35(138). 335–357.

Séguy, Jean. 1973. La dialectométrie dans l'Atlas linguistique de la Gascogne. *Revue de Linguistique Romane* 37. 1–24.

Wmffre, Iwan. 1998. *Central Breton* (Languages of the World/Materials 152). Munich: Lincom.

Chapter 9

Automatically identifying characteristic features of non-native English accents

Jelke Bloem
Amsterdam Center for Language and Communication, University of Amsterdam

Martijn Wieling
Center for Language and Cognition, University of Groningen

John Nerbonne
Center for Language and Cognition, University of Groningen, Freiburg Institute for Advanced Studies, University of Freiburg

> We demonstrate the application of statistical measures from dialectometry to the study of accented English speech. This new methodology enables a more quantitative approach to the study of accents. Studies on spoken dialect data have shown that a combination of representativeness (the difference between pronunciations within the language variety is small) and distinctiveness (the difference between pronunciations inside and outside the variety is large) is a good way to identify characteristic features of a language variety. We applied this method from dialectology to transcriptions of the words from the Speech Accent Archive, while treating L2 English speakers with different L1s as 'varieties'. This yields lists of words that are pronounced characteristically differently in comparison to native accents of English. We discuss English accent characteristics for French, Hungarian and Dutch, and compare the results to other sources of accent information. Knowing about these characteristic features of accents has useful applications in teaching L2 learners of English, since potentially difficult sounds or sound combinations can be identified and addressed based on the learner's native language.

1 Introduction

Dialectologists have taken advantage of computational techniques to study regional language variation, and developed specific measures for quantifying this

Jelke Bloem, Martijn Wieling & John Nerbonne. 2016. Automatically identifying characteristic features of non-native English accents. In Marie-Hélène Côté, Remco Knooihuizen & John Nerbonne (eds.), *The future of dialects*, 155–173. Berlin: Language Science Press. DOI:10.17169/langsci.b81.148

variation. This field of quantitative dialectology is known as dialectometry. Dialectometry research has led to a variety of methods for analyzing large numbers of dialectal features in systematic ways. In particular, aggregation of features made available new methods such as quantification of distances between dialects, and statistical analysis of differences that allowed generalization over the noise inherent in examining any single linguistic feature (Nerbonne 2009). However, dialectologists are still interested in examining single features as well. Typical characteristics of dialects, known as 'shibboleths', are quite salient and frequently discussed among both dialectologists and laymen. Prokić, Çöltekin & Nerbonne (2012) show that quantitative methods can provide insight into this phenomenon as well. They identify the most characteristic words for various Dutch dialects, providing statistical evidence due to the aggregation of data.

The methods that have been developed in dialectometry have not been widely applied to other domains of linguistics, but there are clear generalizations that can be made. Any time a set of language variants is studied, where the languages differ in a quantifiable way, dialectometry methods can potentially be applied. This is certainly the case in second language acquisition, where different language backgrounds lead to a lot of variety among learners. In the acquisition of a particular second language such as English, native Mandarin speakers will produce a different English than native German speakers. These kinds of differences can be studied with dialectometric methods.

In particular, researchers working on accent studies (i.e. Wells 1982; Waniek-Klimczak 2008) could benefit from the use of these methods. It has long been noted that foreign accents can be perceived negatively (Ryan 1983). As a consequence, pronunciation training is a part of second language teaching, in which the goal is to make the students' accents more native-like. Since it is quite difficult to achieve native-like proficiency in second language learning, it has long been acknowledged that learners do not need to learn how to speak perfectly, but that intelligibility is sufficient:

> The learner (...) would have presented to him certain carefully chosen features on which to concentrate, the rest of his pronunciation being left to no more than a general supervision (Abercrombie 1956: 93).

This suggestion has later been developed into the idea of a hierarchy of errors, i.e. pronunciation problems that require the most attention in pronunciation training. A summary of research in this direction is provided by van den Doel (2006: 7–15). He notes that such hierarchies "have been formulated partly on the basis of experimental research, but mainly as a result of impressionistic observational procedures". Obviously, they are also language-specific.

9 Automatically identifying features of non-native English accents

We are not aware of many studies that discuss error hierarchies of phonological errors, or characteristic feature rankings. One example of the use of error hierarchies in a more general sense can be found in Rifkin (1995). This analysis does not go to the level of phonological features, as it discusses grammatical errors and intonation errors. Gynan (1985) discusses phonological features and places them in an error hierarchy, but only on a general level. Based on data from Spanish learners of English and U.S. bilingual native speakers of English, he notes that comprehensibility of accents is related more to phonological than to morphosyntactic characteristics, but problems with morphosyntax are more salient to native speakers.

There are also studies that discuss characteristic pronunciation errors in English by speakers of a specific language. Gao (2005) studied a Chinese L2 student of English in a longitudinal study over 12 weeks, analyzing the errors and determining whether they arose from first-language interference or from being in an early stage of language acquisition. Potential errors were identified from earlier work on Chinese accents, a methodology that is strongly biased against the discovery of less stereotypical errors. The study finds that most errors arise from Chinese interference, though this may be partly due to the bias towards typical Chinese errors. The article also notes the need for research that studies a wider range of speakers.

Another line of work that assumes strong interference effects and makes comparisons to native speaker phonology is automatic accent classification. These methods are often also based on the assumption that the non-native speaker replaces unfamiliar sounds in the second language with sounds from their native language, e.g. by Angkititrakul & Hansen (2006).

One error hierarchy that explicitly includes phonological errors can be found in the thesis of van den Doel (2006). He carried out a large study where native English speakers were asked to detect and evaluate Dutch pronunciation errors, to provide more empirical evidence for attitudes towards specific pronunciation errors for this combination of languages. We will compare this error severity hierarchy approach with our characteristic feature ranking approach, and show that this measure of severity is not the same as measuring characteristic features by comparing results of the two approaches.

Schaden & Jekosch (2006) discuss an interesting data set that has applications in identifying characteristic pronunciation errors: the CrossTown corpus, which contains transcriptions of speakers of several European languages pronouncing place names from other European countries. In Schaden (2004), a rule-based system for accent generation was created from this data set. Rules that encode typical pronunciation errors by speakers of one language in another language were derived manually in this study. Automatic identification of these errors would probably be possible from this data set, but does not appear to have been attempted.

Automatic identification of characteristic features of accents may provide additional empirical evidence for pronunciation difficulties. Since by definition native speakers rarely produce these features, they are likely to stand out. We propose that Prokić, Çöltekin & Nerbonne's (2012) method for detecting characteristics of dialects can be used for detecting characteristics of accents. Based on transcriptions of accented English speech from the Speech Accent Archive (SAA, Weinberger & Kunath 2011), we demonstrate how such characteristic features of accents can be identified. We quantify the most distinctive deviations from the standard English pronunciation for several languages of which native speakers are included in the archive. Note, however, that the method can be used for any language of which transcriptions from native speakers are available. We then compare the segments we identify to phonological features from published literature that are said to be typical of the English accent of that language.

To illustrate the method, we discuss the results for three languages: French, Hungarian and Dutch. First, however, we will explain the measure we use to determine the characteristic features.

2 Measure

Wieling & Nerbonne (2011) proposed two measures to identify characteristic features of dialects. The first measure is REPRESENTATIVENESS, which they defined as how frequently the feature occurred within the dialect area. A high representativeness indicates that the differences between pronunciations within the dialect area are small. The second measure is DISTINCTIVENESS, which they defined as how characteristic the feature is for the dialect. A high distinctiveness indicates that the differences between pronunciations within and outside the dialect area are large.

These measures are comparable to Labov, Ash & Boberg's (2006: p.43) isogloss measures: REPRESENTATIVENESS is identical to their measure of homogeneity, and DISTINCTIVENESS is similar but not identical to their consistency measure. The differences are discussed by Wieling, Upton & Thompson (2014). Furthermore, the representativeness measure is similar to RECALL and distinctiveness to PRECISION, as used in information retrieval.

Prokić, Çöltekin & Nerbonne (2012) showed that even a single dialect word can be used to characterize a dialect area using these measures. The measures proposed by Wieling & Nerbonne (2011) were generalized by Prokić, Çöltekin & Nerbonne (2012) in order to apply them (numerically) to the word level, rather than at the level of the individual features. Given that we are interested in the word level, we follow Prokić et al.'s definition. A further advantage of focusing on the word level is that phonetic context is taken into account. Non-native speakers are likely to use phonological rules from their native language, which may depend on context.

Prokić, Çöltekin & Nerbonne (2012) define the measures from a dialectological perspective in terms of sites and groups — a site is a location where a dialect sample is observed, and a group is a dialect area. Since we are working with accent data, instead we will use the terms speakers and languages — a speaker is one person included in the Speech Accent Archive, and a language is a group of speakers with the same native language.

A very representative feature shows little variation among the English accents of native speakers of one language, and a very distinctive feature shows a large difference between those speakers and native speakers of English. More formally, we assume a native language l, consisting of $|l|$ speaker samples, among a larger group of languages G consisting of $|G|$ speaker samples. G includes the speakers s that speak l as well as the s speaking other languages. In this work, we limit G to only include native speakers of the language of interest l and of English, since we would like to see what features are characteristic compared to native English. However, including more languages in G is possible too.

We also assume a measure of between-speaker difference d, with respect to a given feature f. For representativeness, we then calculate a mean difference $\bar{d}$ with respect to f within the language under investigation:

$$\bar{d}_f^l = \frac{2}{|l|^2 - |l|} \sum_{s,s' \in l} d_f(s, s') \qquad (9.1)$$

To quantify distinctiveness, we calculate a mean difference $\bar{d}$ with respect to f from the speech of native English speakers:

$$\bar{d}_f^{\neg l} = \frac{1}{|l|(|G| - |l|)} \sum_{s \in l, s' \notin l} d_f(s, s') \qquad (9.2)$$

Characteristic features are considered to be those where the difference between $\bar{d}_f^{\neg l}$ and $\bar{d}_f^l$ is relatively large. Following Prokić, Çöltekin & Nerbonne (2012), we normalize these measures by calculating the difference between their z-scores rather than just the raw difference:

$$\frac{\bar{d}_f^{\neg l} - \bar{d}_f}{sd(d_f)} - \frac{\bar{d}_f^l - \bar{d}_f}{sd(d_f)} \tag{9.3}$$

This normalizes the difference scores for each feature separately.

This measure is implemented in the publicly available Gabmap application for dialectology (Nerbonne et al. 2011), and this is the implementation we used to conduct this research.[1] In this application, languages l are represented as clusters of $|l|$ speaker samples. We manually defined these clusters using the native language metadata from the Speech Accent Archive, not applying any of the automatic clustering techniques available in Gabmap to avoid errors.

As for the measure of between-speaker difference d, we used the Gabmap function for finding the aggregated Levenshtein distance between two speakers' transcriptions, described by Nerbonne et al. (2011). This dialectometric method has also been applied to accent studies before. Wieling et al. (2014) found a correlation of $r = -0.81$ between human native-likeness judgments and the Levenshtein distance between native and non-native English speech.

We have applied this measure to transcriptions of the words from the Speech Accent Archive, each time comparing speakers of one particular language to native English speakers. After applying the formula above to the pronunciation distances, we identify lists of words that are characteristically pronounced differently by the non-native speakers, in comparison to native accents of English. To verify the measure and obtain more detail, we examined the top of these lists more closely. For the top five words, we looked at the most frequently occurring transcribed forms of the word in language l to see if they are indeed different from native English speech and if these differences might be called characteristic.

3 Material

Our transcriptions are a subset of transcriptions extracted from the Speech Accent Archive (SAA, Weinberger & Kunath 2011). The SAA has been expanded since we extracted the transcriptions, but we have used this older dataset because it has been segmented and manually checked. The SAA is available at http://accent.gmu.edu and contains a large collection of speech samples in English from people with various language backgrounds, including both native and

---

[1] Available at: www.gabmap.nl

9 Automatically identifying features of non-native English accents

non-native speakers of English. Each speaker reads the same paragraph containing 69 words in English:

> *Please call Stella. Ask her to bring these things with her from the store: Six spoons of fresh snow peas, five thick slabs of blue cheese, and maybe a snack for her brother Bob. We also need a small plastic snake and a big toy frog for the kids. She can scoop these things into three red bags, and we will go meet her Wednesday at the train station.*

While reading out a paragraph may not be the most accurate representation of one's pronunciation ability, this method of elicitation makes sure that there is a set of comparable transcriptions for all speakers. Furthermore, this paragraph has been designed to include the most common phonemes of English, and should be able to serve as a standard for that reason.

To show how much information these transcriptions contain, we provide some example transcriptions from the SAA below. These are the first lines of the elicitation text, spoken by four speakers with different language backgrounds. Example 4 was spoken by a 42-year-old American male from Pittsburgh (english1 on the website). Example 5 is a female Hungarian speaker, who lived in both the UK and the USA for 1.5 years (hungarian1). Example 6 is a male Dutch speaker from the Netherlands, who only spent one month abroad in the UK (dutch1). Lastly, example 7 is a female speaker from France, who spent four months in the USA (french1). More information about the speakers is also available in the archive, but for this study we have not taken any of this metadata into account, except for the native language.

(4) [pʰl̥iːz kʰɑlʸ stɛlə æsk ɚ ɾə bɹɪŋ ðiiːz θɪŋz wɪθ ɚ fɹʌm ðə stɔɹ] (English)

(5) [plis kol stalʌ æsk hɜ tu brɪ̃ŋ d̪is t̪ɪ̃ŋz̪ wit̪ hər frɔ̃m d̪ə stɔr] (Hungarian)

(6) [pliːs kɔl stɛ̬la ask hɜ tu bɹɪŋ ʔðɪs ʔθɪŋs wɪθ hɜ fɹom d̪ə sto₃] (Dutch)

(7) [pʰliz̥ kʰɔl stɛla æsk hɜɹ tu bɹɪŋ zɪs θɪːŋks wɪθ hɜɹ fɹʌm d̪ə stɒɹ] (French)

Even from these single examples, we can already observe some typical foreign accent characteristics. The English speaker strongly reduces the word *her*, which the non-native speakers seem to be more conservative about. The English and French speakers aspirate their unvoiced plosives at the start of the first two words ([pʰ]), while the Hungarian and Dutch speakers do not, since their native languages lack aspirated stops. The open back unrounded vowel [ɑ] is not present in standard Dutch or Hungarian, and none of the speakers use it in the example. We observe these speakers replacing it with more closed varieties of the vowel. We also see that not all stereotypical accent characteristics are always present: both the Dutch and French speakers correctly produced dental fricatives in the sequence *things with*, even though these languages do not include dental fricatives and non-native speakers are known to have trouble with this sound. Furthermore, French does not have aspirated stops just like Dutch and Hungarian, yet the French speaker still produced one (as noted above), while the Dutch and Hungarian speakers did not. Some speakers may be better at English pronunciation than others, and have learned to correctly use foreign sounds. We do see the French speaker substituting [z] for [ð] in *these*, and she aspirates the /p/ and /k/ in the first two words, which is unusual in French. She also devoices the final consonant of *things*, but not in *please*, showing that we not only find variation among native speakers of the same language, but that we also find it within the speech of a single speaker. We can observe one peculiar phenomenon in the Dutch transcription, the glottal stops before *these* and *things*. No other speakers of Dutch or English show this, and no such phoneme is apparent in the sound file, so it appears to be a transcription error. For these and other reasons, it is insufficient to examine the speech of a single speaker in discussing 'characteristic' accents. By aggregating, our method will provide stronger evidence of the characteristic features of accented speech.

4 Results

In this section, we will discuss the results of applying our method to French, Hungarian and Dutch accents. We limit ourselves to showing the top five most characteristic words according to the method, and their two most common transcribed forms. We have examined the French accents because many samples are available in the archive, Hungarian because it has some unusual phonological phenomena that span word boundaries and may be hard to detect, and Dutch, because we can compare our measure to the empirically established pronunciation error hierarchy of van den Doel (2006).

4.1 French

There are 34 speakers of French in the data set, providing us with a large sample of different forms of the words. Table 1 shows the five most characteristic words of the French speakers, ranked by their difference score (see previous section). This is calculated over all of the tokens in the elicitation paragraph. For words

9 Automatically identifying features of non-native English accents

Table 1: Characteristic words of French native speakers

Rank	Word	Score	Characteristic forms	Native forms
1	to	1.26	tu (20/34 : 11/181) tŭ (5/34 : 8/181)	ɾə (0/34 : 112/181)
2	into	1.05	ĭntu (21/34 : 25/181) ĭnt̪u (4/34 : 0/181)	ĭntə (1/34 : 56/181) ĭnɾə (0/34 : 29/181)
3	call	0.88	kɔl (14/34 : 12/181) kɔːl (3/34 : 0/181)	kʰɑlˠ (0/34 : 48/181) kʰɔlˠ (1/34 : 13/181)
4	small	0.78	smɔl (22/34 : 33/181) smol (4/34 : 1/181)	smɑlˠ (1/34 : 59/181) smɔl (22/34 : 33/181)
5	can	0.50	kæ̃n (13/34 : 3/181) kæn (4/34 : 0/181)	kə̃n (1/34 : 82/181) kʰə̃n (0/34 : 23/181)

that occur multiple times in the paragraph, we will refer to their tokens with an index, i.e. *the* [2] for the second instance of the word 'the' in the text. For each word, we also list the two most frequent forms used by French speakers, and the two most frequent forms used by native English speakers. If one form is used overwhelmingly more often than the other ones, we only list one. Behind each form, we list their frequency of occurrence in the following format: (French usage ratio : native usage ratio). For instance, for the first ranked item *to*, we can see that 20 out of 34 French speakers used the form [tu], while 11 out of 181 native English speakers used this form. It is highly characteristic of French. Native English speakers generally use the weakened form [ɾə], while the French speakers do not.

In French, unstressed vowels tend to be pronounced, and French speakers would be unlikely to produce the form [ɾə] anyway. The [ə] does exist in French, but it is phonetically realized only under special circumstances. A word-final schwa is usually elided, and only pronounced when the next word starts with a consonant. However, in the orthography this sound always appears as an <e>. A similar effect can be observed for *into* (ranked 2nd). English speakers use the form [ĭntə], used 56 times, as well as other forms ending in [ə], which are only used by one of the French speakers. The French language does not have vowel reduction to [ə] in word-final position, so it makes sense that French speakers would deviate from standard English here.

For the word *call* (rank 3), we mainly observe the use of [ɔ] as the vowel, while the majority of the native speakers uses [ɑ]. In French, the vowel [ɑ] is used, but it is in the process of merging with [a] (Walker 2001: 60–62). Perhaps for this reason, the French native speakers use [ɔ] in their English. The [ɔ] pronunciation can be observed in the speech of some native speakers as well. British Received Pronunciation (RP) speakers would use [ɔ] here, and this dialect is prestigious. Furthermore, the same difference can be observed in the Dutch and Hungarian data, though not as strongly. It may be the case that [ɔ] is taught to second language learners of English in this context, explaining the effect. The same phenomenon occurs in *small* (rank 4), where there are even some instances of [o] in the French-accented speech.

To continue, we can see that French native speakers do not aspirate the initial consonants of *call* or *can* (5th), for there are no aspirated consonants in Standard French (Walker 1984: p. 35). In the fifth word, *can*, we can also observe the usage of [æ̃] or [æ] instead of [ə] by the French speakers. [æ] is not a phoneme of standard French (Walker 2001), however, it is the vowel used in the full American English form of *can*. It is likely that the speakers have mostly acquired this English sound, but have not or not yet learned to reduce it, as the native speakers do.

Some properties of accents are considered to be effects of being in an early stage of learning regardless of the native language. However, it appears that many of the characteristic differences we found in French accents can be traced back to the phonology of Standard French.

4.2 Hungarian

Our discussion of the Hungarian accent data will refer to the English pronunciation teaching guide of Nádasdy (2006), which contains specific information on errors and substitution by Hungarian native speakers of English. Table 2 shows the most characteristic words of the Hungarian speakers. The top-ranked word *these* indeed shows two properties that seem to be typical of Hungarian accents and follow from the phonology of the language.

First, the dental fricatives [ð] and [θ] do not exist in Hungarian. The language has dental sounds and fricatives, but no dental fricatives, and using dental fricatives is considered to be a speech defect. Hungarian learners of English are said to often perceive these sounds as [f] and [v], but in production, the typical mistake is to replace [θ] with [s] and [ð] with [d] (Nádasdy 2006: p. 71). This is also what we observe in our data: the words *these* (rank 1 and 4) and *the* (rank 5) show [ð] being replaced by [d̪]. Second, we observe that a majority of the Hun-

9 Automatically identifying features of non-native English accents

Table 2: Characteristic words of Hungarian native speakers

Rank	Word	Score	Characteristic forms	Native forms
1	these [1]	2.06	d̥is (5/7 : 3/181)	ði:z (0/7 : 35/181)
			d̥iz̥ (2/7 : 0/181)	ðiz (0/7 : 19/181)
2	please	1.70	plis (4/7 : 1/181)	pʰli:z (0/7 : 39/181)
			pʰli:s (2/7 : 5/181)	pʰli:z̥ (0/7 : 31/181)
3	big	1.69	bɪk (5/7 : 0/181)	bɪg (0/7 : 77/181)
			bɪk̬ (1/7 : 1/181)	
4	these [2]	1.55	d̥is (4/7 : 1/181)	ðiz (0/7 : 59/181)
			d̥iz̥ (1/7 : 1/181)	ði:z (0/7 : 38/181)
5	the [1]	1.52	d̥ə (6/7 : 3/181)	ðə (0/7 : 97/181)
			də (1/7 : 0/181)	n̪ə (0/7 : 64/181)

garian speakers devoices the [z] in *these*, something the English speakers do not do. This is likely to be an effect of Hungarian regressive (or anticipatory) assimilation. When two obstruents in Hungarian are pronounced in sequence, the first one assimilates to the second one — if the second obstruent is voiceless, the first obstruent will be voiceless, too. This can also occur across word boundaries, as long as there is no phonological gap. In the original text, both instances of *these* are followed by the word *things*, which the speakers pronounce with [t̪] (7 times), [t] (1 instance) or [θ] (6 times), which are all unvoiced obstruents. In Hungarian, regressive assimilation would devoice the [z] of *these* here, and this is also what happens in their English pronunciation.

The word *big* (rank 3) shows another clear example of regressive devoicing, but with [g] devoicing to [k]. The context in the elicitation paragraph is *big toy frog*, and the Hungarian speakers mostly pronounce [tɔɪ] as the English speakers do, with the only differences being in aspiration of the [t]. Since the [t] is unvoiced, the devoicing of the [g] in *big* is regressive devoicing. The word *please* (rank 2) shows the devoicing before the unvoiced [k] of *call*, but also a difference in aspiration. There are no aspirated stops in Hungarian (Petrova et al. 2006).

When looking at these characteristic features, one might wonder whether speakers always apply final devoicing in English. This is not the case, however. For example, the word-final [d] in the sequence *red bags* is voiced by all Hungarian speakers. These cases are not characteristic of the Hungarian accent, as English also has no strict final devoicing and English speakers use the [d] as well. The score of the word *red* is only -0.48, the fourth lowest, showing less difference between Hungarian and English native speakers than among the Hungarian speakers. This indicates a quite similar pronunciation to native English.

In summary, our data show that regressive devoicing and the lack of dental fricatives are typical of Hungarian English accents compared to native English speakers' accents.

4.3 Dutch

While it is interesting to have quantitative evidence for characteristic features that can be linked to the phonetics of the native language, this does not tell us much about the ranking of the features. How do we know that the top five words really contain the most characteristic features? We are not aware of any other work that ranks phonetic or segment-based features of accents using a computational measure, but we may be able to find some evidence in perception studies. van den Doel (2006) conducted a large study on how Dutch accents are judged by British (Received Pronunciation) and American native speakers, which was aimed at finding salient pronunciation errors. In his study, he presented native English speakers 32 sentences, each containing a single pronunciation error considered to be typically Dutch, based on a survey. The pronunciation of the sentences was native, except for the error. Not all of the errors are phonemic (and therefore relevant to our study), but the ones that are, are considered by the authors to be representative of a more general phonological error. In the study, van den Doel (2006: 292) established hierarchies of errors consisting of five classes of severity, and separately for British English and American English. The most severe errors according to both groups are stress errors, which are not relevant to our study. We will discuss the most severe phonemic errors mentioned in the study, reproduced in Table 3, and compare them to our most characteristic features of Dutch accents, the top five of which are listed in Table 4.

For the American English data, two phonemic errors were classified in the most severe error class van den Doel (2006): the use of the uvular trill [ʀ], and 'fortis/lenis neutralization' (similar to devoicing, replacing [v] with [f], [d] with [t]). The first error is not observed in our top five. The topmost word where an [ʀ] might be found is *for* [2] at rank 19. However the Dutch speakers either use [ɹ] or no final consonant at all, and this is similar to what the native speakers do. In fact, in all of the words spoken by the 16 Dutch native speakers in the SAA, no instances of [ʀ] occur. The error may be severe and distinctive, but not representative, and therefore not characteristic. Even in native Dutch, [ʀ] is only used in the south, and throughout the Dutch language area, five main categories of *r* are

Table 3: Dutch hierarchy of error including only errors of severity > 2.2, adapted from van den Doel (2006)

Severity	Received Pronunciation	General American
> 3.5	Stress errors	Stress and stress-related errors
		Fortis/lenis neutralization
		Use of uvular-r
2.2 − 3.5	Stress-related errors	Most substitutions of /θ,ð/ by /t,d/
	Fortis/lenis neutralization	
	Use of uvular-r	Glottalisation of final /d/
	Some substitutions of /θ,ð/ by /t,d/	Epenthetic [ə] in /lm/
		/v ∼ w/ confusion
	Glottalisation of final /d/	/æ ∼ e/ confusion
	Epenthetic [ə] in /lm/	Inappropriate post-vocalic r
	/v ∼ w/ confusion	
	Confusion of /æ ∼ e, ʌ ∼ ɒ, ʊ ∼ u:/	
	Unaspirated [t]	

in use, with further subdivisions possible (Sebregts 2015). This illustrates the fact that the perception experiment of van den Doel (2006) identifies perceptually salient errors, which do not necessarily have to be characteristic. To be ranked highly by our measure, a feature has to be used by many non-native speakers of the language under consideration. Nevertheless, the second error, fortis/lenis neutralization, does occur. While *of* (rank 5) is more commonly pronounced with a final [v] by the native English speakers, all Dutch speakers use [f]. In our ranking, we also observe other forms of devoicing at the end of the words *slabs* (rank 3), *bags* (rank 4) and *big* (rank 1), though *big* is more likely to stem from the fact that most Dutch speakers do not use [g]. These phenomena were not included in the study of van den Doel (2006) at all, so it is unclear whether these forms are perceived as severe errors.

Table 4: Characteristic words of Dutch native speakers

Rank	Word	Score	Characteristic forms	Native forms
1	big	1.92	bɪk (13/16 : 1/181)	bɪg (0/16 : 77/181)
				bɪg' (0/16 : 41/181)
2	to	1.22	tu (10/16 : 11/181)	rə (0/16 : 112/181)
			tə (3/16 : 21/181)	
3	slabs	1.12	slæps (5/16 : 0/181)	slæbz (1/16 : 66/181)
			slæb̥s (3/16 : 1/181)	slæ:bz (0/16 : 38/181)
4	bags	1.08	bæks (4/16 : 0/181)	bægz (1/16 : 39/181)
			bæ:gs (3/16 : 2/181)	bæ:gz (0/16 : 33/181)
5	of [1]	1.06	ɔf (7/16 : 7/181)	əv (0/16 : 58/181)
			əf (7/16 : 46/181	əf (7/16 : 46/181)

Out of the remaining errors listed in the second-most severe class for both British and American English, all but one appear to be relatively uncharacteristic for Dutch non-native speakers of English. /v/-/w/ confusion is listed as severe, and might be expected because the Dutch /w/ is usually often pronounced [ʋ]. It almost never occurs in the data. For each word containing a *w*, all but one or two Dutch speakers use [w]. In fact, both instances of *we* in the elicitation paragraph are the two lowest ranked words using our difference scores. Another such confusion, /æ/-/e/ confusion, might be expected in *slabs* (rank 3 in Table 4). This confusion may arise because Dutch does not normally use [æ]. However, no Dutch speakers pronounce *slabs* with an [e], though [a] and [ɛ] are each used by one speaker. The word mainly ranks highly because of devoicing in the final consonant cluster. Another error considered severe, though it can only occur in intermediate stages of learning, is glottalization of final /d/. While Dutch does not have any final glottalization, the hypothesis is that because English has glottalization of final /t/, Dutch speakers may generalize it. There is only one final /d/ in our elicitation paragraph, in *red*, and the phenomenon does not occur there. The word has a score of only -0.05, indicating a very similar distribution of forms as among the native speakers, with the exception of two speakers who did fortis/lenis neutralization. The last uncommon error is the insertion of an epenthetic schwa in [lm] clusters. There are no such consonant clusters in the elicitation paragraph, and there are not many words that end in *lm* in English.

One notable characteristic that van den Doel (2006) classifies in the second-most severe category, is the replacement of dental fricative with other sounds (most likely [t] and [d] in Dutch). The highest ranked word with a dental fricative in Dutch accents is *the*[2] at rank 17. The reason is that various different replacements of the [ð] are used by the Dutch speakers. The expected phoneme [d] was used seven times, and four times [d̪] was used, the dental variety which is used in Flemish Dutch. Only two out of these four speakers were actually Flemish, so it may be used as a closer approximation of a dental fricative when learning English. Three more speakers correctly used [ð]. Since there is so much variation, there is no form that is particularly representative of Dutch accents, and the feature is not judged to be characteristic as a result. However, if we rank the Dutch accent features only by distinctiveness, two instances of *the* are ranked second and third. Consequently, this approach may be use to detect errors which show great variability by the non-native speakers.

5 Discussion

In this paper, we have demonstrated the use of dialectometric techniques to study English accents. We hope to have shown that methods from dialectology can be applied to other domains of linguistics in which there is language variation. We have used a quantitative measure to identify characteristic features of the accents of several languages. By aggregating over the transcriptions of multiple speakers from the Speech Accent Archive, we obtain stronger evidence for these features than one would obtain from the analysis of single transcriptions. We verified the resulting feature rankings by comparing them to three other sources of information relevant to accents: phonologies of the native language (Walker 2001), pronunciation teaching literature (Nádasdy 2006), and an empirical error perception study (van den Doel 2006). From the phonology and pronunciation literature, we learned that most of the characteristic features that we found are indeed a direct effect of interference from the native language, as opposed to some intermediate stage of learning. Furthermore, our method provides quantitative evidence for these observations, something we were not able to find in other work. It also yields a ranking of the words that phonological features occur in, providing more detail than was previously possible.

In the comparison to the perception study, we observed that our measure of characteristic features only somewhat overlaps with the perceived severity of speech errors. In particular, uncommon differences may be severe, but not characteristic due to their rarity. Difficult phonemes that are substituted in various ways by different speakers of an accent, are not deemed characteristic by our method. To identify these errors, the distinctiveness measure can be used.

The identification of characteristic features of accents can provide an additional source of information for teachers of English, since the measure favours features that are widespread, as opposed to some of the more stereotypical errors described by van den Doel (2006). They also differ from these stereotypical errors, indicating that our method may find errors that are not typically considered by teachers. By obtaining these characteristics in an empirical, objective and reproducible way, existing insights on L1-specific pronunciation errors can be validated against a dataset of transcriptions. Our method can also identify characteristic features of non-native speakers in other languages, as long as transcriptions of the SAA elicitation paragraph are available. This information can be applied in teaching L2 learners of English. Potentially difficult sounds or sound combinations can be identified and addressed based on the learner's native language.

One limitation of the method is that we still require a manual step to find phonological features in the transcribed forms of the words. In future work, perhaps this method can be combined with identifying characteristic sound correspondences (Wieling & Nerbonne 2011). An obvious continuation of this line of work is to apply this method to English accents of other languages. Finally, we suggest that dialectometric methods could be applied to the study of accents more often, since the two fields have many common characteristics.

Acknowledgements

We would like to thank Anna Mészáros for suggestions regarding the Hungarian data, and the anonymous reviewers for their helpful comments.

References

Abercrombie, David. 1956. *Problems and principles: Studies in the teaching of English as a second language.* London, New York, Toronto: Longmans, Green.

Angkititrakul, Pongtep & John HL Hansen. 2006. Advances in phone-based modeling for automatic accent classification. *Audio, Speech, and Language Processing, IEEE Transactions on* 14(2). 634–646.

Gao, Lili. 2005. Pronunciation difficulties analysis: A case study using native language linguistic background to understand a Chinese English learner's pronunciation problems. *Celea Journal* 28(2). 76–84.

Gynan, Shaw Nicholas. 1985. Comprehension, irritation and error hierarchies. *Hispania* 68. 160–165.

Labov, William, Sharon Ash & Charles Boberg. 2006. *The atlas of North American English: Phonetics, phonology and sound change.* Berlin, New York: Mouton de Gruyter.

Nerbonne, John. 2009. Data-driven dialectology. *Language and Linguistics Compass* 3(1). 175–198.

Nerbonne, John, Rinke Colen, Charlotte Gooskens, Peter Kleiweg & Therese Leinonen. 2011. Gabmap – a web application for dialectology. *Dialectologia* Special Issue II. 65–89.

Nádasdy, Ádám. 2006. *Background to English pronunciation.* Budapest: Nemzeti Tankönyvkiadó.

Petrova, Olga, Rosemary Plapp, Catherine Ringen & Szilárd Szentgyörgyi. 2006. Voice and aspiration: Evidence from Russian, Hungarian, German, Swedish, and Turkish. *The Linguistic Review* 23(1). 1–35.

Prokić, Jelena, Çağri Çöltekin & John Nerbonne. 2012. Detecting shibboleths. In *Proceedings of the EACL 2012 Joint Workshop of LINGVIS & UNCLH*, 72–80. Association for Computational Linguistics.

Rifkin, Benjamin. 1995. Error gravity in learners' spoken Russian: A preliminary study. *The Modern Language Journal* 79(4). 477–490.

Ryan, Ellen Bouchard. 1983. Social psychological mechanisms underlying native speaker evaluations of non-native speech. *Studies in Second Language Acquisition* 5(02). 148–159.

Schaden, Stefan. 2004. CrossTowns: Automatically generated phonetic lexicons of cross-lingual pronunciation variants of european city names. In *Proceedings of LREC 2004*, 1395–1398.

Schaden, Stefan & Ute Jekosch. 2006. Casselberveetovallarga and other unpronounceable places: The CrossTowns corpus. In *Proceedings of LREC 2006*, 993–998.

Sebregts, Koen. 2015. *The sociophonetics and phonology of Dutch r.* Utrecht: LOT.

van den Doel, Rias. 2006. *An evaluation of native-speaker judgements of foreign-accented British and American English.* Utrecht: LOT.

Walker, Douglas C. 1984. *The pronunciation of Canadian French.* Ottawa: University of Ottawa Press.

Walker, Douglas C. 2001. *French sound structure.* Vol. 1. Calgary: University of Calgary Press.

Waniek-Klimczak, Ewa. 2008. *Issues in accents of English.* Vol. 2. Newcastle-upon-Tyne: Cambridge Scholars Pub.

Weinberger, Steven H & Stephen A Kunath. 2011. The speech accent archive: Towards a typology of English accents. *Language and Computers* 73(1). 265–281.

Wells, John C. 1982. *Accents of English*. Vol. 1. Cambridge: Cambridge University Press.

Wieling, Martijn & John Nerbonne. 2011. Bipartite spectral graph partitioning for clustering dialect varieties and detecting their linguistic features. *Computer Speech & Language* 25(3). 700–715.

Wieling, Martijn, Clive Upton & Ann Thompson. 2014. Analyzing the BBC Voices data: Contemporary English dialect areas and their characteristic lexical variants. *Literary and Linguistic Computing* 29(1). 107–117.

Wieling, Martijn, Jelke Bloem, Kaitlin Mignella, Mona Timmermeister & John Nerbonne. 2014. Measuring foreign accent strength in English. Validating Levenshtein distance as a measure. *Language Dynamics and Change* 4(2). 253–269.

Chapter 10

Mapping the perception of linguistic form: Dialectometry with perceptual data

Tyler Kendall
University of Oregon

Valerie Fridland
University of Nevada, Reno

> In this paper we examine the geographic distribution of perceptual data from over 550 participants from around the U.S. in an experiment testing the categorical perception of vowel continua across several word pairs (e.g. *bet~bait, bid~bead, sad~sod*). Previous research has demonstrated that vowel identification, at least for certain vowel pairs like /e/ and /ɛ/, is significantly different across the major dialect regions of the U.S. and that vowel identification can be influenced by individual participants' own vowel configurations in production (Fridland & Kendall 2012). Here, we focus for the first time on the actual geographic distribution of the participants, to ask to what extent modern methods of dialectometry, in particular spatial autocorrelation (Grieve, Speelman & Geeraerts 2011), can help us to understand these data, and the regional patterning of perception differences more generally.

1 Introduction

In this paper we consider how methods from dialectometry can aid our understanding of regional differences in perception by geospatially examining the results from a large-scale, web-based vowel identification experiment, where listeners throughout many parts of the U.S. were asked to identify which word they heard when stimuli were played with synthesized and somewhat ambiguous vowel acoustics (e.g. a range between *bait~bet*). This work comes from a larger, long-term project in which we have sought to understand regional differences in the perception of U.S. English vowels and linkages between perception

Tyler Kendall & Valerie Fridland. 2016. Mapping the perception of linguistic form: Dialectometry with perceptual data. In Marie-Hélène Côté, Remco Knooihuizen & John Nerbonne (eds.), *The future of dialects*, 173–194. Berlin: Language Science Press. DOI:10.17169/langsci.b81.149

and production at both the regional and individual level (Fridland & Kendall 2012; Kendall & Fridland 2010; 2012), as well as lesser studied aspects of the vowel systems of U.S. English (e.g. Fridland, Kendall & Farrington 2014). Those projects have identified a number of regional patterns in perception. For instance, in Kendall & Fridland (2012) we identified that Southerners performed significantly differently from non-Southerners for the vowel continua probing the relationship between the mid-front vowels, /e/ and /ɛ/. In the present paper, we turn our attention to recent developments in dialectometry, the statistical evaluation and visualization of geographic variation in language, to ask whether we can shed better, more granular light on the regional distribution of perceptual patterns in our data.

In terms of speech production in the traditional domain of dialectology, researchers have long utilized mapping techniques to isolate the use of a feature or form in geographic space. In doing so, dialectology has brought to light much about the way such features interact with social and geographic barriers and, in wave or gravity models, about the way change spreads across space and time (cf. Chambers & Trudgill 1998). Recent work in understanding regional variation has increasingly focused on quantitative and statistical approaches to the analysis and mapping of regional forms. This work, under the heading DIALECTOMETRY, has developed more sophisticated approaches to understanding the regional distribution of variants (cf. Lee & Kretzschmar 1993; Nerbonne & Kretzschmar 2003; Nerbonne 2009; Szmrecsanyi 2012) and intersected modern dialectological work with advances in geographical information systems (GIS) more generally. It has also allowed researchers to take advantage of the vast accumulations of dialectological data now available. However, mapping perception is still in its infancy and researchers have not explored whether the same techniques that have been used on production data by linguistic geographers so successfully might be as useful for understanding regional variation in perception. In this paper, we attempt to tease out some of the ways in which the methods utilized in production contexts can be used to illuminate if and how perception maps across space. We largely draw on work from dialectometry, and in particular recent work by Jack Grieve and colleagues (Grieve 2009; Grieve, Speelman & Geeraerts 2011; 2013), which applies GEOSPATIAL AUTOCORRELATION TECHNIQUES to assess regional patterns in (typically productive) language data. As we consider the future of dialects and dialectology, we hope the work here can suggest new uses for geospatial mapping techniques and also illustrate the value of looking past production to perception in assessing dialect differences. Can these approaches help us identify patterns in perception across and within more traditionally defined dialect regions (e.g. Carver 1987; Labov, Ash & Boberg 2006)? Can we find significant regional patterns in perception like we do for production?

2 Background

To begin to look at the question of whether we can identify regional differences in perception using approaches from dialectology in general and the quantitative methods of dialectometry in particular, we first consider previous dialectological work that has focused on perception. Perhaps the best-known work of this kind is the approach, aptly named PERCEPTUAL DIALECTOLOGY, pioneered by Dennis Preston (1989; 1993). In this type of study, participants are given a map and asked to label where or how people speak differently. Perceptual dialectology is, at its heart, the study of folk-linguistic beliefs (cf. Niedzielski & Preston 1999), correlating overt attitudes and beliefs of speakers with specific locations or regions on a map. Generally, such work finds that listeners' negative attitudes tend to have geographic correlates, namely in the areas where stereotyped dialects are believed to be regularly spoken. For example, in Preston's work (e.g. 1989), negative attitudes toward Southern speech keenly affected how states in the South were rated in intelligence and education compared to non-Southern states. On the other hand, the same areas tended to suffer less on ratings of pleasantness. Thus, in such work we see that dialect regions, despite having a great deal of social and ethnic diversity, are strongly marked by associations with prominent beliefs about speech varieties linked to region. While perceptual dialectology research has long used quantitative and statistical methods, recent work has further incorporated sophisticated GIS methods (e.g. Evans 2013), expanding the use of quantitative and visualization techniques.

However, such studies deal mainly with language attitudes – that is, associations of linguistic forms with social meanings – and often tell us little of how the perception of a linguistic form itself, for example which vowel category a word involves, might be affected by where and how that form is spoken and where it is heard. Place, or belief about place, is known to be a source for variation in production and, one might hypothesize, perhaps variation in perception as well. Certainly, a number of studies have examined how well listeners are able to identify and place samples of regionally distinct talkers (Clopper & Pisoni 2004; 2007; Preston 1996; van Bezooijen & Gooskens 1999), confirming that listeners do interpret (some) production differences as correlating with place. While listeners (typically from one location) tend to do fairly well in such tasks on broad regional placement, especially with highly recognizable dialects (such as Southern dialects in the U.S.), accurate placement of speakers exhibiting sub-regional differences is less successfully demonstrated, suggesting that listeners may not always conceptualize place the same way as dialectologists.

Expanding this line of research, some work has attempted to measure more specifically how speech perception may be affected not only by the actual linguistic forms we hear, but by whom we believe to be uttering them, much like work showing that gender stereotypes can affect phoneme categorization (Strand 1999). In other words, some work in regional speech perception has indicated that the perception of linguistic form itself can be altered simply by labeling a speaker as from a particular location. Such studies have typically used a synthesized continuum of the feature in question and asked participants to identify what sound they think they heard. Most of this work suggests that where a speaker is from (or is believed to be from) influences the categorization of the sound heard or filters how it is processed (e.g. Allbritten 2011; Labov & Ash 1997; Plichta & Preston 2005). So, for instance, participants might anticipate and report having heard different vowels when presented with the same stimuli but given different regional affiliation for the talker as background information (e.g. Niedzielski 1999). Work has also shown that listeners are also affected by other subtle influences, such as the dialect of the experimenter (Hay, Warren & Drager 2006), or whether an item in the experimental context, even as subtle as a stuffed animal, has a regional association (Hay & Drager 2010).

Such work clearly shows that speech processing and speech production are necessarily linked – differences in (and beliefs about) regional speech production affect how speech is processed. However, most of this research is focused on the regional identity of the talker, or aspects of the experimental context, and less has focused on the actual regional identity of the *listener*. So, how might a listener's own geographic "place" affect how speech forms are processed and identified?

There is some evidence that a listener's dialect exposure or geographic mobility can increase success at discerning more subtle regional differences (e.g. Clopper & Pisoni 2007; Evans & Iverson 2004). Such work suggests the locational experience of a listener does have bearing on how speech input is identified. In addition, psycholinguistic work on perception also suggests that a listener's own familiarity with regional speech affects speech processing. For example, work by Sumner & Samuel (2009) found that listeners from the New York City area who were non-rhotic actually showed processing and representation differences compared to listeners from other (rhotic) regional dialects, as well as rhotic listeners who were also from New York City. This suggests that, like production, perception is regionally varied and variable. We might expect then that perceptual differences are likely to accompany geographic divisions among speakers. So, we might well have something yet to learn by looking at speech perception from the perspective of dialect geography.

Our own previous work (Fridland & Kendall 2012; Kendall & Fridland 2012) has demonstrated that listeners' regional affiliations do influence their perceptions of vowel identity, in particular for vowels undergoing regional shifts, such as vowels engaged in the Southern Vowel Shift. However, the bulk of our work has focused exclusively on definitions of region based on patterns in speech production (namely, from *The Atlas of North American English*; hereafter *ANAE*; Labov, Ash & Boberg 2006). Thus, our questions have largely focused on the ramifications of regional identity (via productive dialects) on perception. Sumner & Samuel (2009: 489) argue that "there are three distinct aspects in which a [person] may have a dialect: (1) in production, (2) in representation, and (3) in perception." We find this notion of perception's role in dialect provocative (see Kendall & Fridland 2010 as well). In moving forward in dialectological research, we see a need to examine the role of perception in dialect more fully.

In this paper, we present a new attempt to understand perception as part of what constitutes a regional dialect. We undertake this by exploring whether mapping techniques most often reserved for investigating differences in production are useful and informative for perceptual differences as well. In other words, we inquire whether we can identify, as we do for production, significant regional divisions in perception by examining listeners from a range of locations across and within the major traditional dialect regions. As discussed above, it has amply been demonstrated that region and linguistic form vary in ways that can be correlated to geographic, historical, and social distance, but we ask here if perception shows similar geographical patterns that might help reveal something about such differences.

3 Data

3.1 Overview

The data for our studies come from a computer-based vowel identification task that has been administered in a number of sites around the U.S. As of the time of this writing, we have collected data from 578 informants from seven field sites, with participants drawn primarily from eight U.S. states.[1] Participants were primarily in the 18–25 age range (as they were primarily students at local universities) and had to be raised from the age of 4 in that location. Regional groupings were based on those used in the *ANAE*. The locations of the participants' self-reported hometowns are shown in Figure 1. Elsewhere (e.g. Fridland & Kendall 2012), we have organized the participants categorically, by state or by *ANAE* regional grouping (and these state-level groupings are indicated with colors in Figure 1), but here self-reported hometowns are used to anchor the participants geospatially. An important caveat to the present study is that our participants were not sampled with an aim towards large-scale geospatial analysis and do not distribute across the U.S. in a balanced fashion as would be ideal for such analysis (see, for instance, Grieve 2009). We recognize that this lack of balance and representation across the U.S. hinders the generalizability of findings from our investigation. Nonetheless we believe that our relatively large sample makes an initial inquiry into dialectometry with perception data a useful endeavor, one which can shed important light into our data and point to the general utility of using geospatial analysis techniques for perception data.

3.2 Study design

In the test, vowel tokens from a number of continua were randomly played for listeners who were then asked, in a forced-choice format, to indicate the token they just heard from two choices (Strange 1995; Thomas 2002). Each continuum range was synthesized into 7 steps based on a sample speaker's production values for each of two selected endpoint vowel categories. The stimuli were created using estimated beginning and endpoint values for F1 and F2 for each vowel pair (based on regional vowel patterns). At each analysis frame, a distance in frequency was estimated between the trajectories of each vowel in the pair. Because duration was held constant, each vowel has the same number of analysis frames. Increments of change in frequency were estimated (using a linear interpolation) for consecutive steps of a 7-step continuum spanning the distance in F1 and F2 trajectories across the vowel pair. More information about the perception stimuli,

---

[1] Our seven field sites are: Memphis, Tennessee (South), Reno, Nevada (West), Oswego, New York (Inland North), Blacksburg, Virginia (South), Eugene, Oregon (West), Raleigh, North Carolina (South), and Chicago, Illinois (Inland North). Our recent work (e.g. Kendall & Fridland in progress) includes California (West) as an eighth state/sub-region. A large number of Californians live and attend university in Nevada and Oregon and due to the substantial participation we have been able to obtain from Californians we have treated these participants as their own group.

10 Mapping the perception of linguistic form

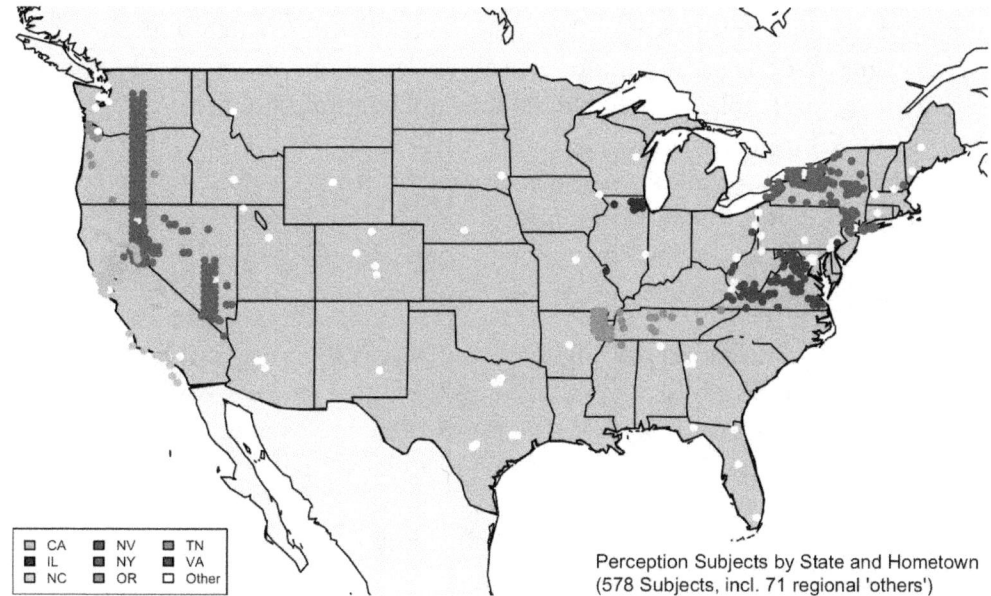

Figure 1: Location of 578 vowel identification participants. Colors indicate regional (i.e. U.S. state) associations for 507 participants included in our earlier work while white dots indicate participants not previously examined or assigned to a regional group; "Stacks" of dots indicate participants from same locale.

as well as details exemplifying the synthesis (for the /e/~/ɛ/ test), is available in Kendall & Fridland (2012).

The sample speaker was a 40 year-old male from Reno, Nevada, who was chosen as representing unmarked dialectal features in line with Clopper & Pisoni (2004). The tokens were embedded between a single consonant onset and single consonant coda (C_C) and two consonant contexts were used for each vowel pair of interest (a post-bilabial context and a post-alveolar context, e.g. for /e/~/ɛ/, *bait* & *bet* and *date* & *debt*). All following environments were alveolar obstruents. For the test, each trial presented a single vowel continuum step (played once) and participants were asked to indicate the token they just heard from two choices drawn from the relevant vowel categories (e.g. for the post-bilabial /e/~/ɛ/ test, *bait* or *bet*). To investigate how much of a role vowel dynamics plays in vowel category perception and whether this varies across dialects, two different conditions were created for each vowel continuum, one which altered dynamic information for each step along with steady state information and another which removed dynamic information. The static tokens were created with target formant values fixed based on midpoint values across the entire vowel trajectory while the dynamic tokens included the formant variability of the original tokens across time. Thus, the test included both versions for all vowels so that each participant's vowel thresholds were measured in both static and dynamic contexts for the two different consonant contexts.

3.3 Test procedure

In order to be simultaneously implemented across regions, the test was developed and administered through a website. Each step in each vowel continuum had four iterations – i.e. was played 4 times randomized over the course of the study. Thus, this vowel identification test included 20 perception continua over a total of 560 trials – 5 vowel pairs (/e/~/ɛ/, /i/~/ɪ/, /æ/~/ɑ/, /ʌ/~/o/, and /ɪ/~/u/) × 2 consonantal environments (post-bilabial and post-alveolar) × 2 conditions (static and dynamic) × 7 steps per continua × 4 repetitions. The study was also randomized by trial.

4 Analysis and results

4.1 Analysis

In our previous work, we have focused entirely on subsets of our total perception data (primarily the tense and lax mid- and high-front vowels) and we have limited our examination to just European American participants from a set of specific sub-regions (and, as explained above, examined those participants in categorical regional groups). In this paper, we examine, for the first time, a more complete set of our perception data from the larger project: 20 perception continua for each of 578 participants from throughout the continental United States (participants in our database as of August 2014).

As noted above, participants in the perception experiment heard vowels synthesized along a 7-step continuum and rated each step as one of two words in a minimal pair (e.g. *bait* or *bet*). The majority of our analyses have examined the data at this level through mixed-effect logistic regression (e.g. Kendall & Fridland 2012). However, we can also examine the data in terms of the participants' crossover points – the place in each 7-step continuum where a subject first "crossed over" the 50% point of hearing predominately one vowel category to predominantly another. We chose this measure of the "first" point at which participants crossed over from recognition of one vowel quality to another to provide a more

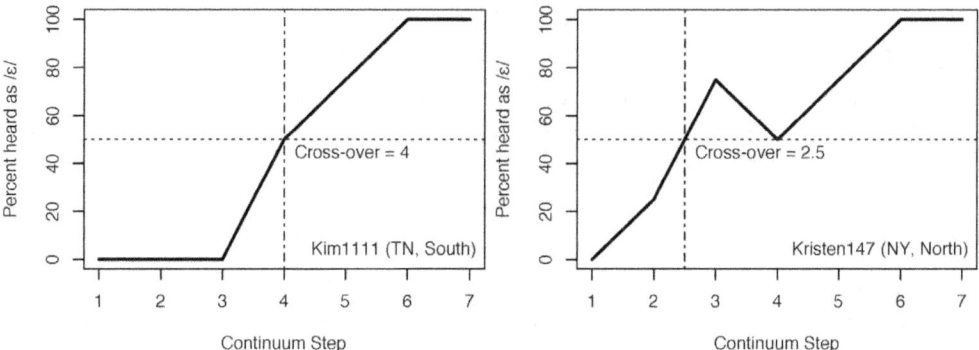

Figure 2: Identification function for /e/~/ɛ/ in dynamic post-bilabial context (*bait~bet*) for two individuals.

simple test case for the present analysis than assessing the full continuum data for stimuli set.[2] Using a cross-over measure provides a single value for each stimuli set (henceforth also referred to as a variable) for each participant and is less complex as input for some of the methods we utilize in this paper. Future work can assess whether the geospatial techniques we employ can be usefully applied to, e.g., full logistic models of the continua data.

To exemplify the cross-over points and perception data more generally, Figure 2 illustrates the identification functions and cross-over points for /e/~/ɛ/ in the post-bilabial context (*bait~bet*) for two individuals, Kim1111, a female from Memphis, TN in the South (on left), and Kristen147, a female from Rochester, NY in the Inland North (on right). Kim1111 highlights a Southern pattern for /e/~/ɛ/, with a relatively later cross-over in comparison to Kristen147, who shows a more Northern pattern, crossing-over to /ɛ/ earlier in the continuum (Kendall & Fridland 2012).

To begin to consider these cross-over data in more detail, we first examine the 507 speakers we have previously grouped into regional categories (South vs. North vs. West; these are the non-white dots in Figure 1). Table 1 presents a breakdown of the results of a series of ANOVA tests, which ask whether region differentiates cross-over points for each variable. The table shows results for Tukey post-hoc tests for the ANOVAs with *p* values below 0.05. Due to the large number of statistical tests, it is judicious to use a Bonferroni corrected *p* value as a more conservative measure of significance. Thus, while the table notes variables with *p* values below 0.05 (noted by *), *p* < 0.0025 (noted by **) is a better assessment of significance.

---

[2] We also examined the cross-over data briefly in Kendall and Fridland (2010; 2012).

Table 1 also includes ANOVA results for the first 3 Principal Components (PCs) from a Principal Components Analysis (PCA) for all 20 variables. PCA is a common dimensionality reduction and cluster analysis technique, and examining the Principal Components (PCs) provides a convenient way to assess trends across the whole (large) set of variables simultaneously. For sake of space, we do not discuss the PCA in depth here but note that PC1 accounts for 32.4% of the variance, PC2 accounts for 14.8%, and PC3 accounts for 11.0%. Focusing on the individual variables (the first 5 rows of Table 1), we see that ANOVAs yield $p < 0.05$ for 11 of the 20 variables and $p < 0.0025$ for 3 of these variables, the static and dynamic post-bilabial /e/~/ɛ/ continua and the dynamic post-alveolar /ʌ/~/o/ continuum. Overall, the majority of cases show the South having higher cross-over points than other regions, a finding inline with our results for the data examined elsewhere that showed, for example, Southerners tending to perceive /e/ farther along the synthesized F1/F2 continuum (e.g. Kendall & Fridland 2012). The general finding of a difference between the South and the North in particular is confirmed in the results for the first two PCs. These patterns align with production differences in regional vowel patterns between the North and the South (e.g. Labov, Ash & Boberg 2006) and demonstrate that, similar to perception, perception is also sensitive to geographic identity (Fridland & Kendall 2012).

Table 1: Results for ANOVA tests with Tukey post-hoc comparisons. - denotes region $p > 0.05$; * denotes region $p < 0.05$; ** denotes region $p < 0.0025$; > indicates e.g. S > W = "South has a significantly higher cross-over than West"; ~ denotes marginally significant (0.075 > p > 0.05 post hoc comparison)

	Bilabial		Alveolar	
Continuum	Dynamic	Static	Dynamic	Static
/i/ ~ /ɪ/	-	-	* S > N, W	* S > N
/e/ ~ /ɛ/	** S > N, W	** S > N, W	* S > N, ~W	* S, W > ~N
/æ/ ~ /ɑ/	-	-	-	* S > N, W
/ʌ/ ~ /o/	-	* S > ~N	** S, W > N	-
/ɪ/ ~ /u/	* S > W	* S > W	-	-
PC1		* S < N		
PC2		* S < N, ~W		
PC3		-		

Beyond noting differences in perception among the major regions of U.S. English, our present interest is in examining the perception data at a finer-level of regional granularity and to move away from our preexisting regional categories, which are based on production patterns and regional assignments from the *ANAE* (Labov, Ash & Boberg 2006). We turn now to spatial autocorrelation techniques to ask whether we can learn anything new from examining the perception data from a geospatial perspective, where participants are considered in terms of the geospatial coordinates of their self-reported "hometowns" rather than as members of a predefined dialect region.

Following Grieve (Grieve 2009; Grieve, Speelman & Geeraerts 2011; 2013) and previous work more generally on geospatial analysis (e.g. Moran 1950; Ord & Getis 1995), we apply two geospatial analysis techniques to the cross-over point data. First, we use Moran's I statistic to ask whether (any of) the 20 variables show overall patterns of regional clustering. Moran's I provides a measure of global spatial autocorrelation, with associated p values that indicate whether there are significant patterns of global (i.e. overall) spatial autocorrelation. Then, we apply Getis-Ord G_i^* z scores to measure local spatial autocorrelation to examine where any regional clusters appear to exist. These analyses are conducted using the spdep package for R (Bivand 2014b).

In this short paper, we limit our description of these methods and point readers to the sources mentioned above for a thorough explication of the techniques. As discussed in several papers by Grieve (see, for instance, Grieve 2014), analysis for both Moran's I and Getis-Ord G_i^* involve the choice of a SPATIAL WEIGHTING FUNCTION, which defines rules for how spatial relationships are assessed among the items being analyzed and which yields the SPATIAL DISTANCE MATRIX used for the analyses. There is no foolproof method for choosing the most appropriate spatial weighting function. For the analyses here, we followed advice from Bivand (2014a) and after assessing a range of different possible functions, used a binary spatial distance matrix using distances within 75% of the maximum distance found from a k-nearest neighbors (kNN) analysis using k=7. Other measures, such as a full kNN (k=7) binary matrix, yielded similar, though not identical, results. Given the unevenness of the distribution of our participants over the U.S. (see again Figure 1), the use of a binary kNN matrix seems most judicious. This somewhat limits skewing that might occur from other choices of matrix types, due to the fact that some groups of participants, like those from around Reno, NV where our sampling has been heaviest, have lots of close neighbors, while other participants, with hometowns farther afield from our sampling sites, have very few proximate neighbors. Further, since multiple participants self-reported the same hometowns (these were shown as stacks of dots in Figure 1) and many geospatial analysis techniques require that each data point has a unique geospatial coordinate, the geospatial coordinates were jittered (using the R function jitter() with a factor of 0.05) to ensure that no coordinates where exactly identical.

For the Moran's I test, we find global spatial autocorrelation at $p < 0.0025$ for six of the 20 perception variables. We do not find significant Moran's I results for any of the Principal Components, with PC1 obtaining a p value of 0.095. The Moran's I results are shown in Table 2. Thus, six of the variables are characterized as having global spatial clustering according to a conservative p value assessment.

Getis-Ord G_i^* analysis allows us to look at the spatial autocorrelation for each individual participant and to ask whether that participant is a member of a spatial cluster of like-valued participants. While examining all of the variables for local spatial autocorrelation would be useful, due to space constraints, we focus our attention on the dynamic variables which showed global spatial clustering by Moran's I. Maps for the static versions of these stimuli are not shown, despite that they also reached significance in the Moran's I analysis, also due to space limitations. Figures 3–6 display the Getis-Ord G_i^* scores overlaid on maps of the U.S. for the three perception variables and for PC1. These maps depict the scores as colors (see the legend of each map for keys to the colors). Light gray lines on the maps indicate the neighbor relationships from the spatial weighting function, so clusters are assessed in terms of relationships between connected participants. These maps highlight important regional and sub-regional clusters. However, before discussing these clusters, we must also note that these clusters are best taken more as visual "suggestions" than as statistically significant proof of regional differences. The G_i^* scores are effectively geospatially smoothed values for the variables (see e.g. Grieve, Speelman & Geeraerts 2013: 37). Ord & Getis (1995) provide a measure of significance for G_i^* values (here, for a dataset of this size, significant values should be $> \sim|3.72|$), but many of our mapped participants do not reach this level. Nonetheless, the maps can provide useful visual clues to fine-grained regional patterns and we see the G_i^* scores as a tool for better understanding our data regardless of the degree of significance of the values obtained. Figure 3 displays the G_i^* scores for /e/~/ɛ/ in the dynamic post-bilabial context, Figure 4 displays the scores for /ʌ/~/o/ in the dynamic post-alveolar context, and Figure 5 displays the scores for /ɪ/~/u/ in the dynamic post-bilabial context. Maps of static scores pattern similarly but, as stated above, are not included for sake of space. Again, while none of the PCs yielded significant Moran's I values, Fig-

Table 2: Results for Moran's I tests. - denotes not significant; ~ denotes 0.1 > p > 0.05; * denotes $p < 0.05$; ** denotes $p < 0.0025$ (Bonferroni corrected significant p value); *** denotes $p < 0.00001$

	Bilabial		Alveolar	
Continuum	Dynamic	Static	Dynamic	Static
/i/ ~ /ɪ/	-	-	~	-
/e/ ~ /ɛ/	**	**	-	*
/æ/ ~ /ɑ/	-	-	~	*
/ʌ/ ~ /o/	-	-	**	**
/ɪ/ ~ /u/	***	***	-	-
PC1		~		
PC2		-		
PC3		-		

ure 6 shows the G_i^* scores for PC1, which helpfully capture some of the larger patterns across the maps.

4.2 Discussion

To a large degree, the Getis-Ord maps demonstrate that speakers within traditionally defined dialect regions often pattern perceptually similarly to each other. Altogether, however, the maps also suggest some finer-grained patterns of interest. We see in these maps that perceptual similarity is not simply aligned with traditional regional divisions – there are a number of intra-regional and cross-regional perceptual clusters. It must be remembered, however, that the mapped patterns are based on heterogeneous samples across the U.S. (with large clusters of participants in areas around Reno, NV, Oswego, NY, and Memphis, TN). Though strong generalizations cannot be made from our data at this point, we can, however, point to some suggestive findings.

First, throughout the maps we see a visual break between our participants in Southern California and those from the rest of the West Coast. We also notice that in all the maps, California and Nevada speakers appear to cluster together more than they cluster with other areas in the West. Figures 3, 4, and 5 all show less clustering with the Pacific Northwest region in particular (as well as several Inland Western states such as Colorado, Wyoming, and Idaho). Similarly, while

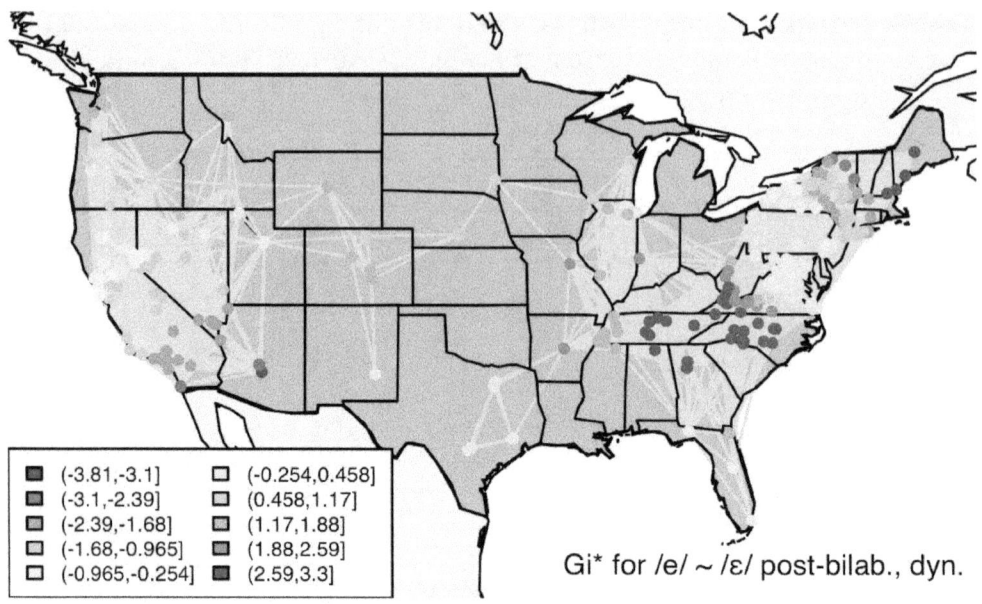

Figure 3: Getis-Ord G_i^* z score values for /e/~/ɛ/ in the dynamic post-bilabial context.

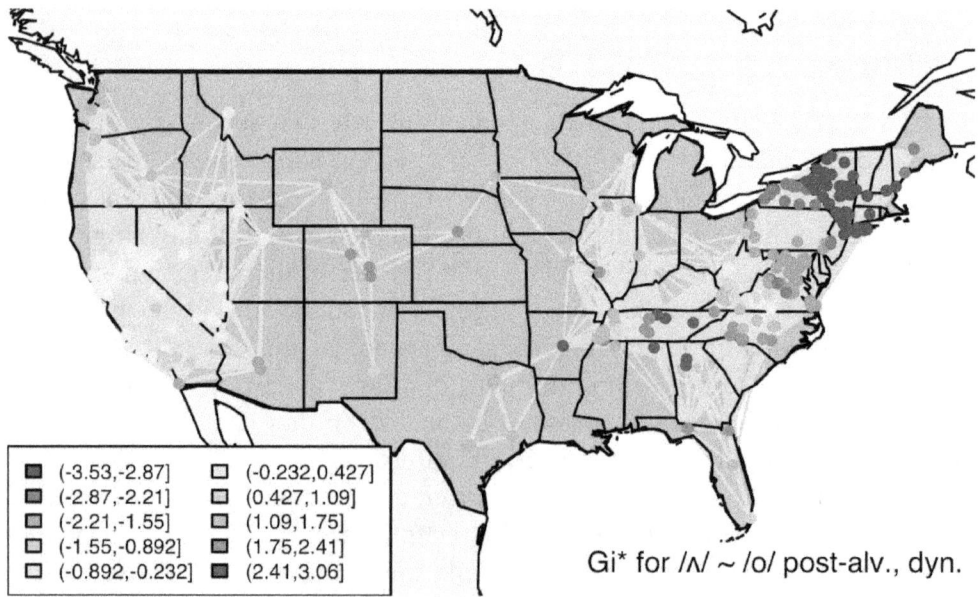

Figure 4: Getis-Ord G_i^* z score values for /ʌ/~/o/ in the dynamic post-alveolar context.

10   Mapping the perception of linguistic form

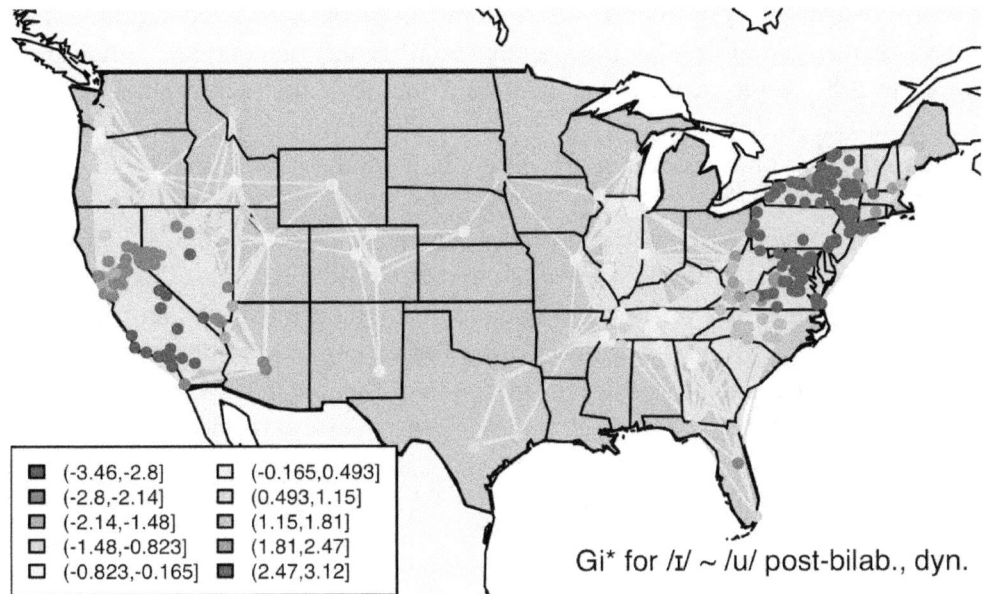

Figure 5: Getis-Ord G_i^* z score values for /ɪ/~/u/ in the dynamic post-bilabial context.

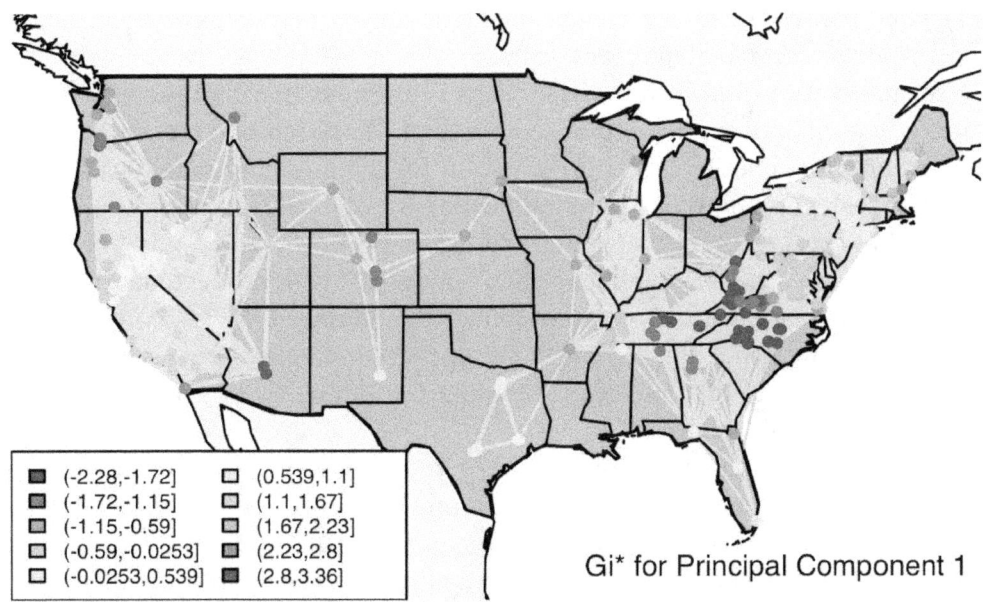

Figure 6: Getis-Ord G_i^* z score values for Principal Component 1.

our cross-over analysis reported earlier in this paper displayed significant differences overall mainly with the way our Southerners perceptually behave compared to other regions, we see in Figures 3, 4, and 6, that sub-regional clusters in the Eastern U.S. and among our Southern site participants suggest that more subtle intra-regional differences in perceptual behavior may also be important to explore.

Looking at these maps without preconceived regional boundaries would lead one to a somewhat different view of shared perceptual behavior than one takes away from imposing traditional dialectological constructs based on production (as we have done in our previous work). For example, although often lumped together according to production norms such as the low back vowel merger into one "Western dialect" region (e.g. in *ANAE*), our Western participants show substantial differences in perceptual clustering. Such clustering is suggestive that dialect, as conceived perceptually, may indeed need to be explored as something different than that of dialect expressed in production, as suggested by Sumner and Samuel's (2009) work. In other words, while "regional" clustering in perception is clear in these maps, perceptual patterns generally fall into smaller clusters than the macro-level regional groups we might assume based on broader generalizations, as we discuss a bit more below. Certainly, while production differences within, in addition to across, regions have been noted in dialectological work, pan-regional vowel shifts, characterizing wide swaths of regions, have been widely researched in recent years.

What emerges overall from these maps is an indication that perceptual similarity and difference may not so cleanly align with traditional dialect regions (based on production), despite the fact that we often impose region as a superordinate categorizing tool. As mentioned above, the Getis-Ord maps generally show that speakers in our sites in the West and the South are not perceptually unified in a way that we might expect given claims about production tendencies (e.g. such as the California Vowel Shift or the Southern Vowel Shift) in those regions (Labov, Ash & Boberg 2006). While these differences are necessarily putative at this point, they do suggest that perception needs to play a role in our understanding of dialect.

Though beyond the scope of this paper to consider in detail, it may be that many of these perceptual differences, like production differences, correlate with historical migratory and settlement patterns. For example, the history of Southern Californian speech influences does stand in contrast with that of Northern California, owing to greater Southern and Spanish influence. In addition, geographic boundaries effectively limited early North-South travel along the West

Coast, leading to sharp differences in lexical patterns in traditional dialect maps for the area (Bright 1967; Reed & Reed 1972). Nonetheless, what is intriguing in the mapping of our perception study results using geospatial techniques is that we can see such influences affecting how sounds are heard, not just produced.

Likewise, perceptual clusters of speakers are also notable within the South – in parts of Middle and Eastern Tennessee and in inland North Carolina and Virginia – which suggest these participants hear the perceptual continuum more similarly than other residents of their own states. For example, our subjects from Memphis (Western Tennessee) show different perceptual tendencies than subjects from Eastern Tennessee. This could partly reflect early settlement patterns and, importantly, contemporary migratory differences within the state. It is perhaps not surprising that such differences emerge, but it reinforces our sense that people use dialect variation to establish place rather than place establishing dialect.

However, we end here and do not attempt to elucidate the reasons for these differences more deeply as to do so would be too speculative at this stage. What is clear is that perception, like production, is a place-based phenomenon, with place here reflecting geo-social similarity and not just superimposed regional categorization. While our preliminary analysis has been suggestive of areas within our data we plan to explore more deeply, our goal here has been a more general one – to assess the benefit of looking at perceptual data using geospatial analysis.

5 Conclusion

Overall, this investigation has shown that dialectometry has a lot to offer the investigation of regional patterns in perception. We gain new insights in the perception of linguistic form by assessing the geospatial patterns of the responses made by participants in perception experiments. The clusters appear to not simply align with regionally demarking isoglosses coming from more traditional dialect surveys, or even the recent phonological survey of *The Atlas of North American English* (Labov, Ash & Boberg 2006).

While the visual patterns in the maps of Figures 3-6 are suggestive of finer regional patterns in perception than we have previously considered, it must be remembered that these patterns are only suggestive. Further analysis and more regionally diverse and balanced data are needed to assess the extent to which these clusters are meaningfully different from one another. We hope that this further analysis will involve increased use of techniques from dialectometry so that we can better assess the extent to which isoglosses in perception align with those in production.[3]

Acknowledgements

This research has been supported by grants # BCS-0518264 & BCS-1123460 (PI Fridland), and BCS-1122950 (PI Kendall) from the National Science Foundation. We thank Craig Fickle and Charlie Farrington at the University of Oregon, and Sohei Okamoto and Kaylynn Gunter at the University of Nevada, Reno, for support with various aspects of this research. We also thank our audience at Methods in Dialectology XV, the editors, and the three anonymous reviewers for their helpful advice about our project.

References

Allbritten, Rachael. 2011. *Sounding Southern: Phonetic features and dialect perceptions*. Washington, D.C.: Georgetown University PhD dissertation.
Bivand, Robert. 2014a. *Creating neighbours. Spdep R Package Vignette*.
Bivand, Robert. 2014b. *spdep. R Package*. et al.
Bright, Elizabeth. 1967. *A word geography of California and Nevada*. Berkeley: University of California, Berkeley PhD dissertation.
Carver, Craig M. 1987. *American regional dialects: A word geography*. Ann Arbor: University of Michigan Press.
Chambers, J. K. & Peter Trudgill. 1998. *Dialectology*. 2nd edn. Cambridge, New York: Cambridge University Press.
Clopper, Cynthia & David Pisoni. 2004. Some acoustic cues for the perceptual categorization of American English regional dialects. *Journal of Phonetics* 32(1). 111–140.

---

[3] Although we leave most of this further analysis for the future, we have begun to follow up on the pattern observed from the Getis-Ord analysis that Southern California differs from the rest of the West Coast. A linear regression on just participants from the West Coast (participants from longitudes west of -116.54°, the longitude of our east-most Californian participant) indeed identifies a significant relationship between latitude coordinate and e.g. perception of the /e/~/ɛ/ dynamic post-bilabial continuum (coef=0.1278, $p < 0.05$) and conditional inference trees find significant breaks at about latitude 39° for many of the continua. We also find significant differences for sub-groupings of West Coast participants based on several separations of these participants into "North" and "South" West Coast based on the visual differences in Figures 3-6.

Clopper, Cynthia & David Pisoni. 2007. Free classification of regional dialects of American English. *Journal of Phonetics* 35(3). 421–438.

Evans, Betsy. 2013. Seattle to Spokane: Mapping perceptions of English in Washington State. *Journal of English Linguistics* 41. 268–291.

Evans, Bronwen & Paul Iverson. 2004. Vowel normalization for accent: An investigation of best exemplar locations in northern and southern British English sentences. *The Journal of the Acoustical Society of America* 115(1). 352–361.

Fridland, Valerie & Tyler Kendall. 2012. Exploring the relationship between production and perception in the mid front vowels of U.S. English. *Lingua* 122(7). 779–793.

Fridland, Valerie, Tyler Kendall & Charlie Farrington. 2014. Durational and spectral differences in American English vowels: Dialect variation within and across regions. *Journal of the Acoustical Society of America* 136(1). 341–349.

Grieve, Jack. 2009. *A corpus-based regional dialect survey of grammatical variation in written Standard American English*. Flagstaff: Northern Arizona University PhD dissertation.

Grieve, Jack. 2014. A comparison of statistical methods for the aggregation of regional linguistic variation. In Benedikt Szmrecsanyi & Bernhard Wälchli (eds.), *Aggregating dialectology, typology, and register analysis: Linguistic variation in text and speech* (Lingua & Litterae 28), 53–88. Berlin, New York: Walter de Gruyter.

Grieve, Jack, Dirk Speelman & Dirk Geeraerts. 2011. A statistical method for the identification and aggregation of regional linguistic variation. *Language Variation and Change* 23(2). 193–221.

Grieve, Jack, Dirk Speelman & Dirk Geeraerts. 2013. A multivariate spatial analysis of vowel formants in American English. *Journal of Linguistic Geography* 1(1). 31–51.

Hay, Jennifer & Katie Drager. 2010. Stuffed toys and speech perception. *Linguistics* 48(4). 865–892.

Hay, Jennifer, P. Warren & Katie Drager. 2006. Factors influencing speech perception in the context of a merger-in-progress. *Journal of Phonetics* 34(4). 458–484.

Kendall, Tyler & Valerie Fridland. 2010. Mapping production and perception in regional vowel shifts. *Penn Working Papers in Linguistics* 16(2).

Kendall, Tyler & Valerie Fridland. 2012. Variation in perception and production of mid front vowels in the U.S. Southern Vowel Shift. *Journal of Phonetics* 40(2). 289–306.

Kendall, Tyler & Valerie Fridland. in progress. The production and perception of low vowels in U.S. English: A cross-regional view.

Labov, William & Sharon Ash. 1997. Understanding Birmingham. In Cynthia G. Bernstein, Thomas Nunnally & Robin Sabino (eds.), *Language variety in the South revisited*, 508–573. Tuscaloosa: University of Alabama Press.

Labov, William, Sharon Ash & Charles Boberg. 2006. *The atlas of North American English: Phonetics, phonology and sound change*. Berlin, New York: Mouton de Gruyter.

Lee, Jay & William A. Kretzschmar. 1993. Spatial analysis of linguistic data with GIS functions. *International Journal of Geographical Information Systems* 7(6). 541–560.

Moran, P. A. P. 1950. Notes on continuous stochastic phenomena. *Biometrika* 37(1-2). 17–23.

Nerbonne, John. 2009. Data-driven dialectology. *Language and Linguistics Compass* 3(1). 175–198.

Nerbonne, John & William A. Kretzschmar. 2003. Introducing computational methods in dialectometry. *Computers and the Humanities* 37(3). 245–255.

Niedzielski, Nancy. 1999. The effect of social information on the perception of sociolinguistic variables. *Journal of Language and Social Psychology* 18(1). 62–85.

Niedzielski, Nancy & Dennis Preston. 1999. *Folk linguistics*. Berlin, New York: Mouton de Gruyter.

Ord, J. Keith & Arthur Getis. 1995. Local spatial autocorrelation statistics: Distributional issues and an application. *Geographical Analysis* 27(4). 286–306.

Plichta, Bartek & Dennis Preston. 2005. The /ay/s have it: The perception of /ay/ as a North-South stereotype in U.S. English. *Acta Linguistica Hafniensia* 37. 243–285.

Preston, Dennis. 1989. *Perceptual dialectology nonlinguists' views of areal linguistics*. Dordrecht: Foris Publications.

Preston, Dennis. 1993. Folk dialectology. In Dennis Preston (ed.), *American dialect research*, 333–377. Amsterdam, Philadelphia: Benjamins.

Preston, Dennis. 1996. Where the worst English is spoken. In Edgar Schneider (ed.), *Focus on the USA*, 297–360. Amsterdam: Benjamins.

Reed, Carroll E. & David W. Reed. 1972. Problems of English speech mixture in California and Nevada. In A. Davis (ed.), *Studies in linguistics in honor of Raven I. McDavid*, 135–143. Auburn: University of Alabama Press.

Strand, Elizabeth A. 1999. Uncovering the role of gender stereotypes in speech perception. *Journal of Language and Social Psychology* 18(1). 86–100.

Strange, Winifred. 1995. Cross-language studies of speech perception: A historical review. In Winifred Strange (ed.), *Speech perception and linguistic experience: Issues in cross-language research*, 3–48. Baltimore: York Press.

Sumner, Megan & Arthur G. Samuel. 2009. The effect of experience on the perception and representation of dialect variants. *Journal of Memory and Language* 60(4). 487–501.

Szmrecsanyi, Benedikt. 2012. *Grammatical variation in British English dialects a study in corpus-based dialectometry*. Cambridge, New York: Cambridge University Press.

Thomas, Erik R. 2002. Sociophonetic applications of speech perception experiments. *American Speech* 77(2). 115–147.

van Bezooijen, Renée & Charlotte Gooskens. 1999. Identification of Language Varieties: The Contribution of Different Linguistic Levels. *Journal of Language and Social Psychology* 18(1). 31–48.

Chapter 11

Horizontal and vertical variation in Swiss German morphosyntax

Philipp Stoeckle
University of Zürich

> This paper deals with the question of how areas with different syntactic variability can be identified. It uses data from the *Syntactic Atlas of German-speaking Switzerland* (SADS) which uses multiple informants in each survey location. As a starting point the well-known doubling construction with the verb *aafange* 'begin' is used to illustrate how the different regions differ with respect to inter-personal variation and how the different variants can be mapped in terms of predominance, i.e. to what extent they co-occur or compete with the other variants. As a quantitative measure, the intensity value of the dominant variant (i.e. the agreement rate between those informants providing the dominant variant as their variant) is used as the basis to create a so-called "variation index". This technique is applied to a larger set of SADS data, and the results are mapped onto the survey points indicating the syntactic variability for each location. To assess the validity of the method, several subgroups are created which turn out to correlate with the whole data set at a significant level. By performing a hot spot analysis, regional clusters of high/low syntactic variability can be identified.

1 Introduction

In traditional dialectological surveys, linguistic variation has been viewed as one-dimensional, i.e. the only level of interest has been the geographical level. The main focus of most atlas projects[1] was documentation, since researchers aimed at investigating the old base dialects. Therefore, only one speaker – who was assumed to represent the dialect in its most original form – was interviewed at each location. While these atlases generally provide a very profound and extensive overview of the traditional linguistic structurings of the areas under inves-

---

[1] An exception would be the *Mittelrheinischer Sprachatlas* (MRhSA; 'Linguistic Atlas of the Middle Rhine'; Bellmann, Herrgen & Schmidt 1994–2002), for which informants with different social backgrounds were taken into account.

Philipp Stoeckle. 2016. Horizontal and vertical variation in Swiss German morphosyntax. In Marie-Hélène Côté, Remco Knooihuizen & John Nerbonne (eds.), *The future of dialects*, 195–215. Berlin: Language Science Press.
DOI:10.17169/langsci.b81.150

tigation, sociolinguistic findings as well as everyday experience suggest that the equation *one place = one variety* does not correspond to linguistic reality, rather we find inter- and even intra-speaker variation at single locations.

A second observation regarding traditional dialect atlases is that (morpho-) syntax has often been largely excluded from surveys. As for the *Sprachatlas der deutschen Schweiz* (*SDS*; 'Linguistic Atlas of German-speaking Switzerland', Hotzenköcherle 1962–1997), only seven maps (0.8%; Bucheli Berger & Glaser 2002: 42) depict syntactic phenomena. The main objections raised by traditional dialectologists were that syntactic phenomena of dialects do not show any geographical distribution and that dialect syntax basically is the syntax of spoken language and thus does not display many differences to the spoken standard language (Löffler 2003: 109).

However, in recent years a growing interest in the study of dialect syntax can be observed, initiated by theoretical linguists who discovered dialects as an ideal empirical basis for the study of microvariation (Kayne 1996). As a result, a number of projects in many different countries were initialized.[2] One of these projects is the *Syntaktischer Atlas der deutschen Schweiz* (*SADS*; 'Syntactic Atlas of German-speaking Switzerland'; Bucheli Berger & Glaser 2002) which provides the data for my analyses in this paper. In contrast to many of the aforementioned traditional atlas projects, in the SADS survey multiple informants were investigated at each location. This gives us the opportunity to analyze syntactic variation not only on one dimension, i.e. on the horizontal level (*between* locations), but to include the vertical level (*between* informants *at* single locations) as a second dimension.[3]

From a theoretical perspective, the concept of variation is important in (at least) two respects: On the one hand, it is seen in a close relationship with language change and is often regarded as an indicator thereof. However, it is not clear whether variation is to be seen as a precondition for language change or as its consequence (Glaser 2014: 39–40) — or if both cases are possible, depending on the linguistic phenomenon and the extra-linguistic context. On the other hand (and closely connected to the first aspect), in recent years there have been

---

[2] The Edisyn (*European Dialect Syntax*) website gives an overview of recent projects on dialect syntax (http://www.dialectsyntax.org/wiki/Welcome [accessed November 2014]).

[3] It should be noted that my approach resembles, to a certain degree, the concept of "two-dimensionality" taken in the MRhSA (Bellmann 1997). While the selection of speakers was more systematic in the MRhSA since informants from two groups of clearly defined social backgrounds were interviewed, in my analysis I deal with multiple informants at each location. This means that for now inter-speaker variation is examined regardless of the informants' social backgrounds.

11 Horizontal and vertical variation in Swiss German morphosyntax

more and more attempts to integrate the concept of variation into syntactic theory (Cornips & Corrigan 2005). The central question guiding this approach is whether variation or optionality can be assumed an inherent part of grammar (Seiler 2008) or have to be generally excluded, in which case variation would be the result of (different) competing grammars (Kroch 1994; cf. Henry 2002 for a general discussion of that matter). While in the first case variation could be seen as "Normalzustand" ('normal state'; Seiler 2008: 56), thus providing a basis for language change, in the latter case variation would be a reflex of change "proceed[ing] via competition between grammatically incompatible options which substitute for one another in usage" (Kroch 1994: 180).

The goal of this paper is to take a closer look at interpersonal variation and to classify the whole research area into regions according to this variation. For this purpose, a variation index will be developed. While the focus of this paper is on the methodology, the measure of variation will nevertheless provide a useful tool for dealing with the theoretical issues described above, and it will help us answer the following questions: Which regions show the most variation and which regions show only little variation? Can a high degree of variability be regarded as an indicator for *dynamism* or *modernism*, and does little variation indicate a linguistically *static* or *conservative* situation? How do the resulting geographic patterns correlate with other findings from Swiss-German dialectology? The answers to these questions shall help us gain a better understanding of speech variation, linguistic change and the relationship between them.

2 An example from the Syntactic Atlas of German-speaking Switzerland (*SADS*)

Before I illustrate the syntactic variability on the basis of one phenomenon, I will provide a quick overview of the database. The SADS project was funded by the Swiss National Science Foundation between the years 2000 and 2008 and was extended through the end of 2014. The survey was conducted using four written questionnaires including 118 questions on 54 different syntactic variables. These questionnaires were sent to informants in 383 locations which were chosen as a subset of the 600 places included in the SDS survey. The goal was to include ten informants at each location: men and women, different age groups and all kinds of professions (Bucheli Berger & Glaser 2002: 52). Apart from the general requirement of localness, the informants were not acquired systematically, so their numbers as well as their socio-demographic backgrounds are not evenly distributed over the research area. Finally, a total of 3187 informants (i.e. an average of 8 informants per location) could be included in the survey. Since not all of them were able to complete all four questionnaires (due to lack of time, migration, illness or death), a total of 2770 informants answered the whole series of questionnaires (Bucheli Berger 2008: 33). For the elicitation of the data, different question types were used: *translation* from the standard language into the informants' dialect, *completion* with a dialectal beginning of a sentence which was to be completed, and *multiple choice* with several given answers from among which the participants could indicate which ones they would accept and which they would prefer.[4]

The following example refers to the syntax of the verb *anfangen* ('to begin'). In Swiss German, the verb *anfangen* (or, in its dialectal form, *aafaa*) belongs to a group of verbs which allow for (or, in some areas, require) a repetition of a reduced form of the verb when governing an infinitive.[5] In the SADS questionnaires, six items addressed the syntax of the verb *anfangen*. Example (1) from the SADS (see below) illustrates the replacement of the particle *an* by the reduced infinitival form AFA.

(1) [dann] fängt das Eis AFA schmelzen.
     [then] begins the ice BEGIN melt.
     'Then the ice begins to melt.'

The main interest in the SADS survey regarding this phenomenon was to investigate in which regions the doubling of AFA[6] would occur and whether it was exclusive or optional. The respective task for the informants was to translate the following sentence into their own dialect (this was the first question of the third questionnaire):

Wenn es so warm bleibt, fängt das Eis an zu schmelzen! ('If it stays this warm, the ice will begin to melt.')

Altogether 2835 answers given by 2761 informants could be used,[7] among which the most frequent were the following:

---

[4] For more information cf. the project website: http://www.ds.uzh.ch/dialektsyntax/ [accessed November 2014].
[5] The other verbs are *gehen* ('to go'), *kommen* ('to come') and *lassen* ('to let'). For more information on the phenomenon cf. Glaser & Frey (2011) and Lötscher (1993).
[6] This is a rather simplified description of the phenomenon as it could be argued that it is rather the element *-fa* which is doubled than the whole form AFA. For more details about the occurrence of AFA in different syntactic contexts cf. Andres (2011).
[7] In very few cases the answers could not be included since the informants had not understood the purpose of the questionnaire properly.

11 Horizontal and vertical variation in Swiss German morphosyntax

1. ... *fängt das Eis an (zu) schmelzen* (begins the ice PART (to) melt; 'the ice begins to melt'; 1417 answers)[8]

2. ... *fängt das Eis AFA schmelzen* (begins the ice BEGIN melt; 959 answers)

3. ... *schmilzt das Eis* (melts the ice; 'the ice melts'; 403 answers)

4. ...[9]

Obviously the variant without AFA, which also corresponds to the standard variant, is the most widespread in German-speaking Switzerland, followed by the variant where AFA replaces the particle *an*. It is noticeable that there is also a third variant (... *schmilzt das Eis*) which makes up 14.2% of all answers and which does not involve the lexeme *anfangen* at all. In the following we will take a look at the geographic distributions of the two most frequent variants. For the creation of the maps as well as for the geostatistical analyses I used the Geographic Information System ArcGIS, a program which has proven to be of great use in linguistic geography since it allows for working with georeferenced data and provides a wide range of tools for analyzing geographically distributed phenomena (Montgomery & Stoeckle 2013; Stoeckle 2014). The data were visualized using a Voronoi diagram instead of point symbols, a technique that is well-known in dialectometry (Goebl 2010; Nerbonne 2010). In the case of the data analyzed here this has the advantage that small value differences between neighboring locations can be perceived more easily. Figure 1 depicts the geographical distribution of the most frequent variant ... *fängt das Eis an (zu) schmelzen*.

The different color hues indicate the percentage of informants at each place who provided the respective translation in the questionnaire. As the map suggests, the form is clearly dominant in the eastern part of Switzerland where we find an agreement of almost 100% of informants in many locations. Moreover, the map shows that the variant seems to be used almost all over the research area apart from some locations in the center and in the west. For a comparison we will consider the distribution of the variant ... *fängt das Eis AFA schmelzen* which is displayed in Figure 2.

As for the AFA variant, we can observe a concentration in the center and (north)western parts of Switzerland, while it is not used at all in the east. A direct comparison of Figures 1 and 2 reveals that in large parts of German-speaking

---

[8] Only 138 of these translations were realized with the infinitival particle *zu*, 1279 were realized without it.

[9] Among the less frequent variants which are not listed here were translations using a periphrastic *do*-construction or the future tense.

Philipp Stoeckle

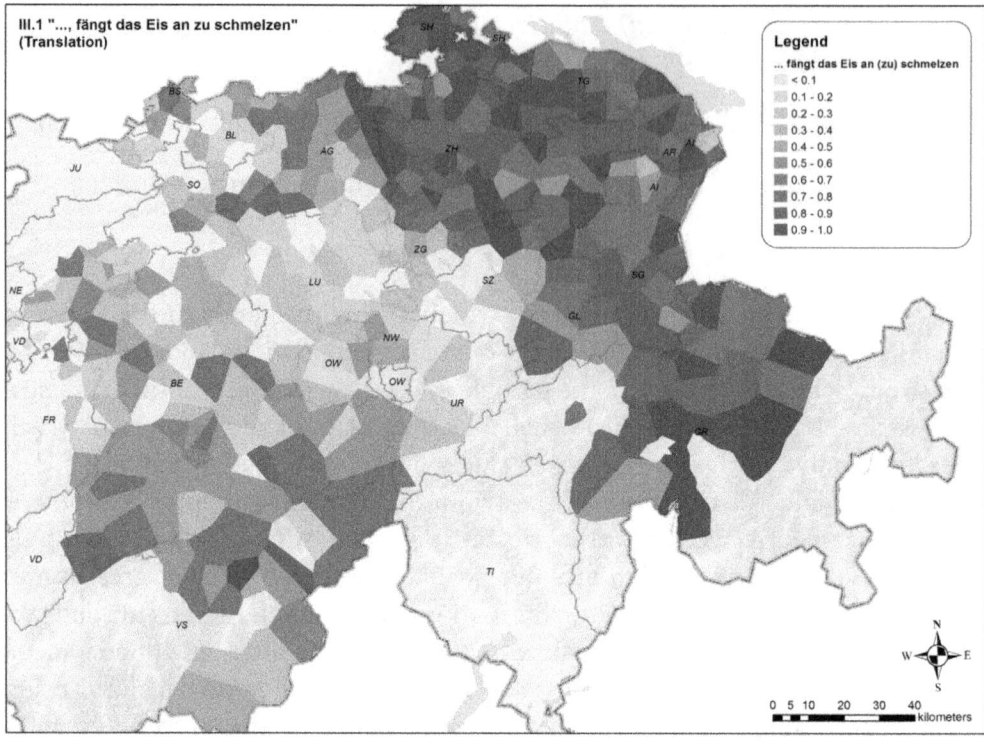

Figure 1: Geographical distribution of the variant ... *fängt das Eis an (zu) schmelzen*.

Switzerland – especially center and west – both variants can be observed, whereas particularly in the east just one variant seems to be used exclusively. At this point we have gained a very precise idea of the distributions of the two variants separately. However, it is difficult to tell what their relationship looks like, especially in the areas where both variants are used. For this purpose I combined both variants on a single map (Figure 3), the dominant variant, i.e. the variant that was provided by the most informants, at each location.

Four things can be observed in Figure 3: First, the dominant variants do not seem to be distributed randomly, rather they seem to shape areas. Especially in the central and (north-)western parts of Switzerland it becomes clear that the variant ... *fängt das Eis AFA schmelzen* appears to be the predominant form – an observation that could hardly be made by regarding the individual maps. Second, the variant ... *schmilzt das Eis* ('the ice melts') is dominant in only seven scattered locations, although a separate look at its geographic distribution reveals that it

11 Horizontal and vertical variation in Swiss German morphosyntax

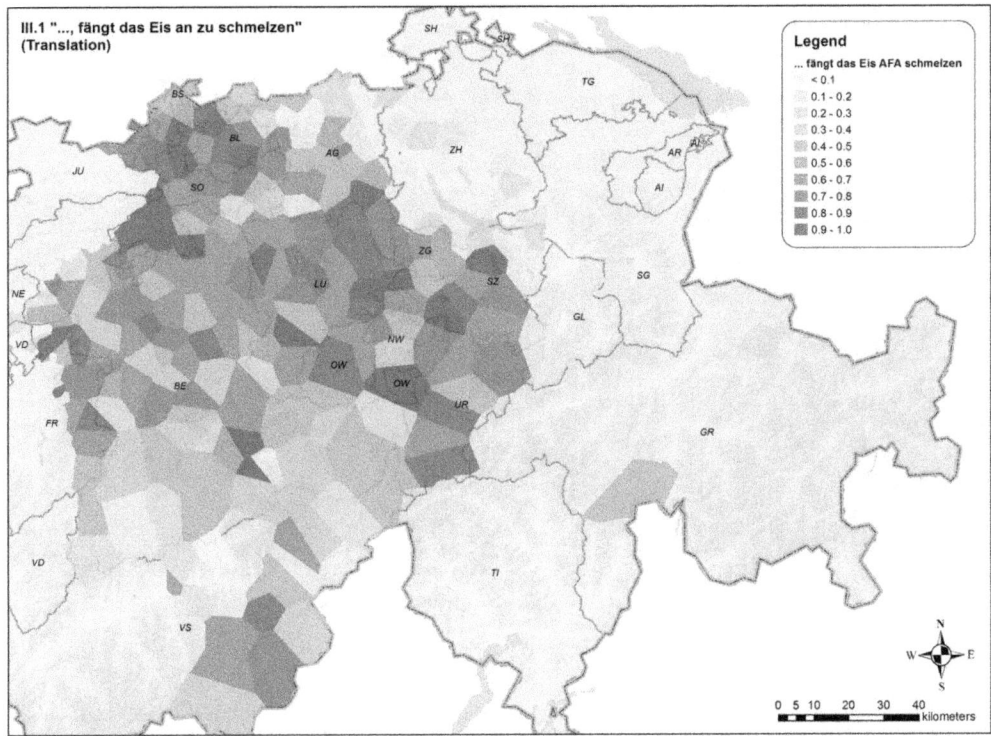

Figure 2: Geographical distribution of the variant ... *fängt das Eis* AFA *schmelzen*.

can be found in almost all parts of the research area. Third, some of the polygons are 'empty', i.e. none of the variants could be assigned to them. This is due to the fact that in these locations no single variant turned out to be dominant, but instead two forms were used by equal numbers of informants.

The fourth – and in this context most important – point regards the percentage values of the dominant variants. If our goal was, like in many 'traditional' approaches, to determine one form for each location, the most obvious procedure would be to choose the dominant variant. This way we would obtain a more or less clear east-west division of our research area with some exceptions in the southern Bernese (BE) area[10] and the canton of Wallis ('Valais', VS). However, if we take the percentage values of the dominant variants into account, it becomes obvious that this division would hide a lot of the linguistic reality. While in some locations we find very high rates of agreement, in other places the highest values for the dominant variant range between only 40 and 50 percent. This means

---

[10] The cantons are indicated by two-letter codes. In the case of the canton Bern, the code is BE.

Philipp Stoeckle

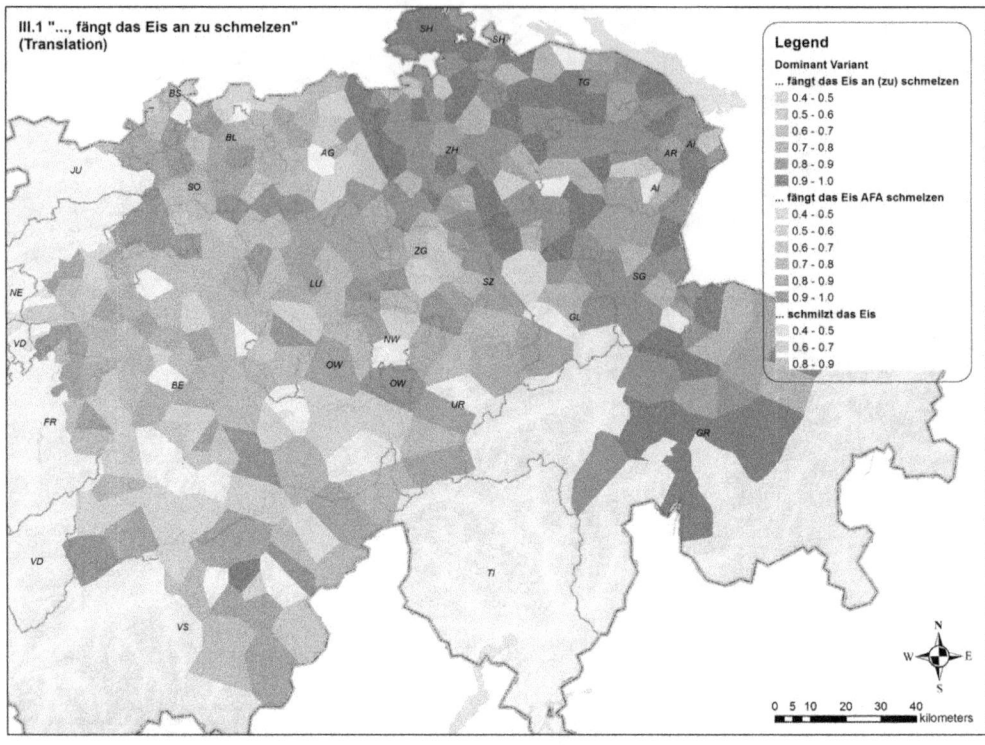

Figure 3: Geographic distribution of the dominant variants.

that there must be at least two or three (or even more) different forms given as translations by the informants.

If we abstract away from the variants themselves and only consider the agreement rate of the dominant variant at each location, we obtain a visualization as depicted in Figure 4. As the map shows, the agreement between the informants seems to be generally higher in the northern and eastern regions (at least for this question), whereas especially in the southern parts of the canton Bern (BE) there is very little agreement, i.e. comparatively, the informants differ greatly in their answers.

The analysis of this single phenomenon has shown that variation turns out to be very frequent once multiple informants are taken into account at one location. It also became obvious that in spite of all the variation, the geographic distribution of the different variants is not random but shows a rather characteristic pattern.[11] As a consideration of more and different phenomena from the

---

[11] Of course, this could be subject to further geostatistical testing.

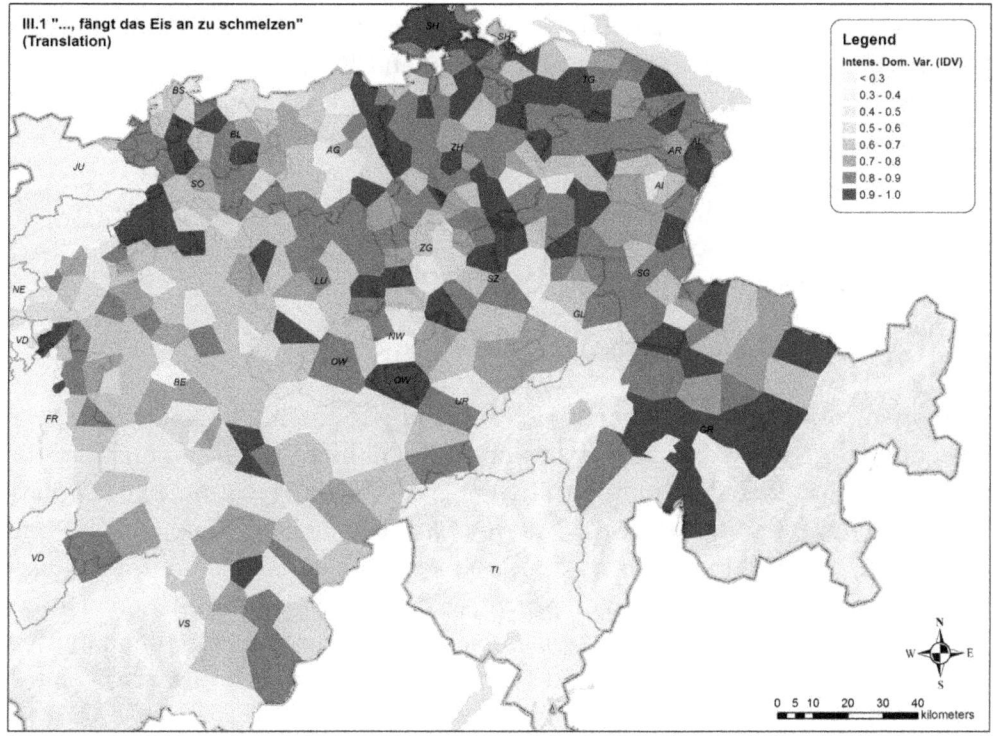

Figure 4: Intensity of the dominant variant.

SADS shows,[12] the observations made in this section do not hold only for this phenomenon but can be generalized for most syntactic variables. Although the geographic patterns are not always the same, some areas seem to display more variation than others. The goal of the following part will be to classify the research area into regions with respect to inter-speaker variation.

3 Variation Index

As the observations in the previous section have shown, the percentage of agreement between the informants regarding the dominant variant can be taken as an indicator for variation. If, for example, we find 100 percent agreement, this

---

[12] Examples of which would be word order variation in verb clusters (e.g. ... *ob er einmal heiraten will* vs. ... *ob er einmal will heiraten*, '... whether he ever wants to get married'; Seiler 2004) or prepositional dative marking (e.g. *Das gehört an/in meiner Schwester* vs. *Das gehört meiner Schwester*, 'It belongs to my sister'; Seiler 2003).

means that all informants gave the same answer and that there is, therefore, no variation at all. Agreement rates between 50 and 100 percent mean that there must be two variants (or more), agreement rates of less than 50 per cent point to at least three variants, and so on. Of course these percentage values do not provide information about the exact number of variants,[13] but they can give us an idea about variation in the following sense:

- high value ~ high agreement ~ little variation

- low value ~ little agreement ~ much variation

In order to classify the research area according to the inter-speaker syntactic variation at the individual survey locations, it will be necessary to quantify the agreement rates including multiple phenomena. At the present time not all questions which were part of the SADS survey have been edited completely, so that their inclusion in the analyses might have been problematic. Therefore a subset of 57 questions from the SADS comprising 26 different syntactic phenomena was chosen as data for the analyses. As a simple mathematical measure of quantification the arithmetic mean of all agreement rates for each location was calculated. We will call it *agreement index*, and it is defined as follows:[14]

$$AI = \frac{1}{n} \sum_{i=1}^{n} IDV_i \qquad (11.2)$$

where

- *IDV* stands for the *intensity of the dominant variant* (i.e. the agreement rate between those informants providing the dominant variant as *their* variant),

- each *i* stands for an individual question from the SADS,

- *n* is the total number of SADS questions taken into account.

---

[13] It should be noted that the total number of variants per phenomenon differs between two and eight. Although a higher total number does not automatically imply a higher inter-speaker variation at the individual locations (the different variants could theoretically be used in separate locations), this fact should be taken into account in a detailed analysis of the variability of the different phenomena. However, since we are primarily interested in the geographic distribution of inter-speaker variation, we can neglect these differences here.

[14] I am aware that the arithmetic mean is a very simple statistic measure which does not necessarily have to be quoted as mathematical formula. Nevertheless, it shall be presented here so that it is easier in the remainder of the article to refer to its elements.

11 Horizontal and vertical variation in Swiss German morphosyntax

Since our main focus is on variation rather than agreement and we would, therefore, like to obtain higher values for more variation and smaller values for less variation (and all values range between 0 and 1), we define our *variation index* as

$$VI = 1 - AI \qquad (11.3)$$

For a first impression of the geographic distribution, the variation indices are mapped to the SADS survey points, the result of which is displayed in Figure 5.

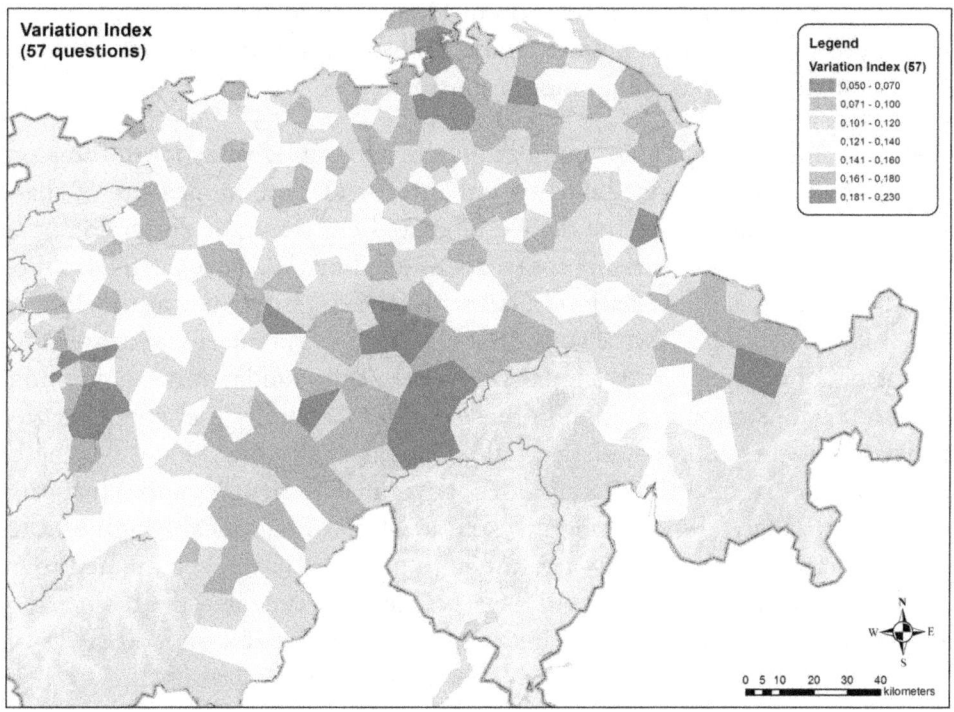

Figure 5: Geographic mapping of the *variation index* including 57 SADS questions.

The different colors indicate different degrees of variation (or agreement between the informants, respectively). Red colors stand for a high variation index, blue colors for low values. At first glance the pattern seems a bit fuzzy, but there are some concentrations of high and low variation observable. While in the north-east there are many blue and almost no red areas, the central part of Switzerland especially shows a clear concentration of high values. Moreover, there seem to be red clusters at the very western (canton of Fribourg, FR) and eastern (canton of Grisons, GR) borders. Although Figure 5 provides a general impression of the geographical pattern of syntactic variation, two questions remain:

1. To what degree is the variation index as displayed in Figure 5 a result of the choice of the SADS questions that were taken into account? Would the geographical pattern look different if we had used a different set of variables?

2. How much is our interpretation of Figure 5 influenced by intuition? Are there more elaborate ways to (statistically) confirm the observed geographical pattern, i.e. to obtain more robust results?

Let us first address question number two. In geography, questions of this type are addressed with the concept of spatial autocorrelation, "a measure of spatial dependency that quantifies the degree of spatial clustering or dispersion in the values of a variable measured across a set of locations" (Grieve 2011: 34). In our case, the variable is the variation index with its different values at the different SADS survey locations. If we assume that in some parts of our research area there are clusters of polygons with similar colors (and thus similar values), we should expect a positive autocorrelation in these parts.[15] Generally there are two types of spatial autocorrelation statistics: "global measures [which] identify whether the values of a variable exhibit a significant overall pattern of regional clustering", and "local measures [which] identify the location of significant high and low value clusters" (Grieve 2011: 34). While both methods have been applied to our data, for illustration purposes I will focus on the latter type in order to determine so-called *hot* and *cold* spots. For this purpose I used the Hot Spot Analysis tool in ArcGIS, which uses the Getis-Ord Gi* statistic (Getis & Ord 1992).

> [It] works by looking at each feature within the context of neighboring features. A feature with a high value is interesting but may not be a statistically significant hot spot. To be a statistically significant hot spot, a feature will have a high value and be surrounded by other features with high values as well.[16] (ESRI 2014)

---

[15] For a more detailed description of spatial autocorrelation and its application to SADS data cf. Sibler (2011: 62–63).

[16] For the exact reference cf. the ArcGIS online help "How Hot Spot Analysis (Getis-Ord Gi*) works": http://resources.arcgis.com/en/help/main/10.2/index.html#/How_Hot_Spot_Analysis_Getis_Ord_Gi_works/005p00000011000000/ [accessed November 2014]

11 Horizontal and vertical variation in Swiss German morphosyntax

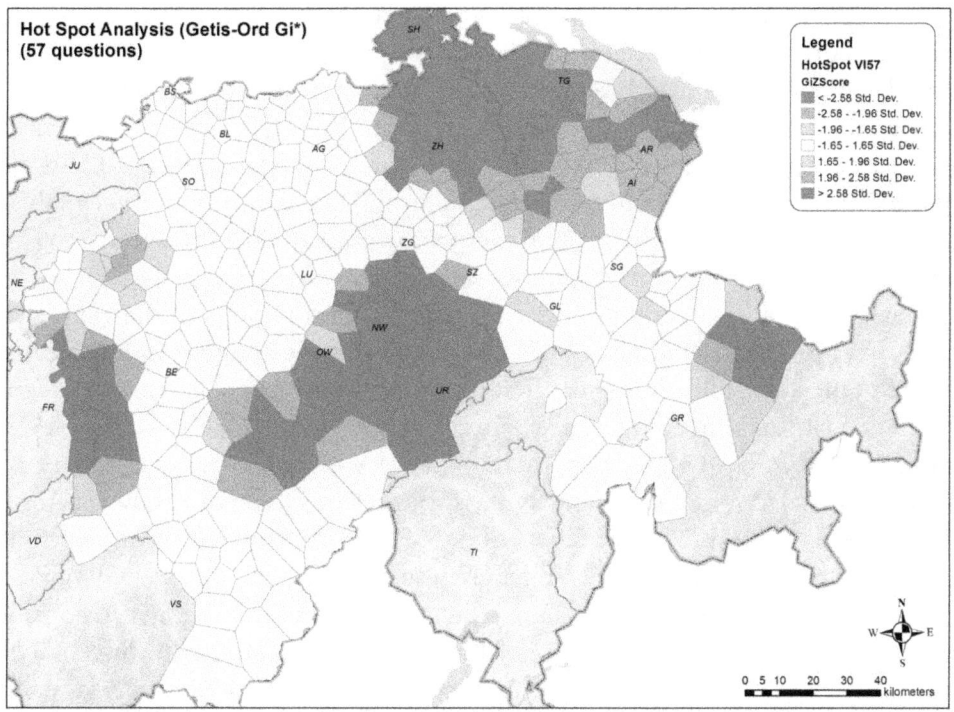

Figure 6: Hot Spot Analysis of the *variation index* (Getis-Ord Gi* statistic; fixed distance band; Euclidean distance; distance threshold: 17.4km).

As a result, for each location the analysis yields a z-score and a p-value, both of which are associated with standard normal distribution. Very high positive z-scores indicate a clustering of values which are higher than the mean value, thus building a hot spot (Sibler 2011: 65). In the case of our data the *VI* for every survey location is compared with all other *VI*s within a distance of 17.4km, a value computed automatically to ensure that each location has at least one neighbor.[17] If a location has a very high positive *VI* and the locations within the defined radius also have high *VI*s, it becomes part of a hot spot. In the opposite case (i.e. high negative values) we find a cold spot. Figure 6 displays the results mapped to the SADS survey locations in order to identify the hot and cold spots geographically.

The map confirms the impression we gained from observing Figure 5: In the north-east we find a cluster of low *VI* values or a cold spot (the blue areas), indi-

---

[17] The requirement of having at least one neighbor to be included in the analysis is especially important for the locations in the periphery. On average, there are twelve neighbors included within the radius of 17.4km for each location.

207

cating little variation or high agreement between the informants regarding their answers. Furthermore, there is a smaller cluster of blue polygons in the west. On the other hand, there are three hot spots, i.e. clusters of high *VI* values which indicate a lot of variation.[18] Of course, one has to be careful interpreting the results, since changes in the analysis settings (e.g. autocorrelation method, distance method, etc.) can yield slightly different pictures. However, as modified analyses of the same data show,[19] the general picture is very similar for each case: While agreement between the informants is rather high in the north-eastern region, especially central Switzerland but also the peripheral regions in the cantons of Fribourg and Grisons show a lot of variation. Before we engage in interpreting these findings, we will address the first question raised above, i.e. to what degree the choice of phenomena influences the results.

It is clear that the list of phenomena that were included in the SADS survey represents a selection of the many syntactic structures that could have been subject to linguistic research. Since the authors of the SADS put a lot of thought into the selection of relevant features (Bucheli Berger & Glaser 2002), we will not deal with this aspect of the question here. However, there is still the fact to consider that it was only possible to use 57 of the 118 SADS questions for our analysis of syntactic variation, a selection which could also have influenced the results. One way to deal with this problem is to build different subgroups of the dataset and see how much they correlate with the entire dataset. I therefore created six different subsets which are listed in the following:

- *VI reduced*: The idea for this subset was to create a balanced dataset that does not contain any questions that display very similar geographic patterns. For this purpose, the pairwise correlations for all *IDV*s were calculated. Finally, from the twelve pairs of questions with the highest correlations, one was omitted in each case, so that the subset consists of 45 instead of 57 SADS questions.

- *VI phenomena*: As previously mentioned, the 57 questions taken into account represent 26 different phenomena. In order to weight these phenomena equally, the arithmetic mean value was calculated for each of them. Therefore this subset consists of 26 phenomena.

---

[18] There is one more cold spot in the east. Since it only consists of two polygons, it will not be considered in the following.

[19] Besides the hot spot analysis, other techniques like cluster analysis using the local Moran's I value or Kriging interpolation were applied to the data.

- *VI M(ultiple) C(hoice)*: For this subset, all multiple choice questions (36 out of 57) were taken into account.

- *VI translation*: Analogously to *VI MC*, all translation questions (21 out of 57) were taken into account.

- *VI random 1 & 2*: Two subsets, each containing 30 randomly chosen questions, were created.

Each of these subgroups were correlated with VI all, i.e. the variation index that was calculated on the basis of all 57 questions. The results are shown in Table 1.

Table 1: Correlations between VI for all 57 phenomena and VIs for different subsets (Pearson method, p-values for all correlations <.001)

	VI reduced	VI phenomena	VI MC	VI translation	VI random 1	VI random 2
VI all	.91	.87	.83	.69	.84	.82

As the table shows, all correlations have high coefficients and are highly significant with p<.001. However, the correlations are not equally high: The subgroup *VI reduced* shows the highest coefficient, followed by *VI phenomena*, *VI random 1*, *VI MC*, *VI random 2* and *VI translation*. The different correlations are reflected in the respective geographic distributions, which show slight differences. Since the geographic patterns mainly differ with respect to the extensions of the hot and cold spots rather than their locations,[20] we can state that the general variation pattern – a low variation index in the north-east vs. a high variation index in the southern areas – holds for all our subsets. For a more detailed account of the little differences it would be necessary to take a closer look at the individual questions from the different subgroups and perform more qualitative analyses with them. Moreover, it should be noted that the methods used to create the subsets differ clearly from each other: While *VI reduced* and *VI random 1 & 2*

---

[20] There are some minor exceptions which cannot be dealt with here.

were created for statistical reasons, the basis for building *VI MC* and *VI translation* was the elicitation method used in the questionnaire. *VI phenomenon* was the only subset created on the basis of a linguistic classification. At this point it should be mentioned that it would be interesting to create further subgroups of that kind focusing on different grammatical domains such as NP, VP, word order etc. Of course, this would require more classification groundwork. The fact that different subsets of the data yield comparable results suggests that the variation index can be considered a quite stable measure for the syntactic variation in our research area.

4 Discussion

The starting point for this paper was the observation that dialectal variation can be analyzed not only on the geographical level, i.e. *between* locations, but also *within* locations, the latter being a merit of the SADS research design including multiple informants at each location. As the inspection of one phenomenon could show (and as many other studies of the SADS data have shown previously), variation occurs in many areas, but it does not appear to be chaotic. In order to get a grasp of the regional distribution of syntactic variation, the agreement rate between all informants at one place regarding the dominant variant was used to create a variation index. A quantification of this simple measure[21] and its mapping to the SADS survey locations showed a characteristic geographic pattern with very little variation in the north-east and a lot of variation in central Switzerland and the peripheral regions in the cantons of Fribourg (FR) and Grisons (GR). A correlation with different subsets of the data showed that the general variation pattern still holds if a reduced version of the dataset is used.

However, so far we haven't dealt with the question of how to interpret the findings. In many (socio)linguistic studies variation is regarded as an indicator for dynamism and linguistic change. In Swiss German dialectology the southern regions where most of our hot spots are located are generally considered rather conservative areas, whereas the north(east) is regarded as the part of Switzerland where the most innovations are found (Haas 2000). So how do these results fit with our findings? If variation is considered an indicator of linguistic dynamics, the geographic pattern of syntactic variation seems to contradict the general findings regarding Swiss German dialects. As a first step toward an explanation

---

[21] One could also think of more sophisticated measures like counting the actual number of occurring variants. However, these would have to be harmonized with the number of possible variants as well as with the number of informants in each case.

we take a closer look at our three hot spots in the south and consider their different geographic contexts. With respect to the two areas in the eastern and western peripheries, we can state that they are both located in linguistic contact zones: the majority of the canton of Fribourg belongs to the French-speaking area, while in the canton of Grisons Romansh and Italian are spoken in addition to German.[22] Linguistically, the latter canton is especially interesting since for historical reasons its German-speaking inhabitants either speak a high Alemannic dialect which spread from the northern regions around the Rhine Valley and the Lake of Constance or a so-called "Walser German" (named after the canton of Wallis), a dialect which was brought by settlers during the Walser migrations that started in the Middle Ages.

Our largest hot spot is located in the center of Switzerland. In the linguistic literature two major dialectal contrasts are generally assumed to be important: one between North and South, the other between East and West (Haas 2000: 61-67). Although these two divisions can be seen as generalizations of many linguistic differences with more or less similar geographic distributions, it is clear that central Switzerland is exposed to many different influences and is often seen as a dialectal transition zone.

If we take a closer look at our own data, we find that the areas with a high variation index – especially those located in the eastern and western peripheries – are those regions where in many cases very distinct variants can be found. Examples would be the missing article before personal names as in *Ich habe Ø Fritz gesehen*[23] ('I have seen Fritz'), or copredicative agreement as in *Fischstäbchen gefroren-e anbraten* (fish fingers:N.PL frozen:N.PL fry; 'to fry fish fingers frozen'; Bucheli Berger 2005). Interestingly, the latter variant is also found in the Wallis, often said to be the dialectally most conservative region in Switzerland. In contrast to the other southern areas, where this variant co-occurs with the other, more widespread 'common' form, in the Wallis it is the only variant.

Based on our findings, what conclusions can we draw regarding the dynamics of syntactic variation in German-speaking Switzerland? Our results suggest that variation and dynamism probably do not point to "modernism", since they are found in the conservative, southern dialect areas. Rather, it seems that many of the forms that are dominant in the north-east are spreading toward the traditional areas which are dynamically being exposed to a lot of variation. Whether

---

[22] Though an influence of the neighboring Romance languages seems obvious, further analyses would be necessary to provide evidence.

[23] Unlike standard German, the common variant used in most parts of German-speaking Switzerland is *Ich habe den Fritz gesehen* with a definite article.

the inter-speaker syntactic variation is 'stable', i.e. distinct variants and more widespread variants continue to co-exist, or can be seen as an indicator for language change, is not clear at the present (Glaser 2014) and will be subject to future research. For this purpose it will be helpful to take a closer look at the sociolinguistic variables and see whether there are indicators for apparent-time change. Moreover, it will be interesting to compare the SADS findings with results from other dialect syntax projects which also have more than one informant per location (e.g. the *Syntax hessischer Dialekte (SyHD)* 'Syntax of Hessian dialects'; Fleischer, Kasper & Lenz 2012).

Acknowledgements

This paper is a revised and extended version of a talk I gave at the Methods in Dialectology XV conference in Groningen (NL), August 2014. I would like to thank Elvira Glaser, Péter Jeszenszky and Gabriela Bart for their helpful comments, as well as three anonymous referees. Moreover, I would like to thank Stephanie Schwenke for correcting my English. All shortcomings are my own responsibility.

References

Andres, Marie-Christine. 2011. Die Verdoppelung beim Verb *afaa* im nord-östlichen Aargau. *Linguistik online* 45(1). 9–18.
Bellmann, Günter. 1997. Zur Technik und Aussagefähigkeit zweidimensionaler Dialekterhebung und Dialektkartographie am Beispiel des Mittelrheinischen Sprachatlasses. In Gerhard Stickel (ed.), *Varietäten des Deutschen. Regional- und Umgangssprachen*, 271–290. Berlin; New York: de Gruyter.
Bellmann, Günter, Joachim Herrgen & Jürgen Erich Schmidt. 1994–2002. *Mittelrheinischer Sprachatlas (MRhSA)*. 5 Bände. Tübingen: Niemeyer.
Bucheli Berger, Claudia. 2005. Depictive agreement and the development of a depictive marker in Swiss German dialects. In Nikolaus P. Himmelmann & Eva Schultze-Berndt (eds.), *Secondary predication and adverbial modification. The typology of depictives*, 141–171. Oxford: Oxford University Press.
Bucheli Berger, Claudia. 2008. Neue Technik, alte Probleme: Auf dem Weg zum Syntaktischen Atlas der Deutschen Schweiz (SADS). In Stephan Elspass & Werner König (eds.), *Sprachgeographie digital – die neue Generation der Sprachatlanten (mit 80 Karten)* (Germanistische Linguistik 190–191), 29–44. Hildesheim: Olms.

Bucheli Berger, Claudia & Elvira Glaser. 2002. The syntactic atlas of Swiss German dialects: Empirical and methodological problems. In Sjef Barbiers, Leonie Cornips & Susanne van der Kleij (eds.), *Syntactic microvariation*, 41–74. Amsterdam: Meertens Instituut (Meertens Institute Electronic Publications in Linguistics 2).

Cornips, Leonie & Karen P. Corrigan (eds.). 2005. *Syntax and variation. Reconciling the biological and the social.* Amsterdam/Philadelphia: John Benjamins.

Fleischer, Jürg, Simon Kasper & Alexandra N. Lenz. 2012. Die Erhebung syntaktischer phänomene durch die indirekte Methode: Ergebnisse und Erfahrungen aus dem Forschungsprojekt 'Syntax hessischer Dialekte' (SyHD). *Zeitschrift für Dialektologie und Linguistik* 79(1). 2–42.

Getis, Arthur & J. Keith Ord. 1992. The analysis of spatial association by use of distance statistics. *Geographical Analysis* 24(3). 189–206.

Glaser, Elvira. 2014. Wandel und Variation in der Morphosyntax der schweizerdeutschen Dialekte. *Taal en Tongval* 66(1). 21–64.

Glaser, Elvira & Natascha Frey. 2011. Empirische Studien zur Verbverdoppelung in schweizerdeutschen Dialekten. *Linguistik Online* 45(1). 3–7.

Goebl, Hans. 2010. Dialectometry and quantitative mapping. In Alfred Lameli, Roland Kehrein & Stefan Rabanus (eds.), *Language and space. An international handbook of linguistic variation*, vol. 2: Language Mapping, 433–457. Berlin: De Gruyter Mouton.

Grieve, Jack. 2011. The use of spatial autocorrelation statistics for the analysis of regional linguistic variation. In Amir Zeldes & Anke Lüdeling (eds.), *Proceedings of Quantitative Investigations in Theoretical Linguistics 4 (QITL-4)*, 34–37. Humboldt-Universität zu Berlin.

Haas, Walter. 2000. Die deutschsprachige Schweiz. In Hans Bickel & Robert Schläpfer (eds.), *Die viersprachige Schweiz*, 2nd edn., 57–74. Aarau: Sauerländer.

Henry, Alison. 2002. Variation and syntactic theory. In J. K. Chambers, Peter Trudgill & Natalie Schilling-Estes (eds.), *The handbook of language variation and change*, 267–282. Oxford: Blackwell.

Hotzenköcherle, Rudolf (ed.). 1962–1997. *Sprachatlas der deutschen Schweiz (SDS)*. Bern; Basel: Francke.

Kayne, Richard. 1996. Microparametric syntax: Some introductory remarks. In James R. Black & Virginia Motapanyane (eds.), *Microparametric syntax and dialect variation*, ix–xviii. Amsterdam/Philadelphia: John Benjamins.

Kroch, Anthony. 1994. Morphosyntactic Variation. In Katherine Beals (ed.), *Papers from the 30th Regional Meeting of the Chicago Linguistic Society*, vol. 2, 180–201. Chicago: Chicago Linguistic Society.

Löffler, Heinrich. 2003. *Dialektologie. Eine Einführung.* Tübingen: Narr.

Lötscher, Andreas. 1993. Zur Genese der Verbverdopplung bei *gaa, choo, laa* und *aafaa* ('gehen', 'kommen', 'lassen' und 'anfangen') im Schweizerdeutschen. In Werner Abraham & Josef Bayer (eds.), *Dialektsyntax,* 180–200. Opladen: Westdeutscher Verlag.

Montgomery, Chris & Philipp Stoeckle. 2013. Geographic information systems and perceptual dialectology: A method for processing draw-a-map data. *Journal of Linguistic Geography* 1(1). 52–85.

Nerbonne, John. 2010. Mapping aggregate variation. In Stephan Rabanus, Ronald Kehrein & Alfred Lameli (eds.), *Mapping Language,* vol. 2: Language Mapping. Part I, 476–495. Berlin: Mouton de Gruyter.

Seiler, Guido. 2003. *Präpositionale Dativmarkierung im Oberdeutschen.* Stuttgart: Steiner.

Seiler, Guido. 2004. On three types of dialect variation, and their implications for linguistic theory. Evidence from verb clusters in Swiss German dialects. In Bernd Kortmann (ed.), *Dialectology meets typology. Dialect grammar from a cross-linguistic perspective* (Trends in Linguistics. Studies and Monographs 153), 367–399. Berlin/New York: de Gruyter.

Seiler, Guido. 2008. Syntaxgeographie und die Plastizität der Grammatik. In Jean-Marie Valentin & Hélène Vinckel (eds.), *Akten des XI. Internationalen Germanistenkongresses Paris 2005,* 49–58. Bern: Peter Lang.

Sibler, Pius. 2011. *Visualisierung und geostatistische Analyse mit Daten des Syntaktischen Atlas der Deutschen Schweiz (SADS).* Zürich: University of Zurich, Department of Geography PhD thesis.

Stoeckle, Philipp. 2014. *Subjektive dialekträume im alemannischen dreiländereck.* Hildesheim: Olms.

Chapter 12

Infrequent forms: Noise or not?

Martijn Wieling
University of Groningen, CLCG

Simonetta Montemagni
Istituto di Linguistica Computazionale "Antonio Zampolli", ILC-CNR

> In this study we ask the question whether simplifying the data in dialectometrical studies by removing infrequent forms is advantageous to uncovering the geographical structure in dialect data. By investigating lexical variation in a large corpus of Tuscan dialect data via hierarchical bipartite spectral graph partitioning, we are able to identify the main geographical areas together with their linguistic basis. In order to assess the influence of infrequent forms, we conduct two analyses: one which includes only lexical variants used by at least 0.5% of the informants, and another which includes all lexical variants in the data. Using this approach we show that using all data enables us to find a geographical characterization with a more adequate linguistic basis than by using the trimmed data.

1 Introduction

Dialectometry (Séguy 1971; see Wieling & Nerbonne 2015 for an overview) proceeds from the idea that aggregating over a large set of linguistic items will yield a better view of dialectal variation than subjectively selecting a few linguistic items (Nerbonne 2009: 190–191). In quantitative linguistics, it is generally noted that infrequent words constitute noise, and are unreliable evidence of linguistic structure (Manning & Schütze 1999: 199). With respect to lexical differences in dialectology, this view is supported by Carver (1987: 17). In contrast to this, however, stands the opinion of Goebl (1984: Vol I: 83–86), who argues that infrequent words (i.e. word forms used by only a few informants) should be considered more informative (i.e. weighted more) when determining the strength of the linguistic relationship between two sites.

Supporting Goebl's (1984) view, Nerbonne & Kleiweg (2007) show that removing infrequent words results in less adequate linguistic distances than including

Martijn Wieling & Simonetta Montemagni. 2016. Infrequent forms: noise or not? In Marie-Hélène Côté, Remco Knooihuizen & John Nerbonne (eds.), *The future of dialects*, 215–224. Berlin: Language Science Press.
DOI:10.17169/langsci.b81.151

all data. Kretzschmar, Kretzschmar & Brockman (2013: 173) are also in favor of including infrequent elements and argue that "[methods in dialectology which only notice the few most frequently occurring variants and ignore the rest] cannot address the underlying complexity of the data."

At present, however, many researchers in dialectometry still ignore infrequent items under the presumption that these are noise. For example, Wieling, Upton & Thompson (2014) only use the top-ten most frequent variants for each concept in a study on English lexical variation, and Szmrecsanyi (2011) ignore infrequent items in a morpho-syntactic dialectometric study.

We believe that the contrasting views reported above are based on two different notions of word frequency, namely that of token and type frequency. Whereas Manning & Schütze (1999) refer to a notion of token frequency (i.e. counting how often a particular form appears in the input), frequency based on dialectal data gathered through questionnaires should be interpreted as type frequency (i.e. the number of distinct lexical items that can be substituted to express the same meaning). Bybee (2001) argues that type rather than token frequency underlies productivity, the diachronic consequence of which may be lexical enrichment. Following this line of reasoning, from a diatopic perspective we can hypothesize that type frequency is related to lexical variation. The question we started with can therefore be reformulated as follows: What is the role and impact of lexical type frequency in dialectometrical studies based on atlas data in uncovering the geographical structure underlying them? To answer this question, we will evaluate the effect of taking into account all data, versus ignoring lexical variants used in at least two locations by 10 informants or fewer (out of a total of 2060 informants).

2 Data

In this study, we investigate Tuscan lexical variation on the basis of the *Atlante Lessicale Toscano* (ALT, Giacomelli et al. 2000), available as an online resource (http://serverdbt.ilc.cnr.it/ALTWEB). The dialect data used in this study contains the results gathered in response to 170 onomasiological questions, i.e. starting from concepts and looking for their lexicalizations, in 213 locations. In each location, multiple informants were interviewed of varying age. Consequently, a total of 2060 informants are included in this dataset. Montemagni & Wieling (2015) provides an extensive overview of this data source. In short, the dataset consists of noun concepts only, which resulted in at most 50 different (normalized) lexical variants, and responses were normalized to abstract away from phonetic variation. This dataset has also been used by Wieling et al. (2014) to investigate lexical variation in Tuscany with respect to standard Italian. While our approach is also applicable to other types of linguistic data (such as phonetic, syntactic or morphological data), the large number of informants behind this dataset ensure low frequent variants can be reliably identified.

3 Methods

We analyze the dataset using hierarchical bipartite spectral graph partitioning (HBSGP; Wieling & Nerbonne 2011). This advanced clustering approach simultaneously clusters the geographic locations together with the linguistic variants, thereby yielding a linguistic basis of the geographical clustering. In short, the method functions by constructing a bipartite graph, which is a graph consisting of two sets of vertices. One set of vertices represents the locations, whereas the other set represents the lexical realizations of the 170 investigated concepts or, in short, lexical variants. Whenever a lexical variant is used in a location, there is an edge between the variant and the location. The width of the edge represents the proportion of informants in a location using the variant. There are no edges between pairs of locations or pairs of variants. The HBSGP algorithm determines which edges to cut in such a way that as few (thick) edges as possible are cut to obtain two separate bipartite graphs (i.e. the two graphs are not connected) and the number of vertices in both graphs is (approximately) balanced. Consequently, the two new bipartite graphs represent two clusters in which lexical variants are grouped together with the locations they are most strongly associated with. The optimal clustering is determined via the singular value decomposition of a (normalized) matrix representation of the original bipartite graph, which is subsequently subjected to the algorithm (with $k = 2$) to determine the two-way clustering. The hierarchical clustering is obtained by recursively applying the HBSGP algorithm to the separate bipartite graphs. A more detailed explanation of the method and the mathematical details can be found in Wieling & Nerbonne (2011). Besides having been applied to pronunciation variation (e.g., Wieling & Nerbonne 2011), HBSGP has been previously applied to analyze English lexical variation (Wieling, Upton & Thompson 2014).

To identify the most important linguistic variants, two measures have been proposed by Wieling & Nerbonne (2011): representativeness and distinctiveness. Representativeness of a variant in a cluster is defined as the relative frequency of the variant in the cluster. In each location the relative frequency of the variant ranges between 0 (no informant uses the variant) and 1 (all informants use the variant). By summing these relative frequencies for all locations in the cluster and dividing this value by the number of locations in the cluster, the representativeness is obtained. Consequently, a representativeness of 0 indicates that the variant is not used in any of the locations in the cluster, while a representativeness of 1 indicates that all informants in all locations in the cluster use the variant.

Distinctiveness measures how frequent the variant occurs within as opposed to outside of the cluster. It also takes the relative size (i.e. the number of locations) of the cluster into account to correct for chance effects. Consequently, distinctiveness requires two values, the relative occurrence of the variant in the cluster and the relative size of the cluster. The relative size is calculated by dividing the number of locations in the cluster by the total number of locations in the dataset. The relative occurrence is calculated by summing the relative frequencies of the variant for all locations in the cluster (as was done for representativeness) and dividing this number by the summed relative frequencies of the variant in all locations in the dataset. Subsequently, distinctiveness is calculated by subtracting the relative size from the relative occurrence and dividing this value by the relative size subtracted from 1. A distinctiveness of 1 indicates that the variant is only used within the cluster, and not outside the cluster, whereas a distinctiveness of 0 (or lower) indicates that the variant is used equally (or less) frequently as would be expected on the basis of the relative size of the cluster. For example, if the relative occurrence is 0.75, and the relative size is 0.25, the distinctiveness is equal to $\frac{0.75-0.25}{1-0.25} = 0.67$.

In previous studies (e.g., Wieling, Upton & Thompson 2014) the importance of a variant has been determined by taking the mean of representativeness and distinctiveness, but here we follow the approach of Montemagni & Wieling (2015) in multiplying the two values (i.e. importance = distinctiveness x representativeness).

In the following, we will evaluate the choice of taking into account all lexical data ("full") versus ignoring variants used by at most 0.5% of the informants ("trimmed": ignoring variants used by 10 or fewer informants out of all 2060 informants) by investigating the importance values of the most characteristic variants associated with the various clusters. The underlying idea is that a better clustering will be characterized by more distinctive and representative linguistic variants. Figure 1 visualizes the typical frequency distribution of the lexical variants associated with a specific concept (i.e. showing the number of informants using each variant, in this case of the concept *susina*, 'plum') and the red dots indicate the low-frequency variants (i.e. those used by a maximum of 10 informants) excluded in the trimmed dataset.

12 Infrequent forms: Noise or not?

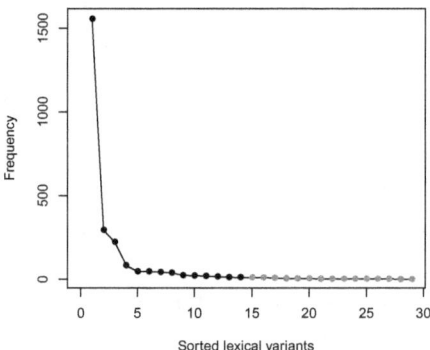

Figure 1: Number of informants in the different locations (i.e. type frequency) using the various lexical variants for the concept 'plum'. The red dots indicate the variants excluded in the trimmed dataset. The variants are sorted by decreasing frequency.

4 Results

Figure 2 shows two cluster maps (seven groups) on the basis of both datasets. Figure 3 shows the top-thirty importance values associated with the most relevant lexical variants for each of the seven groups on the basis of the two datasets. The importance values were calculated for all variants available per dataset (i.e. all 5174 variants for the complete dataset, and the 1996 variants having a frequency

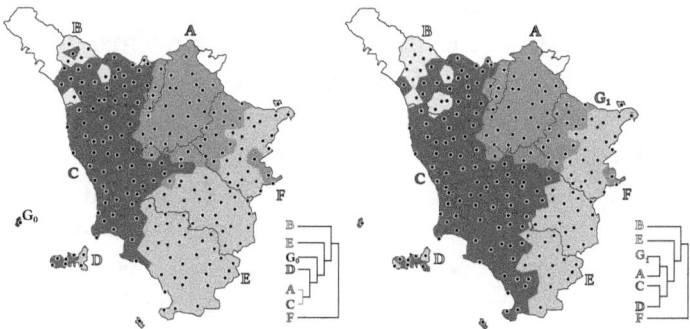

Figure 2: Clustering of Tuscan dialects in seven groups. Left: based on full dataset. Right: based on trimmed dataset.

219

of at least 11 for the trimmed dataset). Only the top-thirty variants are visualized, as the number of associated variants per cluster varied. Clearly, the results on the basis of the full dataset (solid dots) are generally more reliable than those on the basis of the trimmed dataset (open dots). Especially the large clusters (A, C and E) appear to be better characterized on the basis of the full data. For the smaller clusters the results appear to be more mixed. However, when averaging the top-three importance values across the seven groups, the mean importance score for the full dataset is 0.639, whereas it is only 0.478 for the trimmed dataset. This pattern remains similar when looking at the top-ten (0.560 vs. 0.413) or top-thirty variants (0.435 vs. 0.316), and also holds when specifically focusing on distinctiveness (top-three: 0.997 vs. 0.981, top-ten: 0.971 vs. 0.912, top-thirty: 0.881 vs. 0.745) or representativeness (top-three: 0.891 vs. 0.867, top-ten: 0.777 vs. 0.754, top-thirty: 0.630 vs. 0.591). Clearly, taking into account infrequent items helps to improve results on the basis of the HBSGP method. Given that this method takes as input individual variants and their relative frequency in each location, the full dataset obviously contains much more information. By contrast, when calculating distances on the basis of these lexical variants (i.e. by using the matrix representation of the bipartite graph as input for the online dialectometry application Gabmap; Nerbonne et al. 2011), the distance matrices on the basis of both datasets have a correlation of $r = 0.81$. Furthermore, Figure 4 shows that the clustering (7 clusters, on the basis of Ward's method) is hardly affected at all.

5 Discussion

In this study we have shown that cluster quality improves when the analysis is based on all data, rather than using a subset in which infrequent variants are filtered out. This effect appears to be greater for a feature-based clustering method, such as hierarchical bipartite spectral graph partitioning, than for distance-based clustering, where the influence is only limited. In the case of the HBSGP method, the improvement is observed at the level of both the clustering of locations into dialectal areas and the identification of the most important associated lexical variants. These findings support and extend earlier findings of Nerbonne & Kleiweg (2007) and suggest that investigating geographical patterns of dialect variation on the basis of all data might be a worthwhile approach when studying dialects in the future. Further studies on the role of type frequency in dialectometry might investigate whether and to what extent it relates with productivity, to be interpreted here as geographic lexical variability.

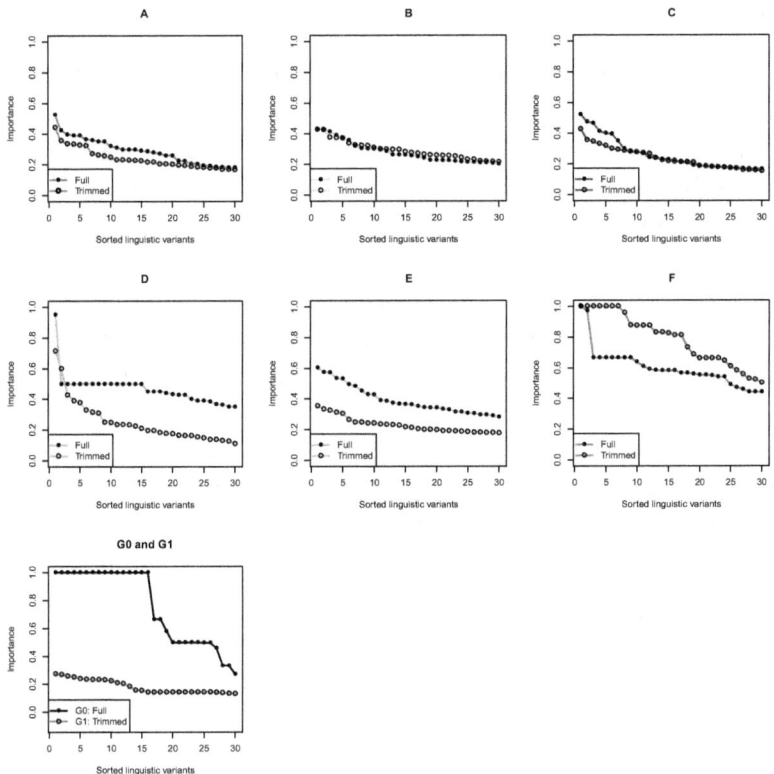

Figure 3: Sorted importance values for each of the seven groups. The solid dots are associated with the full dataset while the open dots are associated with the trimmed dataset. The line color matches the color of the groups in Figure 2.

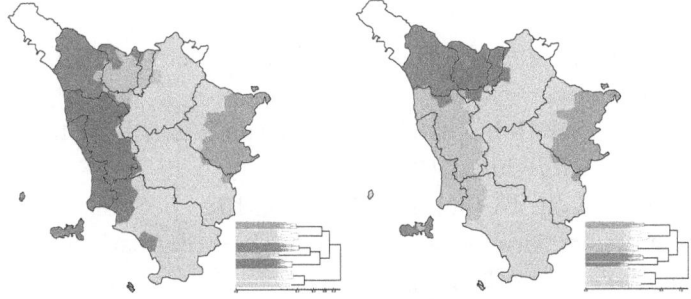

Figure 4: Distance-based clustering of Tuscan dialects in seven groups using Ward's method. Left: based on full dataset. Right: based on trimmed dataset.

References

Bybee, Joan L. 2001. *Phonology and language use*. Cambridge; New York: Cambridge University Press.

Carver, Craig M. 1987. *American regional dialects: A word geography*. Ann Arbor: University of Michigan Press.

Giacomelli, Gabriella, Luciano Agostiniani, Patrizia Bellucci, Luciano Giannelli, Simonetta Montemagni, Annalisa Nesi, Matilde Paoli, Eugenio Picchi & Teresa Poggi Salani. 2000. *Atlante lessicale toscano*. Roma: Lexis Progetti.

Goebl, Hans. 1984. *Dialektometrische Studien: Anhand italoromanischer, rätoromanischer und galloromanischer Sprachmaterialien aus AIS und ALF*. Tübingen: Niemeyer.

Kretzschmar, William A., Brendan A. Kretzschmar & Irene M. Brockman. 2013. Scaled measurement of geographic and social speech data. *LLC: Journal of Digital Scholarship in the Humanities* 28(1). 173–187.

Manning, Christopher D & Hinrich Schütze. 1999. *Foundations of statistical natural language processing*. Cambridge, Mass. [etc.]: The MIT Press.

Montemagni, Simonetta & Martijn Wieling. 2015. Tracking linguistic features underlying lexical variation patterns: A case study on Tuscan dialects. In Marie-Hélène Côte, Remco Knooihuizen & John Nerbonne (eds.), *The Future of Dialects*. Berlin: Language Science Press.

Nerbonne, John. 2009. Data-driven dialectology. *Language and Linguistics Compass* 3(1). 175–198.

Nerbonne, John & Peter Kleiweg. 2007. Toward a dialectological yardstick. *Journal of Quantitative Linguistics* 14(2). 148–166.

Nerbonne, John, Rinke Colen, Charlotte Gooskens, Peter Kleiweg & Therese Leinonen. 2011. Gabmap – a web application for dialectology. *Dialectologia* Special Issue II. 65–89.

Szmrecsanyi, Benedikt. 2011. Corpus-based dialectometry: A methodological sketch. *Corpora* 6(1). 45–76.

Séguy, Jean. 1971. La relation entre la distance spatiale et la distance lexicale. *Revue de Linguistique Romane* 35(138). 335–357.

Wieling, Martijn & John Nerbonne. 2011. Bipartite spectral graph partitioning for clustering dialect varieties and detecting their linguistic features. *Computer Speech & Language* 25(3). 700–715.

Wieling, Martijn & John Nerbonne. 2015. Advances in dialectometry. *Annual Review of Linguistics* 1. 243–264.

Wieling, Martijn, Clive Upton & Ann Thompson. 2014. Analyzing the BBC Voices data: Contemporary English dialect areas and their characteristic lexical variants. *Literary and Linguistic Computing* 29(1). 107–117.

Wieling, Martijn, Simonetta Montemagni, John Nerbonne & R. Harald Baayen. 2014. Lexical differences between Tuscan dialects and Standard Italian: A sociolinguistic analysis using generalized additive mixed modeling. *Language* 90(3). 669–692.

Chapter 13

Top-down and bottom-up advances in corpus-based dialectometry

Christoph Wolk
University of Giessen

Benedikt Szmrecsanyi
KU Leuven

> We present three approaches to corpus-based dialectometry and apply them to morphosyntactic variation in the *Freiburg Corpus of English Dialects*, which covers 34 counties throughout Great Britain. Two of these are *top-down approaches* that start with a predefined feature list; one using a straightforward frequency-based analysis, the other enhancing the raw numbers using probabilistic modeling. Both methods are able to detect the structure of areal variation in Great Britain, and the second approach is able to reduce the influence of textual coverage as a nuisance factor. The final approach is a *bottom-up* method that eschews pre-specified lists and evaluates potential features directly from the data using a permutation-based metric. Again, we find that simple frequency-based metrics are biased, but that derived metrics yield a clearer pattern. Using these methods, we are able to uncover significant geolinguistic structure in Great Britain.

1 Introduction

In this contribution, we sketch novel ways to conduct dialectometry. Let us set the scene by fixing some terminology first. LINGUISTIC CORPORA are principled and broadly representative collections of naturalistic texts or speech. Linguistic corpora thus sample USAGE DATA, and as such are increasingly popular in dialectology (Anderwald & Szmrecsanyi 2009; Grieve 2009) and beyond (see the papers in Szmrecsanyi & Wälchli 2014). CORPUS LINGUISTICS, accordingly, is a methodology in linguistics that bases claims about language on corpora. Corpus linguistics is thus the methodological outgrowth of the usage-based turn in linguistics, in the spirit of, e.g., Bybee (2010); Tomasello (2003). As is well known, CLASSICAL

Christoph Wolk & Benedikt Szmrecsanyi. 2016. Top-down and bottom-up advances in corpus-based dialectometry. In Marie-Hélène Côté, Remco Knooihuizen & John Nerbonne (eds.), *The future of dialects*, 225–244. Berlin: Language Science Press. DOI:10.17169/langsci.b81.152

DIALECTOMETRY in the tradition of Goebl (1984); Nerbonne, Heeringa & Kleiweg (1999) draws on atlas material to explore geolinguistic patterns using aggregation methodologies. By contrast, CORPUS-BASED DIALECTOMETRY (henceforth: CBDM) utilizes aggregation methodologies to explore quantitative and distributional usage patterns extracted from dialect corpora.

Why do we need CBDM? After all, there is some scepticism in the community about the usefulness of non-atlas resources (Goebl 2005a: 499, for example, writes that "Extra atlantes linguisticos nulla salus dialectometrica"). Let us emphasize first that we do not wish to suggest that linguistic atlases are dispensable. Quite on the contrary, we are convinced that they are quite indispensable for some purposes, such as surveying – from a bird's eye perspective – the variable presence or absence of particular features in particular language or dialect areas. But at the same time we believe that also (!) being able to analyze naturalistic corpus data is central to the maturation of the dialectometry enterprise. The reason is that the data in (most) linguistic atlases speak primarily to the issue of explicit, active linguistic knowledge, while corpus data document first and foremost usage (which is, of course, related to knowledge of the more implicit sort, but there is no 1-1 correspondence). Thus turning to corpora will enable dialectologists to address hitherto rather neglected questions about usage versus knowledge, production/comprehension versus intuition, chaos versus orderliness, and so on. We should also add that neighboring linguistic disciplines, such as variationist sociolinguistics, rely empirically almost exclusively on usage data. It is precisely because of this that there is some welcome methodological convergence to be had in the field. The disadvantage of CBDM is that corpus methodologies are not well suited to study low-frequency phenomena; rare things, in other words, are better investigated drawing on atlases and surveys.

In this contribution we sketch three CBDM approaches, two top-down, the third bottom-up. The top-down approaches first define a feature catalogue, then establish the frequencies and/or probabilities associated with the features, and finally aggregate over them. The bottom-up approach, by contrast, lets the features to be aggregated emerge in a data-driven fashion through the identification of significant and/or distinctive part-of-speech n-grams. The case studies which we present to illustrate these approaches summarize work by Szmrecsanyi (2013) and Wolk (2014). All case studies are concerned with grammatical variation in traditional British English dialects.

This contribution is structured as follows. In §2 we sketch the dialect corpus into which we tap. §3 describes the top-down CBDM approach; §4 is dedicated to the bottom-up approach. §5 offers some concluding remarks.

2 The Freiburg Corpus of English Dialects (FRED)

The case studies in this contribution will analyze the *Freiburg Corpus of English Dialects* (henceforth: FRED) (see Hernández 2006 for details). The version of the corpus used in the top-down CBDM study (§3) contains 368 individual texts and covers approximately 2.44 million words of running text (this corresponds to about 300 hours of speech), mainly transcribed so-called 'oral history' material. These were mostly recorded between 1970 and 1990. The typical setting is that a fieldworker interviews an informant about life, work, etc. in the olden days. The 431 informants represented in the corpus are typically elderly people with a working-class background – so-called NORMs (*non-mobile old rural males*) (cf. Chambers & Trudgill 1998: 29). The interviews were conducted in 156 different locations – that is, villages and towns – in 34 different pre-1974 counties in Great Britain including the Isle of Man and the Hebrides. These counties are displayed in Figure 1. Note that we aggregate all texts/interviews from the same county, in order to obtain 34 distinct subcorpora. Individual texts are annotated with longitude/latitude information; county coordinates (mean longitude and latitude) have consequently been calculated by computing the arithmetic mean of all the location coordinates associated with a particular county. Some of the informants had to be removed for the analysis presented in §3.2 due to missing metadata. This led to the complete removal of three counties for that analysis: East Lothian, Denbighshire and Warwickshire.

In the bottom-up CBDM study (§4), we will analyze a smaller version of the corpus: the Freiburg Corpus of English Dialects Sampler (FRED-S) (Szmrecsanyi & Hernández 2007). FRED-S contains a subset of the texts in the full FRED corpus totaling about 1 million words of running text and covering 17 counties in England and the Scottish Lowlands. The big advantage of using FRED-S, though smaller in size, is that it exists in a version that was automatically part-of-speech (POS) annotated by the CLAWS4 tagger (Garside & Smith 1997) using the detailed CLAWS7 tagset.

To illustrate the nature of the material sampled in FRED and FRED-S, (1) is the beginning of an interview conducted in 1978 in St. Ives, Cornwall (FRED text CON003). The informant is an 86 year-old male ('CAVA_PV'), who is interviewed by two interviewers ('IntRS' and 'Inf'). Interviewer utterances are enclosed in curly brackets (note that interviewer utterances are excluded from analysis in the present study).

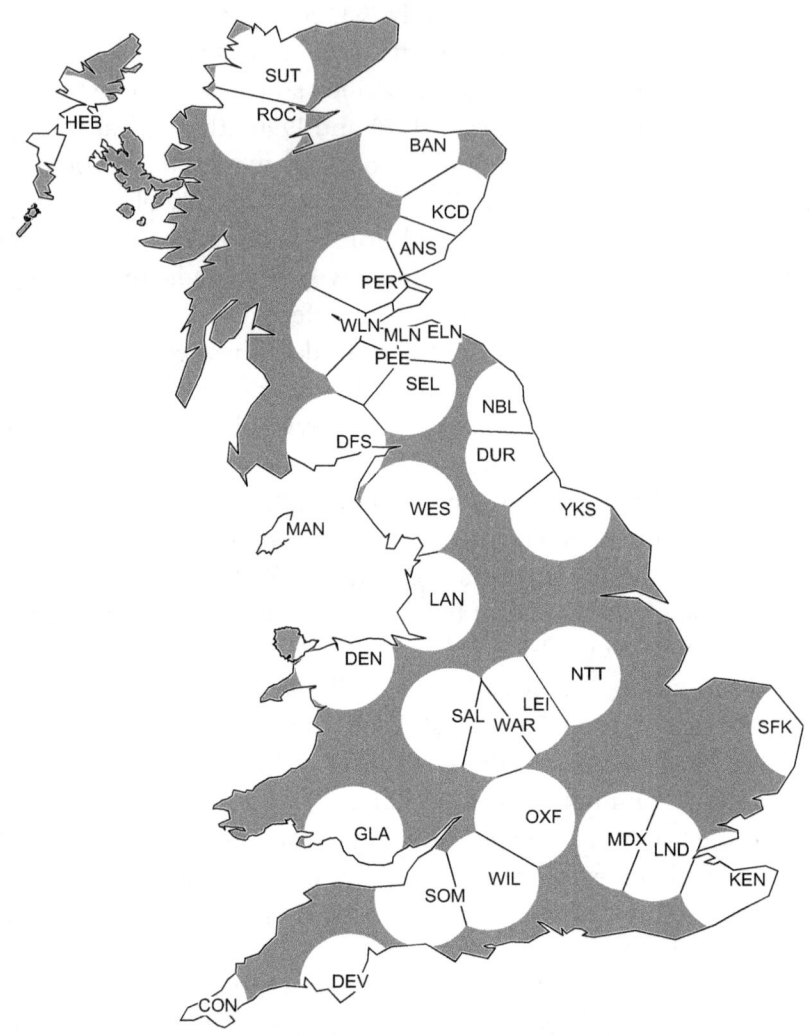

Figure 1: Pre-1974 counties represented in FRED. See http://en.wikipedia.org/wiki/Chapman_code for an explanation of the county codes.

13 Top-down and bottom-up advances in corpus-based dialectometry

(1) {<u IntRS> *Well you're a St. Ives man. Where were you born?*}
  <u CAVA_PV> *Born Belyars Lane, eighteen ninety-two. Eighteenth of December. Worn sovereign in the cupper. Born sovereign. The poor times then, you know (gap 'indistinct') boiling potatoes and t – inkle mosses.*
  {<u IntRS> *Did you, did you, how long did you live there?*}
  <u CAVA_PV> *Oh we lived there about, oh about twelve years, I suppose. Then we went up to a Rosewall Terrace. Hmm. So everything's altered now to what er was then, I mean.*

3 Top-down CBDM

This section will discuss top-down CBDM, which consists of five steps:

Step 1: define the feature catalogue (motto: the more features, the merrier).

Step 2: identify features in the corpus texts (automatically, semi-automatically, or manually).

Step 3: establish raw feature frequencies (per location); subsequently, normalize frequencies and/or model frequencies probabilistically.

Step 4: aggregate: calculate a distance matrix.

Step 5: project to geography, analyze & interpret.

Szmrecsanyi (2013) and Wolk (2014) discuss the method in meticulous detail. Suffice it to say here that the feature catalogue we used to explore grammatical variation in British English dialects consists of $p = 57$ features, which cover all major domains in English grammar as well as the usual suspects in the variationist and dialectological literature, such as non-standard past tense *done* (e.g., *you came home and done the home fishing*), multiple negation (e.g., *don't you make no damn mistake*), and *don't* with third person singular subjects (e.g., *if this man don't come up to it*). These features were identified in the corpus material (automatically, semi-automatically, or manually – depending on the nature of the feature), and their usage frequency established. Subsequently, this information was arranged in an n by p table: 34 counties, each characterized by a vector of 57 feature frequencies. At this point, there are two ways to proceed: the *normalization-based top-down CBDM approach*, pursued in Szmrecsanyi (2013), and the *probabilistically enhanced top-down CBDM approach*, explored in Wolk (2014). We will now discuss these top-down variants in turn.

3.1 The normalization-based top-down CBDM approach

Szmrecsanyi (2013) processed the frequency table in two ways prior to analysis. For one thing, he normalized raw frequencies to frequency per 10,000 words, doing justice to the fact that textual coverage of individual dialects varies. This normalized frequency table tells us, for example, that multiple negation is twice as frequent in Nottinghamshire than in Yorkshire. Additionally, Szmrecsanyi applied a log-transformation to the normalized frequencies for the sake of de-emphasizing large frequency differentials and thus alleviating the effect of frequency outliers. Next Szmrecsanyi converted the normalized, log-transformed frequency table into an N by N distance matrix. This transformation is an aggregation step, in that the resulting distance matrix abstracts away from individual feature frequencies and specifies pairwise distances between the objects considered. To calculate dialectal distances, Szmrecsanyi used the well-known Euclidean Distance Measure (see, e.g., Aldenderfer & Blashfield 1984: 25). The Euclidean Distance Measure defines the distance between two dialects as the square root of the sum of all p squared frequency differentials.

Distance matrices are the customary input to dialectometric analysis and visualization techniques. Let us now explore the normalization-based top-down distance matrix using a particularly popular dialectometric mapping technique, *cluster maps*. Cluster maps are common in all strands of dialectometry, and project the outcome of cluster analysis to geography (cf., for example, Goebl 2007: Map 18; Nerbonne & Siedle 2005: Figure 5; Heeringa 2004: Figure 9.6). First, an N by N distance matrix is subjected to HIERARCHICAL AGGLOMERATIVE CLUSTER ANALYSIS (cf. Jain, Murty & Flynn 1999; we specifically used Ward's method as the clustering algorithm), a statistical technique used to group a number of objects (in this study, dialects) into a smaller number of discrete clusters.[1] Cluster memberships of dialect locations can then be projected to geography via, e.g., color coding.

In the left-hand and center maps of Figure 2 we find two cluster maps that correlate (Goebl 2005b) Great Britain's geographic landscape to its dialect landscape. For expository purposes, both maps display a 3-cluster solution, but we do not wish to claim that this is necessarily the optimal solution. The left-hand map clusters a distance matrix detailing not linguistic distances but as-the-crow-flies geographic distances between dialect sites, thus depicting, for reference purposes, a geographically maximally neatly partitioned map. This map suggests that on strictly geographic grounds, Great Britain can be partitioned into three coherent

---

[1] Simple clustering can be unstable, so we used the "clustering with noise" technique (Nerbonne et al. 2008).

13 Top-down and bottom-up advances in corpus-based dialectometry

Figure 2: Cluster maps – hierarchical agglomerative cluster analysis (displayed: 3-cluster solution). Left: Geographic as-the-crow-flies distances. Center: Normalization-based morphosyntactic distances. See Szmrecsanyi (2013: chapter 6) for details. Right: Probabilistically enhanced morphosyntactic distances.

areas: a red region comprising the South of England plus the county of Glamorganshire in Southern Wales; a green region containing the North of England plus the county of Denbighshire in Northern Wales plus the county of Dumfriesshire in Southern Scotland; and a blue region encompassing Scotland minus the county of Dumfriesshire.

Compare this scenario to the map in the center of Figure 2, which projects a corresponding regionalization on morphosyntactic grounds. There is a good deal of geographic incoherence in the morphosyntax division: For example, there are blue outliers all over England and Wales; Durham in the North of England is categorized as a red (i.e. Southern) county; Glamorganshire in Southern Wales is a green (i.e. Northern) county; and so on. That said, there is clearly some similarity between the geographic and linguistic partitioning, because the tripartite division between Scotland, the North of England, and the South of England is essentially in place. We conclude that our corpus-based measure of aggregate morphosyntactic variability does detect a geolinguistic signal.

3.2 The probabilistically enhanced top-down CBDM approach

While the signal discussed in the previous section seems to broadly match the description in the literature, it also raises some concerns. First, the outliers are difficult to motivate. Why should, for example, Middlesex group with Scotland? For most of the outliers, individual significant differences to their geographically close neighbors can be found (Szmrecsanyi 2013: chapter 7), but this does not sufficiently explain the cluster structure. Second, the results do not confirm two of the most reliable results of the atlas-based dialectometric enterprise: both the shape and the strength of the relationship between linguistic and geographic distances are markedly different. Nerbonne (2013) summarizes several studies, finding that geographic distance (statistically) explains 16 to 37 percent of the variance in linguistic distance, and that the relationship is sublinear: as one considers location pairs that are further apart, the increase in linguistic dissimilarity begins to level off. In contrast the corpus signal yields a very low correlation between linguistic and geographic ("as the crow flies") distances, explaining only approximately 4.4 percent of the variance, and the relationship is linear rather than sub-linear. Using travel time as the operationalization of geographic distance (Gooskens 2005) improves the relationship slightly to almost 8 percent; nevertheless, it is still far below what is typically found. This suggests that some form of bias may exist in the data set.

It is a well-known effect that non-linguistic aspects of the data set and its creation can influence the aggregate results, such as the specific fieldworker cover-

13 Top-down and bottom-up advances in corpus-based dialectometry

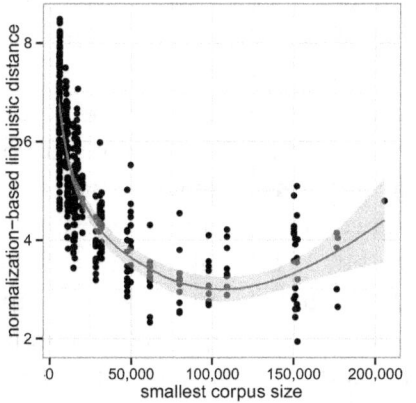 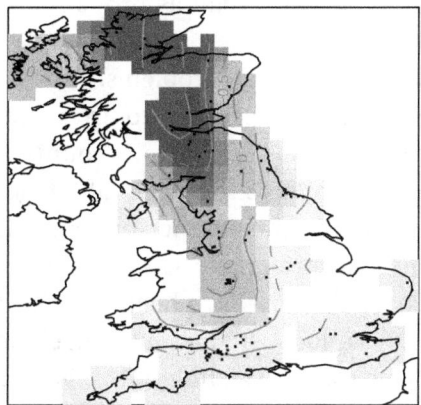

Figure 3: Left: Correlation of minimum subcorpus size and linguistic distance (top down normalization-based approach; $R^2 = 0.61$) Right: Example GAM for multiple negation (log scale). Lighter colors indicate higher frequency. Red lines indicate shape of the frequency gradient.

ing a location ("field worker isoglosses", Trudgill 1982: 241ff.). Similar problems may reside in the corpus at hand. We suggest that one issue in particular causes a substantial amount of the divergences from the usual pattern: the fact that the amount of corpus material per county varies, and in some cases the number of words per county may be very small. Measurements that are based on little data are imprecise, and so are the distances resulting from them. We can test the influence of this factor by exploring the relationship between linguistic distance and an appropriate operationalization of corpus size (and therefore accuracy).

The left-hand part of Figure 3 displays the linguistic distance between county pairings as a function of the smaller of the two subcorpus sizes; a smoother line is included to highlight the general trend. Clearly, there is a strong relationship: distances involving the counties with the worst coverage are consistently too high. At approximately 50,000 words, this relationship largely levels off.[2] The outliers in Figure 2 fall below this threshold. For example, the subcorpus for Durham consists of 28,000 words, and that for Middlesex of 32,000. These three measures of quality – interpretability of groupings, correlation with geography, and influence of the amount of data – suggest that there may be a bias in the data that obscures the pattern. Note, however, that these measures serve more as

---

[2] The small uptick at the end is a combination of data sparsity (due to the small number of subcorpora of that size) and the somewhat atypical, but large Suffolk subcorpus.

"sanity checks"[3] than as proper external validation. A method that fares better under this yardstick is not necessarily correct, but a method that fares worse indicates potential problems.

We therefore propose to use some form of smoothing that takes the accuracy of the measurement into account. Per the Fundamental Dialectological Postulate (Nerbonne & Kleiweg 2007), geographic smoothing seems particularly appropriate: in the absence of compelling evidence to the contrary, we should assume that proximate varieties resemble each other. Several methods of doing such smoothing have been proposed, including intensity estimation (Rumpf et al. 2009), local spatial autocorrelation (Grieve 2009), and generalized additive models (GAMs; Wieling 2012). We believe that GAMs are an especially adequate choice, as they are a variant of regression modeling, and therefore closely resemble the techniques in common use by, among others, variationist sociolinguists (Tagliamonte 2012). Using such models, it is possible to account for other factors that may influence the result, whether language-internal (e.g. subject type) or -external (e.g. speaker age). In Wolk (2014), two language-external factors were included, namely speaker age and gender.[4] We keep these two factors for the analysis presented here, to account for any imbalances in the corpus sampling process. For many features, there are significant effects of these factors, largely in the expected direction (i.e. female speakers use fewer non-standard features and older speakers use more archaic features). Simulations based on these results, however, suggest that the overall effect that the inclusion of these factors has on the resulting distances is marginal (Wolk 2014: 233f.).

In contrast to the GAM-based method used in Wieling (2012), Wolk (2014) did not model the distances directly, but built a separate model for each feature. Furthermore, features that represent binary alternations,[5] such as habitual *would* vs. *used to* or *will* vs. *going to* as future markers, were modeled as such, rather than as individual frequencies. Doing so removes potential bias resulting from base rate differences (e.g. differing frequencies of habitual or future contexts regardless of form) between speakers/counties, and makes the results more comparable to variationist research on these features, which typically utilizes VARBRUL-style modeling. This yields a list of 45 remaining features, and therefore the number of models included in the analysis is also 45. Each model contains a two-dimensional geographic smoother that allows the feature to vary by location in

---

[3] We thank an anonymous reviewer for this phrasing.
[4] As the relevant information was missing for a small number of texts (including all texts from three counties, see §2), they had to be removed from the analysis.
[5] The selection of features to model as alternations was based on the variationist literature and on certain features existing as standard/non-standard variants in the original list.

a gradient fashion. An example for this can be seen in the right-hand map in Figure 3, displaying the smoother for multiple negation. As expected, the feature is rare in Scotland and relatively frequent in the South of England, with the North forming a transition zone. This model is then used to predict the proportion of one realization, or the frequency to be expected in ten thousand words. From here on, the analysis proceeds as outlined above.

A cluster map of the resulting distances is presented in the right-hand part of Figure 2. The tripartite division remains, and the large-scale areas are geographically coherent, with the exception of the young dialects in the Scottish Highlands and the Hebrides, which group with the North of England. Quantitatively, the model fares well. The relationship between geographic and linguistic distances is sublinear and solid ($R^2 = 0.44$ for least-cost travel time; compare the normalization-based value of 0.08). Even more importantly, the influence of subcorpus size has greatly decreased and now accounts for only 16.2 percent of the variance, compared to 61 percent for the normalization-based distances.

We hasten to add that this clean pattern is hardly surprising: the GAMs have geographic coherence built into their assumptions. Therefore, it can be argued that the results may be too homogeneous, that there are true differences that the GAMs smooth over. Nevertheless, the model produces at least an upper boundary for spatial cohesion; and a bias in favor of the Fundamental Dialectological Postulate seems more plausible than a bias toward accidental properties of the corpus compilation process. Furthermore, the resulting association between geography and linguistic distance, while on the high side, is not outside the range of what one would expect based on traditional dialectometric analyses. It is also clearly distinct from 1, indicating that there is still unpredictable dialectal variation left. Finally, it bears noting that the GAM process yields interpretable single feature maps as a byproduct – a rather beneficial property of this approach.

4 Bottom-up CBDM

So far, we have covered methods that rely on a pre-specified feature list. In the following, we explore whether it is possible to eliminate such a list and go directly from the corpus to a distance measurement. Directly measuring corpus (dis)similarity is an important, yet somewhat underresearched, topic in corpus linguistics (Kilgarriff 2001). This is especially true for morphosyntactic measures.[6] The method proposed here builds on an idea proposed by Nerbonne &

---

[6] Scherrer (2012) provides a method for deriving pronunciation distances between corpora automatically, but this approach is not straightforwardly generalizable to morphosyntax.

Wiersma (2006), who employ part-of-speech *n*-grams to compare syntactic differences between two corpora. The method makes use of permutation tests to determine how reliable frequency differences between the corpora are, a technique that is gaining popularity in corpus linguistics (Lijffijt 2013). The first full dialectometric use of such an approach was by Sanders (2010), who used it to explore a Swedish dialect corpus. Let us exemplify the general idea starting with comparisons between county pairs.

Consider the following utterance from the Devon subcorpus of FRED-S:

(2)   We$_{PPIS2}$ started$_{VVD}$ at$_{II}$ three$_{MC}$,, yes$_{UH}$ .. <DEV_005>

Ignoring punctuation, we construct all overlapping sequences of length n (always $n = 2$ here, i.e, *bigrams*), yielding the following result: PPIS2_VVD, VVD_II, II_MC, MC_UH. This is done for all utterances in both subcorpora, and the resulting bigram counts are aggregated on the county level. A normalization procedure that redistributes probability point mass is applied to the resulting absolute frequencies. More specifically, this normalization process keeps the total number of tokens per *n*-gram constant, but scales the per-county numbers according to the amount of *n*-grams in that county.[7]. Then, the data is randomly resampled (without replacement) based on turns[8] and the procedure is repeated on the new corpus. In other words, a new corpus is created, in which each county subcorpus contains the same amount of turns, but each turn is randomly assigned to a county. We can now, for each *n*-grams, calculate the difference in normalized values between the two counties both in the "true" (i.e. original) corpus and the randomly resampled one. If this difference is smaller in the original corpus, we can count this as evidence that the original difference may have occurred purely by chance - after all, a random process yielded a greater difference. Finding that the difference for the permuted corpus is smaller, however, would be consistent with the hypothesis that there is a genuine difference between the counties. If this process is not only done once, but a large number of times, the proportion of cases where the original difference was actually greater yields a probabilistic measure of how significant an *n*-grams frequency difference between the two

---

[7] This method was chosen based on the process described in Nerbonne & Wiersma (2006) The difference to a more familiar normalization scheme seems to be marginal – the correlation between raw distances derived using this method and those from simple per 10,000 *n*-grams normalization is greater than 0.99.

[8] Nerbonne & Wiersma (2006) resample based on sentences; in later work (Wiersma, Nerbonne & Lauttamus 2011), this was changed to resampling based on speakers to increase the reliability of the result. This was not feasible for this study, as the number of speakers for some of the counties was low (see also Sanders 2010).

counties is. In a similar fashion, the overall distance (computed using a suitable distance metric, such as the Manhattan distance) can be evaluated.

In addition, we can run the permutation not only on county pairs, but over all counties at the same time. Instead of comparing differences between counties, we calculate the proportion of random corpora in which the normalized frequency exceeds that of the true corpus, counting runs where they are equal as one half. This yields a *reliability matrix* that indicates how reliably this *n*-gram appears more (or less) frequently than expected by chance. Using either the pairwise number of significant differences or a measure of the extremeness of the distribution derived from the reliability matrix, we can evaluate particularly distinctive patterns. For example, consider AT_NN1, the definite article followed by a singular noun, the most frequent pattern. This pattern was significantly different in 84 of all the 136 possible pairwise county combinations; this amounts to being the 29th most distinct *n*-grams according to this metric, If, on the other hand, we use the number of divergences per *n*-gram from maximally consistent whole-corpus permutations, we obtain a value of 2.42 percent. This is still one of the top patterns, but ranks quite a bit lower at number 83 on the corresponding list. In general, a similar pattern seems to hold: there is a strong correlation between the two measures of distinctiveness, but the number of pairwise significant differences is more strongly influenced by *n*-grams frequency. Both the normalized frequency matrix and the reliability matrix are suitable for distance calculations. Details about the process can be found in Wolk (2014: 64-74).

Figure 4 displays the results. For comparison, the left-hand map displays the results of the normalization-based[9] top-down approach on the texts that are available in FRED-S. First, we note that the approach fares better here than on the complete data set: the clusters are spatially mostly coherent, geographic distance explains 27.6 percent of the variance in linguistic distances, and text size differences account for a slightly lower share of 48.5 percent. This results from the removal of most counties with particularly restricted textual coverage. The center map, showing a cluster analysis of normalized bottom-up frequencies, yields a much messier picture; moreover the quantitative match of the linguistic distances is considerably worse: the R^2 for geographic distances is much lower at 0.10, and that for text size considerably higher at a staggering 0.67. The right plot, finally, shows the clusters resulting from the reliability matrix, restricted to bigrams with at least seven pairwise significant differences. Here, the match between geographic and linguistic distances is almost as good as for

---

[9] This comparison is more appropriate than that to the model-based variant, as both do not employ geographic smoothing.

Figure 4: Cluster maps – hierarchical agglomerative cluster analysis using Ward's method as clustering algorithm (displayed: 3-cluster solution). Left: Top-down normalization-based approach on FRED-S. Center: Bottom-up normalized frequencies. Right: Bottom-up reliability scores.

the top-down result on the left at 26.2 percent, and the influence of corpus size is significantly lower ($R^2 = 0.16$). Qualitatively, we find that contiguous regions emerge. This analysis finds a division between Scotland and the North of England only at a position of lower importance, and instead emphasizes a transition area between the North and South of England. Finally, we add that both measures of distinctiveness identify dialectologically meaningful patterns. Among the ten most distinctive n-grams, for example, we find many known features of British dialect grammar: several bigrams related to *was/were* variation (PPH1/PPHS1/PPHS2_VBDR, *it/(he/she)/they were*, and PPHS2_VBDZ, *they was*), *them* as a determiner (in particular after temporal nouns, as in *them days*), *used to* as a marker of habituality (in particular following nouns), and *is n't/not*, which competes with the non-standard form *ain't*.

In short, then, our results suggest that bottom-up CBDM is practicable and worthwhile; the best method yielded results comparable to those for the manually selected feature set. The normalized frequencies, however, fared rather badly, and only after the permutation process smoothed off the rough edges did the areal signal emerge.

Finally, it bears mentioning that the nature of the tag set and the tagging procedure used have a strong influence on the linguistic patterns that emerge, and therefore most probably also on the aggregational results. Exploring the effect of changes in the data pipeline will be crucial in the further development of this approach.

5 Conclusion

In this contribution, we have sketched some recent advances in corpus-based dialectometry (CBDM). CBDM bases claims about geolinguistic patterns in aggregate linguistic variability on language usage as observed through naturalistic corpus data (as opposed to e.g. linguistic knowledge). Early studies in CBDM (e.g. Szmrecsanyi 2011) aggregate normalized text frequencies of features in an a-prioristically defined feature catalogue. This approach we have called the normalization-based top-down CBDM approach (see §3.1). What we have shown is that top-down CBDM profits from the probabilistic modeling of usage frequencies prior to aggregation. The other major advance we have dwelt on in this contribution is bottom-up CBDM, which does not draw on a pre-defined feature catalogue but lets the features to be aggregated emerge in a data-driven fashion through the identification of significant and/or distinctive part-of-speech n-grams. Both probabilistically enhanced top-down CBDM and bottom-up CBDM are valuable additions to the dialectometry toolbox.

With regard to the theme of the present volume, *The Future of Dialects*, we have discussed in this contribution new ways of analyzing dialect data. These new ways are in line with usage-based methodologies customary in related disciplines such as variationist sociolinguistics. As we have argued in the Introduction section, we believe that the future of dialectology will crucially include the ability to analyze actual usage data. As for the future of dialects *per se*, we would like to stress that a focus on more realistic, usage-oriented data sources is likely to reflect the many-faceted nature of dialects more faithfully than other methodologies do.

Acknowledgments

We wish to thank Peter Kleiweg for creating and maintaining the RuG/L04 package. The audience at the Workshop on 'Frontiers in the study of language variety' at the Methods XV conference in Groningen (August 2014) provided very helpful and valuable feedback on an earlier version of this paper. We also thank three anonymous reviewers for their extensive and constructive feedback. The second-named author gratefully acknowledges an Odysseus grant awarded by the Research Foundation Flanders (FWO, grant no. G.0C59.13N). The usual disclaimers apply.

References

Aldenderfer, Mark S. & Roger K. Blashfield. 1984. *Cluster analysis*. Newbury Park, London, New Delhi: Sage Publications.

Anderwald, Lieselotte & Benedikt Szmrecsanyi. 2009. Corpus linguistics and dialectology. In Anke Lüdeling & Merja Kytö (eds.), *Corpus linguistics. An international handbook* (Handbücher zur Sprach- und Kommunikationswissenschaft / Handbooks of Linguistics and Communication Science 29/1), 1126–1139. Berlin, New York: Mouton de Gruyter.

Bybee, Joan L. 2010. *Language, usage and cognition*. Cambridge, New York: Cambridge University Press.

Chambers, J. K. & Peter Trudgill. 1998. *Dialectology*. 2nd edn. Cambridge, New York: Cambridge University Press.

Garside, Roger & Nicholas Smith. 1997. A hybrid grammatical tagger: CLAWS4. In Roger Garside, Geoffrey Leech & Tony McEnery (eds.), *Corpus annotation: Linguistic information from computer text corpora*, 102–121. London: Longman.

Goebl, Hans. 1984. *Dialektometrische Studien: Anhand italoromanischer, rätoromanischer und galloromanischer Sprachmaterialien aus AIS und ALF*. Tübingen: Niemeyer.

Goebl, Hans. 2005a. Dialektometrie. In Reinhard Köhler, Gabriel Altmann & Rajmund G. Piotrowski (eds.), *Quantitative linguistics / Quantitative Linguistik. An international handbook / Ein internationales Handbuch* (Handbücher zur Sprach- und Kommunikationswissenschaft / Handbooks of Linguistics and Communication Science 27), 498–531. Berlin, New York: Walter de Gruyter.

Goebl, Hans. 2005b. La dialectométrie corrélative. Un nouvel outil pour l'étude de l'aménagement dialectal de l'espace par l'homme. *Revue de Linguistique Romane* 69. 321–367.

Goebl, Hans. 2007. A bunch of dialectometric flowers: A brief introduction to dialectometry. In Ute Smit, Stefan Dollinger, Julia Hüttner, Gunter Kaltenböck & Ursula Lutzky (eds.), *Tracing English through time: Explorations in language variation*, 133–172. Wien: Braumüller.

Gooskens, Charlotte. 2005. Traveling time as a predictor of linguistic distance. *Dialectologia et Geolinguistica* 13. 38–62.

Grieve, Jack. 2009. *A corpus-based regional dialect survey of grammatical variation in written Standard American English*. Flagstaff: Northern Arizona University PhD dissertation.

Heeringa, Wilbert. 2004. *Measuring dialect pronunciation differences using Levenshtein distance*. Groningen: University of Groningen PhD Thesis.

Hernández, Nuria. 2006. *User's Guide to FRED*. Freiburg: University of Freiburg.

Jain, Anil K., M. Narasimha Murty & Patrick J. Flynn. 1999. Data clustering: A review. *ACM Computing Surveys* 31(3). 264–323.

Kilgarriff, Adam. 2001. Comparing corpora. *International Journal of Corpus Linguistics* 6(1). 97–133.

Lijffijt, Jefrey. 2013. *Computational methods for comparison and exploration of event sequences*. Espoo: Aalto University PhD thesis.

Nerbonne, John. 2013. How much does geography influence language variation? In Peter Auer, Martin Hilpert, Anja Stukenbrock & Benedikt Szmrecsanyi (eds.), *Space in language and linguistics: Geographical, interactional, and cognitive perspectives*, 220–236. Berlin, New York: Walter de Gruyter.

Nerbonne, John, Wilbert Heeringa & Peter Kleiweg. 1999. Edit distance and dialect proximity. In David Sankoff & Joseph Kruskal (eds.), *Time warps, string edits and macromolecules: The theory and practice of sequence comparison*, v–xv. Stanford: CSLI Press.

Nerbonne, John & Peter Kleiweg. 2007. Toward a dialectological yardstick. *Journal of Quantitative Linguistics* 14(2). 148–166.

Nerbonne, John & Christine Siedle. 2005. Dialektklassifikation auf der Grundlage aggregierter Ausspracheunterschiede. *Zeitschrift für Dialektologie und Linguistik* 72(2). 129–147.

Nerbonne, John & Wybo Wiersma. 2006. A measure of aggregate syntactic distance. In John Nerbonne & Erhard Hinrichs (eds.), *Linguistic distances. Workshop at the joint conference of International Committee on Computational Linguistics and the Association for Computational Linguistics, Sydney, July, 2006*, 82–90.

Nerbonne, John, Peter Kleiweg, Franz Manni & Wilbert Heeringa. 2008. Projecting dialect differences to geography: Bootstrapping clustering vs. clustering with noise. In Christine Preisach, Lars Schmidt-Thieme, Hans Burkhardt & Reinhold Decker (eds.), *Data analysis, machine learning, and applications. Proceedings of the 31st Annual Meeting of the German Classification Society*, 647–654. Berlin: Springer.

Rumpf, Jonas, Simon Pickl, Stephan Elspaß, Werner König & Volker Schmidt. 2009. Structural analysis of dialect maps using methods from spatial statistics. *Zeitschrift für Dialektologie und Linguistik* 76(3). 280–308.

Sanders, Nathan C. 2010. *A statistical method for syntactic dialectometry*. Bloomington: Indiana University PhD thesis.

Scherrer, Yves. 2012. Recovering dialect geography from an unaligned comparable corpus. In *Proceedings of the EACL 2012 Joint Workshop of LINGVIS & UNCLH (EACL 2012)*, 63–71. Avignon, France: Association for Computational Linguistics.

Szmrecsanyi, Benedikt. 2011. Corpus-based dialectometry: A methodological sketch. *Corpora* 6(1). 45–76.

Szmrecsanyi, Benedikt. 2013. *Grammatical variation in British English dialects: A study in corpus-based dialectometry*. Cambridge, New York: Cambridge University Press.

Szmrecsanyi, Benedikt & Nuria Hernández. 2007. *Manual of Information to accompany the Freiburg Corpus of English Dialects Sampler ("FRED-S")*. Freiburg: University of Freiburg.

Szmrecsanyi, Benedikt & Bernhard Wälchli (eds.). 2014. *Aggregating dialectology, typology, and register analysis: Linguistic variation in text and speech* (Lingua & litterae 28). Berlin: Walter de Gruyter.

Tagliamonte, Sali. 2012. *Variationist sociolinguistics: Change, observation, interpretation*. Malden, Oxford, Chichester: Wiley-Blackwell.

Tomasello, Michael. 2003. *Constructing a language: A usage-based theory of language acquisition.* Cambridge, Mass: Harvard University Press.

Trudgill, Peter. 1982. The contribution of sociolinguistics to dialectology. *Language Sciences* 4(2). 237–250.

Wieling, Martijn. 2012. *A quantitative approach to social and geographical dialect variation.* Groningen: University of Groningen PhD thesis.

Wiersma, Wybo, John Nerbonne & Timo Lauttamus. 2011. Automatically extracting typical syntactic differences from corpora. *Literary and Linguistic Computing* 26(1). 107–124.

Wolk, Christoph. 2014. *Integrating aggregational and probabilistic approaches to language variation.* Freiburg: University of Freiburg PhD thesis.

Chapter 14

Imitating closely related varieties

Lea Schäfer
Philipps-Universität Marburg

Stephanie Leser
Philipps-Universität Marburg

Michael Cysouw
Philipps-Universität Marburg

> In this article we present basic reflections into investigating the mechanisms of imitating closely related language varieties. We first conducted a survey for which speakers of German had to imitate one of five continental West Germanic lects. Furthermore, we carried out a study on imitations of Yiddish in German literature of the 19th century. In this short overview we will summarize our main results and methods from these studies, and offer some perspectives on future research in this field, which will play an important role in perceptual dialectology, psycholinguistics and even the study of language change.

1 The field of language imitation

Imitation is an ability that plays an important role during every process of learning.[1] It is one of the fundamental skills in the evolution of human communication and forms the basis of every kind of language acquisition (e.g. Fitch 2010; Hauser, Chomsky & Fitch 2002; Petkov & Jarvis 2012; Užgiris 1981; Markham 1997; 1999; Meltzoff & Moore 1977; Meltzoff & Prinz 2002; Tomasello & Carpenter 2007: 123). Therefore, it is astonishing that there are barely any core linguistic works on the imitation of natural languages. The few existing studies focus mainly on phonetic

---

[1] The data of this article was presented in two posters at *Methods in Dialectology XV* (2014) at the University of Groningen. We thank Clinton Ford, Jeffrey Pheiff and Ricarda Scherschel for checking our English. We also thank our anonymous reviewers for their useful comments.

Lea Schäfer, Stephanie Leser & Michael Cysouw. 2016. Imitating closely related varieties. In Marie-Hélène Côté, Remco Knooihuizen & John Nerbonne (eds.), *The future of dialects*, 245–261. Berlin: Language Science Press.
DOI:10.17169/langsci.b81.153

and phonological questions of dialect perception; they simply use the human ability of imitation as a method for collecting data of lay concepts without questioning the mechanisms behind dialect imitation (e. g. Segerup 1999; Siegel (2010); Adank, Hagoort & Bekkering (2010); Purschke (2010); Babel (2009); Neuhauser (2012); Dossey (2012)). These experiments only measure isolated non-standard features. We are advocating for experiments that simulate a situation of natural language contact and an analysis of imitation data with regard to more than just one language level, we focus upon lexis, phonology, morphology and syntax and using somehow natural stimuli instead of isolated features.

2 Aspects of dialect imitation

The imitation of closely related varieties, like dialects of one language, differs from the imitation of non-related varieties since there is a common typological ground given in the first case, while in the second case there is not. In this article only imitation of closely-related varieties is examined. In this case we assume that the imitation can be specified as an emulative imitation. Emulation is defined as an imitation of a system through another system. The imitation of a closely related language is based on manipulations of the imitators' own system (I-language). Exploring how these manipulations are created and what conditions influence them can be investigated by the tools of modern dialectology. Using the terminology from Myers-Scotton's (1993, 2002) *Matrix Language Frame Model*, which was originally designed as a model for codeswitching, imitation is made using a matrix language (ML) to which structures of a target language (TL) or what the imitator thinks of as a TL-structure are applied. Used as a model for language imitation, the ML is the speaker's own I-language, while the TL is the language to be imitated. This is basically a simple binary model of two languages playing a role, when in fact there is a grey area in defining the ML and TL; depending on the imitator's perception, he/she can shift between his/her own orality, the TL and what the imitator thinks is the TL.

Therefore, a language imitation model should be at least ternary. Based on the imitation of natural languages, we have to consider that the imitators have a knowledge of varieties of their own language, learned either through media, which may broadcast actual regional dialect as well as medialects[2] found on television, the internet or radio and their own experience (e. g. migration, travelling).

---

[2] Medialects, as we call it, can be defined as artificial lects that are only used in the media. There where some investigations on the influence of dialects on such medialects from TV or internet i. a. by Kleiner (2013), Androutsopoulos (2012), Riemann (2009) or Mayer & Zimmerer (2009).

Once imitators recognize structures of the TL, they can match those with their concepts of a dialect or medialect. It is plausible that imitators will use structures that are not native for the TL but that are native for a similar dialect or medialect. Investigating the imitation of closely related varieties always involves separating what the imitators actually know about the TL from what they believe they know. In addition, other important aspects of dialect imitation we do not focus on are mutual intelligibility and lay concepts of closely related varieties, and of course the yet not quite well defined and investigated dialectological concept of *salience*. We are mainly interested in how imitation can be used as a laboratory for the ML's synchronic variability and how that could represent diachronic variability. This also gives hints on innovative tendencies for the future of a dialect.

Not only can we learn from dialect imitation how imitators interact with the lects of their surroundings, but we can also learn a lot about the ML itself. While the TL delivers the forms that *could* be imitated, the ML decides what form *can* be imitated and how. Furthermore, there are two additional interesting aspects of dialect imitation. The first is the imitator's spoken language (orality): imitators of a dialect will produce forms of their own orality. As a result, data from dialect imitation can be used as a source of (perhaps subconscious) structures of the ML and in general of the imitator's orality. The second is a much deeper aspect of the ML. Through emulative imitation we gain insight into the ML's variability. It is a fascinating fact that we can produce (and process) language structures that do not conform with the structures we usually apply. This variability represents one avenue for change that the ML possesses.

Through emulative imitation we may even learn about the diachronic variability of the ML. As Haider (2007: 135) shows in his analysis of a fictional language by Ernst Jandl (an Austrian poet of the 20th century), constructed languages based on a natural ML show structures known from older periods of the language or distantly related varieties. To use a simplistic picture, we can compare a structure of a certain language to a fluid with its own viscosity. Some structures are very rigid and just show little potential for variability. Thus other structures are not that rigid and allow more variation. Our idea is that this viscosity is motivated typologically and diachronically. In this particular case of dialect imitation, the imitators can produce structures or forms that are not common for their ML (and maybe not even used in the TL). However, these imitators will not invent structures that differ fundamenally from the potential of their own variety. For example, when it comes to imitations of closely related varieties in discourse, like fiction, film or theater, the imitators have to make sure that the intelligibility of what they want to say is guaranteed. With regard to this, evidence for fictitious forms and structures can teach us about the typological variability of the ML. With the aid of dialect imitation we can see which language structures are stable and which ones are not. To what degree this synchronic variability reflects diachronic changes has yet to be tested. The diagram in Figure 1 represents the factors influencing dialect imitation. As we know from developmental psychology: "In imitating, the person constructs a match between some aspect of the external world and his or her own activity" (Užgiris 1981: 2). With two different data sets, presented in the following paragraph, we tried figuring out which structures of emulative dialect imitation come from the imitators' language and which derive from external languages.

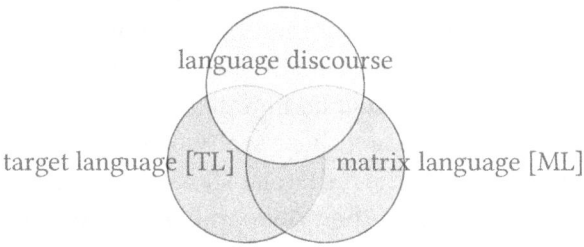

Figure 1: Sources of dialect imitation

Imitation of closely related varieties as we see it, is in its pure state an emulation of one dialect (TL) through an other (ML) influenced and stimulated by the ML's potential of variability which in turn is the basis of language change, which leads us to the history (and future) of the dialect that imitates (ML).

3 Experimental testing

3.1 Internet survey with five West Germanic varieties

To obtain a closer look at how the imitation of modern dialects works and to determine if our assumptions are correct, we designed an online survey in which a short oral story was presented to the participants. The story itself is filled with several linguistic variables; especially morpho-syntactic features like relative particles, verb-second, pronouns, progressive constructions, negative concord, infinitive constructions and verb clusters. The story was translated and recorded by female native speakers of the following five West Germanic varieties: Belgian Dutch (BD), Low German (Westphalian, WP), Central German (Central Hessian, CH), Upper German (Alemannic, AL) and Central Eastern Yiddish (YI).

These recordings were integrated into an internet survey which was completed by German-speaking informants, who listened to one random recording of the five versions of the story accompanied by a transliteration written according to the rules of Standard German orthography (for the story and its four transliterations see Appendix in Section 5, p. 256). The survey was online for the whole of April 2014 using the platform https://www.soscisurvey.de/. Using social networks and mailing lists from the University of Marburg, students and staff of the faculty were recruited.

After hearing and reading the story, the informants had to make true/false decisions about seven statements concerning the content of the story. Then the actual imitation tasks began, in which Standard German sentences were given and the participants were asked to translate them by imitating the language heard beforehand. The sentences presented were structured as follows: five of the sentences were identical to sentences in the story (e. g. 1a), five showed lexical similarity to those in the story (e. g. 1b), five showed syntactic similarity, but differed lexically from those in the story (e. g. 1c) and three showed no relation to sentences in the story (e. g. 1d; cf. the presented story in the Appendix in Section 5, p. 256).

(1)   a. *Julia backt Kuchen* "Julia bakes cake"
      b. *Julia braucht Milch, um einen Kuchen zu backen* vs. "Julia needs milk to bake cake"
      c. *Oli schläft gerade* "Oli is sleeping"
      d. *Ich weiß nicht, wie spät es ist* "I do not know what time it is"

In addition, the informants were asked to judge their comprehension of the language of the recording and to identify the language by name. Furthermore, the informants answered questions about their social background (e. g. age, gender, native language(s), education, place of longest residence). Over 600 participants completed the survey. Unfortunately, most of the German informants came from western Germany and hardly any from the East. So we can not draw any firm diatopic conclusions on the whole of the German language area.

The following results are based on a sample of 353 Germans that rated themselves as non-native speakers of the heard dialect. The distribution is as follows: 61 informants imitate BD, 85 imitate WP, 84 CH, 62 AL, and 61 YI. 100 of the participants identify as male, the rest as female. The average given age of the participants is 47. The selected participants where all German native speakers and non-bilingual. 76% (269) of the informants stated the act of imitation as "difficult", 22% (76) as "feasible" and only 2% (7) as "easy". This does not agree with the self-assessment of the informants' understanding of the story. Following them, the understanding of German dialects was relatively good. On a scale from 1 (understand nothing) to 100 (understand everything), the hearers of WP, CH and AL rate their average all with 96 points (with a standard deviation of the WP data of 10, CH 11 and AL 8). BD was rated with a high standard deviation of 19 with 77 points as understandable. The Yiddish recording received the worst understanding. According to the self-assessment it only achieved 67 points in average. Here we find a huge standard deviation of 24.

For further analysis, we used an alignment tool that divides the relevant structures (e.g. phonetic/phonological segments or larger units, like orthographic words) into different columns so that they can be compared with one another (cf. Mayer & Cysouw 2012). Our data was aligned at four language levels: syntax, lexis, morphology, phonology. With the help of this alignment, we determined that there are four possible imitation strategies based on the empirical data:

(1) A form can represent the correct form of the TL (*follow*), which means that the imitation of the TL was successful. For example, this can be seen in the correct imitation of the Central Hessian vokal in (CH) *bis'* (Standard German *böse*) "evil" as *bis*.

(2) A form can represent neither a form of the TL nor of the ML (*fictitious*); due to overgeneralization, interference with a third variety or made up form based on the potential variability of the ML. For example, the periphrasis with "do" (*tun*-periphrasis) in the imitation of AL *D Julia isch am Kuaha baha* lit. *Julia is at baking cake* as *Julia duat kuacha bacha* "Julia does bake cake".

(3) The imitator ignores the form of the TL and uses the ML (*ignore*), means that a feature just follows the given standard language (in our case German); we do not imply any conscious act of ignoring. For example, an imitator does not produce the anaptyxis given in the Low German (WP) story as *kücket* → *kückt*

(4) Due to the closeness of the TL and ML it is possible that a form could represent either language, in which case we cannot decide if this is a product of the imitation (like 1) or if it is an ignored form (like 3) (*default*). As a very simple example the presented Central German (CH) form *steht* "stays" is equivalent with the Standard German form.

In sum, the imitations were predominately (80%) correct, i. e. cases in which we find the strategies (1) or (4). We compared the aligned data from all of the lects

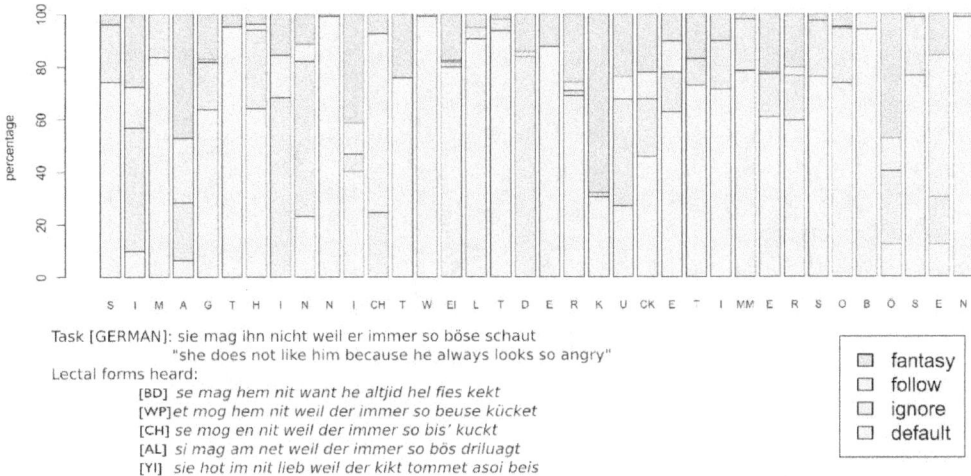

Figure 2: Orthographic/phonological alignment for one sentence (all varieties)

with the four imitation strategies (cf. Figure 2). The distribution of the aligned features shows groups that are more easily accessed by certain strategies than others. For example, in Figure 2 the phonological analysis of one sentence reveals that there is more variation in vowels than in consonants and that the onset is more stable than the nucleus and the coda. Here we see aspects of variability and stability that can be measured by emulative imitation data. Additional domains with vast variability can be seen as easily accessible for language change.

Illustrating the influences of language perception, lay concepts and the imitators' own orality we will take a closer look into the lexico-syntactic structure of pronominal adverbs. The short pronoun doubling construction (***dadavon** ist Julia nicht begeistert* "Julia is not excited about that" lit. ***therethereabout** Julia is not excited*) that was given in the Central Hessian TL was reproduced by 43% of the imitators (like in 2a), while the stranding construction (***da** ist Julia nicht begeistert **von*** lit. ***there** is Julia not excited **about***) given in the Low German (2b) and Belgian Dutch (2c) recordings occurred in only 6% and 3% of the imitations of those languages, respectively (e. g. Figure 3). It is remarkable that we find the short pronoun doubling solely in the imitations of Central Hessian, where it is used in the recording. However, we do find the doubling construction in some isolated imitations of 10% of the Alemannic variety but not in imitations of dialects that do not double their adverbs. In the case of the few instances of short pronoun doubling in the imitations of Alemannic (2d), it has to be considered that this construction is generally possible in this dialect area (e. g. Fleischer

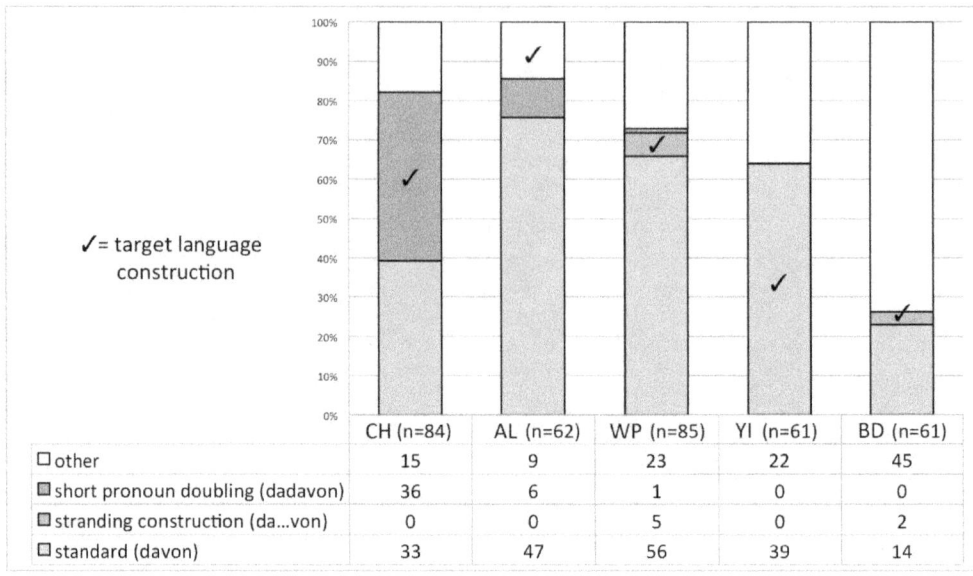

Figure 3: Pronominal adverbs in dialect imitations (all varieties)

(2002); Elspaß & Möller (2001–: Round 1 Questions 11, 12; Round 2 Question 21)), but was not used by the native speaker that translated the text into her dialect and recorded it. Here we can find an example of the influence of external factors on the imitators' knowledge which is based on their orality or/and lay concepts.

(2) a. *dadafo is Julia nit begeisderd* (Imitation of CH)
 b. *Do is Julia net begeistert von* (Imitation of WP)
 c. *da is julia net begeistered von* (Imitation of BD)
 d. *Dodefo isch s Juli net begeischtert* (Imitation of AL)

To stick with the phenomenon of pronominal adverb constructions, We can see the imitations of pronominal adverb constructions by our Hessian informants (e.g. Figure 4). Speakers from Hesse have nearly no trouble producing the construction given in the Hessian recording (*dadavon*). But when it comes to other less common constructions, Hessian imitators scarcely imitate and just keep the structure in its Standard German form (*davon*). The diatopic distribution of the correctly imitated forms of pronominal adverb constructions also fits with the diatopic distribution of this phenomenon in Hessian colloquial speech where the doubling construction is common (cf. Leser 2012; Elspaß & Möller 2001–: Round 1 Questions 11, 12; Round 2 Question 21). Furthermore, this picture could be caused

14 Imitating closely related varieties

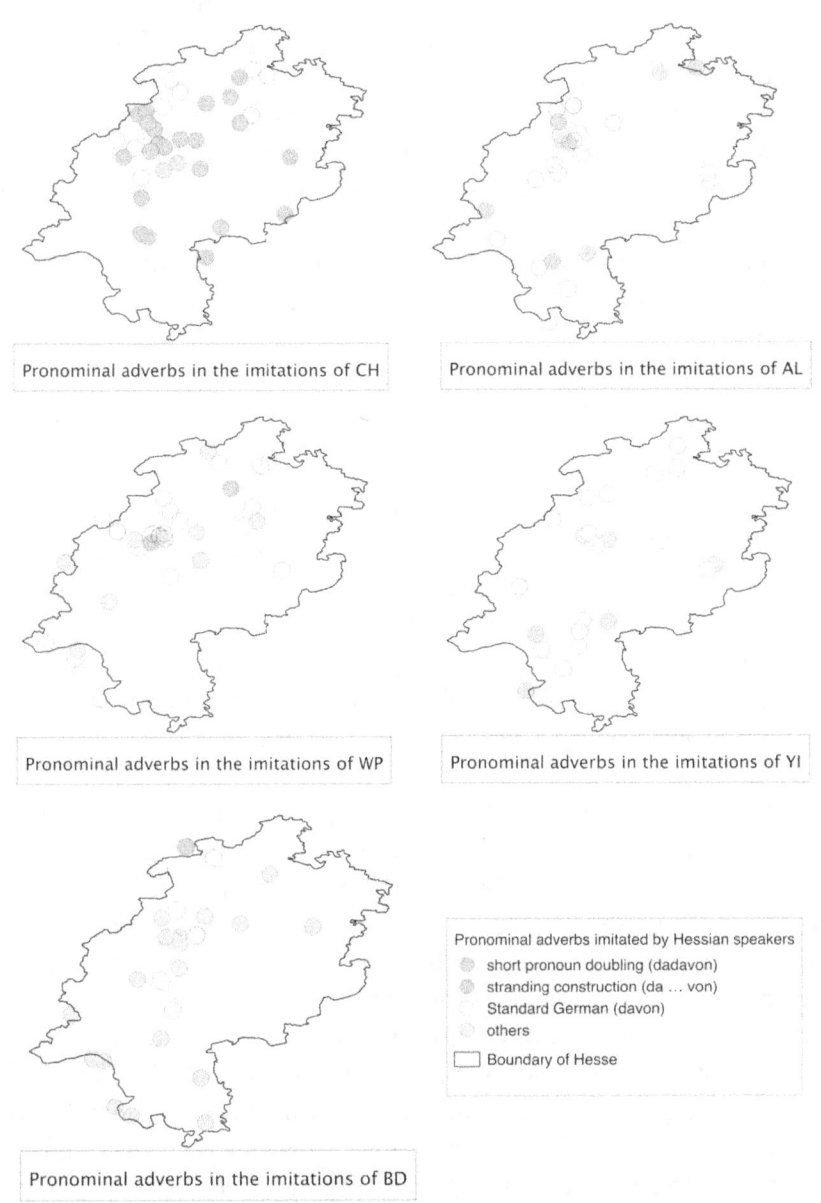

Figure 4: Pronominal adverbs imitated by Hessian speakers (all varieties)

by the factor of markedness: Pronound doubling may stand out more than stranding because it is a simple reduplicative construction while the stranding is just a splitting of the Standard German form. The doubling construction *dadavon* compared to the Standard German *davon* simply represents an increase of morphological material, while stranding *da ... von* is not marked by a rise or decline of material. The latter is simply a usage of the German sentence bracket (*Satzklammer*). The stranding construction with *da ... von* is common in Northern German varieties and has begun entering Standard German. In the course of doubling, we deal with the derivational phenomenon of reduplication, whereas stranding is a syntactic feature. This difference leads us to the question of whether syntactic structures play a less important role for lay concepts than lexical-morphological structures do.

3.2 Corpus study on fictional Yiddish

The second data set for language imitation dates to the 18th and the 19th century. In this period, it became fashionable in German fiction – mostly in theater plays – to mark Jewish characters via speech (cf. Richter 1995). Using *typical Jewish* language is one strategy for evoking anti-Semitic stereotypes. Until the early 20th century, the vernacular of Jews in German speaking countries was Western Yiddish. During the 19th century Western Yiddish was given up in favor of German. In contrast to Eastern Yiddish, which is still a vivid Germanic variety and still spoken today especially by Ultra-Orthodox Jews (e.g. in Israel, USA, or Antwerp), Western Yiddish is not spoken anymore. The fictional adaptations of the Western Yiddish language in German literature, dating back to the 18th and 19th century, can be interpreted as an effect of the language discourse on that variety. These speech styles are imitations of the Western Yiddish variety spoken in Germany, Austria, Switzerland and Alsace. These imitations contain many idiosyncratic structures known from Yiddish varieties, such as the merger of Middle High German /ei/ and /ou/ > /a:/. Yiddish acts here as a medialect that we will call "fictional Yiddish" (fiYi) following Richters (1995) German term "Literaturjiddisch". To be precise, Modern Yiddish is not a dialect of German. But sharing Middle High German as a common origin it is one of Standard German's closest varieties. In the 18th and 19th century it was part of the German dialect continuum. We can assume that Western Yiddish was perceived as a High German variety in that period; thus fiYi is a result of a closely related variety imitation.

The research corpus on fiYi is based on 53 texts of Christian authorship with at most two sources per every 5–year-interval from 1711 to 1948. Through a descriptive and qualitative analysis of the texts, 56 grammatical elements that differ from New High German were highlighted. These fiYi elements, which were observable at all linguistic levels (lexis, phonology, morphology, syntax), were then compared with data from Western and Eastern Yiddish and German dialects of the late 19th century (based on the survey by Georg Wenker, see Lameli 2013). This comparison established that all (!) 56 elements were common forms in West Germanic varieties and most of them represent forms known from Yiddish varieties. There is not a single instance of fictitious fantasy structures in the entire fiYi corpus that does not exist in a Germanic lect. Although texts from the 18th and 19th century fiYi brings together forms we would never find in a natural language. Figure 5 shows the cluster analysis of all elements used in the 53 sources plus ten fictional texts from Jewish authors from 19th century and seven sources of texts from the 21th century[3]. The given forms are all feasible for West Germanic varieties, but they never occur in one variety alone. Sources of fiYi sources form a cluster of their own, while the Yiddish languages build their own cluster. This evidence thus strengthens our theory that emulative imitation happens only within the bounds of its ML's typological possibilities.

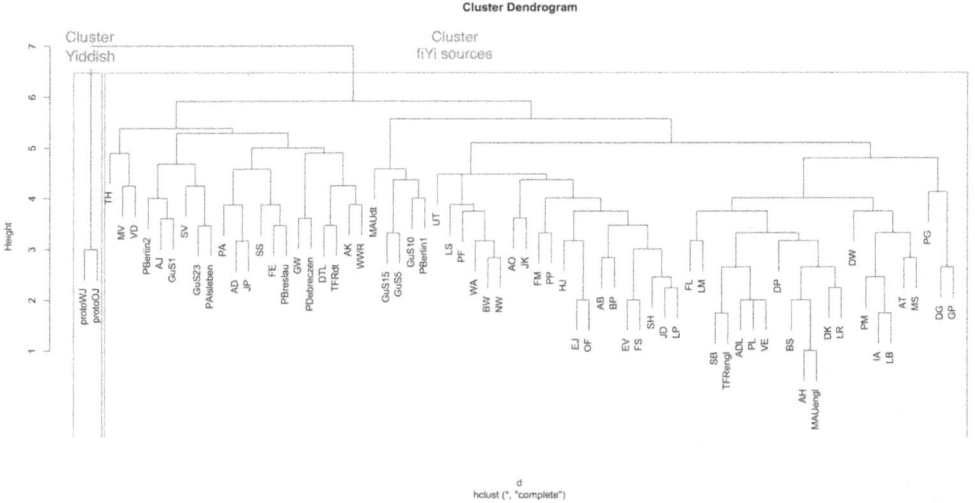

Figure 5: Ward-cluster of fiYi sources compared to Eastern and Western Yiddish

---

[3] The acronyms stand for the single sources and data from Eastern and Western Yiddish

4 Outlook

In this paper, we have presented some data and a number of hypotheses and presumptions on the mechanisms of the imitation of closely related varieties. We emphasize that imitation of closely related varieties show some hidden structures of the ML that may explain to former and future changes that language did or will do. Beyond this survey, further investigations should focus on other important attributes of language imitation, such as regional influences of the imitators' lects, conscious versus unconscious structures used in imitation and the training curve developed during repeated imitation. We would also like to propose that those investigating dialect imitations cooperate with experts in psychology, particularly psycholinguistics, in order to benefit from their knowledge of imitation. In addition to this, there is a need for expanding the West Germanic focus of this study to include other language groups in order to determine whether the isolated mechanisms of dialect imitation can be generalized or not.

5 Appendix

The presented story in its four translations and transcriptions as they where presented in the internet survey. The transcriptions are guided by the Standard German orthography for making them available for the German probands.

Hessian [CH]
Die Julia steht in der Kisch un is am Kuche backe.
Do merkt se, dass se für den Kuche, den se backe will, ach Milsch brauch.
Se kuckt nooch und stellt fest, dass se kah Milsch mehr hot.
'S is Sonndach un die Geschäfte hon zou.
Also will se ihren Freund Max freje, ob der noch Milsch hot.
Do fällt er ober in, dass der Max gesagt hot, er tet's Wochenende fott foan.
Also versucht se 's bei der Frau Hirsch ihrer Nochbursche.
Die hot ober ach kah Milsch un schickt Julia bei den Herr Weiss.
Dodofo is se gornit begeistert, weil der immer so bis' kuckt.
Ober se versuchts trotzdem.
Se kloppt oh sei Tir un seit, se bräuch Milsch im e Kuche ze backe.
Un wer het des gedocht, der Herr Weiss hot Milsch un is fruh, dass er der Julia helfe kann.
Julia bäckt de Kuche un bringt dem Herr Weiss a gruß Stick.

Yiddish [YI]
Julia steiht in Kich un backt a Kichn.
Demolt bamerkt sie, ass sie badarf Milich farn Kichn, wos sie will backen.

Sie git a Kik un bamerkt, ass sie hot nischt kein Milich.
Es is Sunntig un die Kromen sennen farmacht.
Geiht sie freign ihr Freind Max, oib er hot efscher a bisl Milich far ihr.
Demolt gedenkt sie, ass Max hot ihr derzeilt, ass er will awekfuhrn dem Sof-Woch.
Geiht sie zu Frau Hirschn, ihr Schochente.
Jene hot oich nischt kein Milich un schickt sie zu Herr Weissn.
Derfin is Julia nischt bageistert, weil der kikt tommet asoi beiß.
Aber fundestwegen geiht sie.
Sie klappt un in der Tir seiner un sugt, as sie badarf Milich z' backen a Kichn.
'n take, wer wollt sich af dem gericht, Herr Weiss hot Milich un is glicklech ass er kenn ihr helfen.
Julia backt dem Kichen un brengt Herr Weissn a grois Stick.

Low German [WP]
Et Julia steiht in der Kücke un is an Koken backen.
Da merket et, för den Koken, den backen will, nach Milk broket.
Et kücket no un stellt fest, dat et keine Milk mehr do is.
Et is Sundach un die Jeschäfte han to.
Also willt se em Freund Max frochen, of der noch welke het.
Dann fällt 'n aber in, dat Max en vertallt hät, he wör am Wekenenne wech fahren.
Also forsöket et bi Frau Hirsch der Nachbarin.
Die het aber auch kinne Milk un schicket et Julia tu Herr Weiss.
Do is et nit begeistert von, weil der immer so beuse kücket.
Aber et versöket et trotzdem.
Et kloppet an sine Döre un seiet, dat et Milk brucket um en Koken to backen.
Un we hedet det jedacht, der Herr Weiss het Milk un freuet sik det he dem Julia helfen kann.
Julia bicket den Koken un brenget Herrn Weiss 'n grautet Stücke.

Belgian Dutch [BD]
Julia is en de Köken un backt en Tart.
Da merkt se op, dat se vor de Tart, die se will backen, noch Milk nodich heft.
Se kontruliert en merkt op, dat er keen Milk mehr is.
Höt is Sundach un die Winkel sen dicht.
Des wil se haar Friend Max freign of he er noch heeft.
Dan schoot het er te binnen, dat Max haar verteeltede, dat he dat Weekend wech ching sein.
Düs probiert se hüt be mer Frau Hirsch, her Bürfrau.
Ma se heft ok keen Milk en stürt Julia nach min Herr Weiss.
Da is se nit blei um wat he altjid hel fies kekt, ma se probert het doch.
Se kloppt op de Dür en secht, dat se Mild nodich heeft om Taart te backen.
Wi het dat jedeicht, min Herr Weiss heft Milk un is blee dat er Julia heft könne helpe.
Julia backt de Tart en brengt min Herr Weiss er en grot Stück von.

Upper German [AL]
D Julia isch in dr Kuhi am Kuaha baha.
Do merkt si, dass für an Kuaha, wo si am baha isch, noch a Milch fehlt.
Sie luagt nooch und sacht, dass ka Milch mer do isch.
Es isch Sunntig und Gschäfter hon zua.
Drum goht si ihr Freund dr Max froga, ob er noch ane hot.
Denn fallt ira aber i, dass dr Max ira verzählt hot, er tei am Wochanende wegfahra.
Drum probiert sies bei dr Frau Hirsch irer Nachbürin.
Dia hot o ka Milch und schickt d Julia zum Herr Weiss.
Vo dem isch d Julia net begeischtert, weil der immer so bös driluagt.
Aber sie probierts trotzdem.
Sie klopft bei ihm an dr Tür und set dass sie Milch brucht zum Kuacha bacha.
Wer het des denkt, dr Herr Weiss hot Milch und freut sich, dass er ihra helfa könna hot.
D Julia backt dr Kuacha und bringt am Herr Weiss a großes Stück.

References

Adank, Patti, Peter Hagoort & Harold Bekkering. 2010. Imitation improves language comprehension. *Psychological Science* 21. 1903–1909.

Androutsopoulos, Jannis. 2012. Intermediale Varietätendynamik: Ein explorativer Blick auf die Inszenierung und Aushandlung von ‚Dialekt' auf YouTube. *Sociolinguistica* 26. 87–101.

Babel, Molly. 2009. *Phonetic and social selectivity in speech accommodation.* University of California, Berkeley PhD thesis.

Dossey, Ellen E. 2012. *Spontaneous phonetic imitation across regional dialects.* Honors project Macalester College. http://digitalcommons.macalester.edu/ling_honors/8/ (23 June, 2014).

Elspaß, Stephan & Robert Möller. 2001–. *Atlas zur deutschen Alltagssprache.* http://www.atlas-alltagssprache.de/ (29 October, 2014).

Fitch, William Tecumseh Sherman. 2010. *The evolution of language.* Cambridge: Cambridge University Press.

Fleischer, Jürg. 2002. *Die Syntax von Pronominaladverbien in den Dialekten des Deutschen: Eine Untersuchung zu Preposition Stranding und verwandten Phänomenen* (Zeitschrift für Dialektologie und Linguistik, Beiheft 123). Stuttgart, Wiesbaden: Steiner.

Haider, Hubert. 2007. Poetenpidgin – über Ernst Jandls Grammatik einer heruntergekommenen Sprache. In Wolfgang U. Dressler & Oswald Panagl (eds.), *Poetische Lizenzen*, 133–145. Wien: Praesens.

Hauser, Marc D., Noam Chomsky & William Tecumseh Sherman Fitch. 2002. The language faculty: What is it, who has it, and how did it evolve? *Science* 298. 1569–1579.

Kleiner, Stefan. 2013. Medienbairisch – Eine variationslinguistische Untersuchung der Dialekttiefe des Mittelbairischen in Film- und Fernsehproduktionen. In Rüdiger Harnisch (ed.), *Strömungen in der Entwicklung der Dialekte und ihrer Erforschung. Beiträge zur 11. Bayerisch-österreichischen Dialektologentagung in Passau September 2010* (Regensburger Dialektforum 19), 429–449. Regensburg: edition vulpes.

Lameli, Alfred. 2013. *Schriften zum Sprachatlas des Deutschen Reichs: Gesamtausgabe* (Deutsche Dialektgeographie Bd. 1–3). Hildesheim: Olms.

Leser, Stephanie. 2012. Zum Pronominaladverb in den hessischen Dialekten. Eine Untersuchung zum Verlauf syntaktischer Isoglossen. In Robert Langhanke, Kristian Berg, Michael Elmentaler & Jörg Peters (eds.), *Niederdeutsche Syntax* (Germanistische Linguistik 220), 79–100. Hildesheim: Olms.

Markham, Duncan. 1997. *Phonetic imitation, accent, and the learner* (Travaux de l'Institut de linguistique de Lund (Bd. 33)). Lund: Lund University Press.

Markham, Duncan. 1999. Listeners and disguised voices: The imitation and perception of dialectal accent. *Forensic Linguistics* 6(2). 289–299.

Mayer, Benedikt & Peter Zimmerer. 2009. >>Mia san daily<< – Versuch einer Messung von Dialektalität in der Fernsehserie >>Dahoam is Dahoam<< im Bayerischen Fernsehen. In Ulrich Kanz, Alfred Wildfeuer & Ludwig Zehetner (eds.), *Mundart und Medien. Beiträge zum 3. Dialektologischen Symposium im Bayerischen Wald, Walderbach, Mai 2008* (Regensburger Dialektforum 16), 233–242. Regensburg: edition vulpes.

Mayer, Thomas & Michael Cysouw. 2012. Language comparison through sparse multilingual word alignment. In *Proceedings of the EACL 2012 Joint Workshop of LINGVIS & UNCLH*, 54–62. Avignon: Association for Computational Linguistics.

Meltzoff, Andrew & M. Keith Moore. 1977. Imitation of facial and manual gestures by human neonates. *Science* 198. 75–78.

Meltzoff, Andrew & Wolfgang Prinz. 2002. *The imitative mind. Development, evolution, and brain bases.* Cambridge: Cambridge University Press.

Myers-Scotton, Carol. 1993. *Duelling languages: Grammatical structure in codeswitching.* Oxford: Oxford University Press.

Myers-Scotton, Carol. 2002. *Contact linguistics: Bilingual encounters and grammatical outcomes.* Oxford: Oxford University Press.

Neuhauser, Sara. 2012. *Phonetische und linguistische Aspekte der Akzentimitation im forensischen Kontext: Produktion und Perzeption* (Tübinger Beiträge zur Linguistik (529)). Tübingen: Narr.

Petkov, C. I. & E. D. Jarvis. 2012. Birds, primates, and spoken language origins: Behavioral phenotypes and neurobiological substrates. *Frontiers in Evolutionary Neuroscience* 4(12).

Purschke, Christoph. 2010. Imitation und Hörerurteil – Kognitive Dialekt-Prototypen am Beispiel des Hessischen. In Christina Anders, Markus Hundt & Alexander Lasch (eds.), *Perceptual dialectology: Neue Wege der Dialektologie*, 151–178. Berlin/New York: De Gruyter.

Richter, Matthias. 1995. *Die Sprache jüdischer Figuren in der deutschen Literatur (1750–1933). Studien zu Form und Funktion.* Göttingen: Wallstein.

Riemann, Andreas. 2009. Neue >Sprache<, neue >Heimat<, neues >Bayern<? In Ulrich Kanz, Alfred Wildfeuer & Ludwig Zehetner (eds.), *Mundart und Medien. Beiträge zum 3. Dialektologischen Symposium im Bayerischen Wald, Walderbach, Mai 2008* (Regensburger Dialektforum 16), 273–287. Regensburg: edition vulpes.

Segerup, My. 1999. Imitation of dialects: From South to West. *Fonetik*. Gothenburg papers in theoretical linguistics 81 99. 1253–1256.

Siegel, Jeff. 2010. *Second dialect acquisition*. Cambridge: Cambridge University Press.

Tomasello, Michael & Malinda Carpenter. 2007. Shared intentionality. *Developmental Science* 10. 121–125.

Užgiris, Ina Čepėnaitė. 1981. Two functions of imitation during infancy. *International Journal of Behavioral Development* 4. 1–12.

Chapter 15

Spontaneous dubbing as a tool for eliciting linguistic data: The case of second person plural inflections in Andalusian Spanish

Víctor Lara Bermejo
Universidad Autónoma de Madrid

> In this paper, I present an innovative methodology employed to analyse the sociolinguistic evolution of a Peninsular Spanish phenomenon that has not been researched in depth until now. The use of a single pronoun to address a group of people is attested in the southern Spanish region of Andalusia and it induces both 2nd person and 3rd person agreements, unlike the standard pattern. These mismatches correspond to several social factors analysed statistically. The most recent information available on this phenomenon dates back to the 1930's, so the new data collected, through a methodology that lends itself to eliciting a high quantity of data (spontaneous dubbing), illustrates the development of this phenomenon.

1 Introduction

Second person pronouns in most Peninsular Spanish varieties distinguish perfectly the number of addressees and the degree of politeness. There are four: two singular, two plural. For each grammatical number, there is one for formality and another one for informality (Table 1).

All informal pronouns induce 2nd person inflections, whereas the formal pronouns must agree in 3rd person (Table 2). This is the standard usage in Peninsular Spanish or Spanish spoken in the Iberian Peninsula (Spain, except the Canary Islands).

However, at some time in the past, the western part of Andalusia, the most southern region in Spain, eliminated the 2nd person plural pronoun, *vosotros*, and began using *ustedes* for all 2pl, regardless of the formality or the informality.

Víctor Lara Bermejo. 2016. Spontaneous dubbing as a tool for eliciting linguistic data: The case of second person plural inflections in Andalusian Spanish. In Marie-Hélène Côté, Remco Knooihuizen & John Nerbonne (eds.), *The future of dialects*, 261–281. Berlin: Language Science Press. DOI:10.17169/langsci.b81.154

Table 1: Standard second person pronouns

	Singular	Plural
Formality	usted	ustedes
Informality	tú	vosotros

Table 2: Standard person agreement for second person pronouns

	Singular	Plural
Formality	3rd person	3rd person
Informality	2nd person	2nd person

In spite of this feature, Lara (2010) proved that *ustedes* can agree both in 2pl and 3rd person plural with verbs, clitics or possessives (1–3).

(1) Ustedes sois hermanos.
 You-NOM.2PL.HON be-2PL.PRES.IND siblings
 'You are siblings.'

(2) Ustedes se casáis mañana.
 You-NOM.2PL.HON refl.3pl. marry-2PL.PRES.IND tomorrow
 'You are getting married tomorrow.'

(3) A ustedes os vi ayer.
 To you-NOM.2PL.HON 2pl.acc. see-1SG.PRET.IND yesterday
 'I saw you yesterday.'

These agreement mismatches between the stressed pronoun and the other syntactic elements anchoring *ustedes*, have not been explained or sufficiently investigated until now.

The literature about this phenomenon is found in works on historic grammars or monographs dealing with the Andalusian dialect (Mondéjar 1974; Lapesa, Cano Aguilar & Echenique Elizondo 2000; Cano Aguilar 2004; Penny 2004; Menéndez Pidal & Catalán Menéndez-Pidal 2005). These authors state that this vernacular feature is observed in the provinces of Córdoba, Málaga, Cádiz, Huelva and Seville (See the map in Figure 1).

15 Spontaneous dubbing as a tool for eliciting linguistic data

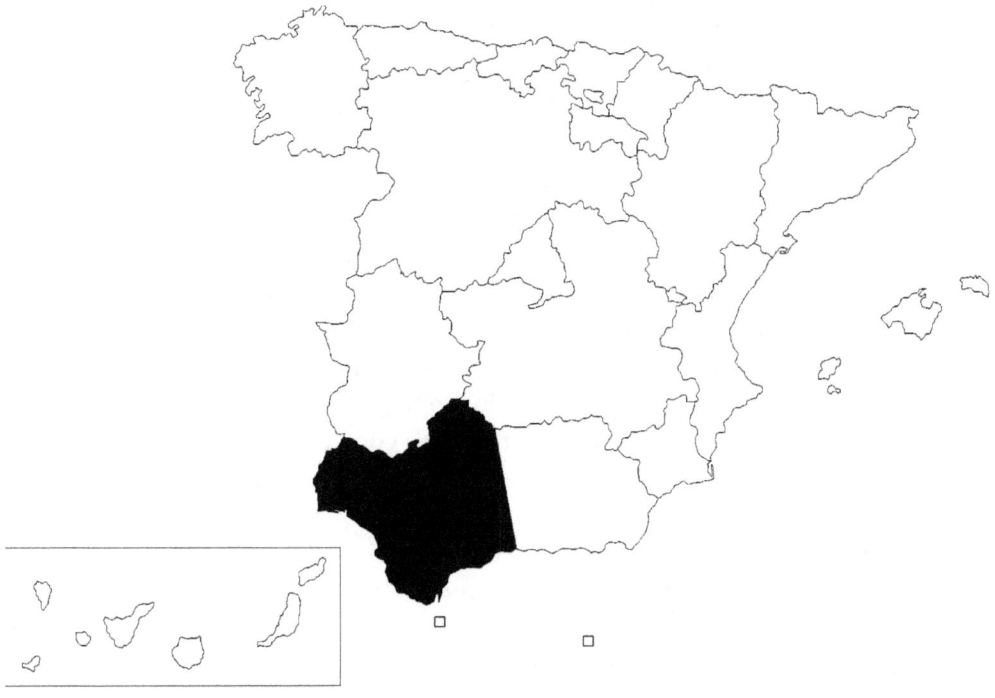

Figure 1: Ustedes phenomenon inside Spain

They also state that it is stigmatised and it has always been considered as illiterate and rural. Furthermore, *ustedes* always agrees in 2pl, unless the verb is in the simple past. In this case, 3pl agreement is preferred. Reflexive pronouns agree in 3pl, as well. All these linguists also assure us that the possessive has changed into the prepositional phrase *de ustedes*, instead of the normative 3rd person *su* or the 2pl *vuestro* (table 3). The adoption of one specific person agreement does not take into account the politeness of the communicative situation.

As for many other phenomena, whenever a linguistic change arises, it does not do so in all the syntactic contexts it should (Labov 1995; Corbett 2006). To illus-

Table 3: Allocutives person agreements in Andalusia

	Stressed pronoun	Verb	Simple past	Possessive	Reflexive pronoun	Object pronouns
Formality	Ustedes	2pl	3pl	3pl	3pl	2pl
Informality	Ustedes	2pl	3pl	3pl	3pl	2pl

263

trate, *voseo* (the use of the plural pronoun *vós* to address one person in an informal context) first emerged in the stressed pronoun and its inflections spread gradually: first to the imperative, then to the present indicative, later to the present subjunctive but they are not attested yet in clitics and possessives (Fontanella de Weinberg 1979; Abadía de Quant 1992; Bertolotti & Coll 2003). In the case of *ustedes*, the 3pl was initially used in the stressed pronoun but it has not yet forced all its syntactic elements to be inflected in the 3pl, as will be shown later. It is reasonable to expect that the 3pl will spread gradually, until it is attested in all the *ustedes* syntactic references.

As will be argued, some techniques employed in dialect data elicitation have not been useful to obtain 2pl inflections due to their low probability of emergence. The method I describe in this article represents a good pointer for the future study of dialects, thanks to the use of video dubbing and audiovisual stimuli. It can produce a large quantity of tokens to be analysed statistically, while avoiding any priming. In fact, this method has allowed to establish that the Andalusian dialect is beginning to comply with standard patterns. Thus, this paper is structured as follows: firstly, I describe previous methods for the collection of 2pl inflections in Andalusia; what has been found about the *ustedes* linguistic behaviour and the shortcomings of these techniques. Later, I introduce my corpus and methodology and how they have compensated the lack of linguistic data from other sources. Then, I apply two statistical tests to the results of this new methodology. Finally, I focus on the development of the dialect phenomenon under study, in order to demonstrate the findings that my technique has led to.

2 ALPI data

The most recent information available on this phenomenon can be found in the Linguistic Atlas of the Iberian Peninsula (ALPI, by its Spanish acronym), uploaded on Heap (2003). This dialect atlas was conceived by Menéndez Pidal. However, it was a group of researchers who obtained the data by travelling throughout the Iberian Peninsula, with the aim of collecting the phonological, lexical and morpho-syntactic phenomena of all the Romance languages in the peninsula. Their interviews were carried out between the 1930's and the 1950's and these consisted of pre-established sentences and words that the informants had to repeat based on their vernacular variety (Sanchís Guarner 1962). The lack of spontaneity could have tainted the informants' responses. Although they could not rely on the electronic devices currently available, a great many of their linguistic findings are being validated in most recent research.

Within the ALPI pre-established sentences, there are eleven with a reference to a 2pl. These provide data about the stressed pronoun, the reflexive pronoun, the accusative pronoun, as well as main verbs tensed in imperative and present indicative. A sentence with an embedded verb is also included. Thanks to this invaluable work, some information on the geographic diffusion pattern, the grammatical behaviour and the pragmatic incidence of this phenomenon could be disseminated.

2.1 Geography

With respect to geography, this phenomenon is attested in Western Andalusia, specifically in the provinces of Cádiz, Seville, Huelva, Córdoba (except the northern part) and Málaga (excepting the eastern part). Moreover, its diffusion pattern followed the wave model, as presented by Chambers & Trudgill (1980) or Wolfram & Schilling-Estes (2003). This model states that a specific linguistic phenomenon arises in a specific geographic point, called focus or epicentre, from which all the further innovations concerning the phenomenon also emerge in the first place.

The hypothesis predicts that in an innovation in which three changes (C) have occurred, C1 arises in a specific point from which it is diffused toward its outlying area. When C1 has extended to the periphery, C2 appears in the same point where C1 had originated earlier. In a later evolution, C2 reaches the outlying area of the focus, while C1 leaps to an even more distant area, while, at the same time, a C3 arises at the focus point.

If all this information is applied to the phenomenon under investigation, based on the ALPI data in the map in Figure 2, several conclusions can be drawn.

The *ustedes* phenomenon produced four changes, as map 2 shows. Level 1 is characterised by change 1; level 2 by changes 1 and 2; level 3, by changes 1, 2 and 3, and, finally, level 4 shows four changes. This spatial diffusion proves that the *ustedes* phenomenon arose in Cádiz and southern Seville, as it is the region where all the changes initiate. The closer a site is to this area, the more changes are shared with it; the farther away, the fewer changes shared, until the *ustedes* phenomenon fades.

2.2 Grammar

In terms of its grammatical behaviour, this phenomenon predicts the extension of the 3pl in all the syntactic elements anchoring *ustedes*. Since *ustedes* induces 3pl inflections, these must appear gradually, until they are settled in all the elements

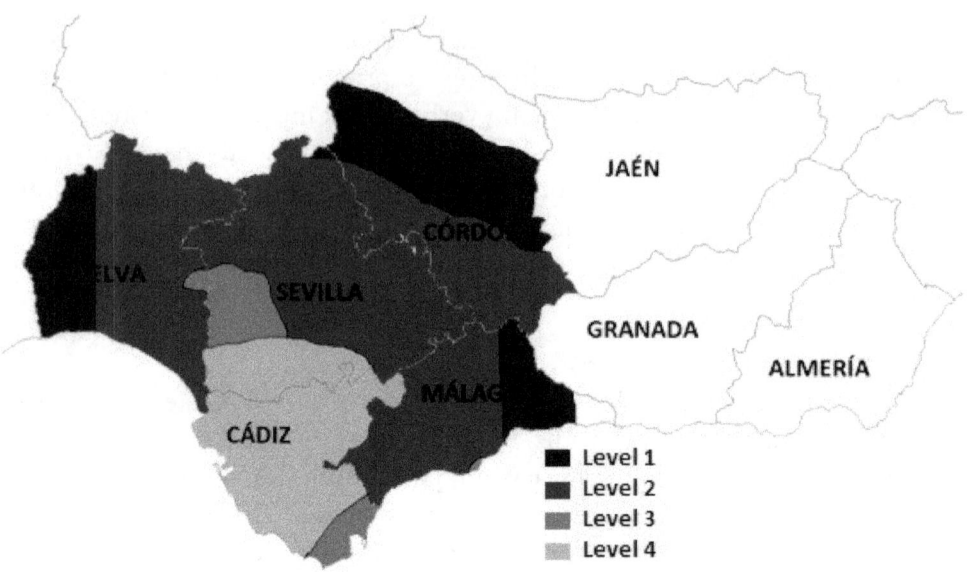

Figure 2: Andalusian geographic diffusion pattern (Lara 2012: 85).

with reference to *ustedes*. According to the map in Figure 2, the extension of the 3pl agreement follows the implicational hierarchy expressed in (4).

(4) Stressed pronoun > reflexive pronoun > accusative pronoun > embedded verb

The continuum must be read as follows: the adoption of the 3pl in a specific grammatical element implies its emergence in the ones to the left. So, if the 3pl is attested in the accusative pronoun, it is also attested in the reflexive pronoun and, of course, in the stressed pronoun. The extension to new grammatical contexts proceeds to the right in the hierarchy.

Level 1 is thus characterised by the use of the 3pl in the stressed pronoun (5); level 2 is characterised by the extension of the 3pl use to the reflexive pronouns (6); level 3, by the spread of the 3pl in the accusative pronoun (7); and, finally, at level 4 the 3pl is established in the embedded verb (8) as well.

(5) Ustedes sois parientes del alcalde.
 you-NOM.2PL.HON be-2PL.PRES.IND relatives of.the mayor
 'You are the mayor's relatives.'

(6) Ustedes   se   vais   de viaje.
    you-NOM.2PL.HON REFL.3PL go-2PL.PRES.IND on trip
    'You are going on a trip.'

(7) A ustedes   los   han   engañado.
    to you-NOM.2PL.HON   acc.3PL   have-3PL.PRES.IND   lie.PCP
    'You have been deceived.'

(8) Haced   ustedes   lo   que quieran.
    do-2PL.IMP you-NOM.2PL.HON that what want-3PL.PRES.SUBJ
    'Do whatever you want.'

2.3 Pragmatics

In terms of pragmatics, the informants' grammatical agreement do not change based on the degree of politeness. According to the ALPI data, *ustedes* is used both formally and informally. The adoption of the 3pl or the maintenance of 2pl inflections are not affected by the type of addressees, as (9) and (10) show.

(9) ¿Adónde vais   ustedes?   (to children).
    where   go-2PL.PRES.IND   you-NOM.2PL.HON
    'Where are you going to?'

(10) Lo   queréis   para ustedes   (to elderly
     acc.3SG.NEUT   want-2PL.PRES.IND   for you-NOM.2PL.HON
     people).

    'You want it for yourselves.'

3 Corpus and methodology

In a typical sociolinguistic interview, the 2pl pronouns are the least likely to appear in a conversation. Thus, to analyse a phenomenon like the one studied here, it is not useful to collect data using this type of elicitation, since the informants tend to speak about themselves, about other people's lives and they are also very likely to only address one interviewer although there may be two people posing questions. Pre-established sentences do not trigger a great many tokens, as ALPI demonstrates, since only one example for each pre-established sentence was recorded.

In order to compensate for the shortcomings that arise when using in pre-established sentences and questionnaires, as well as to remedy the low frequency of 2pl inflections in material elicited using other more recent methods, I have devised another type of eliciting. It consists in having the informants dub a series of scenes compiled from the popular sitcom *Friends* and the Spanish sitcom *Aquí no hay quien viva* ('It is impossible to live here'). Video stimuli have become quite an important tool for eliciting spontaneous and quantitative data in order to carry out an ulterior statistical analysis (Chelliah & de Reuse 2011; Mallinson, Childs & van Herk 2013; Thieberger 2011; Lara 2015). The reason for choosing these two programmes lies in the dynamics that the scripts trigger since multiple dialogues, in which one or two characters have to address a group of people, naturally take place. In addition, these characters speak to addressees, with whom they either maintain a formal or informal social relationship: elderly people, bosses, flatmates, friends, neighbours, acquaintances, children, etc. It is, therefore, a great opportunity to analyse possible mismatches in the informants' grammatical agreement, by taking also into account the formality of the given situation.

The scenes are shown to informants, who are given a description with some lead sentences (cf.I), while they are watching the video. The scenes do not contain any sound and these provide a prompt, since the dubbing of the informants does not have to synchronise with the speech of the character they have to dub. Once they have understood the activity, they are asked to dub the character that is addressing the others, based on the previous oral synopsis and lead sentences. Each scene predicts the emergence of a specific syntactic element (verb, reflexive pronoun, object pronouns, and so on) thanks to these cue sentences. I have compiled several scenes so that each syntactic context can appear, in order to ensure the quantitative part of the corpus and its further analysis. No conditioning of the informants is possible, because the description of the scene is always carried out with references to third persons. Therefore, no 2pl is previously mentioned at all. All the fieldwork was carried out in 2012 and, thanks to this method, I have obtained approximately 4,500 occurrences from about 250 different informants. All of them were contacted through different educational institutions, depending on their level of literacy.

3.1 Friends

This sitcom was broadcast between the years 1994 and 2004, and it deals with the personal and social relationships that a group of close friends have with each other. Below, I describe some of the lead sentences that the informants had to reproduce in 2pl.

15 Spontaneous dubbing as a tool for eliciting linguistic data

I The main character is meeting some friends and they are all celebrating that she is getting married very soon. However, she is not as happy as she should be and starts pointing out to her friends all the things they can still do because they are single. (symmetrical communicative situation)

Syntactic context: Present indicative and present subjunctive in embedded sentence.
Lead sentence: She says that they can do whatever they want.
Expected sentence:

(11) Podéis / pueden [ustedes / vosotros] hacer lo que
Can-PRES.IND.2PL/3PL [NOM.2PL.HON. / NOM.2PL.] do whatever
[ustedes / vosotros] queráis / quieran.
[NOM.2PL.HON. / NOM.2PL.] want-2PL / 3PL
'You can do whatever you want.'

Syntactic context: Imperative, reflexive pronoun.
Lead sentence: She urges them not to get married.
Expected sentence:

(12) No os / se caséis / casen
Neg. REFL.2PL / 3PL get married-PRES.SUBJ.2PL. / 3PL.
[ustedes / vosotras].
[nom.2pl.hon. / nom.2pl.]
'Don't get married.'

II The boss of one of the characters is in a meeting with the main character and a workmate. The boss asks them for their opinion on the new collection of clothing, which is about to be distributed on the market. (asymmetrical communicative situation)

Syntactic context: Present indicative, interrogative modality
Lead sentence: She asks them for their opinion about the new collection.
Expected sentence:

(13) ¿Qué pensáis / piensan [ustedes / vosotros]?
What think-PRES.IND.2PL / 3PL [NOM.2PL.HON. / NOM.2PL.]?
('What do you think about it?')

Syntactic context: Conditional / reflexive pronouns / interrogative modality.
Lead sentence: She asks them whether they would wear the new collection.
Expected sentence:

(14) ¿Os / se   pondríais / pondrían   [ustedes / vosotros]
     REFL.2PL / 3PL wear-COND. 2PL. / 3PL. [NOM.2PL.HON. / NOM.2PL.]
     la nueva colección?
     the new   collection?

('Would you wear this?')

3.2 Aquí no hay quien viva

This sitcom was broadcast between the years 2003 and 2006, and it deals with the daily lives and relationships among neighbours of a residential building in the centre of Madrid. Some of the pre-established lead sentences are described below.

III A pair of friends wish to pretend to be a couple and they ask a friend of theirs how they can succeed in their pretence. Their friend answers by enumerating the conditions they have to fulfill if they want others to believe them. (symmetrical situation)

Syntactic context: Future or present indicative.
Lead sentence: He says that they have to know many things about each other.
Expected sentence:

(15) Tendréis / tendrán / tenéis / tienen
     Have-FUT.IND.2PL / 3PL /-PRES.IND.2PL / 3PL
     [ustedes / vosotros]   que saber cosas el uno del otro.
     [NOM.2PL.HON. / NOM.2PL.]   to know   things about each other

('You have to know things about each other.')

IV The director of a bank office informs a couple that the bank cannot grant them a loan. (asymmetrical communicative situation)

Syntactic context: Dative pronoun
Lead sentence: He tells them that the bank cannot grant them a loan.
Expected sentence:

(16)　No　os / les　　　podemos　　　otorgar
　　　NEG. DAT.2PL / 3PL can-PRES.IND.1PL. grant
　　　[a ustedes / vosotros]　　el　préstamo.
　　　[OBL.2PL.HON. / NOM.2PL.] the loan

('We cannot grant you the loan.')

4 Analysis

Each occurrence is tagged based on its extra-linguistic and linguistic factors. To illustrate, every example provides information about the social factors of the informant that has produced it: gender, age, educational level, locality, province, ALPI zone (cf. map 2) and size of the population of the locality. Moreover, the linguistic factors that have been established to analyse the agreement are the stressed pronoun, the reflexive pronoun, the accusative pronoun, the dative pronoun, the possessive, the verb tense, the verb mood, the modality, the type of embedded sentence and the communicative situation (formal or informal). Below, I reproduce the number of tokens and informants, on the basis of a number of their social features.

Table 4: Informants and tokens (gender)

	Informants	Occurrences
Men	117 (48,3%)	2007 (44,6%)
Women	125 (51,7%)	2484 (55,4%)
Total	242 (100%)	4491 (100%)

All the data have been processed with a statistics programme (SPSS). I have applied two statistical tests: the Pearson's chi-squared test and a logistic regression. The former gives the real significance of an independent variable (ie: gender, age, etc.) and the latter orders the degree of affectedness of each significant variable. Below, I detail the results of this methodology, applied to the *ustedes* phenomenon, taking into account three parameters: the geographical factor, the sociolinguistic factor and the linguistic factor.

Table 5: Informants and tokens (age)

	Informants	Occurrences
Young	94 (38,8%)	1956 (43,5%)
Working population	94 (38,8%)	1930 (42,9%)
Elderly	54 (22,4%)	605 (13,6%)
Total	242 (100%)	4491 (100%)

Table 6: Informants and tokens (educational level)

	Informants	Occurrences
Higher education	58 (24%)	1086 (24,1%)
Lower education	184 (76%)	3405 (75,9%)
Total	242 (100%)	4491 (100%)

4.1 Geography

I have classified the occurrences of the phenomenon, based on their percentages. Hence, the map in Figure 3 shows extent to which the *ustedes* phenomenon is attested in speakers. This map is based on the ALPI zones (cf. map 2). As Figure 3 shows, in the area marked A, the informants manifest the *ustedes* misagreement feature over 66% of the time. In area B, the informants are characterised by an intermediate degree of dialectalism (33% - 66%). Finally, part C represents the area in which the *ustedes* phenomenon appears less than 33% of the time.

Table 7: Informants and tokens (size of the population)

	Informants	Occurrences
-5.000 inhabitants	28 (11,5%)	489 (10,9%)
5.000 – 10.000 inhabitants	67 (27,7%)	1202 (26,7%)
10.000 – 20.000 inhabitants	63 (26%)	1149 (25,6%)
20.000 – 100.000 inhabitants	18 (7,5%)	252 (5,6%)
100.000 – 500.000 inhabitants	41 (17%)	872 (19,4%)
+500.000 inhabitants	25 (10,3%)	527 (17,8%)
TOTAL	242 (100%)	4491 (100%)

15 Spontaneous dubbing as a tool for eliciting linguistic data

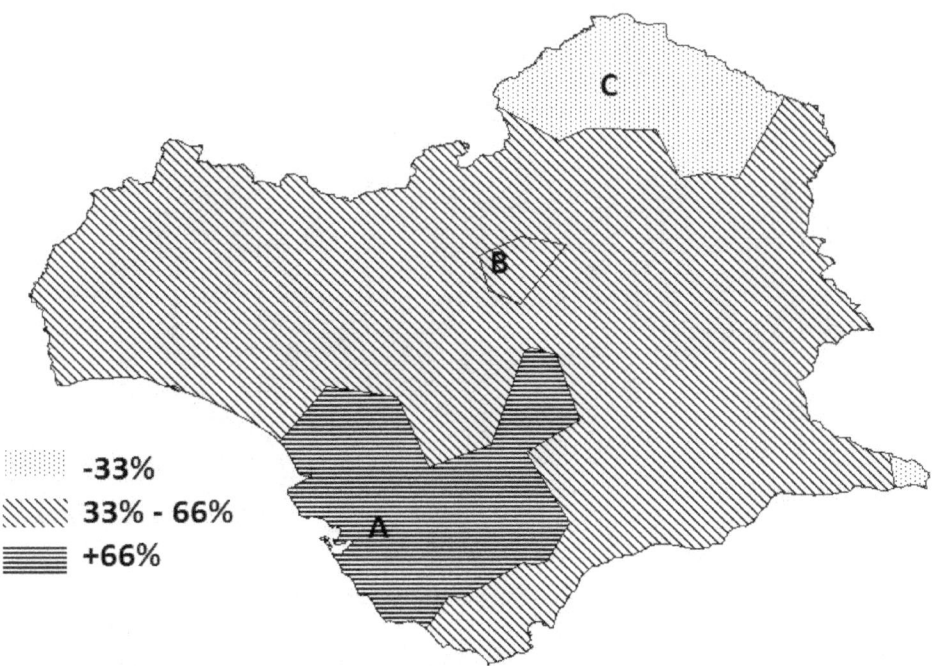

Figure 3: Percentage of use of ustedes, based on the ALPI zones

While Cádiz and Seville are the districts with a higher proportion of maintenance of the phenomenon, Córdoba and Málaga behave in the opposite fashion, and Huelva takes up the middle ground. The *ustedes* phenomenon has not extended further than it had almost one hundred years earlier. Indeed, in some parts where ALPI had recorded this phenomenon I have not found any instances. We find it likely that the *ustedes* phenomenon has retreated geographically. This retreat has taken place in northern Córdoba. Nevertheless, the conclusion is that the further away from the focus, the likelier to imitate the standard usage: the closer to the ALPI focus or epicentre (Cádiz and southern Seville), the greater the likelihood that this vernacular phenomenon is maintained.

If the percentages are divided on the basis of the size of the population of the locality surveyed, the results are quite different, as the map in Figure 4 shows.

This map reveals that the use of the vernacular feature is greater when the city or town has fewer inhabitants. Despite the high variation, there seems to be a clear distinction between large cities, such as Seville and Málaga, and towns (Marbella and Algeciras) and villages (Ayamonte and Pedrera). The first try to adopt the standard usage, while the remaining two are more conservative and prefer

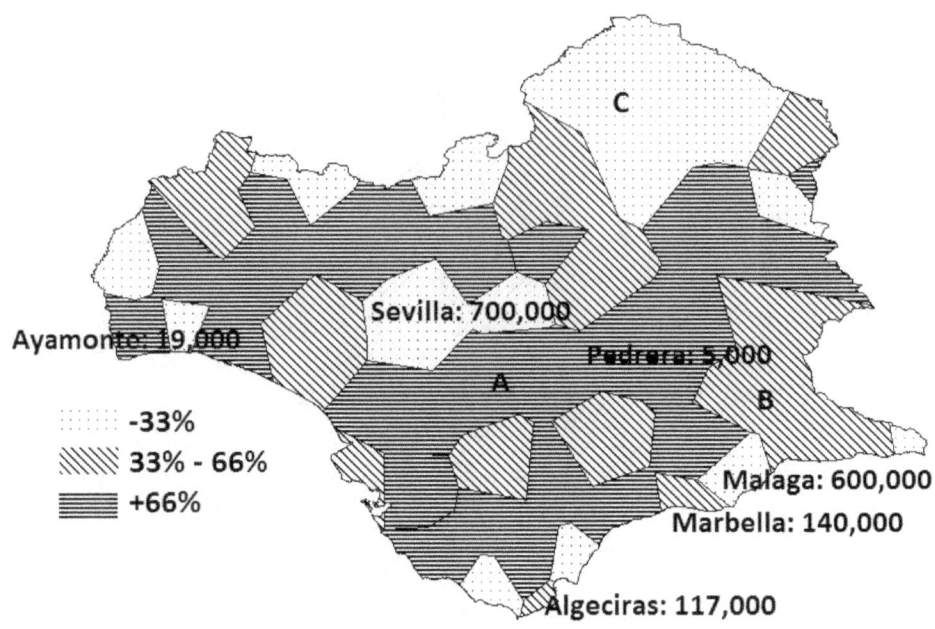

Figure 4: Percentage of use of ustedes, based on the locality surveyed

to maintain the vernacular phenomenon. In all the statistical results related to population, the smaller the town is, the likelier they maintain the vernacular phenomenon. This may lead to the conclusion that another kind of spatial diffusion of the standard use is taking place in detriment of the dialect feature: the gravity model. This pattern predicts that a given linguistic phenomenon will be extended depending on the population density of two points (Wolfram & Schilling-Estes 2003).

4.2 Sociolinguistic factor

The Pearson's chi-squared test for the *ustedes* phenomenon has proved that the use of the vernacular or the standard pattern depends on the informants' age, educational background and the municipality in which they live. In addition, the logistic regression shows that the first factor that conditions the use of the vernacular feature is the educational background, followed by the age and, then, the size of the population of the locality. This implies that the higher the educational background of the informants, the lower their tendency toward the vernacular. As a sample of this, I reproduce the table and figure taken from the statistical analysis (Figure 5).

15 Spontaneous dubbing as a tool for eliciting linguistic data

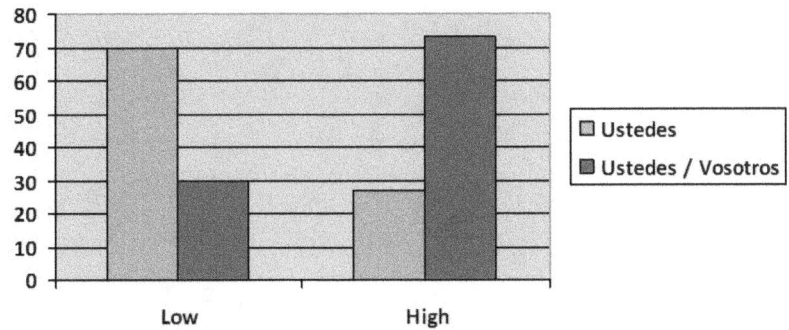

Figure 5: Percentage of use of ustedes, based on the educational level

Table 8 and Table 9 show that the educational level influences the frequency of use of *ustedes* vs. *vosotros*. Only 53 speakers out of the 169 informants with a low educational level distinguish between *vosotros* and *ustedes*, while 44 people (out of 60) with a high educational background do so. This means that nearly 80% of informants with a higher education prefer to follow the standard pattern (to distinguish *ustedes* and *vosotros*) while barely 30% of those with a lower education draw this distinction. Furthermore, if the variable age is taken into account (Figure 6), other conclusions can be drawn.

Table 8: Occurrences in informants, based on their educational level

		Educational level		Total
		Low	High	
SUBJECT U / V	U	116	16	132
	U / V	53	44	97
Total		169	60	229

Table 9: Pearson's chi squared test applied to educational level

Pearson's chi squared			
	Value	gl	Sig. (bilateral)
χ^2	31,9	1	$< 0,001$
Valid cases	229		

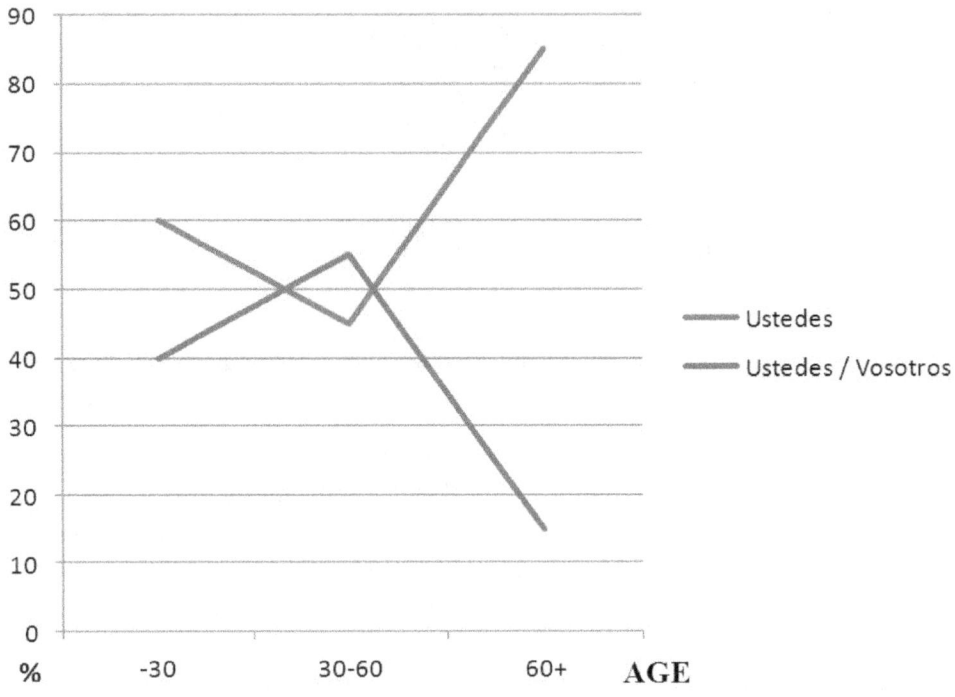

Figure 6: Percentage of use of ustedes, based on the informants' age

Figure 6 clearly shows that the informants that have reached working age choose the prestigious norm, as they favour the standard in a higher proportion. They are closely followed by speakers younger than 30. At the opposite end, the elderly informants have little sensitivity to the standard form. According to Chambers & Trudgill (1980), a situation like the one described here is due to the fact that young people are less pressured by the standard and their linguistic behaviour responds to the uses their social networks positively value. The elderly also follow this pattern, since they do not belong to the labour environment, which, on the other hand, is crucial to the working-age population. In fact, these assume a different behaviour than the rest of the age groups. Their integration into the work force leads them to adopt the prestige form in order to succeed in their careers (Macaulay & Trevelyan 1977; Bourdieu 1978; Seara 2000). According to Chambers & Trudgill (1980), a result like this is not a solid proof of a change in progress. Moreover, this result predicts that the new speakers will behave the same way, depending on the age group to which they belong. So, the new young people will imitate this behaviour because they are less pressured by the standard; once they are of working age, they will try to adopt the prestige and, when that phase is over, they will be freer to readopt their most vernacular features.

4.3 Linguistic extension

As mentioned at the beginning of this article, the 3pl was not attested in all the syntactic elements anchoring *ustedes* and the extension of the 3pl was expected to occur gradually in syntax. The results obtained through my methodology have demonstrated that the syntactic elements agreeing with *ustedes* adopt the 3pl as follows:

(17) Stressed pronoun > reflexive pronoun > verb > accusative pronoun > dative pronoun

The hierarchy must be read this way: if the 3pl appears in the accusative pronoun, it must also arise in the verb, the reflexive pronoun and the stressed pronoun. Only when the 3pl is established at one point in the hierarchy, may it pass to another, always to the immediate right. Unlike ALPI data, the data collected using our dubbing methodology has allowed the elicitation of all the syntactic elements referring to *ustedes*. Contrary to the statements made by Mondéjar (1974), Lapesa, Cano Aguilar & Echenique Elizondo (2000), Cano Aguilar (2004), Penny (2004) or Menéndez Pidal & Catalán Menéndez-Pidal (2005), possessives hardly agree in 3pl – indeed, they are the elements the least likely to adopt it. Object pronouns behave more independently than the reflexive pronouns. In fact, dative pronouns are quite reluctant to agree in 3pl (Table 10).

Table 10: Extension of the innovative 3pl in the *ustedes* phenomenon

	Stressed pronoun	Reflexive pronoun	Verbs	Accusative pronoun	Dative pronoun	Possessives
Stage 1	3pl	2pl	2pl	2pl	2pl	2pl
Stage 2	3pl	3pl	2pl	2pl	2pl	2pl
Stage 3	3pl	3pl	3pl	2pl	2pl	2pl
Stage 4	3pl	3pl	3pl	3pl	2pl	2pl
Stage 5	3pl	3pl	3pl	3pl	3pl	2pl
Stage 6	3pl	3pl	3pl	3pl	3pl	3pl

As explained above, the extension of innovations follows implicational hierarchies. Blake (2004) states that in many languages, any innovation usually obeys the continuum reproduced in (12).

(18)   Nominative > accusative > dative > ablative > genitive

This means that if a language allows a rule to apply to one case, it will also allow the rule to apply to the cases on the left. Blake states that in some languages, relativisation follows this continuum. If a language can relativise direct objects, it can also relativise subjects. The same applies to passive sentences. Spanish can passivize direct objects, but not indirect objects. Since English can promote indirect objects in the passive, it follows that accusatives may also be passivized. In the *ustedes* phenomenon, this hierarchy is completely fulfilled, as the 3pl emerges on the nominative and shifts over to the next syntactic context until the 3pl is established in the whole continuum.

5 Conclusions

To summarise, the innovative methodology designed for obtaining quantitative and qualitative data about the *ustedes* phenomenon has been a success, in comparison to other traditional methods, unable to collect instances of 2pl inflections. Therefore, thanks to my fieldwork, it is possible to know that nowadays some Andalusian speakers are characterised by a high rate of alternation between the standard and the vernacular feature with respect to the 2pl pronoun system. On the one hand, there is a dramatic tendency toward the prestige and standard usage, and this behaviour is led, above all, by middle-aged speakers with a high educational background, and who live in large urban environments. This new change seems to be spreading hierarchically, unlike the wave diffusion pattern attested last century. The standard pressure is firstly observed in the populous cities of Seville and Málaga. In contrast, the smaller towns are more likely to maintain the vernacular phenomenon.

On the other hand, rural, elderly and not very educated speakers maintain the vernacular in their linguistic behaviour. In this case, the 3pl extends linguistically across an implicational continuum. The stressed pronoun is the one where it is first attested, then it passes onto the reflexive pronoun, followed by the verb and it extends to the accusative and the dative pronouns, in this order. Finally, possessives are the syntactic contexts with the least probability to be inflected in 3pl.

This method for eliciting linguistic data is an important tool in order to obtain a large amount of tokens for their ulterior statistical analysis without priming. Furthermore, having informants carry out an activity that may be perceived as leisurely can lead to more spontaneous data. Audiovisual prompting is a productive method for the collection of dialect data and the method I have introduced here will certainly be useful to others in the future.

References

Abadía de Quant, Inés. 1992. La relación pronominal-verbal de segunda persona singular en el español de Corrientes durante el siglo XIX, su comparación con la situación en Buenos Aires. *Revista argentina de lingüística* 8. 31–46.

Bertolotti, V. & M. Coll. 2003. A synchronical and historical view of the tú/vos option in the Spanish of Montevideo. In Silvina Montrul & Francisco Ordoñez (eds.), *Linguistic theory and language development in Hispanic languages: Papers from the 5th Hispanic Linguistics Symposium and the 4th Conference on the Acquisition of Spanish and Portuguese*, 1–12. Somerville: Cascadilla Press.

Blake, Barry J. 2004. *Case*. Cambridge; New York: Cambridge University Press.

Bourdieu, Pierre. 1978. El mercado lingüístico. In Pierre Bourdieu (ed.), *Questions de sociologie*, 121–137. Paris: Éditions de Minuit.

Cano Aguilar, Rafael (ed.). 2004. *Historia de la lengua española*. Barcelona: Ariel.

Chambers, J. K. & Peter Trudgill. 1980. *Dialectology*. Cambridge, New York: Cambridge University Press.

Chelliah, Shobhana L. & Willem J. de Reuse. 2011. *Handbook of Descriptive Linguistic Fieldwork*. London / New York: Springer Netherlands.

Corbett, Greville G. 2006. *Agreement*. Cambridge, UK; New York: Cambridge University Press.

Fontanella de Weinberg, Beatriz. 1979. La oposición *cantes/cantés* en el español de Buenos Aires. *Thesaurus* 34. 72–83.

Heap, David. 2003. *Atlas Lingüístico de la Península Ibérica (ALPI)*. London: University of Western Ontario.

Labov, William. 1995. *Principles of linguistic change*. Cambridge, Oxford: Blackwell.

Lapesa, Rafael, Rafael Cano Aguilar & Maria Teresa Echenique Elizondo. 2000. *Estudios de morfosintaxis histórica del español*. Madrid: Gredos.

Lara, Víctor. 2010. *El uso de ustedes por vosotros en Andalucía occidental*. Madrid: Universidad Autónoma de Madrid.

Lara, Víctor. 2012. *Ustedes* instead of *vosotros* and *vocês* instead of *vós*: An analysis through the Linguistic Atlas of the Iberian Peninsula (ALPI). *Dialectologia* Special Issue 3. 57–93.

Lara, Víctor. 2015. *Los tratamientos de 2pl en Andalucía occidental y Portugal: Estudio geo- y sociolingüístico de un proceso de gramaticalización.* Madrid: Universidad Autónoma de Madrid Ph.D. dissertation.

Macaulay, Ronald K. S. & G. D Trevelyan. 1977. *Language, social class and education: A Glasgow study.* Edinburgh: Edinburgh University Press.

Mallinson, Christine, Becky Childs & Gerard van Herk (eds.). 2013. *Data collection in sociolinguistics: Methods and applications.* New York: Routledge.

Menéndez Pidal, Ramón & Diego Catalán Menéndez-Pidal. 2005. *Historia de la lengua española.* Madrid: Fundación Ramón Menéndez Pidal ; Real Academia Española.

Mondéjar, Jose. 1974. *El verbo andaluz formas y estructuras.* Málaga: Ágora.

Penny, R. 2004. *Variación y cambio en español.* Madrid: Gredos.

Sanchís Guarner, M. 1962. El Atlas lingüístico de la Península Ibérica (ALPI). In *Trabajos, problemas y métodos. Actas del IX Congreso Internacional de Lingüística Románica*, 113–120. Universidade de Lisboa: Centro de Estudios Filológicos.

Seara, I. C. 2000. A variação do sujeito nós e a gente na fala florionapolitana. *Organon* 14. 179–194.

Thieberger, Nick. 2011. *The Oxford handbook of linguistic fieldwork.* Oxford; New York: Oxford University Press.

Wolfram, Walter & Natalie Schilling-Estes. 2003. Dialectology and linguistic diffusion. In Brian D. Joseph & Richard D. Janda (eds.), *The handbook of historical linguistics*, 713 –735. Malden: Blackwell.

Chapter 16

Dialect levelling and changes in semiotic space

Ivana Škevin
University of Zadar

> The Betina variety is a local Čakavian Croatian variety spoken on the island of Murter in central Dalmatia. The influence of Romance languages has left visible traces on the island's vocabulary, just as it has in many other Čakavian varieties of the Eastern Adriatic coast. The Betina variety, through contact with other, more dominant dialectal varieties or the Croatian standard variety, and as a consequence of language accommodation, is losing many of its most salient, mostly Romance, characteristics. This process is leading to a loss of local distinctiveness. The paper proposes a semiotic approach to the problem of dialect levelling. It assumes that it occurs not only because of language accommodation, but also as a consequence of the alteration and transformation of the culture and of the ways of life referred to as semiotic spaces. Since a language or dialect can function only in interaction with its semiotic space, its change leads to language change. The analysis was conducted on a collection of words of Romance origin and involved interviews with young speakers living in Betina. The results of this study are expected to confirm that in Betina, particularly in the vocabulary of young speakers, Romance elements are disappearing. It occurs as a consequence of the disappearance of human practices and of utilitarian and sociocultural objects that once had an important role and which used to create very particular and distinctive semiotic spaces.

1 Introduction

Over the centuries, our needs as humans change. The objects we use and the activities we engage in disappear and get (re)constructed. Our way of life changes together with the ways in which we make a living, eat, get our food, and dress. All these components of life are intimately connected. One cannot exist without the other. They all create meaning and are generally considered to be secondary modeling systems. These systems are secondary in relation to the primary system of language because, like all semiotic systems, they are constructed on the model of language (Lotman, Grishakova & Clark 2009: viii). It is possible to suggest that, in reality, clear and functionally mono-semantic systems do not exist in isolation. No one system, in fact, is effective when taken individually. The starting point of this research is Lotman's assumption that, without the semiosphere-that is, the semiotic space of the culture in question-language not only does not function but does not exist (Lotman 1985 [2015]: 218–219). Accordingly, the current article deals with linguistic and semiological signs. Barthes (1968: 41) claims that a semiological sign, like its linguistic model, comprises a signifier and a signified, but that it differs from a linguistic sign at the level of the substance of its expression, the essence of which is not to signify but to have function and utility in everyday use.

2 Linguistic, historical, geographic and socioeconomic background

The Croatian language has three main groups of dialects: *Kajkavian*, *Čakavian*, and *Štokavian*. Their names derive from the form of the interrogative pronoun (*kaj*, *ča*, and *što* 'what') used in each dialect. Standard Croatian is based on Štokavian. The dialects of the Čakavian group, one of which is the subject of this study, are spoken along the East Adriatic Coast. Čakavian has many local varieties, which vary in terms of accentuation, morpho-syntax, or lexicon. The local dialect spoken in Betina belongs to the group of Southern Čakavian Ikavian varieties. In the Ikavian varieties the reflex of the Slavic *jat* phoneme is /i/, and in standard Croatian it is /ije/ or /je/. Thus, in Ikavian, we have *lipa divojka* 'beautiful girl', as opposed to the Croatian standard form *lijepa djevojka*. One of the main characteristics of Betina dialect, which it shares with most other Čakavian varieties, is that a significant portion of its technical vocabulary in specific fields is of Romance origin.[1] Romance lexical elements originate from the now extinct Dalmatic languages as well as from old dialectal varieties of Italian that functioned as proper languages in past centuries (Venetian and Triestine, as well as

---

[1] Research undertaken in 2008, 2009, and 2010 has revealed that in the Betina dialect, loanwords of Romance origin account for 61.96% of fishing terminology, 65.12% of maritime terminology, 29.41% of wine terminology, 36.73% of olive cultivation terminology, 57.14% of barrel-making terminology, and finally, 61.54% of agricultural terminology (tools and maintainance of arable land) (Škevin 2010: 254–255).

16 Dialect levelling and changes in semiotic space

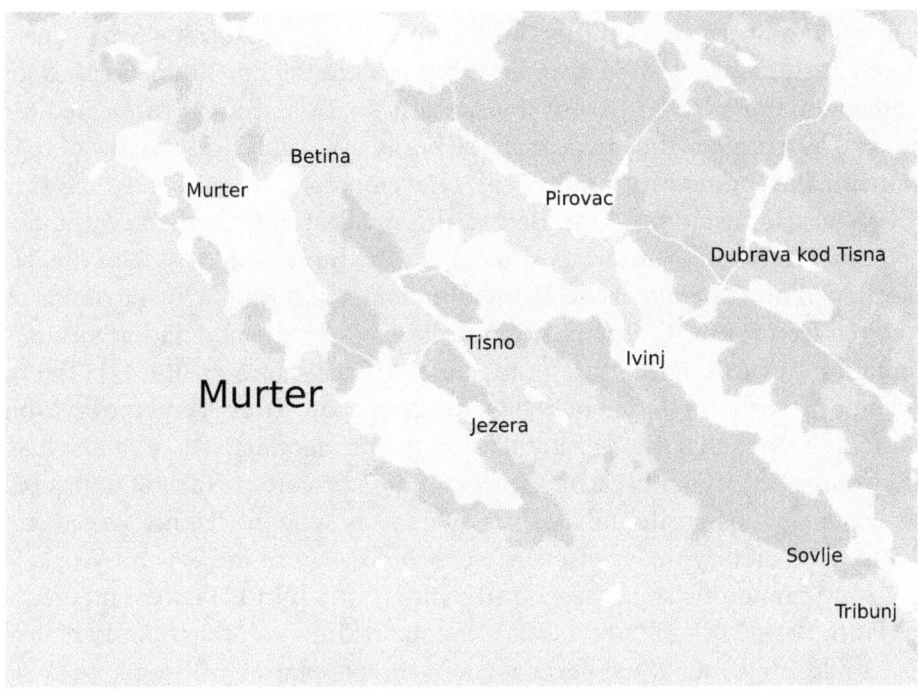

Figure 1: The location of Betina. ©OpenStreetMap contributors, licensed under ODbL

Italian).² Previous research and etymological analysis have shown that a great majority of the loanwords used in the Čakavian variety of Betina are of Venetian origin (Filipi 1997; Škevin 2010). Croatians borrowed from the Venetians the objects and the corresponding words they needed to understand and sail the sea, to build boats, and to cultivate wine and olives, thus creating their semiotic space. The borrowed words naming these everyday needs and ways of life became integral lexical forms and structures of the Čakavian Croatian Adriatic varieties.

This research concentrates on the case of Betina, though we claim that in fact it reflects the dialectal situation of many other small local varieties of central Dalmatia. As shown in Figure 1, Betina is situated on the island of Murter, which

---

² Dalmatic languages were spoken on the eastern Adriatic coast from the 9th until the 13th century in central Dalmatia, until the 16th century in Dubrovnik, and until the 19th century on the northeastern Adriatic island of Krk. Venetian, very often referred to as Colonial Venetian, was the *lingua franca* of the eastern Adriatic for many centuries. Its influence was the strongest between the early 16th and the late 18th century. After the fall of the Serenissima, Trieste became the centre from which spread a new Venetian variety – Triestine. At the beginning of the 20th century, especially during the First World War, began the expansion of the Italian language, which lasted until the Second World War.

stretches in a northwest-southeasterly direction in the Adriatic Sea, in central Dalmatia. Although situated on an island, we cannot define Betina as an isolated island community, but as part of the Adriatic coast, since it is connected to the mainland by a bridge. The bridge makes it easily accessible and was one of the key factors for the community's rather early development of tourism, which started in the 1960s (Kulušić 1984: 138). Betina, the smallest of four villages (the others are Tisno, Jezera and Murter), is situated on the northeastern side of the island. It developed on the edge of the Murter-Betina fertile zone, which extends close to the sea (see Figure 1). The position itself explains the population's extensive orientation towards agriculture in the past (Čuka & Lončar 2010: 12). The main economic activities in Betina in 1971 were agriculture, fishing, and the building of traditional wooden boats. Agriculture was the primary activity of most villagers and a source of income because the inhabitants produced fruits and vegetables, olive oil, and wine for sale and for their own needs, whereas fishing served mostly to satisfy the dietary needs of every household. Before the Second World War, there were numerous small private shipyards, which in 1948 were merged into one (Filipi 1997: 21).[3] In 2014, besides the main shipyard, there are two smaller ones. Table 1 represents the percentage of the population of Betina working in different economic sectors in the years 1971 and 2001 (Čuka & Lončar 2010: 21).

Table 1: Percentage of the population of Betina employed in different economic sectors in the years 1971 and 2001 (Čuka & Lončar 2010).

Economic sector	1971	2001
agriculture, fishing	38%	21%
industry (wooden boat building)	30%	18%
service (tourism)	9%	45%
public sector	0%	6%
people working abroad	20%	8%

There was a noticeable decline in the primary (agriculture and fishing) and secondary (industrial) sectors, as well as an increase of 36% in the tertiary sector (tourism), during the period between 1971 and 2001. The population's reorienta-

---

[3] In 1926 there were one large and nine small shipyards. Betina's shipyards covered a total of 11,200 square meters, which was greater than the total surface area of shipyards in the rest of Northern Dalmatia, which was 10,330 square meters. In 1930, ten private shipyards were registered in Betina. The 1930s marked the beginning of a crisis in the sector of traditional wooden boat building (Filipi 1997: 19).

Table 2: Decrease of the number of people living in Betina from 1971 to 2011 (Čuka & Lončar 2010: 15 and *1. Stanovništvo prema starosti i spolu po naseljima, popis 2011*)

Year	1971	2001	2011
No. of inhabitants	988	774	697

tion to the tertiary sector of the economy led to the abandonment of arable land, excessive urbanization, and the degradation of the natural and cultural identity of the island. As a consequence of these social changes, the dialectal identity of Betina's population changed as well. Besides that, as Table 2 shows, the population of Betina has dropped by almost 30% in the last four decades.

3 Methodology and hypothesis

This study focused on a collection of words of mostly Romance origin, and it involved interviews conducted by the present author (an in-group researcher) with seven young adult speakers (ranging in age from 22 to 40) living in the village of Betina on the island of Murter in central Dalmatia. The questionnaire consisted of 70 lexemes. This collection is a small subset of a much wider corpus collected and registered during interviews with older speakers between the ages of 50 and 90 conducted in Betina during the years 2008, 2009 and 2010 (Škevin 2010). The lexemes were chosen so that they would belong to different spheres of life: household, maritime and fishing, viticulture and olive cultivation, folklore and church. These are (or at least used to be) very important aspects of the life and culture of Betina.

This study concerns intergenerational variation mainly in connection with the social context of variation and change. It is expected to confirm a hypothesis that in Betina, particularly in the vocabulary of young speakers, the Romance elements are disappearing for two reasons:

1. as a consequence of the local variety's convergence toward the Supra-regional Dalmatian Dialect (SRDD) and toward Standard Croatian (SC)

2. as a consequence of the disappearance of human practices and utilitarian objects that once had an important role and which used to create very specific and distinctive semiotic spaces.

Ivana Škevin

Since a language or a dialect can function only in interaction with its semiotic space, changes in that space should lead to language change.

4 Sociolinguistic and semiotic approach to dialect levelling

The results presented in Table 3 suggest that there is a pattern which determines the speakers' knowledge and usage of the variants. The least-known variants (numbers 1-34, with the exception of the variant *gvantijera* 'a tray') refer to referents or concepts that have lost importance in the daily life of Betina (e.g., *batusić/batusigaj* 'an inside, hollowed-out part at the bottom of a well where water gets trapped', *gaštaldo* 'a person who helps the priest in the church', *štiva* 'the interior part of a boat under the bow') or whose referent is not in use any more (e.g., *bujo(l)* 'a wooden bucket held on traditional Dalmatian boats, used to remove sea water', *burača* 'a leather sack for keeping wine', *dumplir* 'a wooden candlestick carried during a funeral'). The second group of variants (from number 35 onwards), which the users know better and use more often, mostly, but not always, name referents or concepts whose function in everyday life has not changed. These include words that, for example, refer to household objects (such as *prsura* 'a frying pan', *kočeta* a bed', *škabelin* 'a nightstand', *čikara* 'a mug'). In this second group, though, there are also variants that name objects whose function in the daily life of Betina has changed. For example, variants like *škohuni* 'type of shoes worn during work in the fields', *bukara* 'a large wooden wine cup', *brganja* 'a type of a fishing tool', *kajin* 'a round metal vessel used for washing clothes', *pičona* 'a metal cup with a handle' name objects that are out of use, whereas *burtižati* 'to sail into the wind', *paj* 'a scoop used for throwing sea-water out of a boat' and *rehud* 'a sudden, brief gust of wind' name referents or concepts whose role in the daily life of Betina has become less prominent. These results suggest that, contrary to the anticipated hypothesis, a change in the semiotic space does not always lead to dialect change. They also show that in some cases there is a divide between familiarity with a variant and its actual use. For example, all speakers know the meaning of the variants *bruncin* and *kočeta*. However, all of them also declare that they do not use them in any communication situation. In this article we propose two approaches to the challenges of dialect levelling: a sociolinguistic approach, which concerns changes in the use of variants in different social contexts, and a semiotic approach, which concerns change in the way of life of the community and the transformation of its semiotic spaces.

Table 3: Vitality of lexical variants

	lexeme	meaning	informants who knew the word's meaning		informants who use the word	
			n	%	n	%
1	brganjaš	'the wind that favors bottom trawling with a *brganja*'	0	0	0	0
2	bujo(l)	'a wooden bucket held/kept on traditional Dalmatian boats, used to remove sea water'	0	0	0	0
3	goče	'a part of a fishing net'	0	0	0	0
4	koslata	'a type of a barrel vertically placed on a trailer'	0	0	0	0
5	tinac	'a type of a vessel similar to *mastač*, but smaller and without handles'	0	0	0	0
6	batusić/ batusigaj	'an inside, hollowed-out part at the bottom of a well where water gets trapped, so there's water even when the well is almost empty'	1	14.28	0	0
7	burača	'a leather sack for keeping wine'	1	14.28	0	0
8	dumplir	'a wooden candlestick carried during a funeral'	1	14.28	0	0
9	gaštaldo	'a person who helps the priest in the church'	1	14.28	1	14.28
10	komoštra	'one of the metal rings of the chain used to hang pots over the fire'	1	14.28	0	0
11	murtar	'a stone container used for storing olive oil. It comes in different sizes'	1	14.28	1	14.28
12	taraban	'a church custom that consists in making lots of noise by striking an object with one's hands or with a stick'	1	14.28	0	0
13	štiva	'the interior part of a boat under the bow'	2	28.57	2	28.57
14	butarga	'fish eggs'	2	28.57	1	14.28
15	baraškada	'a small sea storm'	2	28.57	1	14.28

	lexeme	meaning	informants who knew the word's meaning		informants who use the word	
			n	%	n	%
16	brenda	'a flat wooden vessel carried on one's back or on a donkey, used for the transportation of grapes'	2	28.57	0	0
17	buklija	'a flat wooden wine container'	2	28.57	0	0
18	kopanja	'a wooden vessel used for kneading dough'	2	28.57	2	28.57
19	maškul	'an iron part of a steering wheel' (Filipi 1997: 163)	2	28.57	1	14.28
20	šijun	'a squall, a sudden, strong and sharp increase in wind speed'	2	28.57	1	14.28
21	hildošpanja / fildošpanja	'wrapping nylon thread (used in fishing)'	3	42.85	3	42.85
22	bava	'a very small gust of wind which you can hardly feel'	3	42.85	3	42.85
23	gvantijera	'a tray'	3	42.85	0	0
24	konistra	'a type of a wicker basket'	3	42.85	3	42.85
25	mankul	'a thick wooden post around which a mooring rope is tied (there are usually two, one on each side of the boat)'	3	42.85	0	0
26	ogrica	'a shirt, part of the national costume'	3	42.85	3	42.85
27	soha	'boat oar holder made of wood'	3	42.85	3	42.85
28	škapular	'an image of a saint held around the neck or sewn onto clothes'	3	42.85	3	42.85
29	zmorac	NE	3	42.85	2	28.57
30	lustra	'fish scales'	4	57.14	2	28.57
31	kaca	'a wide wooden vessel used for the transportation of grapes'	4	57.14	0	0
32	karutula	'a type of braided cake made for children at Easter'	4	57.14	4	57.14
33	koha	'a type of a wicker basket, flat and rounded'	4	57.14	4	57.14
34	lebić	'a type of SW wind'	4	57.14	2	28.57
35	burtižati	'to sail into the wind'	5	71.43	5	71.43
36	bušt	'a red vest, part of the national costume'	5	71.43	5	71.43
37	dekmar/ drkmar	'a small anchor-shaped object used to grab and lift a bucket out of a well or a fishing net out of the sea'	5	71.43	5	71.43

16 Dialect levelling and changes in semiotic space

	lexeme	meaning	informants who knew the word's meaning		informants who use the word	
			n	%	n	%
38	puca	'a stone frame or a kind of a small wall around a well'	5	71.43	4	57.14
39	bruncin	'a large cylindrical pot with handles (in the past it hung above the fire)'	6	85.71	0	0
40	dontrina	'religious education'	6	85.71	0	0
41	herijada	'a small barred window'	6	85.71	0	0
42	kandelir	'a candlestick used in church'	6	85.71	6	85.71
43	kurenat	'sea current'	6	85.71	4	57.14
44	lehunara/ lohunara	'a type of a small fishing net in the form of sack on a long stick'	6	85.71	6	85.71
45	mastač	'a type of a vessel with handles used for squeezing grapes and for wine making'	6	85.71	6	85.71
46	mašte	'a type of a deep plastic vessel, mostly used for washing clothes'	6	85.71	6	85.71
47	paj	'a (usually wooden) scoop used for throwing sea-water out of a boat'	6	85.71	6	85.71
48	pot, potić	'a smaller metal bowl with a handle'	6	85.71	6	85.71
49	škohuni	'type of shoes worn during work in the fields'	6	85.71	6	85.71
50	tangati	'to dye, such as fishing-nets, clothes'	6	85.71	5	71.43
51	trmuntana/ tremuntana	'a northern wind'	6	85.71	5	71.43
52	bukara	'a large wooden wine cup'	7	100	7	100
53	gučica	'undershirt'	7	100	7	100
54	brganja	'a type of a fishing tool used to collect different kinds of seashells by dragging it across the sea floor'	7	100	7	100
55	bublija	'a round Easter cake, a type of sweet bread'	7	100	7	100
56	čikara	'a mug'	7	100	7	100
57	hrtuna	'a very strong and sudden storm'	7	100	7	100
58	intimela	'a pillowcase'	7	100	7	100

	lexeme	meaning	informants who knew the word's meaning		informants who use the word	
			n	%	n	%
60	kamara	'a bedroom'	7	100	0	0
61	kamenica	'a large stone container used to store olive oil'	7	100	7	100
62	kočeta	'a bed'	7	100	0	0
63	loštijera	'a baking tray'	7	100	7	100
64	pajoli	'each of the wooden boards that cover the floor of a boat'	7	100	7	100
65	pičona	'a metal cup with a handle'	7	100	7	100
66	prova	'a bow'	7	100	7	100
67	prsura	'a frying pan'	7	100	7	100
68	rehud	'a sudden, brief gust of wind'	7	100	7	100
69	škabelin	'a nightstand'	7	100	7	100
70	torkulati/ trkulati	'to produce olive oil or wine'	7	100	7	100
		Average %		61.42		48.16

5 Salience of Romance loanwords

Etymological analysis has revealed that all of the lexical variants listed in Table 3 are of Romance origin, besides *kopanja* and *soha*, which are of Slavic origin, while the origin of the variant *dumplir* is not clear. A systematic approach to the research of Romance loanwords is essential for three reasons. Firstly, they are integral lexical forms and structures of the Čakavian Croatian Adriatic varieties. Secondly, they are a cultural and a linguistic specificity of Betina and of other Čakavian varieties. Thirdly, they, as primary semiotic systems, name everyday needs and ways of life, thus creating and reflecting the cultural and social distinctivness of Betina and of wider Dalmatian semiotic spaces. All of these characteristics make them an expression of the Čakavian language, regional and cultural identity. In some cases, it is not possible to decide whether a dialect feature is salient or not, but in our case it is the variants' Romance origin that makes them overtly stigmatised in comparison with standard Croatian (e.g., *prsura* 'a frying pan' as opposed to SC *tava*; *tangati* 'to dye, such as fishing-nets, clothes', as opposed to SC *bojati*; *čikara* 'a mug' as opposed to SC *šalica*). Some of the Betina examples can be considered stigmatised in comparison with their equivalent SRDD Romance variants as well, such as *loštijera* 'a baking tray' as opposed to the more common variant *roštijera* or to the SRDD *padela*, or *škabelin* 'a nightstand' as opposed to the more common *kantunal*. Their overt stigmatisation in comparison with their SC or SRDD lexical variants makes them more liable to change. Jutronić (2010: 30–32) claims that the dialect levelling of Čakavian varieties is mostly caused by the fact that those dialect features which a speaker of a standard or of a dialect variety perceives as socially stigmatised or salient (that is, as some kind of error) first disappear from a dialect. As a rule, stigmatised and salient features disappear faster, while features that are less stigmatised and less salient last longer. Romance loanwords are perceived as markers of geographical differentiation, often in connection with stereotypes, but also as markers of geographic affiliation, when it can play a role in the process of linguistic accommodation among young adult speakers (see Auer, Hinskens & Kerswill 2004: 44–45). The dialect convergence of the Betina variety towards broader regional dialect varieties or standard Croatian implies the abandonment of Betina features (such as lexemes or accentuation). Thus, dialect levelling in Betina can be manifested in phonetic/accent levelling and in lexical levelling, which concerns the reduction of intrasystemic-especially quantitative lexical-variation.

6 Linguistic accommodation among young adults

So far, the research undertaken in Betina has shown that young speakers are influenced by the current process of globalisation and language homogenisation (mostly through schools, media, and tourism) and that they use and know significantly fewer Romance loanwords than older speakers. The results of a study done in 2011 (Škevin 2012)[4] show a significant decline in the use of Romance loanwords.

The results of the interviews held in 2014 have confirmed the decline in the knowledge and use of the Romance lexical variants. They have shown that 7 interviewed speakers between the ages of 22 and 40 know 61.42% and use 48.16%[5]

---

[4] This study, conducted in 2011, involved questionnaire-based interviews with 21 speakers living in Betina and belonging to four different generational groups. The questionnaire contained a collection of 100 words of Romance origin, and the informants were asked whether they knew the meanings of the words. The study confirmed that in Betina, particularly in the vocabulary of young speakers, Romance elements are rapidly disappearing.

[5] Both percentages are relative and used for illustrative purposes only because the complexity of speakers' answers cannot be simplified and displayed in numbers. Sometimes they would claim that they would use the variant if they've seen the object that is no longer in use; sometimes they would say that they would use it only in specific situations or only with other speakers of the Betina dialect. In either of these cases, we would mark their answer as if they had claimed that they use it in all social contexts and situations.

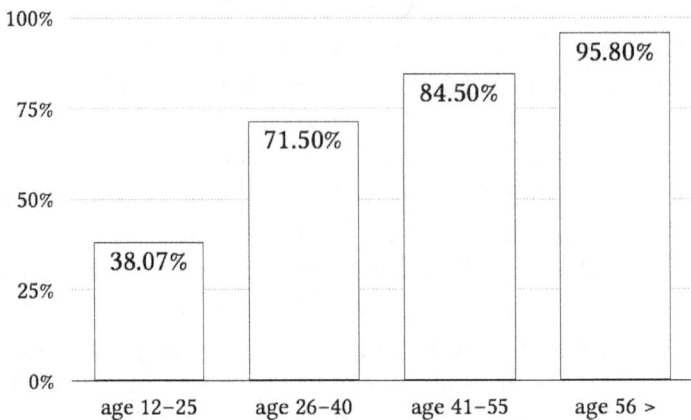

Figure 2: Knowledge and use of Venetian loanwords vs. age of informants (Škevin 2012: 175).

of the words from the questionnaire. The speakers of the Betina dialect in some cases claim to avoid a number of lexical variants, as shown in Table 4. Even though 6 out of 7 speakers know the meaning of words like *bruncin* 'a type of a cooking bowl', *dontrina* 'religious education' and *herijada* 'a small window', they also say that they would never use them in a conversation with speakers of either their own or of another dialect variety because, according to them, these words are rare or no longer used. For the same reason, they claim not to use words like *kamara* 'room' and *kočeta* 'bed'. This means that these Betina variants have already been replaced by SC or SRDD variants. As far as the variants *gučica* 'undershirt', *intimela* 'pillowcase', and *trkulati* 'to produce olive oil' are concerned, they would use them only in conversations with speakers from Betina. This means that, over time, these variants are also likely to be replaced by SRDD or SC expressions.

On the other hand, there are variants (which are listed in Table 5) that can also be considered salient because they are used only in the Betina dialect (e.g., *lohunara/lehunara*) or only in the varieties of the island of Murter (e.g., *bublija*). Still, the speakers claim that they use them in communication with speakers of other varieties. It is unlikely that the speakers are not aware of their markedness, so we can presume that, for some reason, these variants signal the speaker's identity as a member of a group (Chambers & Trudgill 1998: 85).

Table 4: Examples of intrasystemic quantitative reduction as a consequence of a convergence toward SRDD and toward SC.

Betina lexical variant	Meaning	No. of informants of the seven interviewed who know the meaning	No. of informants of the seven interviewed who claim to use the word	SRDD variant	SC variant
Variants that have already been replaced by an SRDD or SC variant					
bruncin	'a type of cooking bowl'	6	0	–	lonac
dontrina	'religious education'	6	0	–	vjeronauk
herijada	'a small window'	6	0	ponistr(ic)a	–
kamara	'a room'	7	0	–	soba
kočeta	'a bed'	7	0	posteja	–
Variants that the speakers use only in conversations with speakers of the Betina dialect. In conversations with other speakers they use either the SRDD or the SC variant					
gučica	'an undershirt'	7	7	kanotijera	potkošulja
intimela	'a pillowcase'	7	7	–	jastučnica
trkulati	'to produce olive oil'	7	7	napraviti ulje; (u)činiti uje	–

Table 5: Examples of divergence

Betina lexical variant	Meaning	No. of informants of the seven interviewed who know the meaning	No. of informants of the seven interviewed who claim to use the word with speakers of their own and of other varieties
lehunara/ lohunara	'a type of a small fishing net in the form of sack on a long stick'	6	6
bublija	'a round Easter cake, a type of sweet bread'	7	7
čikara	'a mug'	7	7
loštijera	'a baking tray'	7	7
prsura	'a frying pan'	7	7
škabelin	'a nightstand'	7	7

7 Semiotic space as the space of identity

Objects that seem to be merely utilitarian are often part of a particular space; they signify and issue messages about the society's priorities, ways of life, culture, and traditions (see Hawkes 2004: 110). Each utilitarian object, such as *brganja*, *lohunara*, *hildošpanja*, *karutula* and *pot* acknowledges the way people used to organize their lives and the way they structured their social and cultural identity. *Brganja*, *lohunara* and *hildošpanja* issue presuppositions concerning inhabitants' adherence to fishing and to the sea. *Karutula* 'a type of braided cake' was traditionally prepared for children at Easter. As an additional gift, one whole egg would be baked inside the cake on the bottom end of the cake. Also, *pot* is not merely 'a metal container with a handle' out of which people used to drink, but the manifestation of a custom to make *bevanda* (red wine with water) and to pass it around the table so that everyone could drink out of the same *pot*. The meaning of an object is largely attached to its function, its utility in relation to the repertoire of human needs (Moles 1972: 48); that is, as soon as there is a society, every usage is converted into a sign of itself (Barthes 1968: 41). In this work we use the Lotmanian term of semiotic space to refer to all aspects of human existence and to stress that external factors, such as culture, society, fishing, wooden boat building, and ways of earning money or getting food, can acquire semiotic meaning. In Lotman's words, they influence the consciousness of man only when they have corresponding signifiers to name them because "for human thought all that exists is that which falls into any of its languages" (Lotman, Grishakova & Clark 2009: 134). This means that, even if some social or cultural aspects of Betina still exist, if the speakers don't know the signifiers to name these aspects, it is as if they did not exist, which means that the local identity and distinctiveness are lost to their thought. It also works the other way around: if the cultural and social aspects are lost, it won't take long for the signifier, emptied of its signified, to be lost as well.

8 Changes in semiotic space *vs.* the reduction of intrasystemic variation

In the case of dialect levelling caused by the linguistic accommodation of speakers, the replacement of dialect variants with SRDD or SC variants occurs. In the case of dialect levelling caused by changes in the semiotic space, no such replacement occurs because the object or a human practice that has been lost doesn't need a new signifier. Nonetheless, dialect levelling still occurs because there is a reduction in intrasystemic variation, which leads to simplification, homogenization and the levelling of a dialect variety and of its cultural and local distinctiveness, making it more similar to a supra-regional or standard variety.

Changes in semiotic space are parallel to changes in human needs and praxis, and can be analysed from three standpoints:

1. the complete disappearance of utilitarian objects that used to be very effective sociocultural signs

2. the loss of an object's utilitarian and functional importance in everday life

3. the transfer of such an object from one semiotic space to another.

These are three hypothetical reasons that supposedly cause the loss of intrasystemic quantitative variation as a consequence of change in a semiotic space. To illustrate these points and to show our interest in the cognitive effect on the interpreter, the variants and their referents are represented through Peirce's semiotic triangle. The semiotic triangle begins with an understanding of the sign as the primary element of any semiotic system. Strictly speaking, semiosis, and not the sign, is the proper object of semiotic study. The realization of a semiological sign in a communication process depends on the interlocutors, on the objects, and on the context in which the communication occurs. In this case, the analysis of the communication process is relevant both to the addresser and to the addressee.

8.1 The disappearance of utilitarian objects

It is common knowledge that very often a word survives even though the object it represents has disappeared, which is the case with the word *dumplir*. All of the older speakers who participated in the 2008, 2009 and 2010 interviews knew its meaning, while only one of the young speakers was familiar with its meaning.

8.2 The loss of an object's utilitarian and functional importance in everyday life

Table 1 shows that in Betina the traditional wooden boat building sector decreased by 12% in the period from 1971 to 2001. The same happened to agriculture and fishing, which in the same period decreased by 17%. These trends lead to a loss of importance in these human practices and consequently of the utilitarian objects affiliated with them. They also affect the general familiarity of speakers with other topics of conversation, such as the weather, the winds, the behaviour of the sea, the points of the compass, fishing tools, boat-building tools, and boat parts. Consequently, they also affect the speakers' recognition and awareness of the signifiers. For example, young speakers know the terms for some of the most prominent parts of a traditional boat (e.g., *prova* 'bow' or *pajoli* 'wooden floor of a boat'), but they are uncertain when asked about less prominent and smaller parts, such as *mankul* 'a thick wooden post around which a mooring rope is tied' or *maškul, soha* or *štiva*. In the case of *mankul*, 3 out of the 7 speakers interviewed guessed that it was something on a boat but could not identify the exact referent. *Why should they know these words?* someone might ask. Because they used to be, and on paper still are, signs that create the semiotic space of Betina, whereas today they belong to very specialized semiotic spaces whose language is accessible only by those who work in that field. Just as people live nowadays with their tablets, computers, and smart-phones, people in Betina, only a few decades ago, used to live with the sea and their boats. This is in fact what Lotman refers

16 Dialect levelling and changes in semiotic space

Older speakers	Young adults	Loss of the lexical variant
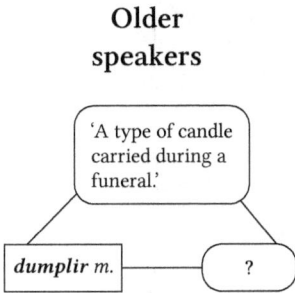	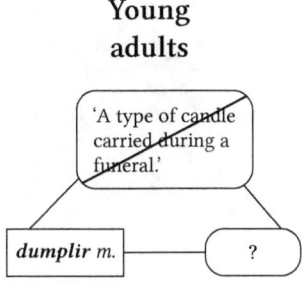	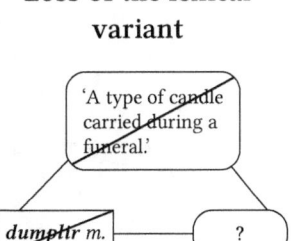

Dumplir 'a wooden candlestick carried during a funeral' is not in use anymore, although the older speakers still have a mental picture of it in their minds and are able to describe it.

Over time, there will not be any speakers who can describe it (unless it has been described in some written text such as a dialectal glossary).

When an object has disappeared, the addresser and the addressee cannot communicate, the object as a semiological sign cannot have any cognitive effect on the addressee, and it is no longer possible to close the circle of semiosis by finding exclusively the same interpretant at both ends of the communication process. Meaning without communication is not possible, so, over time, the word disappears as well.

Figure 3: Loss of intrasystemic quantitative variation.

Figure 4: A *mankul*.

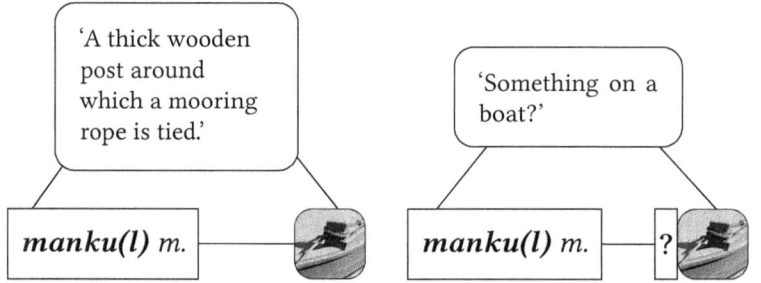

(a) **Older speakers** can identify without any problem the referent as 'a thick wooden post around which a mooring rope is tied'.

(b) **Young speakers** suppose that it is something on a boat, but cannot identify the referent.

Figure 5: Restriction of the number of users.

to as a secondary modeling system interwined with a primary modeling system, that is, with a natural language. The different substructures of the semiosphere are linked in their interaction and cannot function without the support of each other. (Lotman 1985 [2015]: 219).

This analysis has shown that speakers know 53.05% of the words that name objects and concepts that have lost importance in everyday life in Betina. This means that there is still some adherence to the traditional and that the identity of Betina is still recognized in some traditional crafts, although the average speaker's knowledge of words does not always keep pace with this identity projection. To this list belong the names of parts of the National costume (*bušt, ogrica*), parts of some fishing tools (*hildošpanja/fildošpanja*), fish parts (*lustra, butarga*), or the names of the winds and sea storms (*brganjaš, baraškada, šijun*). There are also variants whose meanings are more well known, which can be explained by the fact that they also belong to the lexis of SRDD (e.g., *trmuntana/tremuntana*) or by their semantic transparency (e.g., *kamenica, mastač*).

8.3 The transfer of an object from one semiotic space to another

8.3.1 The resemantization and refunctionalization of traditional utilitarian objects

Brganja is a Venetian loanword *par excellence*. To this day, it has always had a very imporant role in the everyday life of Betina. The fact that, through the centuries, new words were formed by adding Croatian endings to the original Venetian form *bragagna* testifies to the importance of its uses in the past. For example, the verb *brganjati*, meaning to collect sea shells with this tool', or the name of the wind *brganjaš*, which favors bottom trawling with a *brganja*. With

 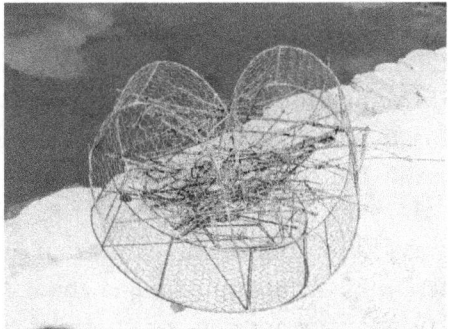

Figure 6: A *brganja* (l.) and a *vrša*.

the birth and development of tourism, a new expression, *Dan Brganje* (Brganja Day) has also been coined. This is the name of a festival celebrated in Betina every summer on the first Sunday of August. Today, the use of this fishing tool is forbidden. Still, *brganja* is one of the most vital fishing terms in Betina, and all of the interviewed speakers knew the word.

This is an example of the extension, or rather, the commercialization of the meaning, since *brganja*, removed from its original semiotic space, that of a fishing tool, has produced a new one, closer to and more appropriate for today's society and economy, which is oriented mostly toward tourism and no longer toward fishing. Trudgill explains this phenomenon in the following way:

> The remaining variation, i.e. the forms that are not removed during koineisation… will tend to be re-assigned according to certain patterns. This reallocation can cause variants to take on a specialised linguistic (allophonic) or extra-linguistic (social, stylistic, or geographical) function. (1986: 110-126 in Auer, Hinskens & Kerswill 2004: 46)

There are other examples of semantic extension, such as the variant *škohuni*, which used to refer to a type of shoes, usually made of rubber and rags, worn to work in the field, whereas today, young speakers, besides the original meaning, also know a metaphoric one, i.e., 'cumbersome, usually old and not very elegant shoes'.

8.3.2 The aestheticisation and refunctionalization of traditional utilitarian objects

A change in the utilitarian value of the objects, through their aestheticisation and refunctionalisation as decorative items or objects primarily used to re-evoke tradition, can cause a shift in the stylistic meaning of the variants such as in the case of the use of traditional cups and dishes (*pot, potić, pičona*, or *bukara*) or of different kinds of baskets and vessels (*koha, konistra*, or *kopanja*).

The refunctionalization of the objects listed in Table 6 consists in using them as decorative or even utilitarian items in traditional restaurants, hotels, and houses for rent. Their purpose is to re-evoke tradition and old customs such as kneading dough in a *kopanja* or serving wine in a *bukara*. They still serve a purpose by means of their traditional utilitarian function being switched to a new aesthetic function: to attract tourists in a changed context and in a changed economy that today relies on tourism up to 45% (as illustrated in Table 1). Thanks to these processes, some of the variants, like *bukara, pot*, and *pičona*, by taking on a new social and stylistic function, are better known to the speakers.

16 Dialect levelling and changes in semiotic space

Older speakers	Young adults: semantic extension	
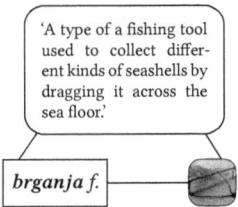	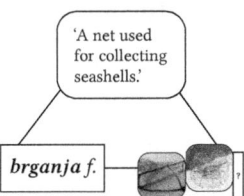	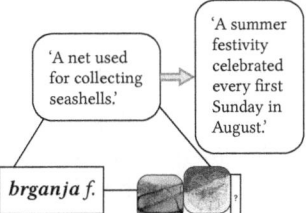
'A type of a fishing tool used to collect different kinds of seashells by dragging it across the sea floor.' / *brganja f.*	'A net used for collecting seashells.' / *brganja f.*	'A net used for collecting seashells.' → 'A summer festivity celebrated every first Sunday in August.' / *brganja f.*
This is a triadic relation formed in the mind of an older speaker but not in the minds of the young informants. This word has a different effect on young speakers.	This is a triadic relation formed in the mind of a young speaker. The second element of Peirce's semiotic triangle, the *thing signified* or *referential object*, varies. Five out of seven speakers are unsure about the correct referential object; they either describe another fishing tool, or they don't know how to describe it. But all of them, without exception, know its function. Thus, communication is still fulfilled at the pragmatic level.	Young speakers know this word thanks to the fact that the community of Betina has refunctionalized it; that is, it has changed its function and accordingly its semiotic space. This word traditionally signified a tool which for centuries was used by the inhabitants of Betina on a daily basis, mostly to get food. A few decades ago, a new substance was attributed to this word: the value of tradition and of collective memory through the name of the festival *Dan Brganje* (Brganja Day).

Figure 7: Change in intrasystemic qualitative variation through resemantization and refunctionalization of the utilitarian objects.

Table 6: The aestheticisation and refunctionalization of objects

Lexeme	meaning	No. of informants of the seven interviewed who know the meaning	No. of informants of the seven interviewed who claim to use the word
bukara	'a large wooden wine cup'	7	7
pičona	'a metal cup with a handle'	7	7
pot, potić	'a smaller metal bowl with a handle'	6	6
koha	'a type of a wicker basket, flat and round'	4	4
kopanja	'a wooden vessel used for kneading dough'	2	2

9 Conclusions

This study has confirmed that young speakers, when talking about familiar and everyday subjects, converge in their communication with speakers of other dialect varieties by eliminating salient lexical variants that they consider rare or "out of use" (*kamara, kočeta*). On the other hand, it has also shown that the informants diverge from their interlocutors by using lexical variants typical of island varieties (*bublija*) or of the Betina variety in particular (*lehunara/lohunara*). This indicates that young adults still want to be identified with their speech community and recognized as members of that group of speakers.

The study has also confirmed that a change in semiotic space can lead to quantitative or qualitative intrasystemic variation or to a reduction of the number of users.

A complete disappearance of objects causes a reduction in intrasystemic quantitative variation, i.e., a loss of lexical variants, which leads to cultural and dialect levelling. Therefore, a loss of referents will over time cause a loss of local variants such as *bujo(l), dumplir, murtar, taraban,* and *škapular*.

There are cases in which, due to the object's refunctionalization, resemantization, or aestheticisation, no such loss occurs. It has proven that the transfer of objects from one semiotic space to another, when an object gets refunctionalized, leads only to semantic change because of the extension of the meaning of the variants (*brganja, škohuni*). However, only a very small number of lexical variants belong to this group. If refunctionalization and resemantization does not occur, over time this will lead to a reduction of intrasystemic lexical variation, as well as cultural and dialect levelling.

The analysis shows that speakers know the meanings of 53.05% of the words referring to objects and concepts that still exist but have lost their utilitarian and functional importance in everday life (e.g., *mankul, butarga, šijun, fildošpanja/hildošpanja, burtižati*). Since these words have ceased to be important to the wider speech community, this implies a restriction in the number of users and consequently, a loss of cultural and dialect diversity as well as cultural and dialect levelling.

Since the interviews and the analysis have shown that young adults in Betina converge and diverge in more or less the same number of situations and variants, this research has shown that changes in semiotic space (at least in the case of Betina) are in fact the most prominent reason for dialect levelling.

Naturally, with this change of approach we do not claim to have found all the reasons for dialect levelling. We just claim that this is another possible approach to understanding this phenomenon. On the contrary, in our corpora there are some lexical variants whose status in the lexis of the Betina dialect cannot be explained by means of any of the proposed approaches (i.e., the saliency factor, linguistic accommodation, or the loss of utilitarian objects and human praxis). For example, we could not find a valid answer to why the variant *gvantijera*, which refers to such an ordinary and everyday object as a tray is almost lost to the knowledge and usage of the young adults (3 out of 7 speakers know its meaning, but none of them uses the word), whereas *kajin* 'a round metal vessel used for washing clothes', a household object as well, but no longer in use, is very familiar to all the speakers, and all of them claim that they would use the word if they saw the object. This and many other questions on the future of dialects have yet to be answered and can be explained neither through the semiotic nor through the sociolinguistic approach.

References

Auer, Peter, Frans Hinskens & Paul Kerswill. 2004. The study of dialect convergence and divergence: Conceptual and methodological considerations. In Peter Auer, Frans Hinskens & Paul Kerswill (eds.), *Dialect change: Convergence and*

divergence in European languages, 1–51. Cambridge, New York: Cambridge University Press.
Barthes, Roland. 1968. *Elements of semiology;* New York: Hill & Wang.
Chambers, J. K. & Peter Trudgill. 1998. *Dialectology*. 2nd edn. Cambridge, New York: Cambridge University Press.
Čuka, Anica & Nina Lončar. 2010. Otok Murter – prirodne i društvenogeografske značajke. In Vladimir Skračić (ed.), *Toponimija otoka Murtera*, 5–31. Zadar: Sveučilište : Centar za jadranska onomastička istraživanja.
Državni zavod za statistiku Republike Hrvatske. *1. Stanovništvo prema starosti i spolu po naseljima, popis 2011.*
Filipi, Goran. 1997. *Betinska brodogradnja: Etimologijski rječnik pučkog nazivlja*. Šibenik: Županijski muzej.
Hawkes, Terence. 2004. *Structuralism and Semiotics*. London/New York: Routledge.
Jutronić, Dunja. 2010. *Spliski govor, od vapora do trajekta: Po čemu će nas pripoznavat*. Split: Naklada Bošković.
Kulušić, Sven. 1984. *Murterski kraj*. Murter: Društveni centar.
Lotman, Juri. 1985 [2015]. On the semiosphere. *Sign Systems Studies* 33(1). 215–239.
Lotman, Juri, Marina Grishakova & Wilma Clark. 2009. *Culture and explosion*. Berlin; New York: Mouton de Gruyter.
Moles, Abraham A. 1972. *Théorie des objets*. Paris: Ed. Universitaires.
Škevin, Ivana. 2010. *Etimološka i leksikološka obradba posuđenica romanskog podrijetla u govoru mjesta Betina na otoku Murteru*. Zadar: University of Zadar Ph.D. dissertation.
Škevin, Ivana. 2012. Između arhaičnog (romanskog) i standardnog (hrvatskog) jezičnog elementa: Koineizacija otočnih varijeteta. *Aktualna istraživanja u primijenjenoj lingvistici. Hrvatsko društvo za primijenjenu lingvistiku* 25. 171–184.

Chapter 17

Code-switching in the Anglophone community in Japan

Keiko Hirano
University of Kitakyushu, Japan

> The present study investigates code-switching in native speakers of English (NSsE) who live in an Anglophone community in Japan and examines the impact of the speakers' social networks on their use of code-switching in a language contact situation. Sets of natural, spontaneous conversations in English between two NSsE from the same country were collected from the same informants on two separate occasions a year apart. The linguistic variable focused upon is Japanese words and phrases that could easily and naturally be expressed in English. More than 1200 Japanese words and phrases were observed in the linguistic data from 39 NSsE living in Japan as English teachers. Statistical analyses revealed that there was a significant correlation between the speaker's use of Japanese and his/her social networks with English teachers (both Japanese and NSsE). The analysis of social networks with linguistic behaviour suggests that their identity as being not just that of "foreigner teaching English in Japan", but rather "English teacher within a team made up of both Japanese and native-speaker English teachers" is likely to encourage high frequency in the use of code-switching among the NSsE in Japan.

1 Introduction

The purpose of this study is to investigate code-switching in relation to social networks in native speakers of English (NSsE) who live in an Anglophone community in Japan. The members of this Anglophone community start forming new social networks with NSsE from their home country and other countries as well as local Japanese people as soon as they arrive in Japan. The current study observes the use of Japanese words and phrases during conversations in English between NSsE and examines the impact of the NSsE's social networks formed in Japan on their use of code-switching in a language contact situation.

Sets of natural, spontaneous conversations in English between two NSsE from the same country were collected from the same informants on two separate oc-

Keiko Hirano. 2016. Code-switching in the Anglophone community in Japan. In Marie-Hélène Côté, Remco Knooihuizen & John Nerbonne (eds.), *The future of dialects*, 305–313. Berlin: Language Science Press.
DOI:10.17169/langsci.b81.156

casions a year apart. Each informant was also interviewed to collect information about people with whom he/she has a close relationship and regular contact in order to define his/her social networks. The linguistic variable focused upon is Japanese words and phrases (except proper nouns) that could easily and naturally be expressed in English. The frequency of usage of such Japanese vocabulary is examined. Statistical analyses revealed that there was a significant correlation between the speaker's use of Japanese and his/her social networks with English teachers (both Japanese and NSsE). Analysis of social networks with linguistic behaviour suggests that a sense of solidarity is likely to encourage high frequency in the use of code-switching among the NSsE in Japan.

2 Code-switching

NSsE who come to Japan as English teachers are in a bilingual situation with English as their mother tongue and Japanese as their second language (L2). In such a language contact situation, code-switching between the two languages is likely to occur during conversation. Code-switching means that 'bilingual or bidialectal speakers switch back and forth between one language or dialect and another within the same conversation' (Trudgill 2003: 23). According to Azuma (1997: 26), code-switching only occurs if the interlocutor is capable of speaking the two languages at the same level as the speaker. He says that one possible reason for code-switching occurring is the speakers having *dual identities* (29-30). In performing code-switching, the speakers attempt to confirm the fact that they both belong to dual societies synchronically and establish membership between them. It is assumed that NSsE in Japan have dual identities: their original membership and a new membership as an English teacher in Japan. For the present study, the occasional use of Japanese words and phrases during conversation in English between NSsE, as shown in Examples (1) and (2), is considered to be code-switching.

(1) Cathay ... it's ... like twelve *man* or something
　　　　　　　　　　　　　　(ten thousand)

(2) there're about ...ten when we had the *eikai-* not the
　　　　　　　　　　　　　　　　　　　(English conver-...)
　　eikaiwa　　　　　　the *enkai*
　　(English conversation)　(party)

3 Hypotheses

In order to verify the code-switching behaviour of NSsE living in Japan, this paper proposes two hypotheses: (1) Due to long-term language contact with the Japanese language, code-switching to Japanese occurs among NSsE in Japan during conversations in English between NSsE more frequently one year after their arrival in Japan; and (2) The speaker's use of code-switching is strongly correlated to his/her social networks with native-speaker (NS) English teachers. The second hypothesis assumes that the speakers who have strong social networks with NS English teachers like themselves tend to use Japanese words and phrases more frequently than those whose comparable networks are weaker.

4 Methodology

4.1 Informants and data collection

The data used for the present study were collected from thirty-six language teachers on the Japan Exchange and Teaching (JET) Programme, which is sponsored by Japanese ministries (Council of Local Authorities for International Relations [CLAIR] 2013), and three conversation instructors at private institutions. Fifteen English informants (5 males and 10 females), 11 Americans (7 males and 4 females), and 13 New Zealanders (3 males and 10 females) – a total of 39 NSsE – participated in the data collection. The informants were aged between 21 and 34 at the time of the first data collection, averaging 25 years of age. They all lived in Kyushu, mainly in the prefecture of Fukuoka and the surrounding prefectures of Kumamoto and Saga.

In order to examine linguistic changes observed over a period of one year from arrival in Japan, the data used for this study were collected from the same informants on two separate occasions – immediately after the informants' arrival in Japan (2000) and then one year later (2001). The current research used a method designed to elicit more naturally occurring conversation from the informants. The interviewer was not present while the informants were being recorded in order to lessen the possibility of speech modification that might result from the presence of a researcher from Japan who is a non-NSE. In both sessions, casual conversations between two NSsE from the same country were recorded for 45 minutes. The data used for the present study comprised a total of 34 hours of speech.

For the purposes of this study, Japanese words and phrases used by the informants during the conversation in English were extracted and analysed. Proper nouns such as those shown in Examples (3) and (4) were excluded from the data. For the analysis, only Japanese words and phrases that could be expressed in English as shown in Examples (5) to (7) were included. The study includes 487 Japanese words and phrases that could be expressed in English in the first dataset and 759 Japanese words and phrases in the second dataset.

(3) I stayed at the youth hostel ...by *Kawaguchiko* it's a lake at the base (Lake Kawaguchi) of *Fuji*.

(4) And then we're going to *Arita* again on Mon- on the twentieth to look at the ... you know the *Kakiemon* factory

(5) I'm sure you were there when we were in the big room in the *kencho* (prefectural office)

(6) there's a *Monbusho* scholarship isn't there (Ministry of Education)

(7) my *kyoto-sensei* 's really nice actually (vice principal)

4.2 Social network

The current study investigates an Anglophone community in Japan which consists of NSsE who are living temporarily in Japan as English teachers on the JET Programme and at private institutions, and who mix with speakers of different regional varieties of English in an L2 setting. Currently over 4,000 university graduates from about 40 countries participate in the JET Programme (Council of Local Authorities for International Relations [CLAIR] 2013). They form relationships with people from a wide range of social contexts such as English speakers of different dialects and non-NSsE including Japanese. Thus they create a community in a new linguistic environment which differs vastly from those in their home countries.

The influence of speakers' strong social networks on their linguistic behaviour has been studied by researchers including Cheshire (1982), Eckert (1988), Hirano (2013), Labov (1972) and Milroy (1987). Their studies revealed that there was a strong relationship between speakers' network structures and their linguistic behaviour. Milroy (1987) studied communities in Belfast whose social networks were close-knit. Using the degree of density of the network and the multiplexity of each tie, she measured the strength of networks. Members of the Anglophone community in Japan, however, are socially and geographically mobile, and are always in multilingual and multidialectal contact situations. They create many network ties that form ramifying structures but their networks are loose-knit due to their relatively short stay.

In order to gather information about the social networks that the informants for the present study had created in Japan they had a short interview with the researcher and were asked about their close friends at the end of the second data collection session. The present study took into account their self-assessed closeness to other Anglophones or with Japanese, the frequency of contact with them, and network size, and developed a number of quantitative indices.[1] A score for each relationship was calculated using the rank order of closeness and the frequency of actual and virtual contacts with the person as follows:

Score for each relationship = rank order score × (score for meeting frequency + score for telephone call frequency)

These individual relationship scores were then grouped into different social network categories. For this paper, the social network of each informant was first grouped into two networks – a network with NSsE and a network with non-NSsE – and then further divided into seven sub-groups as shown in Table 1. Network with English teachers (7) combines network strength with NS English teachers (2) and Japanese teachers of English (6) to create another network group. These index scores of social networks were used to examine relationships with individual informants' frequency of code-switching and shifts between the two datasets.

5 Results

Multiple regression (stepwise method) was performed to analyse the correlation between frequency in the use of Japanese words and phrases in individual informants a year after their arrival in Japan as the dependent variable and their social network strengths with NSsE and non NSsE as independent variables. The result suggests that the network with English teachers and the network with Japanese who use Japanese as their main language in speaking with the informants (JJML) are statistically significantly influencing the level of Japanese usage positively, as shown in Table 2. The stronger such networks the informants have, the more

---

[1] See Hirano (2013) for a detailed description of the index scores of networks.

Table 1: Types of Social Networks

Network Members	Social Networks	
NSsE	(1)	Native speakers of English
	(2)	Native-speaker English teachers
Non-NSsE	(3)	Japanese people
	(4)	Japanese who use English as their main language in speaking with the informants
	(5)	Japanese who use Japanese as their main language in speaking with the informants (JJML)
	(6)	Japanese teachers of English
English Teachers	(7)	English teachers (2) + (6)

they tend to insert Japanese words and phrases into their conversations in English with another NSE a year after their arrival in Japan.

Table 3 shows the result of multiple regression analysis between the change in frequency in use of Japanese words and phrases from the first dataset to the second dataset in individual informants and their social network strengths. The result suggests that the network with English teachers is the only statistically significant predictor influencing the level of Japanese usage positively. The stronger this network is, the more informants tend to increase use of Japanese in their conversations in English a year after their arrival in Japan.

According to Pearson correlation analysis, other social networks, such as the network with NSsE and the network with NS English teachers, showed strong correlations with the level of Japanese usage in the second dataset or with the change between the two datasets. Those networks, however, are not significant predictors according to multiple regression anayses.

Table 2: Multiple regression for use of Japanese and social networks after a year in Japan. Adjusted $R^2=.344$; $F_{2,36}=9.425$; $p=.001$ (Stepwise method).

Predictor Variables	Beta	p
English teachers NW	.509	.001
JJML NW	.338	.017

Table 3: Multiple regression for change in frequency in use of Japanese and social networks. Adjusted R2=.078; F1,37=4.193; p=.048 (Stepwise method).

Predictor Variable	Beta	p
English teachers NW	.319	.048

6 Discussion

The increase in the amount of code-switching performed by the informants from 487 cases in the first dataset to 759 in the second dataset seems to verify the first hypothesis that "due to long-term language contact with the Japanese language, code-switching to Japanese occurs among NSsE in Japan during conversations in English with other NSsE more frequently one year after their arrival in Japan". The second hypothesis that "the speaker's use of code-switching is strongly correlated to his/her social networks with NS English teachers" was partly verified. The results above showed that the strongest network effect on code-switching was the one with English teachers which combines networks with NS English teachers and Japanese teachers of English. This combined network effect was much stronger than individual network effects. The informants for the current study have possibly established their identity as being not just that of 'foreigner teaching English in Japan'; but rather 'English teacher and contributor to English education in Japan within a team made up of both Japanese and NS English teachers'.

One of the possible reasons why the informants increased their frequency of usage of Japanese that could be easily expressed in English may be explained by the concept of group phraseology. One of the applications of group phraseology offered by Yonekawa (2009: 8) is its usage by certain functional social communities as a language for professional groups. The informants of the current study were all teaching English at schools. A large portion of words and phrases used by them are actually work-related and are mutually understandable even in Japanese. It might be easier to use and to understand the work-related terms in Japanese rather than those translated into English for NS English teachers when the conversation interlocutor is also in the same profession.

Another useful concept which might help to explain the linguistic behaviour of this particular social group is community of practice (Eckert 1988). This concept is described as being active amongst 'people who share a concern, a set of problems, or a passion about a topic, and who deepen their knowledge and expertise in this area by interacting on an ongoing basis' (Wenger, McDermott & Snyder 2002: 4). NSsE who have come to Japan voluntarily to teach English are supposed to belong to a community of practice. Solidarity or competition among NSsE could be other possible reasons for this linguistic behaviour. Further investigation will hopefully help to reveal the mechanisms of code-switching in the Anglophone community in Japan.

Acknowledgement

This work was supported by JSPS KAKENHI Grant Number 25284082.

References

Azuma, Shoji. 1997. *Shakai gengogaku nyumon [An introduction to sociolinguistics]*. Tokyo: Kenkyusha.
Cheshire, Jenny. 1982. *Variation in an English dialect: A sociolinguistic study*. Cambridge: Cambridge University Press.
Eckert, Penelope. 1988. Adolescent social structure and the spread of linguistic change. *Language in Society* 17(02). 183–207.
Hirano, Keiko. 2013. *Dialect contact and social networks: Language change in an anglophone community in Japan*. Frankfurt: Peter Lang.
Labov, William. 1972. *Language in the Inner City*. Philadelphia: University of Philadelphia Press.
Milroy, Lesley. 1987. *Language and social networks*. Oxford [etc.]: Blackwell.
Trudgill, Peter. 2003. *A glossary of sociolinguistics*. Edinburgh: Edinburgh University Press.
Wenger, Etienne, Richard A McDermott & William Snyder. 2002. *Cultivating communities of practice: A guide to managing knowledge*. Boston, Mass.: Harvard Business School Press.
Yonekawa, Akihiko. 2009. *Shudango no kenkyu, Jokan [Study of group phraseology, Vol. 1]*. Tokyo: Tokyodo.
Council of Local Authorities for International Relations [CLAIR]. 2013. *Jet programme participant numbers*.

Chapter 18

Tongue trajectories in North American English /æ/ tensing

Christopher Carignan
North Carolina State University

Jeff Mielke
North Carolina State University

Robin Dodsworth
North Carolina State University

Ultrasound imaging is of interest to many dialectologists, due to the relative transportability and low cost associated with this technique for imaging the tongue. The current study introduces a method for examining the temporal dynamics of articulatory correlates of sociolinguistic variables directly from ultrasound video. This technique is demonstrated with data from North American English /æ/.

Short-a tensing is one of the most well-studied regional variables in North American English (NAE): /æ/ is variably realized as [æ], [eə], [eɪ], etc. depending on region and segmental context (Ash (2002); Becker & Wong (2009); Boberg (2008); Boberg & Strassel (2000); Labov, Ash & Boberg (2006); Plichta (2005), *inter alia*). The reason for these differences remain largely unknown (e.g., why /æ/ tenses before /d/ in some Mid-Atlantic varieties but before /g/ in some Northern varieties). The dimension of /æ/ tensing is commonly operationalized as the front diagonal of the acoustic vowel space—i.e., along a line approximating the axis between [a] and [i] quantified as Z2-Z1 (normalized F2 - normalized F1, see Labov, Rosenfelder & Fruehwald 2013). /æ/ has also been observed to involve both falling and rising diphthongal qualities along this axis (Assmann & Katz 2000; Fox & Jacewicz 2009; Labov, Ash & Boberg 2006). The realization of a particular variant of /æ/ along this acoustic diagonal is often interpreted as a correlate of tongue fronting and raising, but the F1 and F2 differences can be due to other factors such as nasalization (De Decker & Nycz 2012) or changes in oral

Christopher Carignan, Jeff Mielke & Robin Dodsworth. 2016. Tongue trajectories in North American English /æ/ tensing. In Marie-Hélène Côté, Remco Knooihuizen & John Nerbonne (eds.), *The future of dialects*, 313–320. Berlin: Language Science Press. DOI:10.17169/langsci.b81.157

cavity shape due to velum lowering (Baker, Mielke & Archangeli 2008). Therefore, while Z2-Z1 is clearly an appropriate measure for describing /æ/ tensing, the effort to understand the phonetic motivations for /æ/ tensing is aided from observing lingual articulation directly and the ability to derive time-varying measures of tongue postures.

De Decker & Nycz (2012) showed from single ultrasound frames that speakers vary in the amount of tongue raising associated with their acoustic tensing. The current study extends this approach to allow the study of tongue trajectories. Selecting one time point to represent a token of a speech sound is a common simplifying technique in acoustic and articulatory studies of variation. For ultrasound studies, this simplification is often motivated by the amount of work involved in data processing, which typically involves tracing of the tongue surface in individual video frames (Li, Kambhamettu & Stone 2005). The method described here applies principal component analysis (PCA) and linear regression to derive linguistically meaningful time-varying articulatory signals directly from ultrasound video, in order to characterize the temporal aspects of /æ/ tensing.

Ultrasound and acoustic data was collected from 20 speakers (13 male, age range 20–72) from regions of North America previously known to exhibit distinct regional patterns of /æ/ tensing: seven from the Southern U.S. (tensing before nasals expected), seven from the Northern U.S. and three from Ontario (tensing before nasals and /g/ expected), one from Newfoundland (no tensing expected), and two from Philadelphia (Philadelphia system expected). Participants read a randomized list containing three repetitions of 120 monosyllabic words, while lingual ultrasound images were captured at 60 frames per second using a Terason T3000 ultrasound system with a 8MC3 microconvex array ultrasound probe, Ultraspeech software (Hueber et al. 2007), and an Articulate Instruments ultrasound stabilization headset. Audio was collected using an omnidirectional microphone attached to the headset and recorded through a USB preamplifier in Audacity. A phone-level segmentation of each audio recording was carried out using the Penn Phonetics Lab Forced Aligner (Yuan & Liberman 2008). All images within one second of segmented speech were subject to analysis.

The initial feature extraction from the ultrasound video uses the technique described by Hueber et al. (2007): images for each participant's session are filtered to reduce noise and enhance edges, cropped, and downsampled, and then PCA is applied.[1] Similar techniques have been described by Story (2007) for point-tracking data, and Carignan et al. (2015) for MRI data. The PCA model yields

---

[1] Matlab scripts and instructions for performing PCA of ultrasound video as described here are available from http://phon.wordpress.ncsu.edu/lab-manual/

principal components (PCs) that represent independent axes of variation within a set of speech data, and scores for each PC for each image, which represent how strongly an individual image is correlated with each PC. Thus, the analysis allows an ultrasound video to be represented by a matrix with a column for every PC the researcher wishes to retain, and a row for every video frame. This is comparable to deriving a matrix of linear predictive coding (LPC) or Mel-frequency cepstral (MFC) coefficients from a waveform, both in data compression and in the interpretability of the coefficients.

The articulatory PCs themselves are hard to interpret in any meaningful way. To generate an articulatory signal representing the lingual contribution to tensing (tongue body raising/fronting), the PC score vectors are transformed to correlate with the front diagonal of the acoustic vowel space (Z2-Z1). To find the range of lingual configurations correlated with this acoustic front diagonal, F1 and F2 were measured every 6 ms in all vocalic intervals. The articulatory PCs were interpolated temporally in order to match the acoustic time points, and a linear regression was performed with dependent variable Z2-Z1 and independent variables PCs 1-20. Data was every frame during a vowel lying along the front diagonal [a æ ɛ e ɪ i]. The coefficients from the linear regression model are used to transform the articulatory PC score matrix to match the articulatory diagonal, resulting in a tongue height signal composed of a single score for each ultrasound frame. For any given ultrasound frame, the higher the score is the more raised and fronted the tongue body is. Since it is derived from ultrasound images instead of acoustic data, the articulatory signal is continuous throughout the recording, even during consonant and silence intervals.

We present a sampling of the results in selected contexts for particular speakers, to demonstrate how ultrasound-derived articulatory signals can be applied to questions about the phonetic origins of the observed dialect patterns. Figures 1–3 display examples of this lingual tensing signal for /æ/ before different coda consonants, using Smoothing-Spline ANOVA (Gu 2002) to compare articulatory trajectories across contexts. In these figures, the tensing signal is on the y-axis and normalized time is on the x-axis, with the interval [0,1] representing the vowel. Unlike formants, ultrasound-derived articulatory signals are observable during all kinds of consonants.

For most of the speakers, pre-/m n/ tensing is characterized by a peak aligned approximately with the vowel midpoint, while there is no such peak before /ŋ/. These observations are consistent with previously observed formant trajectories for /æ/, and they are illustrated for three speakers in Figure 1. The coda consonant closure intervals are to the right of time=1.0 in the figures. Because it involves

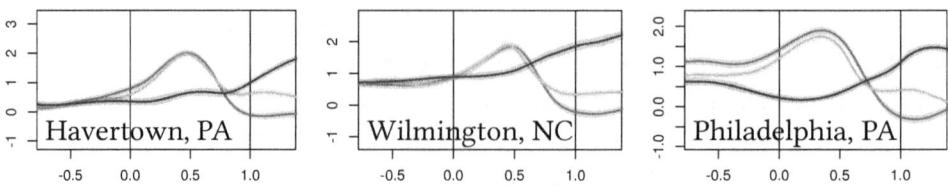

Figure 1: Tongue height for /æ/ before /m/ (red), /n/ (green), and /ŋ/ (blue).

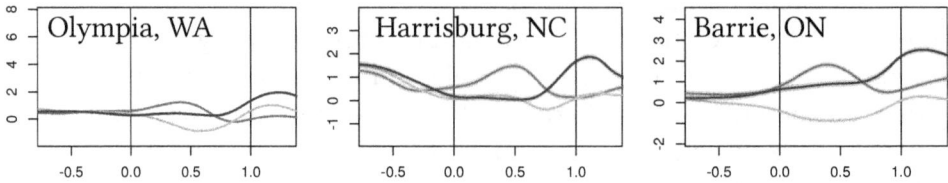

Figure 2: Tongue height for /æ/ before /n/ (red), /d/ (green), and /g/ (blue).

tongue raising, /ŋ/ is high on the tongue raising scale. The raising observed at the end of /æ/ before /ŋ/ can be interpreted as coarticulatory, but the tongue raising in /æ/ before the other nasals is clearly due to a distinct phonetic target. While the *consonant* /n/ trivially involves higher tongue position than /m/, this is clearly not the basis of /æ/ tensing before /n/, which is the same as before /m/. Pre-/ŋ/ tongue raising is less extreme than pre-/n/ tongue raising, except for the speaker from Fargo, ND, whose /æ/ has higher tongue position before /ŋ/ than before /n/, and the speaker from Barrie, Ontario, who raises to the same degree in both contexts.

Figure 2 shows /æ/ before /n d g/ for three speakers. This is an important comparison because pre-/n/ tensing is widespread, pre-/d/ tensing is observed primarily in the Mid-Atlantic region, and pre-/g/ tensing is observed primarily in parts of the North and Canada. All speakers in the sample manifest higher tongue position before /g/ than before /d/, at least by the end of the vowel. This is consistent with /g/ being a velar consonant. For some speakers, including the Philadelphia speaker who tenses more before /d/ in select lexical items, this is true *only* at the very end of the vowel, and it appears to be a purely coarticulatory raising of the tongue body in anticipation for [g]. For the others, the tongue body raising starts earlier in the vowel, which we interpret as a pattern that is not solely due to anticipatory velar coarticulation. This greater tongue height before /g/ compared to /d/ begins in the second half of the vowel for the mid-Atlantic and Buffalo speakers and all but one of the Southern speakers, and from

18 Tongue trajectories in North American English /æ/ tensing

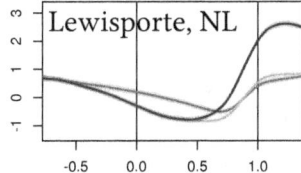 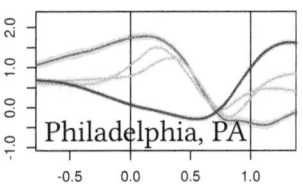

Figure 3: Left: Tongue height for /æ/ before /n/ (red), /d/ (green), /g/ (blue) in Newfoundland; Right: Tongue height for /æ/ before /f/ (red), /θ/ (green), /s/ (cyan), and /ʃ/ (violet) in Philadelphia.

the first half of the vowel for all of the other Northern speakers and one Southern speaker. /æ/ before /g/ has higher tongue body throughout the entire vowel for all of the Ontario speakers. The similarity in the rising trajectories before /ŋ/ and /g/ (seen in Figures 1 and 2), indicates that /ŋ/ patterns with the other velar /g/ rather than the other nasals /m n/. Figure 3 shows two more expected patterns. The speaker from Newfoundland shows very little tongue raising even before a nasal (Boberg 2008), and a speaker from Philadelphia shows tongue raising before anterior fricatives, with a trajectory similar to what is observed in other speakers only before /m n/.

The method we have described generates time-varying articulatory signals from ultrasound video at a high frame rate (60 fps for the system used in this study). This allows the observation and quantification of temporal changes and co-articulatory effects, from an articulatory imaging technique that is fairly accessible to linguists, with minimal manual data processing. Unlike formant measurements, these articulatory signals are present in consonants and even silent intervals, and they do not require any kind of tracking. Using this method, we have analyzed temporal characteristics of NAE /æ/ tensing in different segmental contexts for speakers from different regions known to have different /æ/ tensing patterns. At an articulatory level, most speakers' patterns of tongue height before /m n/ suggest a completely different vowel target in these contexts, much like the tense /æ/ observed in a superset of these contexts in the Philadelphia split short-a system. In speakers who have tongue raising before the velars /g N/, a completely different trajectory is observed, in which tenseness increases throughout the vowel. The observed regional variation in the timing of tongue raising before velars suggests that pre-velar /æ/ tensing can be studied as coarticulation that has been phonologized to different degrees in different dialects.

References

Ash, Sharon. 2002. The distribution of a phonemic split in the Mid-Atlantic region: Yet more on short a. *Penn Working Papers in Linguistics* 8(3). 1–15.

Assmann, P. F. & W. F. Katz. 2000. Time-varying spectral change in the vowels of children and adults. *The Journal of the Acoustical Society of America* 108. 1856.

Baker, Adam, Jeff Mielke & Diana Archangeli. 2008. More velar than /g/: Consonant coarticulation as a cause of diphthongization. In Charles B. Chang & Hannah J. Haynie (eds.), *Proceedings of the 26th West Coast Conference on Formal Linguistics*. Somerville, MA: Cascadilla Proceedings Project.

Becker, K. & A. W. Wong. 2009. The short-*a* system of NYC English: An update. *Penn Working Papers in Linguistics* 14. 11–20.

Boberg, Charles. 2008. Regional phonetic differentiation in Standard Canadian English. *Journal of English Linguistics* 36(2). 129–154.

Boberg, Charles & S. Strassel. 2000. Short-a in Cincinnati: A change in progress. *Journal of English Linguistics* 28. 108–126.

Carignan, C., R. Shosted, M. Fu, Z.-P. Liang & B. B. Sutton. 2015. A real-time MRI investigation of the role of lingual and pharyngeal articulation in the production of the nasal vowel system of French. *Journal of Phonetics* 50. 34–51.

De Decker, P. M. & J. R. Nycz. 2012. Are tense [æ]s really tense? The mapping between articulation and acoustics. *Lingua* 122(7). 810–821.

Fox, R. A. & E. Jacewicz. 2009. Cross-dialectal variation in formant dynamics of American English vowels. *The Journal of the Acoustical Society of America* 126(5). 2603.

Gu, Chong. 2002. *Smoothing spline ANOVA models*. Springer Series in Statistics. New York: Springer-Verlag.

Hueber, T., G. Aversano, G. Chollet, B. Denby, G. Dreyfus, Y. Oussar, P. Roussel & Maureen Stone. 2007. Eigentongue feature extraction for an ultrasound-based silent speech interface. In *Proceedings of the 2007 International Conference on Acoustics, Speech, and Signal Processing*, I–1245–I–1248.

Labov, William, Sharon Ash & Charles Boberg. 2006. *The atlas of North American English: Phonetics, phonology and sound change*. Berlin, New York: Mouton de Gruyter.

Labov, William, Ingrid Rosenfelder & Josef Fruehwald. 2013. One hundred years of sound change in Philadelphia: Linear incrementation, reversal, and reanalysis. *Language* 89(1). 30–65.

Li, M., C. Kambhamettu & Maureen Stone. 2005. Automatic contour tracking in ultrasound images. *Clinical Linguistics and Phonetics* 19(6–7). 545–554.

Plichta, Bartek. 2005. *Interdisciplinary perspectives on the Northern Cities Chain Shift*. Michigan State University Unpublished Ph.D. thesis.

Story, Brad H. 2007. Time dependence of vocal tract modes during production of vowels and vowel sequences. *Journal of the Acoustical Society of America* 121(6). 3770–3789.

Yuan, J. & M. Liberman. 2008. Speaker identification on the SCOTUS corpus. In *Proceedings of Acoustics '08*.

Chapter 19

s-retraction in Italian-Tyrolean bilingual speakers: A preliminary investigation using the ultrasound tongue imaging technique

Lorenzo Spreafico
Free University of Bozen-Bolzano

> This paper presents a preliminary description of the articulation of /s/ in Italian as spoken by Italian-Tyrolean simultaneous and sequential bilingual speakers. The objective is to discuss whether they articulate /s/ differently. To this aim, articulatory differences across monolingual and bilingual speakers are commented upon, in particular focusing on s-retraction, which is attested to different degrees in Italian-Tyrolean simultaneous bilingual speakers and in Tyrolean-dominant sequential bilinguals, but not in Italian-dominant sequential bilingual speakers.

1 Introduction

South Tyrol - an Italian region located on the border with Austria and Switzerland - is characterized by societal bilingualism with two distinct linguistic communities - the Tyrolean and the Italian - that present asymmetries in their linguistic repertoires. The members of the Tyrolean community are multilingual and speak Tyrolean, an East Upper German dialect (Wiesinger 1983; 1990), as their first language, and standard German (Ciccolone 2010) and regional Italian (Mioni 2001) as their second and third languages respectively. In contrast, the members of the Italian community are mostly monolingual and speak Italian: hardly anybody in the Italian community masters Tyrolean and few members of the Italian community use German, a language they learn at school. After years of segregation,[1] the degree of interaction between the Italian and the Ty-

---

[1] One relevant aspect of segregation of the two main linguistic communities is in the separated school system that operates within the province of South Tyrol. Baur & Medda (2008: 237) note

Lorenzo Spreafico. 2016. S-retraction in italian-tyrolean bilingual speakers: a preliminary investigation using the ultrasound tongue imaging technique. In Marie-Hélène Côté, Remco Knooihuizen & John Nerbonne (eds.), *The future of dialects*, 321–330. Berlin: Language Science Press.
DOI:10.17169/langsci.b81.158

rolean community is steadily increasing and the number of bilingual speakers is gradually growing.

In this research note, I focus on s-retraction, the phenomenon in which /s/ is realized as an [ɕ]-like or as an [ʃ]-like sound. There is no previous research done on s-retraction in Italian as spoken by mono- or bilingual speakers. Nevertheless quite often monolingual speakers of Italian make fun of bilingual speakers from the Tyrolean community because they articulate a backed sound instead of the Italian alveolar [s]. For example, they are said to utter [ˈɕkwillo] and [ˈʃkonto] instead of standard Italian [ˈskwillo] 'ring' and [ˈskonto] 'sale'. s-retraction in Italian as spoken by bilingual speakers might be due to an influence from the Tyrolean substratum, since in this dialect the voiceless sibilant is articulated with the body of the tongue raised against the hard palate whenever it is followed by a consonant. This is attested in word-initial position, as well as in medial and final position (Alber 2001; Alber & Lanthaler 2005). Consequently, s-retraction might be indexically important to discriminate between monolingual and bilingual speakers of ITA from South Tyrol.

2 Informants and data collection

To investigate preliminarily the question of the possible sociophonetic relevance of /s/-retraction in Italian, I selected four speakers aged between 22 and 27 all born and living in Meran. In order to exclude possible gender-induced variation (Fuchs & Toda (2011)), I only selected female speakers. All informants had a comparable socio-demographic status but different rates of bilingualism as inferable on the basis of two parameters: the age of first exposure to Italian and/or Tyrolean; and the rate of dual language exposure. According to these parameters the sample included two late sequential (LS) bilingual speakers and two simultaneous bilingual (SB) speakers. The late sequential speaker LS1 is an almost monolingual speaker of Italian who stems from a strictly monolingual Italian family and attended only the Italian section of the South Tyrolean school system. The late sequential speaker LS2 is a Tyrolean-dominant informant who grew up in a Tyrolean-speaking family and attended the German school section only. The simultaneous bilingual speakers SB1 and SB2 originate from two different bilingual families, have both been exposed to Italian and Tyrolean since their birth, and attended the Italian as well as the German sections of the South Tyrolean school system.

---

that the institution of the division along linguistic lines in the field of education is used by the political representatives of the Tyrolean community to protect "the German mother tongue against 'foreign' influence and 'mixture' with other languages".

In order to describe /s/-retraction, I employed the Ultrasound Tongue Imaging (UTI) technique (Stone 2005). UTI involves the use of an ultrasound transducer fixed under the speaker's chin to obtain images of the tongue. The system I used is based on the SonixTablet machine equipped with a microconvex probe recording up to 160 fps at a variable depth of 8 mm to 9 mm (according to the anatomy of the speaker). The machine was synchronized to the audio via the Ultrasonix module in the AAA software by Articulate Instruments. All speakers were recorded in the Alpine Laboratory of Phonetics and Phonology (ALPs) at the University of Bozen. Shortly before the experiment, all informants received detailed instructions on the test procedure. In order to activate the bilingual mode (Grosjean 1998), instructions were given both in Italian and in Tyrolean. Each speaker was instructed to read aloud a list of sentences prompted on a screen. The prompt list consisted of 40 Italian items with word-initial and word-internal /s/, /sV/, /sC/ (C={p, t, k}; V={a, i, u}) groups. The prompt list also contained distractors and three Tyrolean words *schtruuze* '(kind of) bread', *odminischtrativor* 'administrative', *schtrimpf* 'stockings'. For each informant, I was able to obtain a minimum of one to a maximum of three repetitions of the whole sentence list, depending on their resistance to the probe stabilization helmet I used.

3 Data analysis

For the within-speaker comparison, I followed the proposal in Davidson (2006): firstly, I calculated the smoothing spline estimates; secondly, I computed the Bayesian confidence intervals for each set of curves. My aim was to contrast the tongue shape of Italian /s/ in /sV/ sequences vs. the tongue shape of Italian /s/ in /sCV/ sequences to test if, as documented for Tyrolean, the consonant following the sibilant triggered /s/-retraction in the productions of simultaneous bilinguals and/or of the Tyrolean-dominant sequential bilingual.

Figure 1 shows the results of the comparison of /s/ in the two words /ˈsano/ 'sane' and /ˈskanno/ 'I slaughter' for the Italian-dominant speaker. For the purpose of this paper, the main regions of interest are the rightmost part of the tongue, corresponding to the anterior part of the tongue including the blade and tip, and the central part of the tongue, corresponding to the body. The tracings display a tip-down post-alveolar constriction, with the apex of the tongue stopping before the point of contact for /t/ as well as some instances of tongue flexion in the pre-palatal region. The constriction location for /s/ is kept constant across repetitions, but the tongue body is kept higher in /ˈskanno/ and pointing to the constriction location for the following velar stop. The interaction effect graph

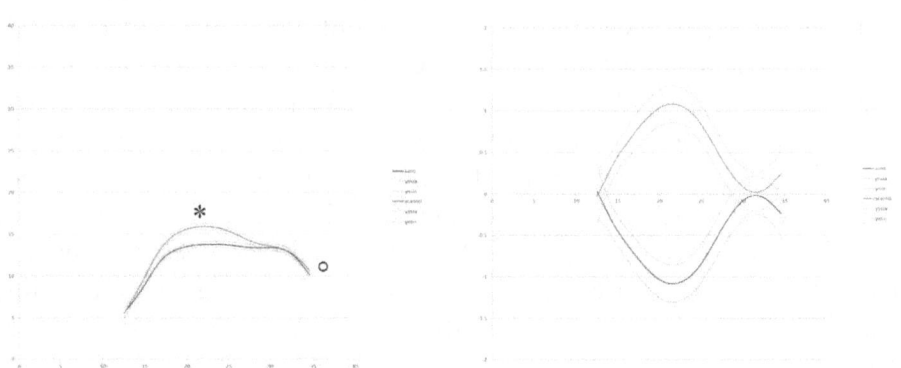

Figure 1: Smoothing spline estimate with 95% Bayesian confidence interval (left) and interaction effects (right) for comparison of the mean curves for /s/ in /ˈsano/ (blue) and /ˈskanno/ (red) for subject LS1. No palate shapes were exported for this study, but in each Figure * and ° point to the place of articulation for /t/ and /k/ respectively. The tip and blade of the tongue are on the right-hand side; the root of the tongue is on the left-hand side. In the Bayesian confidence interval graph, when confidence intervals of the main effects curves overlap, the differences between the two curves are not significant.

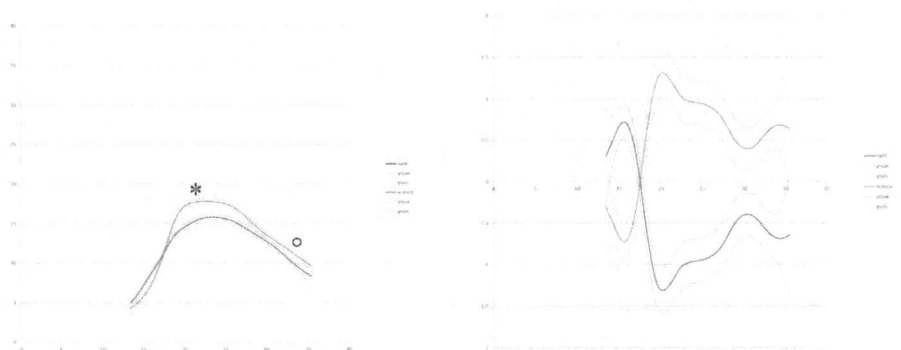

Figure 2: Smoothing spline estimate and interaction effects for subject LS2.

19 s-retraction in Italian-Tyrolean bilingual speakers

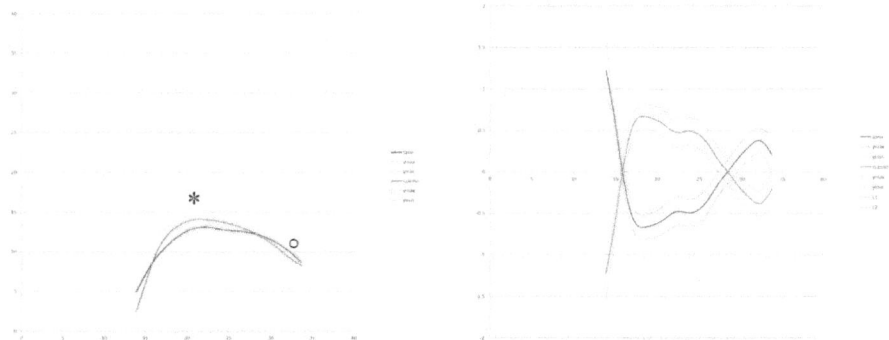

Figure 3: Smoothing spline estimate and interaction effects for subject SB1.

confirms the visual impression and indicates that for both stimuli, the tongue blade and tip have comparable contours while the tongue body significantly differs.

Figure 2 displays data for the Tyrolean-dominant speaker. Visual inspection, confidence intervals and the interaction effect graph show that the silhouettes are significantly different for the entire length of the tongue. With regard to the /s/ in /ˈsano/, the posterodorsum is raised towards the hard palate and the anterodorsum and the tip are down. Regarding the /s/ in /ˈskanno/, the tongue body, blade and tip are higher, while the root is lower. There is an increased constriction degree in the velar region.

Figure 3 shows data for the simultaneous bilingual speaker SB1. Notwithstanding the visual impression of affinity and notwithstanding the tongue tip pointing to the same constriction location in the alveolar area for both smoothed profiles, tracings are significantly different as displayed by the interaction effect graph. Regarding the tongue shape of /s/ in /ˈskanno/, the blade and tip are somehow lower than in /ˈsano/, while the body is higher and pointing to the hard palate. In /ˈsano/, the tongue body is lowered in the pre-palatal region thus showing tongue flexion.

Figure 4 presents data for the simultaneous bilingual speaker SB2. Visual investigation of the smoothing spline estimate shows that the tongue profiles almost coincide. The confidence intervals and the interaction curves confirm that there is no significant difference anywhere in the profiles, except for a few points at the tongue blade and tip and, to a lesser extent, two points in the postero-dorsum. The /s/ of /ˈskanno/ is articulated keeping the tongue apex slightly higher than in /ˈsano/.

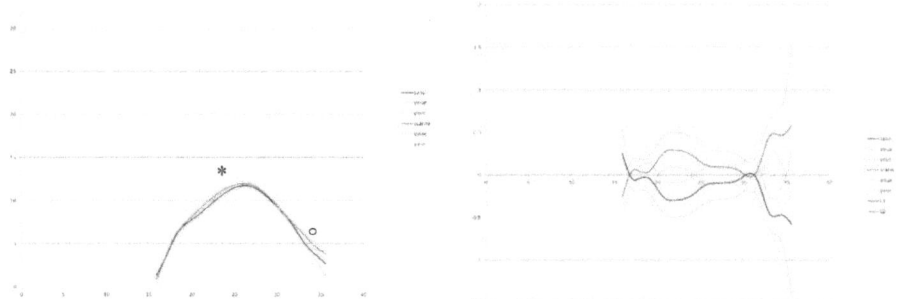

Figure 4: Smoothing spline estimate and interaction effects for subject SB2.

4 Data discussion

Figures 1–4 demonstrate that as far as Italian /s/ in /sV/ vs. /sCV/ sequences are concerned, the Italian-dominant sequential bilingual speaker LS1 does not differentiate the location nor the degree of constriction for the tongue tip and blade. Conversely, the Tyrolean-dominant speaker and the simultaneous bilingual speakers all display differentiated tongue apex profiles for /s/. Such dissimilarities are reflected in the interaction effects, whose absolute difference values are higher in the Tyrolean-dominant informant than in the simultaneous bilinguals.

Besides, and again with respect to tongue apex differences, it impressionistically emerges that the Italian-dominant sequential bilingual speaker presents an apical articulation, which contrasts with the laminal articulation of the Tyrolean-speaking informants.

Figures 1–4 also indicate that all speakers differentiate the tongue body position and keep it higher for /s/ in /ˈskanno/ than for /s/ in /ˈsano/. This evidences coarticulatory sensitivity of /s/ to the subsequent velar stop. However, the values of interaction effects are more relevant for the late sequential bilinguals than for the simultaneous bilinguals. While this is not surprising for LS1 (as apical fricatives are less resistant to coarticulation than laminals; Recasens 1999), this is of interest for LS2 as this might indeed reveal an influence from the Tyrolean substratum.

In order to test if this is the case and to investigate the possible retraction for the Italian sibilant, I contrasted the tongue shapes for /s/ in Italian and Tyrolean in a comparable phonetic environment. Unfortunately in the dataset there were no Tyrolean words containing the cluster /sk/ that I could have contrasted with the word /ˈskanno/ I commented on in the previous figures, so I used tracings of the fricative taken from Italian *castra* 's/he castrates' and from Tyrolean *odminischtrativor* 'administrative'.

Elicited data show that concerning the Tyrolean-dominant speaker, smoothing splines for the Italian and the Tyrolean fricatives are significantly different and, in particular, that in Italian, the possible retraction is very limited compared to the shape and position of the tongue for the comparable Tyrolean context. A similar variation is found in the almost monolingual speaker of Italian who, when pretending to speak Tyrolean, excludes tongue flexion and keeps the body much higher than when speaking Italian. In line with Figure 4, the simultaneous bilingual speaker SB1 appears not to change the overall shape of the tongue but, nevertheless, to articulate significantly different profiles.

According to two independent evaluators, within-speaker articulatory differences displayed in Figure 5 are perceptually relevant and can be reported to Italian [s] and Tyrolean [ʃ] respectively. On the contrary, within-speaker articulatory differences shown in Figures 2-4 are statistically significant but perceptually negligible, possibly because of the coincidence of the normalized rear-most points of contact of the tongue. Non-audible s-retraction in Italian as spoken by LS2, SB1 and SB2 – namely the informants in the database who had Tyrolean in their linguistic repertoire – would indicate that, irrespective of the rate or age of first exposure to Italian, these speakers do not transfer but instead control the allophonic alternation [s, ʃ] characteristic of TYR. Non-perceptible, but UTI-visible gradient articulatory effects nevertheless indicate that, depending on the familiarity with Italian, the production of /s/ in that language by the simultaneous bilingual speakers is less influenced by the [s, ʃ] allophony characteristic of the Tyrolean language.

5 Conclusion

At this stage of investigation, the possible indexical value of s-retraction in Italian as spoken by sequential and simultaneous bilinguals from South Tyrol cannot receive a full, positive answer if approached from an ultrasound-tongue-imaging-based sociarticulatory approach, if only because more (varied and accurate) data are needed. Nevertheless, this approach points to promising directions of investigation because there appears to be non-audible differences in tongue positioning between Italian-dominant vs. sequential and simultaneous Italian-Tyrolean bilingual speakers. Seemingly, these differences generate little or no acoustic consequence but might be sociophonetically relevant and need to be scrutinized.

Acknowledgements

I thank the editors and two anonymous reviewers for their comments, which helped me improve the manuscript.

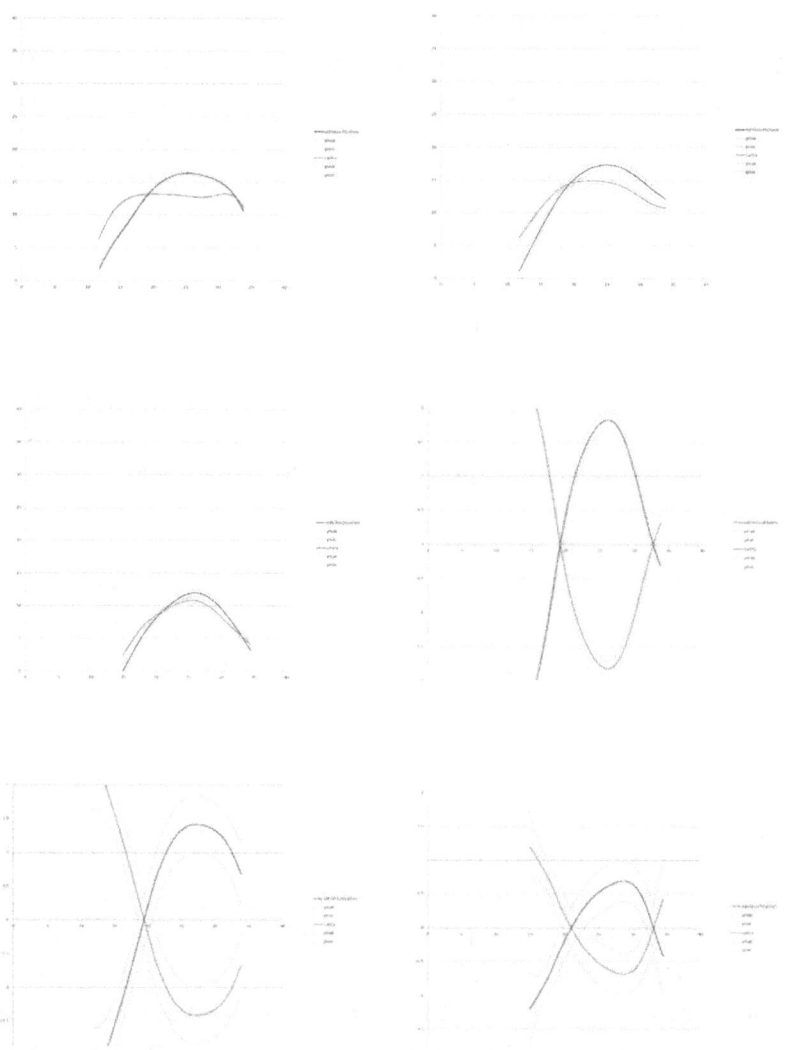

Figure 5: Smoothing spline estimate (above) and interaction effects (below) for comparison of the mean curves for /s/ in *castra* (red) and *odminischtrativor* (blue) for subjects LS1, LS2, SB2 (from left to right). Tracings for *odminischtrativor* in SB1 were corrupted hence discarded.

References

Alber, Birgit. 2001. Regional variation and edges. *Zeitschrift für Sprachwissenschaft* 20(1). 3–41.

Alber, Birgit & Franz Lanthaler. 2005. Der Silbenonset in den Tiroler Dialekten. In Claudio Di Meola, Antonie Hornung & Lorenzo Rega (eds.), *Perspektiven Eins*, 75–88. Rome: IISG.

Baur, Siegfried & Roberta Medda. 2008. The educational system in South Tyrol. In Jens Woelk, Francesco Palermo & Joseph Marko (eds.), *Tolerance through law. Self governance and group rights in South Tyrol*, 235–258. Leiden; Boston: Martinus Nijhoff Publishers.

Ciccolone, Simone. 2010. *Lo standard tedesco in Alto Adige: L'orientamento alla norma dei tedescofoni sudtirolesi*. Pescara: LED.

Davidson, Lisa. 2006. Comparing tongue shapes from ultrasound imaging using smoothing spline analysis of variance. *Journal of the Acoustical Society of America* 120(1). 407–415.

Fuchs, Susanne & Martine Toda. 2011. Do differences in male vs. female /s/ reflect biological or sociophonetics factors? In Susanne Fuchs, Martine Toda & Marzena Żygis (eds.), *Turbulent sounds an interdisciplinary guide*, 281–302. Berlin; New York: De Gruyter Mouton.

Grosjean, François. 1998. Transfer and language mode. *Bilingualism: Language and Cognition* 1(3). 175–176.

Mioni, Alberto. 2001. L'italiano nelle tre comunità linguistiche tirolesi. In Kurt Egger & Franz Lanthaler (eds.), *Die Deutsche Sprache in Südtirol*, 65–76. Vienna: Folio.

Recasens, Daniel. 1999. Lingual coarticulation. In William J Hardcastle & Nigel Hewlett (eds.), *Coarticulation: Theory, data, and techniques*, 81–104. Cambridge, UK; New York, NY, USA: Cambridge University Press.

Stone, Maureen. 2005. A guide to analyzing tongue motion from Ultrasound images. *Clinical Linguistics and Phonetics* 19(6-7). 455–502.

Wiesinger, Peter. 1983. Die Einteilung der deutschen Dialekte. In Werner Besch, Ulrich Knoop, Wolfgang Putschke & Herbert Ernst Wiegand (eds.), *Dialektologie. Ein Handbuch zur deutschen und allgemeinen Dialektforschung. Zweiter Halbband*, 807–900. Berlin/New York: de Gruyter.

Wiesinger, Peter. 1990. The Central and Southern Bavarian dialects in Bavaria and Austria. In Charles V. J. Russ (ed.), *The dialects of modern German: A linguistic survey*, 438–519. London: Routledge.

Part III

Japanese dialectology

Chapter 20

Developing the Linguistic Atlas of Japan Database and advancing analysis of geographical distributions of dialects

Yasuo Kumagai
National Institute for Japanese Language and Linguistics, NINJAL

The Linguistic Atlas of Japan (LAJ) was published from 1966 to 1974. A total of 285 items (mainly from the lexical field) and 2400 localities were surveyed. In 1999, we started constructing the Linguistic Atlas of Japan Database (LAJDB) with the aim of preserving the original survey materials (540000 cards) and advancing various uses of the LAJ. To explore the potential of the LAJDB in advancing quantitative approaches to the LAJ, I made some preliminary observations at the locality level concerning, for example, (1) geographical distributions of the frequency of standard forms, multiple answers, and informants' (speakers') comments on standard forms; (2) geographical distributions of degrees of linguistic similarities among localities; and (3) network representation of the degrees of linguistic similarities. These nationwide "high resolution" patterns of 2400 localities showed clear patterns and structures. Comparing these patterns and structures with each other and with extra-linguistic features, such as the network of roads, enables us to examine their relations in detail. The former nationwide, prefecture-level quantitative studies using the LAJ could not achieve such examination. I present some of these preliminary results and discuss several implications for advancing quantitative analysis using the LAJ.

1 Introduction

The *Linguistic Atlas of Japan* (*LAJ*), with six volumes (Kokuritsu Kokugo Kenkyû-jo (NLRI) 1966–1974), is the first nationwide Japanese linguistic atlas based on a linguistic geographical survey method. Published from 1966 to 1974, it is one of the basic research materials in Japanese dialectology. Many studies on Japanese dialects have utilized the LAJ—including studies based on an interpretation of each linguistic map, such as Satô (1986), Tokugawa (1993), and Kobayashi (2004),

Yasuo Kumagai. 2016. Developing the Linguistic Atlas of Japan Database and advancing analysis of geographical distributions of dialects. In Marie-Hélène Côté, Remco Knooihuizen & John Nerbonne (eds.), *The future of dialects*, 333–362. Berlin: Language Science Press.
DOI:10.17169/langsci.b81.159

as well as quantitative studies based on an accumulation of maps, such as Takada (1969), Hondô (1980), Kasai (1981), Ichii (1993), and Inoue (2001).

However, quantitative studies that use the LAJ have certain limitations. First, such studies, which used each survey point as a unit of calculation, were restricted to examination of small areas. Next, the nationwide studies were mainly based on prefecture-unit calculations. For example, nationwide geographical distributions of standard word forms in the LAJ have been one of the most analyzed subjects in quantitative studies using the LAJ (e.g., Inoue 2001), but such studies are based on prefecture-level calculations,[1] mainly due to difficulties in generating LAJ data at the locality level (e.g., Hondô 1980: 485, 498). In these studies, researchers prepared their data individually by reading the printed maps. It would have been very laborious to prepare data in such a manner, and it would have been difficult to achieve accuracy everywhere. The lack of digital data certainly restricted the methods of quantitative studies utilizing the LAJ.

We have been developing the Linguistic Atlas of Japan Database (LAJDB), aiming to preserve the original survey materials and advance the utilization of the LAJ. The LAJDB provides data from 2400 survey localities. Calculations at the locality level enable researchers to observe "high resolution" geographical distribution patterns (approximately 50 times the resolution of 47 prefectures). These "high resolution" patterns enable researchers, for example, to trace various diffusion routes that former studies could not detect. Compared with the former studies using the LAJ, studies using the LAJDB can compare such diffusion routes with extra-linguistic features, such as road networks, to examine the relation among them in detail. The LAJDB provides not only the geographical distribution data of word forms but also the original survey card images. This feature proves useful for advancing the utilization of the LAJ. In section 2, I provide an overview of the LAJ and LAJDB. In section 3, I describe some results of preliminary observations to elucidate the potential of the LAJDB.

2 LAJ and the LAJ Database (LAJDB)

The survey for the LAJ was conducted from 1957 to 1965 by the National Language Research Institute (NLRI), which preceded the present National Institute for Japanese Language and Linguistics (NINJAL). A total of 285 questionnaire items (Kokuritsu Kokugo Kenkyûjo (NLRI) 1966: 105–118), mainly pertaining to

---

[1] Japan has 47 prefectures.

the lexical field (nouns, verbs and adjectives), and 2400 localities[2] were surveyed by 65 fieldworkers through personal interviews. In principle, one male informant (speaker) born before 1903[3] and born at the given location (or, at least, who spent time there without interruption from the age of 3 to 15) was chosen as informant.[4] As far as possible, those representing the general trend of occupation in their locality were chosen. Here, we may note that approximately 80% of all localities are agricultural communities (Kokuritsu Kokugo Kenkyûjo (NLRI) 1966: 22, 42). Consequently, for practical reasons, male informants were chosen at 2392 localities (99.7%) and female informants were chosen at eight localities. Concerning informants, 97% were born between 1879 and 1903. Moreover, 63% of informants were engaged in agricultural work, 21% in commerce, and the rest in five other occupation categories (Kokuritsu Kokugo Kenkyûjo (NLRI) 1966: 24–26, 42, 43). Almost all informants of the LAJ can be described as "NORMs," that is, non-mobile, older, rural males (Chambers & Trudgill 1998: 29). It was reported that "on an average about 6 localities were surveyed in every 1000 square kilometers, or an average of about 12 kilometers separates each surveyed locality" (Kokuritsu Kokugo Kenkyûjo (NLRI) 1966: 41). The LAJ covers the whole of Japan, and the maximum geographic distance for a locality pair is approximately 2960 km. Figure 1 provides an example of maps from the LAJ.

During the survey period of the LAJ, after completing the questionnaire, each informant's answer was copied to a separate card by fieldworkers. These cards, which number approximately 540000 (Kokuritsu Kokugo Kenkyûjo (NLRI) 1966: 38, 43) and represent the materials of each answer from each locality, were used as original survey materials while editing the LAJ. On these cards, we can see the original phonetic transcriptions by the fieldworkers, informants' comments, fieldworkers' and editors' notes and so on, which were utilized in editing the

---

[2] The number of surveyed localities was not equal for each item. The approximate numbers are as follows: Of 285 items, 128 items were surveyed at 2400 localities, 36 items at 2000 localities, 55 items at 1700 localities, 62 items at 1000 localities, and 4 items at 400 localities (Kokuritsu Kokugo Kenkyûjo (NLRI) 1966: 22, 41).

[3] "One inhabitant was interrogated of each 40,000 people, but since the survey chose only male informants born before 1903, and since we know that there were 4,800,000 males of that age in the whole of Japan (1960 figures), our survey actually reproduces the speech of one out of 2000 of that stratum of the population" (Kokuritsu Kokugo Kenkyûjo (NLRI) 1966: 41–42).

[4] In principle, those whose residence in the locality had been interrupted by absences longer than 36 months were avoided.

Yasuo Kumagai

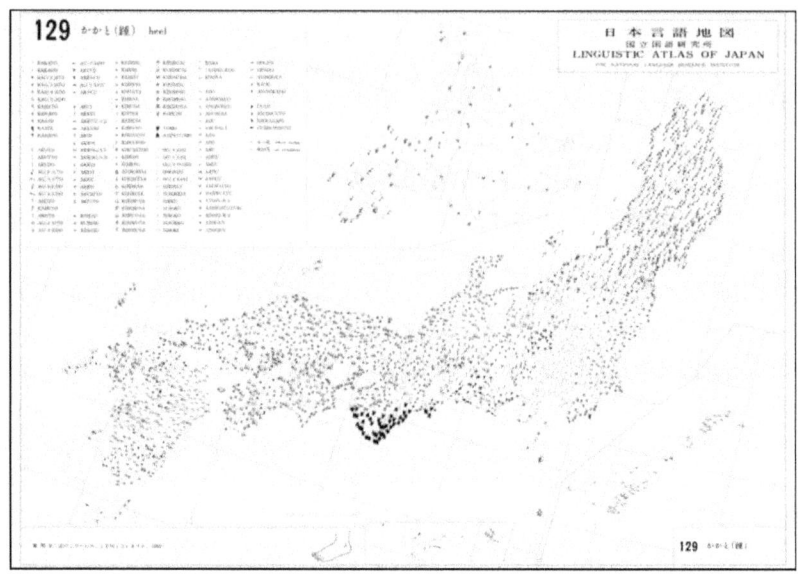

Figure 1: A map from the LAJ (map 129: heel).

maps. However, the published LAJ hardly provided any of this information for users.[5]

In 1999, with the aim of preserving these original survey materials and promoting the utilization of the LAJ, we began constructing the LAJDB (Kumagai 2013a, b).[6] The LAJDB comprises an image database of the original survey cards (Figure 2) and coded data corresponding to the published maps. The items of coded data include (a) locality number (systematically corresponding to degrees of longitude and latitude), (b) item name, (c) linguistic form on the legend of each map, (d) prefecture, (e) number of answers, (f) pattern of multiple answers, and so on.

---

[5] The editors of the LAJ prepared the materials "Nihon gengo chizu shiryô," which listed the varieties corresponding to every linguistic form presented in the LAJ and the comments of informants and fieldworkers (Kokuritsu Kokugo Kenkyûjo (NLRI) 1966: 32, 33). These materials were recorded from the original survey cards in handwritten form. They need further proofreading, and the list is partially incomplete. To use this material, it is necessary to check the original survey cards for confirmation. The editors planned to publish the comments and notes (Kokuritsu Kokugo Kenkyûjo (NLRI) 1966: 44), but this plan was not realized.

[6] After the LAJ was published, the Grammar Atlas of Japan (GAJ, 6 volumes) was published between 1989 and 2006 by the NLRI (NLRI 1989–2006). Surveys were conducted from 1979 to 1982 in 807 localities. In the course of editing the GAJ, the use of computer in publishing the GAJ was developed and the GAJ data was made accessible to the public. However, in the days of the LAJ, computers were in the early stages of development and not available for publishing linguistic atlases.

20 Developing the Linguistic Atlas of Japan Database

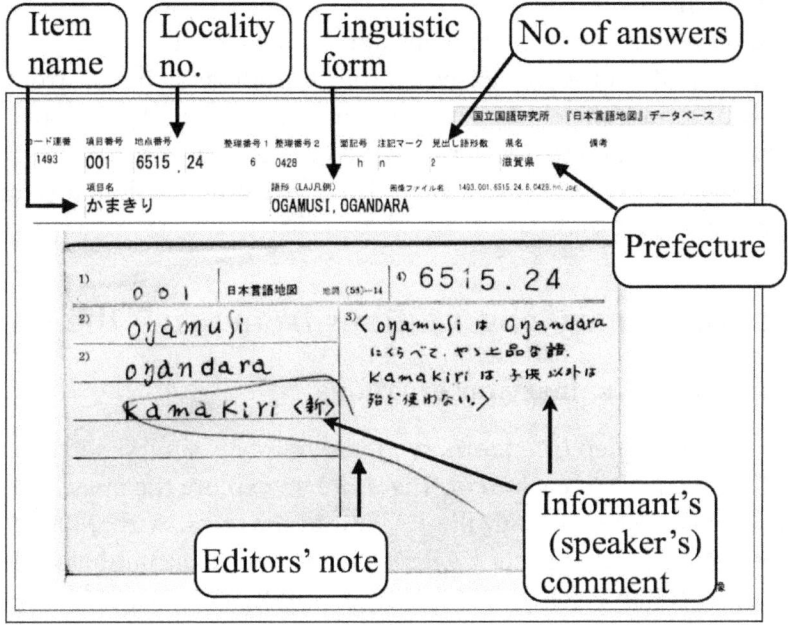

Figure 2: A snapshot of the LAJDB image database.

The original survey card images are linked to each entry of the coded data. While the linguistic forms shown on the maps from the LAJ are the result of the editor's classifications of varieties recorded by the fieldworkers, the LAJ does not provide us with detailed information about the classifications. Combining the coded data from the LAJ and the original survey material card images, the LAJDB allows, for example, tracing of the classifications and interpretations completed by the editors. Moreover, the LAJDB facilitates close examination of the LAJ as a research material, reclassification of linguistic varieties based on other viewpoints, and utilization of informants' comments and field workers' and editors' notes.

Currently, 119 items have been completed, corresponding to 43% of the number of surveyed items (285 items) and 49% of the number of items published as maps (240 items). The progress of the scanning of the original survey cards has reached approximately 90% of the total number of items (Kumagai 2013a: 159).

In addition, we have been preparing the following data for the LAJDB: (1) informant's information provided in the LAJ (Kokuritsu Kokugo Kenkyûjo (NLRI) 1966: 47–102), such as (a) address (without house number), (b) year of birth, (c) occupation, (d) educational background (number of years), (e) absence from the locality (number of months), (f) experience of military service, (g) sex, (h) name of interviewer (fieldworker), (i) year of survey, and (j) questionnaire used; and (2) digital maps—in shapefile format, a standard file format for geographic information system (GIS) software—based on the "Introductory maps" from the LAJ compiled by the editors, including (a) basic maps from the LAJ, (b) topographical maps (showing mountain systems, river systems, etc.), (c) main roads in the Meiji period (approximately 1885), (d) the boundaries of the feudal domains during the Edo period (1664), and so on.

3 Some preliminary observations from using the LAJDB

3.1 Dataset for preliminary observations

As previously mentioned (see footnote 2), the number of surveyed localities for the LAJ was not equal for each item. Therefore, to explore the possibilities of the LAJDB, I selected 55 items from the LAJDB, in progress, with 2400 ± 1 survey points. We will call this dataset LAJDB55 data. The item numbers selected for LAJDB55 are as follows: (001), (005), 006, 007, (012), 032, 036, 038, 039, 048, 051, 052, (056), 057, 059, 060, 063, 064, 066, 067, 072, 076, 083, 089, 103, [104], [105], 110, 111, 116, 118, 119, (122), 124, (127), 129, 148, 149, (165), 174, 179, 185, (186), (187), (188), 191, 194, 200, 214, 215, (216), 219, 220, 221, and 223.

Furthermore, I created a subset—LAJDB42—of LAJDB55 to explore the distribution of the standard forms. In most cases, an item has one standard form; however, two or more forms were occasionally recognized as standard by the LAJ's editors. In the above item numbers, those enclosed in parentheses are the ones in which two or more standard forms were recognized by the editors. No standard forms were explicitly stated for the items enclosed in square brackets []. For convenience in processing standard forms, I omitted the 13 items in parentheses from LAJDB55 and acquired them from LAJDB42. Using the LAJDB55 and LAJDB42 datasets, I made some preliminary observations.

3.2 Geographical frequency distributions of standard forms

Leading studies using quantitative analysis of the LAJ have been performed by Fumio Inoue (Inoue 2001, etc.). Inoue (2001), in a collection of his research of approximately 20 years, analyzed the usage rates of the standard forms of 84 LAJ items, summed up by prefecture (47 prefectures and Hachijô island, which belongs to Tokyo metropolitan area but whose dialect differs significantly from that of Tokyo). This data was originally prepared by Hisako Kasai (1981) by hand.

Inoue input the data for quantitative analysis (Inoue 2001: 89). This data is known as the Kasai data. Inoue (2001) analyzed the Kasai data via multivariate analyses, quantitative techniques, and so on, in order to explore dialect areas, the geographical diffusion of dialects, the distribution of standard forms, and so on.

Figure 3[7] shows the distribution of the usage rates of the standard forms of Kasai data on the map. With the Tokyo metropolitan area as the peak, the usage rate gradually declines toward the periphery, resembling a wave-like diffusion with Tokyo at its center. Hokkaido is an exception as it was a new settlement with people from mainland Japan.

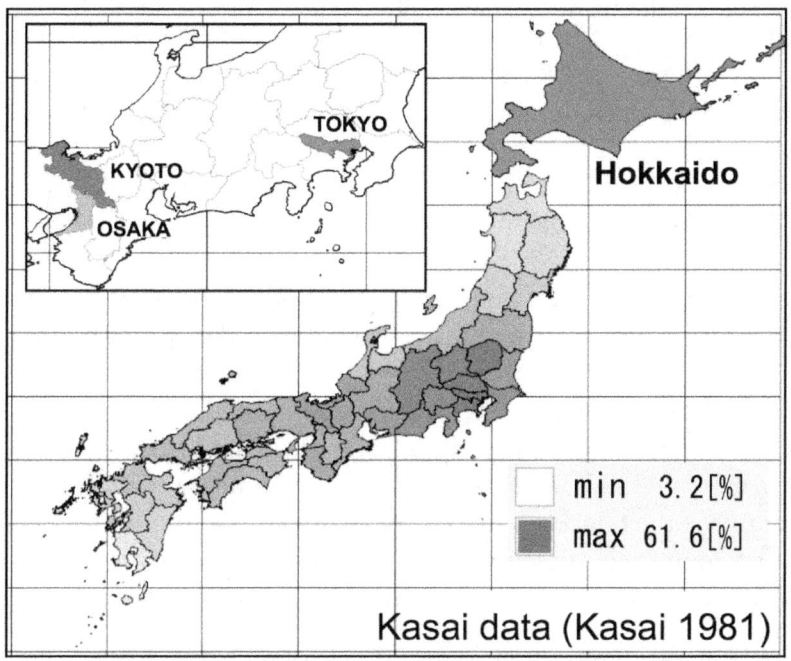

Figure 3: Usage rates of standard forms of 84 LAJ items, summed up by prefecture.

It should be noted that the gridlines of the map are drawn based on the locality number system of the LAJ. The locality number system was based on topographical maps with a scale of 1:50000. Each block in the grid corresponds to 100 topographical maps of a 1:50000 scale. The size of each block in the grid is 2°30' east–west, 1°40' north–south. The gridlines that appear hereafter are similar.

---

[7] Figure 3 was created based on Kasai's (1981) calculation. Okinawa, located in the southernmost part of Japan, is not displayed in this figure due to space constraints.

Figure 4 shows the usage rates of the standard forms according to LAJDB42 data based on the same calculation method as Kasai data, which shows similar distribution of Kasai data. In Figure 5, the usage rates of the standard forms of Kasai and LAJDB42 data are plotted in the descending order of the values of Kasai data for comparison. Figure 5 indicates that Kasai data and LAJDB42 data show a very similar pattern overall. Figure 6 shows the geographical distributions of the frequency (GDF) of the standard forms of LAJDB42 data by 2400 survey points. The GDF of standard forms was calculated by simply totaling the number of standard forms at each locality in the dataset. Patterns can be observed in detail, which could not be obtained from the prefecture-unit calculations of former studies. These "high resolution" patterns obtained using the LAJDB enable us to observe the diffusion routes more precisely. Comparing these distributions with the road networks, which play an important role in dialect diffusion, reveals interesting relationships.

Figure 7 shows the main roads in Japan in approximately 1885 (Honshu, Shikoku, and Kyushu areas). This map was created based on "Introductory Map V,"[8] a road map of the modern period, in the LAJ. An explanatory note from the LAJ states that this map provides an overview of land transport at the time during which the informants were growing up. This historical map is useful for comparing land transport—an important extra-linguistic factor—with dialect distributions. (Certainly, other means of transportation existed, but they were excluded as items for future incorporation into studies of the LAJ.) The thick purple lines denote the national roads, and the thin blue lines denote the prefectural roads.

Now let us see the relation between the main roads and geographical distributions of the frequency of standard forms. To illustrate this relation more precisely, Figure 8 focuses on the central part of the Honshu area, which includes Tokyo

---

[8] Here, it must be noted that "Introductory Map V: The main roads in Meiji period (around 1885)" aimed to provide an overview of the relationships between the surveyed localities and road networks. Roads were drawn on the basic map of the LAJ with reference to 1:200000 scale maps compiled via the Army Land Survey conducted by the General Staff of the Imperial Japanese Army (153 maps compiled and published from 1884 to 1893). The editors of the LAJ selected the national roads and prefectural roads that form the maps. The explanatory note stated that although there may be some roads that had been planned but not realized, "Introductory Map V" contained the most important roads around 1885. Figure 7, a digital map, was made by tracing the roads on "Introductory Map V," and the projection system of the map from the LAJ was not explained in its documentation. Thus, the map shown in Figure 7 is an approximation and involves some deviation (This map will be checked against the original compiled maps). Nonetheless, it is valuable and useful for explorative observation. Further, in the following observation, I consulted some related maps, books, and so on to confirm the observations. See also footnote 9.

20 Developing the Linguistic Atlas of Japan Database

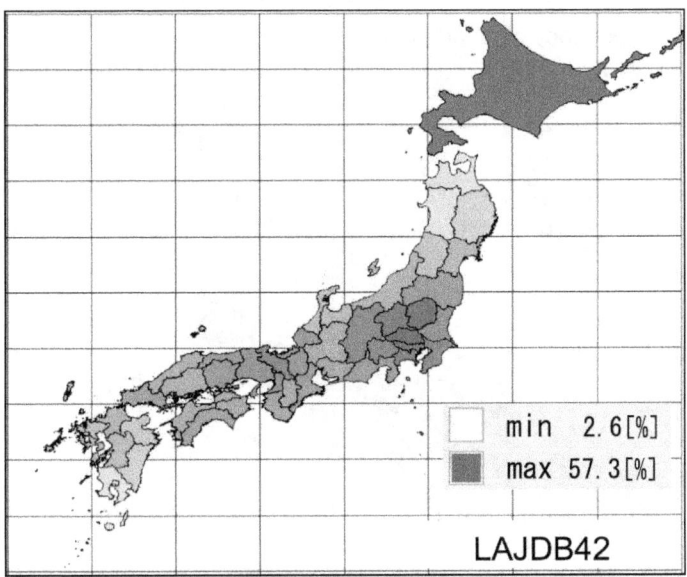

Figure 4: Usage rates of standard forms of LAJDB42 data, summed up by prefecture.

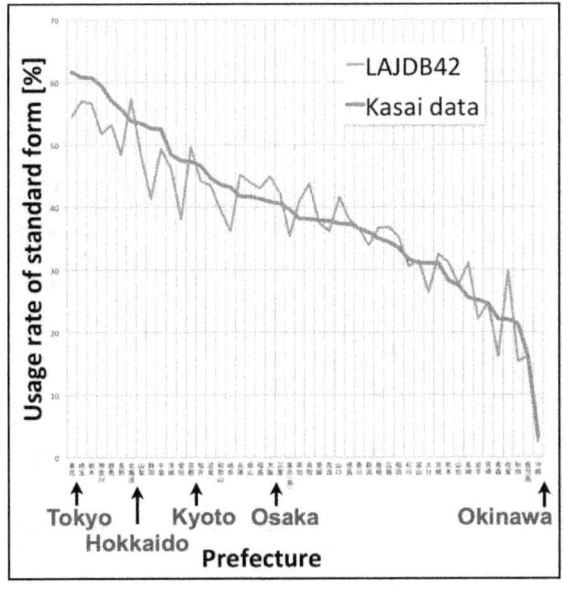

Figure 5: Comparison between Kasai data and LAJDB42 data.

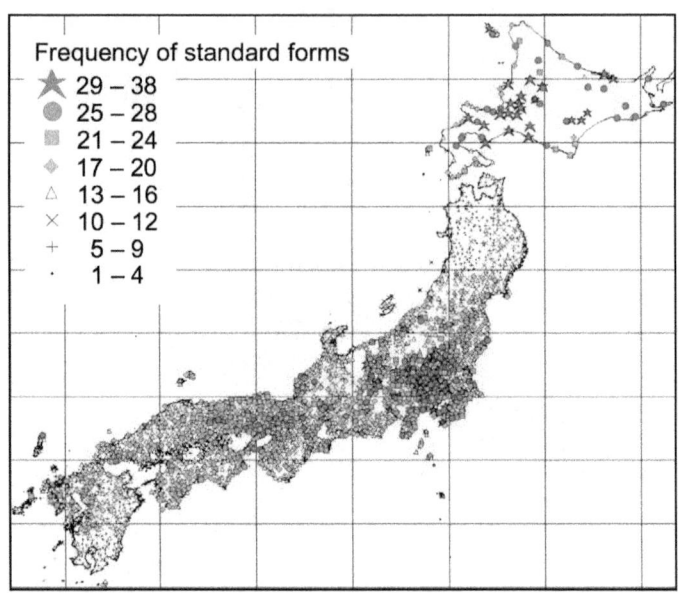

Figure 6: Geographical distributions of frequency (GDF) of standard forms from LAJDB42 data.

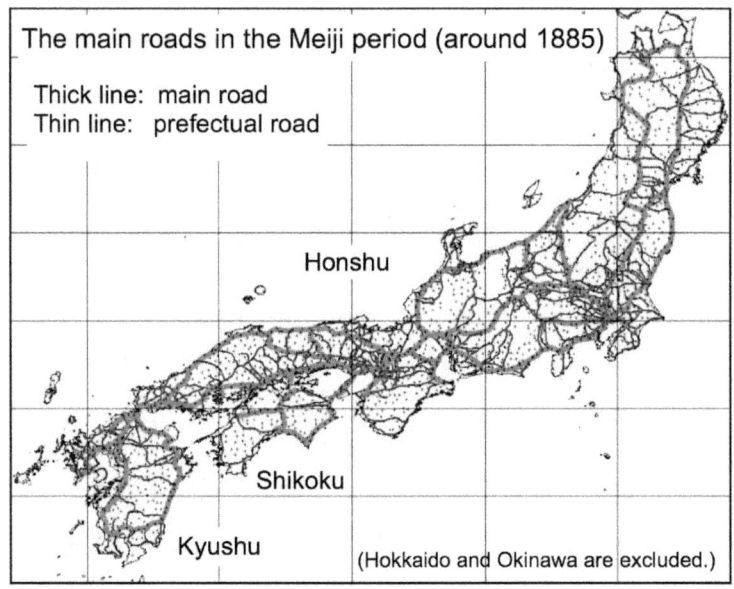

Figure 7: The main roads in the Meiji period (around 1885, Honshu, Shikoku, Kyushu areas).

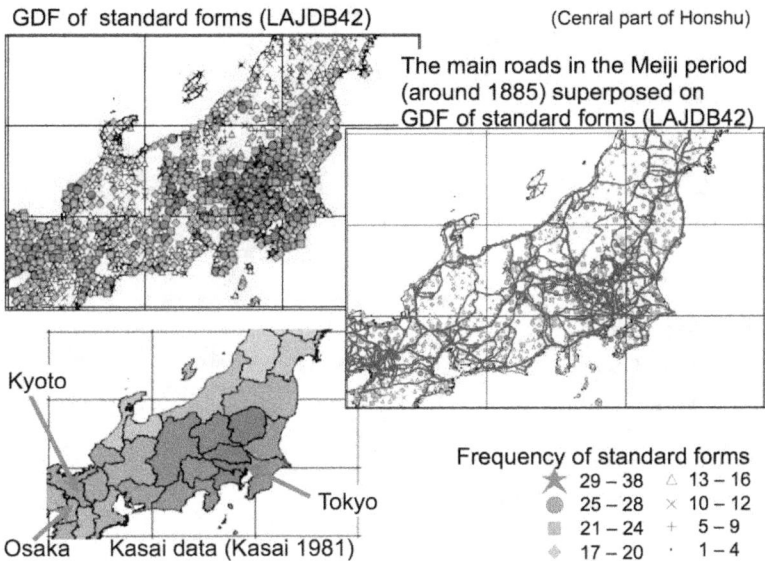

Figure 8: Comparison between Figure 6 and Figure 7 (Central part of Honshu).

(the current capital city) and Kyoto (the former capital city). The roads are superimposed on the distributions of the frequency of standard forms. Interesting observations can be formed regarding the relation between the distributions and the roads.

The map in Figure 9 includes Tokyo (current capital), Kyoto (former capital), and Osaka (large commercial city). The roads connecting Tokyo, Kyoto, and Osaka are very important. There are main roads ("Kaido"), side roads ("Wakikaido"), and others. Tokaido and Nakasendo are the two major main roads connecting these principal cities (Figures 11 and 12). Based on the Kasai data mentioned previously (see Figure 3), Tanaka (1991: 184) observed that the distribution of relative high frequency usage rates along the Tokaido route is interesting and noteworthy. The Nakasendo route runs through the mountainous areas, and Tokaido was the route used by feudal lords in the Edo period (17th century to the middle of the 18th century) to travel to Edo (present Tokyo). The Japanese tend to consider the Tokaido route rather than the Nakasendo route as the major road connecting Tokyo and Kyoto. However, based on LAJDB42 data, the Nakasendo route stands out. Localities with a high frequency of standard forms are plotted along the Nakasendo route. Comparisons drawn between the Tokaido and Nakasendo routes produce interesting results. Future studies on transportation history facilitate deeper insights pertaining to this observation.

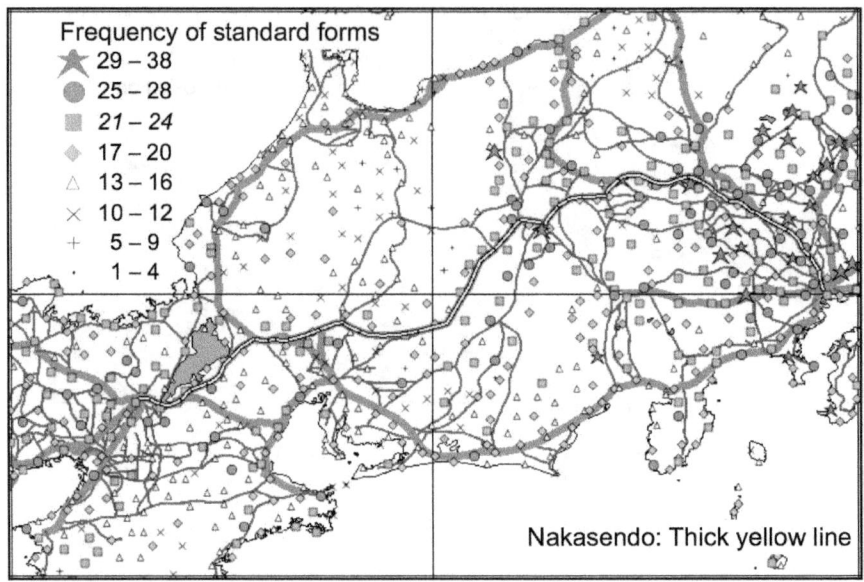

Figure 9: GDF of standard forms superimposed on the main roads in the Meiji period [Nakasendo].

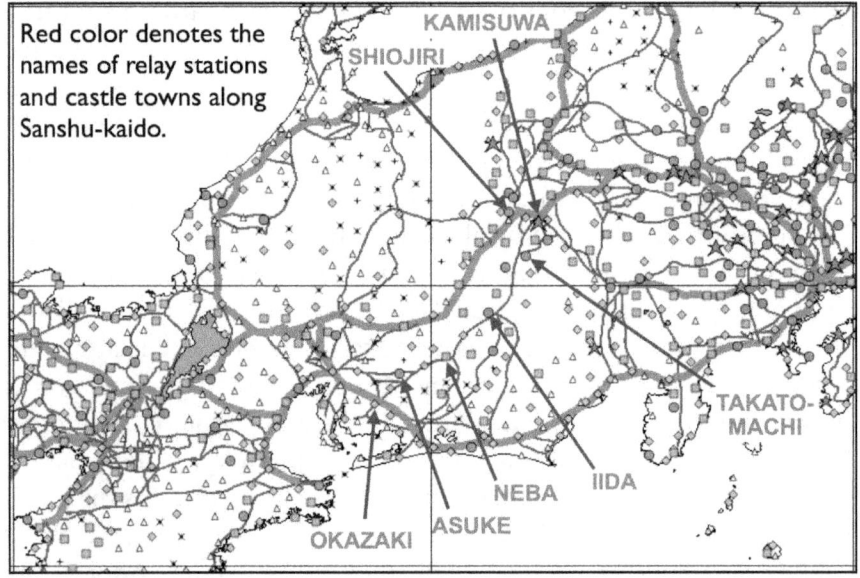

Figure 10: GDF of standard forms superimposed on the main roads in the Meiji period [Sanshu-kaido].

20 Developing the Linguistic Atlas of Japan Database

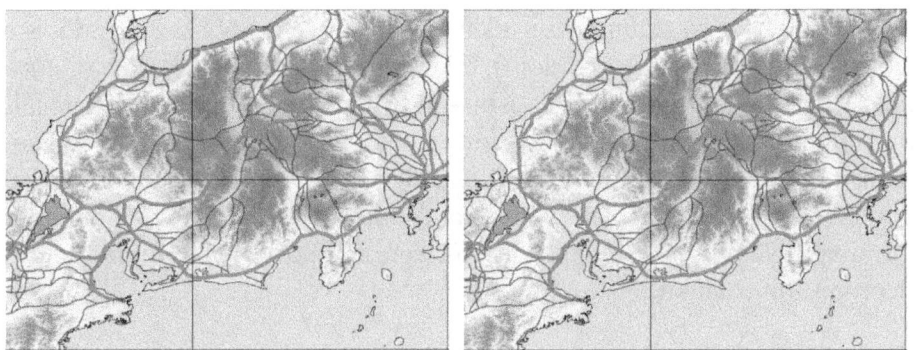

Figure 11: Left: Tokaido route. Right: Nakasendo route.

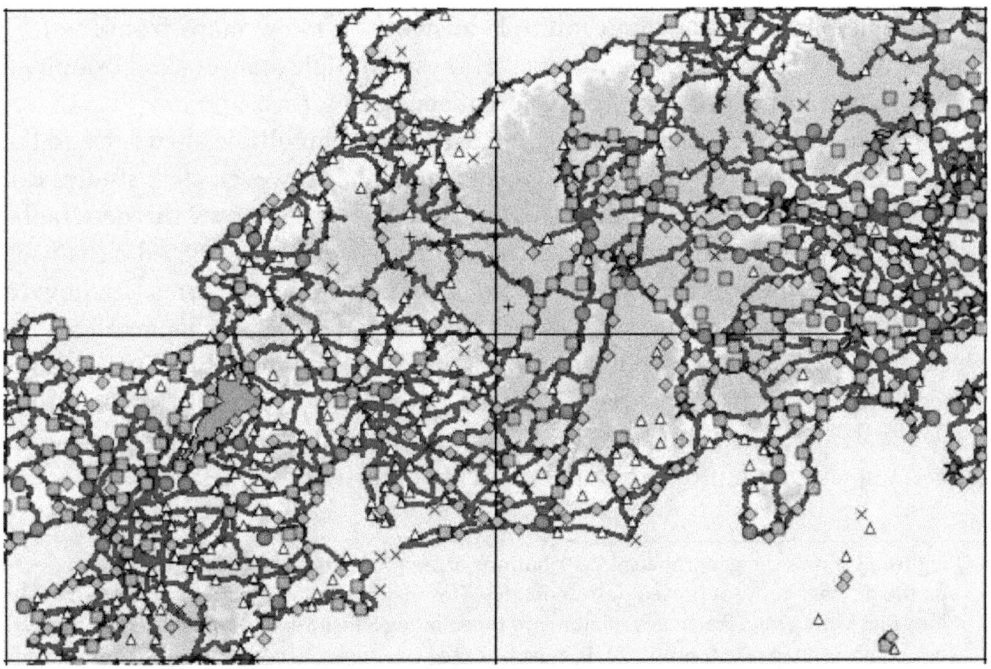

Figure 12: GDF of standard forms superimposed on current road network.

Another interesting example is Sanshu-kaido, a side road of Nakasendo. Sanshu-kaido is a route that connects Shiojiri, Iida, Neba, Asuke, and Okazaki (Figure 10). Similar to the Nakasendo route, Sanshu-kaido appears prominent, with localities with a high frequency of standard forms observed along this route.[9] Sanshu-kaido is not a major road; instead, it was developed as a road for transporting goods. Further systematic observations and analysis should lead to more interesting findings. Notably, these observations were not possible based on the former prefecture-unit calculations of the LAJ.

3.3 Geographical frequency distributions for multiple answers

In some localities, two or more linguistic forms were recorded. These multiple answers play an important role in the interpretation of maps, as they form relations between language contacts, diffusions, and changes. Inagaki (1980) provided some observations about multiple answers on a few maps from the LAJ, and Inoue (2004) noted the importance of these multiple answers and examined their position in the process of diffusion of standard forms.

Few quantitative studies examine the distribution of multiple answers, and the actual status in the LAJ was only partially examined. However, such studies can be easily conducted using computerized data. Figure 13 shows the geographical distributions of the frequency of multiple answers. LAJDB55 data is used here. This distribution contains all items including standard forms. It shows a significant distribution and is not distributed randomly all over Japan. Figure 14 shows the localities color-coded according to the fieldworkers. As Fumio Inoue noted,[10] it is probable that some fieldworkers tended to record more multiple answers, while others tended to record fewer. As a rule, the LAJ survey was designed to maintain uniformity[11] among fieldworkers; however, it is important to

---

[9] Figure 12 shows the geographical distributions of frequency of standard forms superimposed on the primary route at present (around 2010). This map is prepared for double-checking. The localities with a high frequency of standard forms along Sanshu-kaido coincide with the route better in this map (see footnote 8). It must be noted that new roads are sometimes built along old roads and other times are not. As a whole, this observation also supports the observation above. Road network data: Geospatial Information Authority of Japan (2011); Global Map Japan in Global Map ver. 2.0. Elevation data: Geospatial Information Authority of Japan (2000); Global Map Japan in Global Map ver. 1.0.

[10] A comment by Fumio Inoue, recorded in Inagaki (1980: 6).

[11] During the LAJ survey, to maintain uniformity in the fieldworker's surveys, various attempts were incorporated into the survey design. For example, "to assure a greater uniformity in the questioning, one of the members of the directing dialect bureau from Tôkyô, accompanied the local fieldworkers during the survey of one or more of the assigned localities. The technique

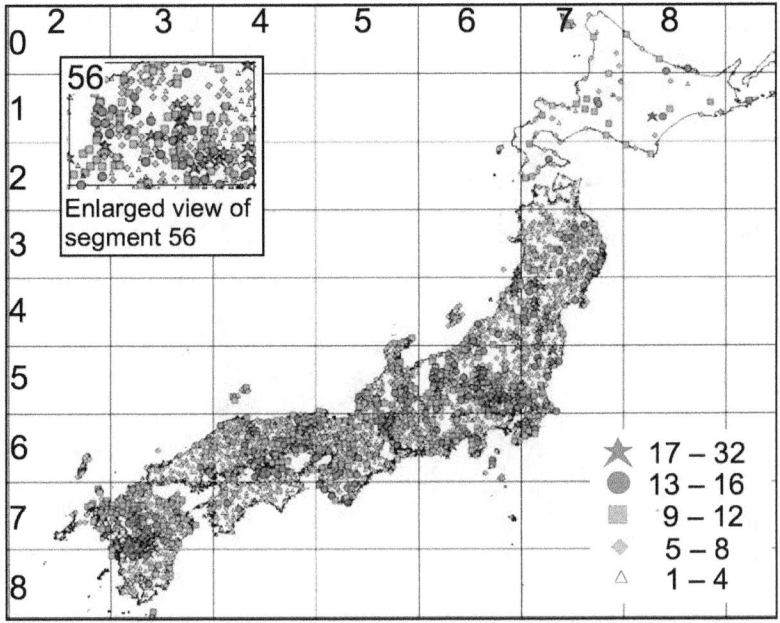

Figure 13: GDF of multiple answers, LAJDB55.

be careful about such risks and verify the observations from multiple perspectives. Accordingly, I compared the distributions of the localities assigned to each fieldworker and the distributions of the frequency of multiple answers. We can see the continuous distribution patterns of the GDF of multiple answers, which spread beyond the boundaries of the fieldworkers' distributions. In other words, we can observe that the boundaries do not limit the continuity of the distribution patterns of the GDF (see, e.g., the enlarged views in Figure 13 and Figure 14).

3.4 The frequency of informant's comments on standard forms among multiple answers

For the LAJ, the editors maintained a principle called the "principle of processing multiple answers." When two linguistic forms were recorded in one locality, both were marked on the map. However, when one of the two forms was the standard language form and, in addition, this fact was noted by the informant—such as in

---

of selecting an informant and the method of questioning was then demonstrated." Furthermore, "221 localities were surveyed by one of the directors" and "these localities are equally distributed over the whole territory," (Kokuritsu Kokugo Kenkyûjo (NLRI) 1966: 23, 40–41).

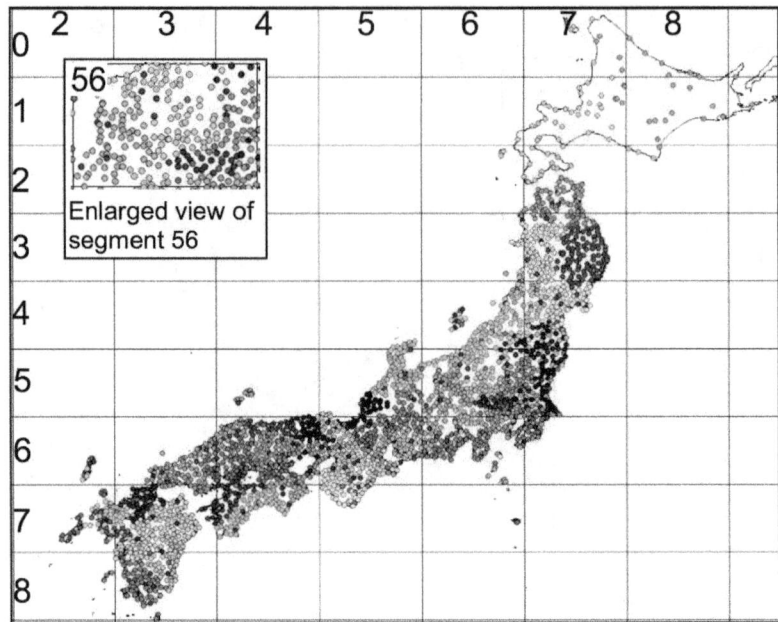

Figure 14: Localities color-coded according to fieldworkers.

the answers "This is a new polite form." or "This is the word used in school."—then the editors would omit the standard forms from a map. This method was followed because the LAJ survey aimed to record informants' personal speech used in their familiar and daily surroundings. Certainly, dialectical forms identical with standard forms were not omitted if there were no informant comments. The principles for processing multiple answers to the LAJ are as follows.

> Further elements of interpretation are given by the informant's comment ("old word," "new form," etc.) or by the fieldworker's notes. These have been helpful for the map interpretation, and they will be published in a later volume.[12] When two linguistic forms have been recorded in the same locality, they have been both marked on the map. When, however, one of the two is the standard language form, and when, in addition, this fact has been noted by the informant ("this is the new polite form," "this is the word used in the school," etc.), in this case only, we have omitted the forms marked this way from the maps (Kokuritsu Kokugo Kenkyûjo (NLRI) 1966: 44).

---

[12] The publication of comments and notes was not realized. Also see footnote 5.

To study the multiple answers, the omitted standard forms that informants had commented on (e.g., "This is new," and so on) are important. In the course of compiling the LAJ, the editors assumed that the standard forms that were commented on as "new" were distributed randomly. However, using one LAJ item as an example, Satô (1986: 152–153) plotted the omitted answers on a map and found that by adding the omitted answers, the distribution pattern of the standard forms became clearer. However, this observation was based on only one item. The real state of the multiple answers of the LAJ is yet to be explored. Fumio Inoue[13] stated that the editors of the LAJ were aware of some regional differences of the standard forms that were commented on as new and considered these differences as interesting. However, the editors did not plot these words and were unsure about their significance. Using the LAJDB, it is possible to analyze the distribution of the word forms omitted from the atlas.

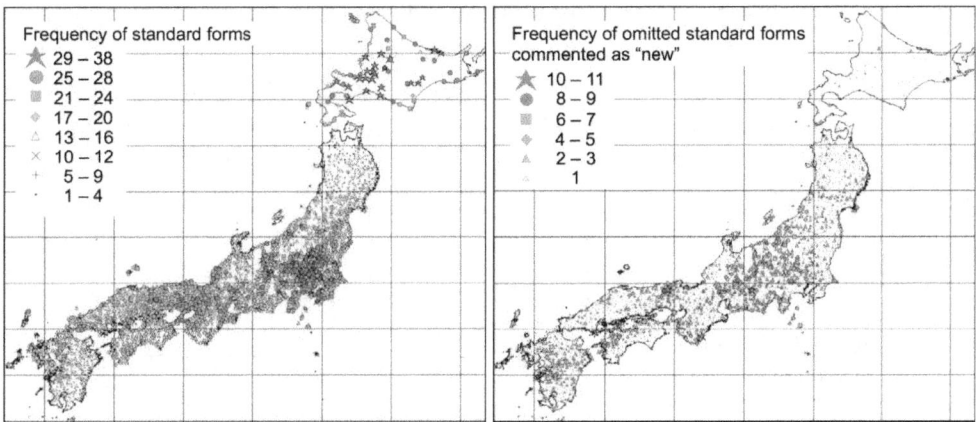

Figure 15: Comparison between GDF of standard forms and omitted standard forms. Left: GDF of standard forms. Right: GDF of omitted standard forms commented as "new".

On the card images provided by the LAJDB, we can see the omitted words and the editors' markings, which signify the application of the principle of processing the multiple answers. In addition, there are lists of localities which record the notes, extracted from the original material cards, with some information about the word omissions performed by the editors. Based on these notes, I formulated data on the omitted word forms using LAJDB42. Figure 15 shows the geographical distribution of the frequency of standard forms and that of omitted standard

---

[13] A comment by Fumio Inoue, recorded in Inagaki (1980: 5).

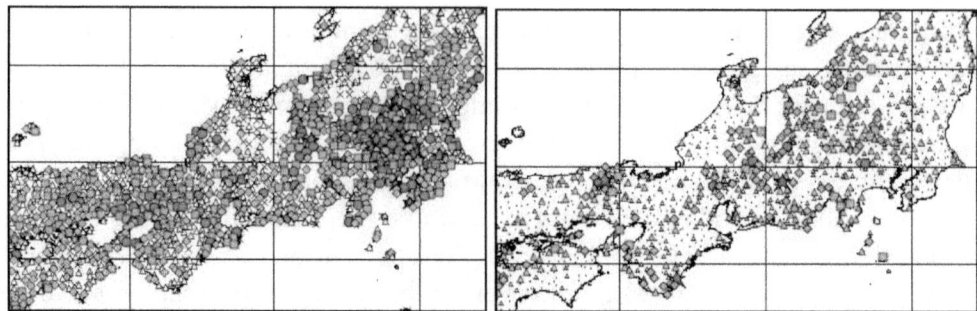

Figure 16: Comparison between GDF of standard forms and omitted standard forms (Central Honshu). Left: GDF of standard forms. Right: GDF of omitted standard forms commented as "new".

forms for comparison. Is there any relation between the distribution of the standard forms and the distribution of omitted standard forms? To observe this relation more precisely, Figure 16 provides a zoomed-in image. By displaying these two maps alternately as an animation, we compared these two maps visually. For our observation, we focused on the Kinki area and the area surrounding it (Figure 17).

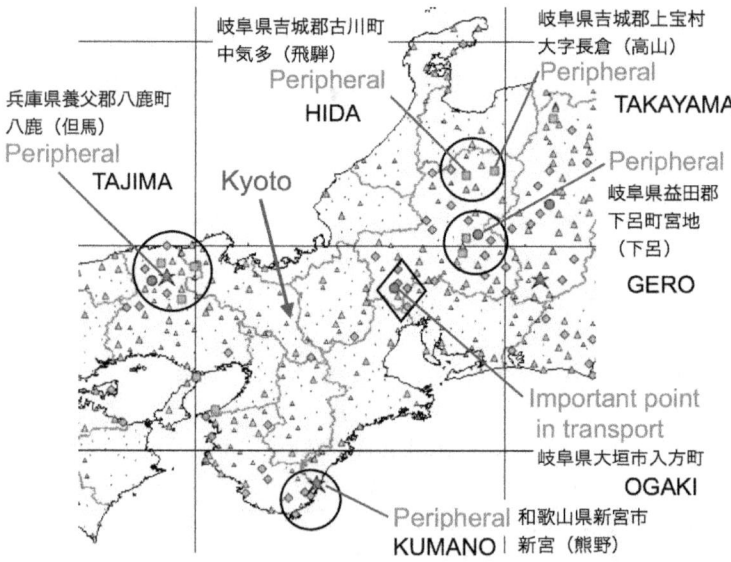

Figure 17: GDF of omitted standard forms commented as "new" (Kinki area).

20 *Developing the Linguistic Atlas of Japan Database*

Figure 17 shows that in areas marked by circles, the areas where standard forms are frequently omitted are surrounded by or adjacent to those where standard forms are very frequent. In areas marked by a diamond shape, the high frequency areas of the two distributions are overlapped. Localities indicated by arrows show the highest frequency in each area marked above. The places marked by circles are the typical peripheral areas. The places marked by diamonds are important areas for transport. In this case, the marked places are clearly separated into two types. Although further investigation is required for other places, these indications are interesting. Possibly, the circled places are at the forefront of the diffusion of the standard forms. More studies should be conducted on areas indicated by diamond shapes.

Figure 18 shows the geographical distribution of the frequency of omitted standard forms superimposed on the main roads in the Meiji period (approximately 1885). Further systematic observations and analysis should present interesting findings. Studies on the history of transportation and other types of knowledge of the regions will be helpful for further studies.

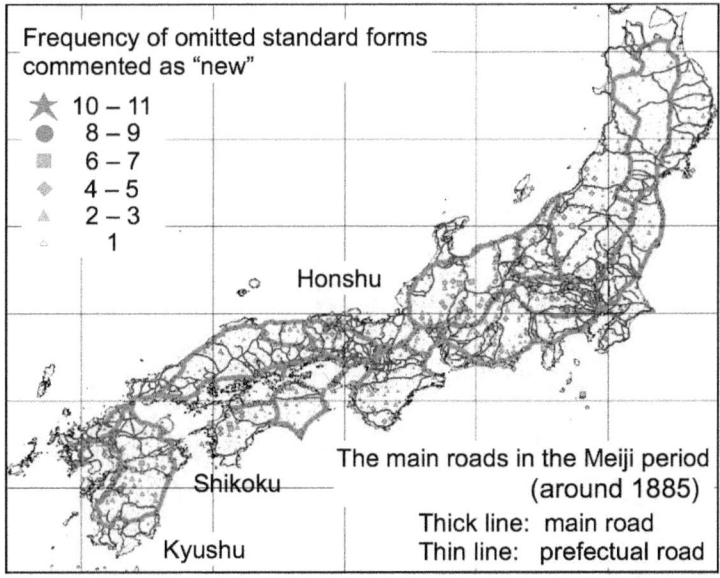

Figure 18: GDF of omitted standard forms superimposed on the main roads in the Meiji period.

3.5 Geographical distributions of degrees of similarity

In this section, the linguistic similarities among the localities based on the LAJDB data will be provided. This information will help present an overall image of the linguistic similarities spread over Japan based on the LAJ. LAJDB55 is used in this section. The previous observations were made mainly with reference to the standard forms. The following maps are based on all word forms including the standard forms. Here, linguistic similarity between two localities is measured by the number of linguistic features shared by the localities. The measure of linguistic similarity used is referred to as NC, that is, a number of common linguistic features. In this paper, NC denotes a number of common word forms (the NC between any two localities is calculated by adding the total number of the same word forms of each item in a dataset). Figure 19 provides some examples[14] of

---

[14] At the Methods XV conference, the geographical distributions of similarities were represented using animation (total number of frames or maps was 2400). In this case, similarity maps are played after they are sorted by locality number. This animation shows the maps in quick succession. This is an impressionistic form of representation; nevertheless, it allows for observation of reoccurring patterns, transition of patterns, and so on. Such a method of observation should be utilized as an exploratory tool. Figure 19 provides some samples of similarity maps.

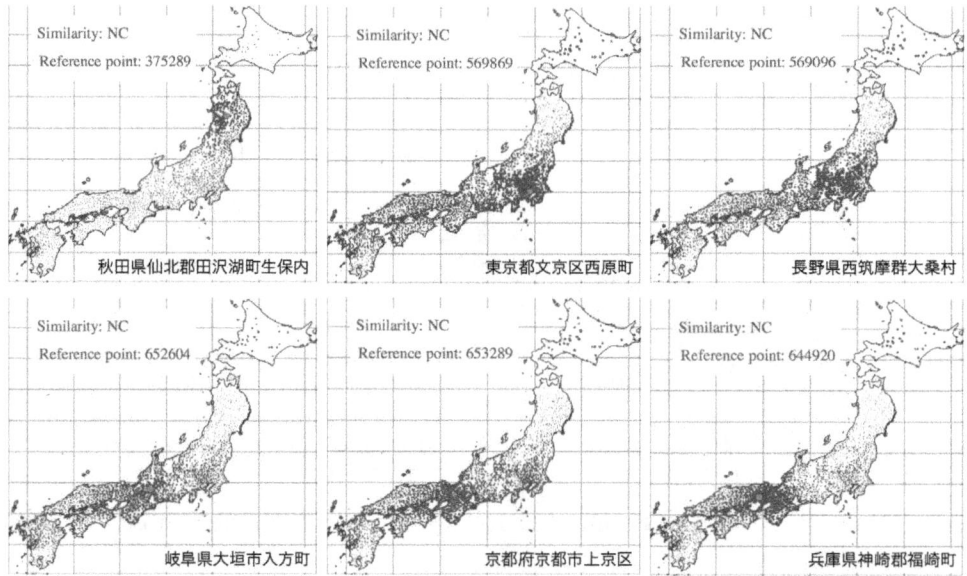

Figure 19: Some example maps of geographical distributions of the degrees of similarity.

20 *Developing the Linguistic Atlas of Japan Database*

geographical distributions of the degrees of similarities. A higher NC value corresponds to a larger radius of circle points. The red points are reference points.

Figure 20 presents similarity maps along the Nakasendo route. A total of 87 points along the Nakasendo route are selected by generating a buffer. Thus, we generated a series of similarity maps of points along a route (Nakasendo). The red line represents the Nakasendo route and the yellow points represent the selected localities. Playing the maps successively from Tokyo to Kyoto as animations

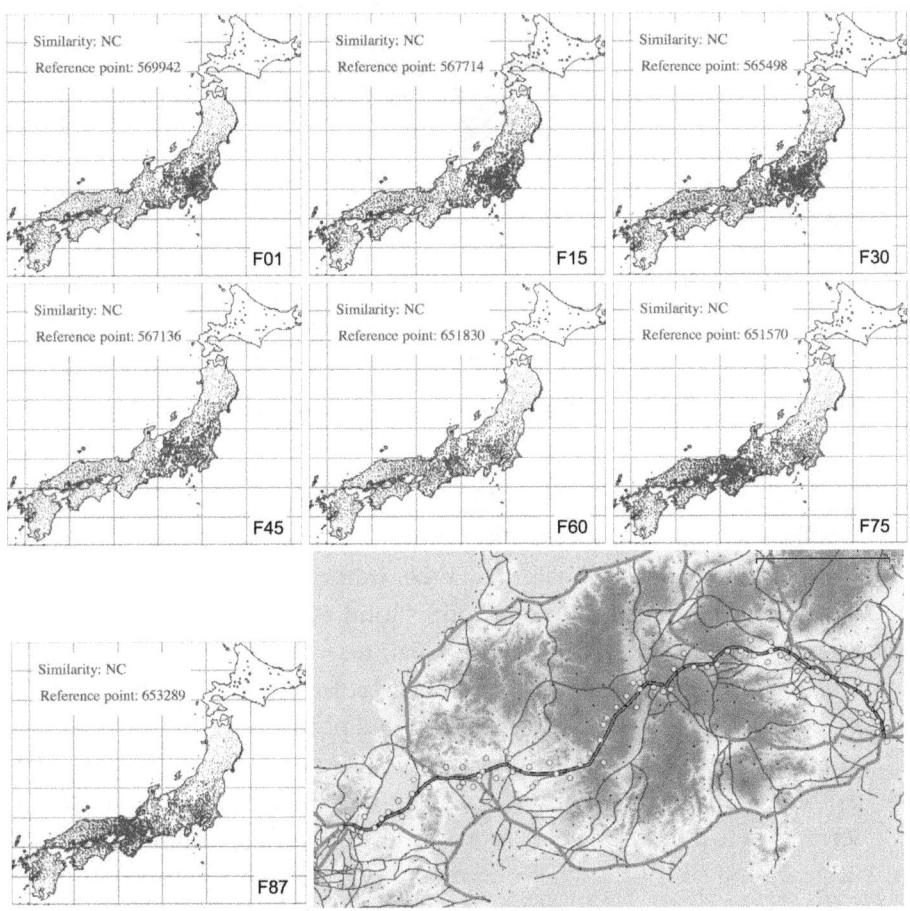

Figure 20: Some examples of similarity maps (frames of the animation) along the Nakasendo route. The number following F is a frame number. F01: Tokyo, F87: Kyoto. Bottom right: The 87 localities selected by buffer along the Nakasendo route (red line: Nakasendo; yellow points: selected localities).

353

Yasuo Kumagai

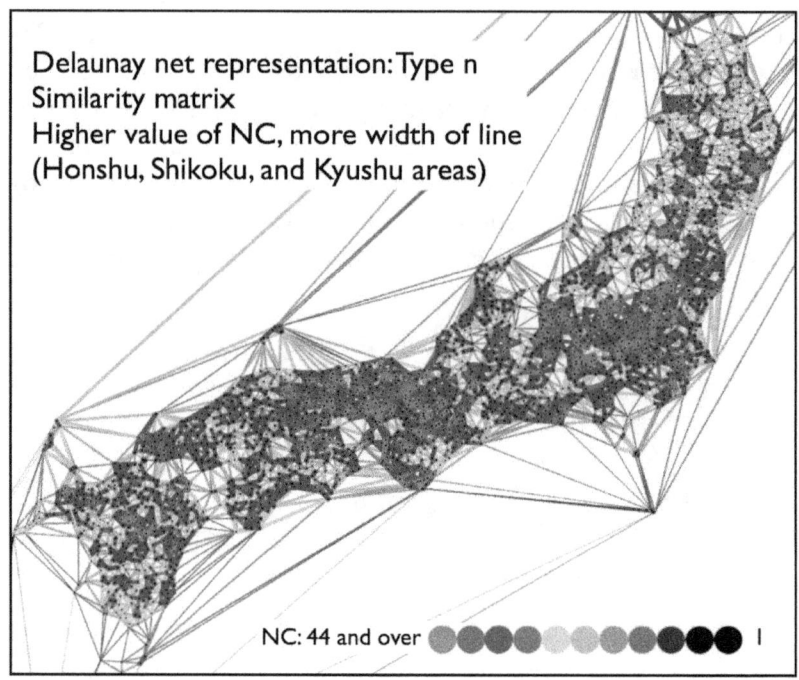

Figure 21: Network representation of degrees of similarity on Delaunay net: Type n.

facilitates observation of the changing patterns along the route. In Figure 20, some examples from the similarity maps (i.e. frames) are shown.

Figure 21 displays an example of another kind of representation of linguistic similarity measured by NC among the localities. Delaunay triangulation — a computational geometrical method to generate a triangular network that connects adjacent points from randomly distributed points on a plane—is used as an approximation to represent continuity among survey points on the geographical space in a formal manner. A network of the points made by Delaunay triangulation is termed as a Delaunay net. We assign a value of NC (number of common linguistic features) to a line which connects two adjacent points of the Delaunay net to visualize the varying degrees of linguistic similarity among survey points distributed on a map. This representation is a network representation on a Delaunay net and is termed type n. Here, "n" represents NC (Kumagai 2013b: 2, 4). Figure 22 presents another example; it provides a network representation of the degrees of similarities on a Delaunay net: type d ("d" denotes distance). The degree of linguistic similarity between adjacent localities is measured by the

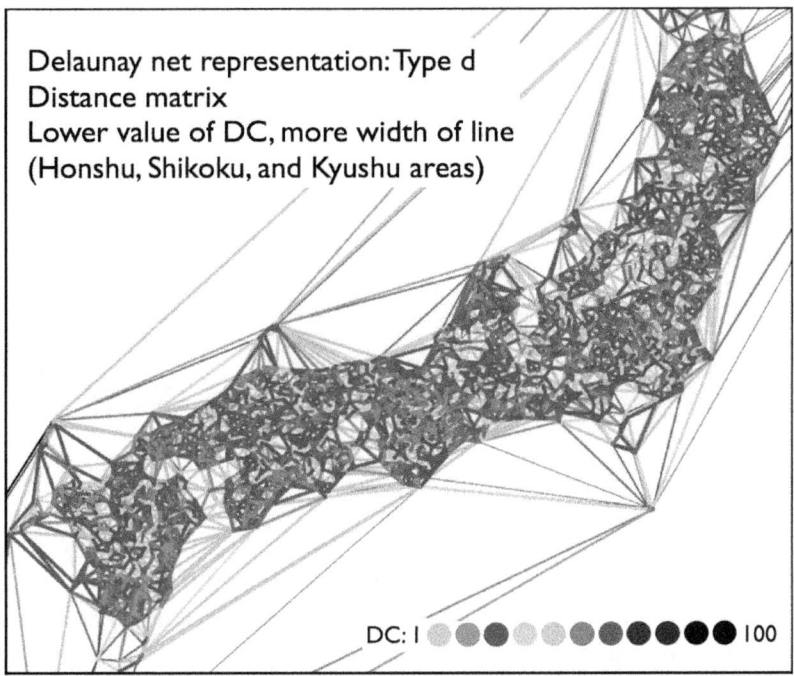

Figure 22: Network representation of degrees of similarity on Delaunay net: Type d.

degree of similarity between the two NC distribution patterns of the localities. A distance matrix is calculated for this purpose. The degree of linguistic similarity between any two localities is measured by the Euclidean distance between the two NC distribution patterns (Kumagai 2013b: 2, 4), and is termed DC. The values of DC are categorized in the range of 100 in Figure 22. Due to space constraints, DC and these maps cannot be discussed in detail; however, clear patterns can be observed on these maps.

Figure 23 shows the NT-1(r)n representation.[15] NT-1(r)n is one of the series of methods we have developed to observe linguistic similarities among localities on a map (Kumagai 2013b: 2). In NT-1(r)n, any two localities that show similarities more than the threshold condition (Lcond) are connected by a line. The red points denote the localities. The measure of similarity used is NC. Any two localities that satisfy the threshold condition (NC ≧ Lcond) are connected by a line. In Figure 23,

---

[15] In the Methods XV conference, this figure was represented as an animation with changing Lcond stepwise from 48 to 30. In Figure 23, some frames selected from the animation of NT-1(r)n are shown (LAJDB55).

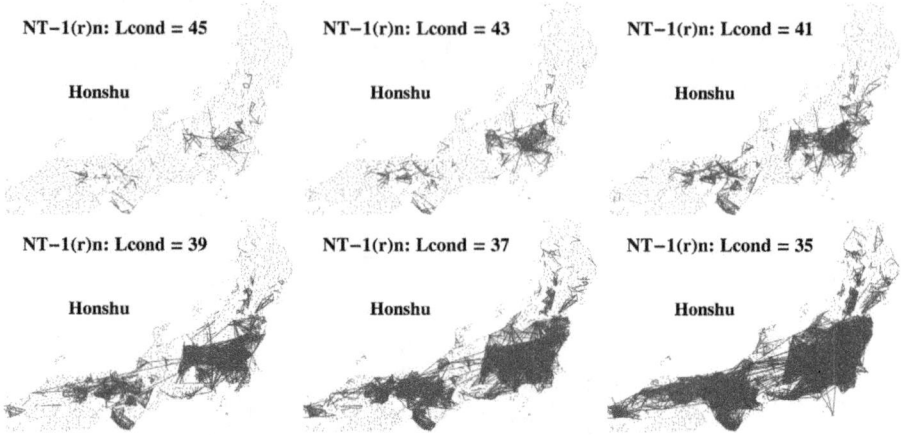

Figure 23: Network representation of NT-1(r)n (Lcond = 45, 43, 41, 39, 37, 35).

only the lines that connect localities inside the Honshu area are displayed to allow focus on observations inside this area. On changing the Lcond from 45 to 30, we can observe how the similar localities are distributed and how the clusters of similar localities grow. Figure 24 displays a superimposition[16] of the network representation NT-1(r)n on the Delaunay net type 2^{17} representation (Kumagai 2013b: 6–7). All figures in this section exhibited clear patterns and structures.

It will be interesting to compare these patterns and structures with one another and with extra-linguistic features, such as road networks, to examine the relations among them. The previous observations made on the standard forms must be studied in relation to these observations.

4 Conclusion

We have been developing the LAJDB to preserve the original survey materials and advance the utilization of the LAJ. With 2400 localities, LAJDB data facilitates detailed observations of nationwide distributions, which are not possible

---

[16] By overlaying two types of representation, we can simultaneously observe the distribution of similarities along the continuity and on the entire map (which is not restricted to neighbors). In transitional zones and homogeneous zones, Nt-1(r) shows the different network structures. By overlaying the two kinds of representation, we can distinguish two types of distribution patterns of similarities, which cannot be distinguished by the representation of the Delaunay net (Kumagai 2013b: 7).

[17] In the type 2 representation of the Delaunay net, a higher NC value corresponds with a lesser line width.

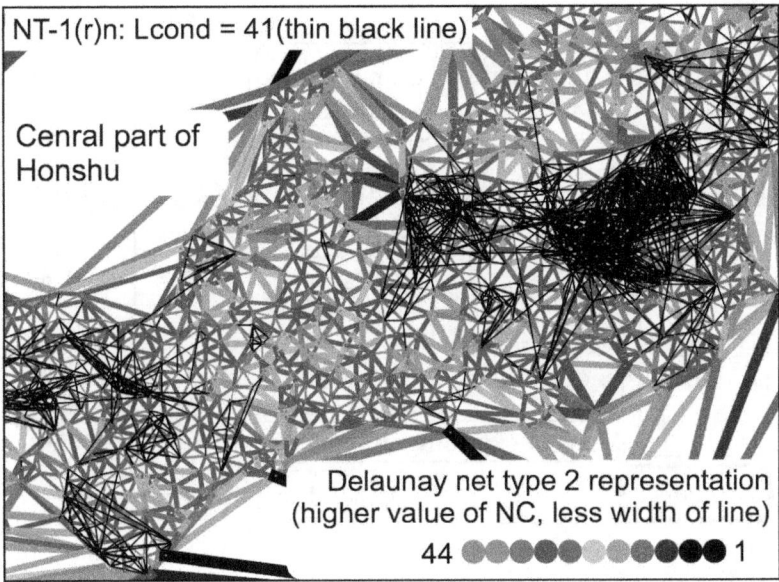

Figure 24: Network representation NT-1(r)n on Delaunay net of type 2 representation.

with the prefecture-unit calculations in the LAJ. In linguistic maps, geographical distribution patterns of each word are usually recognized as distribution areas, that is, planar regions. However, the distributions recognized as planar regions are formed through contact between localities, such as transportation and intercommunication, which refers to contact between individuals (i.e., speakers). By accumulating items for 2400 localities, we will be able to observe the networks responsible for the formation of regions and the phenomena occurring in such networks. Further, we are developing methods for analyzing the geographical distribution data aimed at extracting latent information and finding hidden structure in a manner appropriate to the nature of the data, which will facilitate visualization of the dynamics, flows, and trends of dialectal distribution and understanding of the distribution pattern of dialects in relation to the dynamics of language change (Sibata & Kumagai 1993; Kumagai 2013c,b, etc.). The researchers who conducted the LAJ survey designed many features and devices; however, these tools have not been sufficiently utilized. This shortcoming might partly result from the lack of computerized data, computers, and many other tools which are available today.

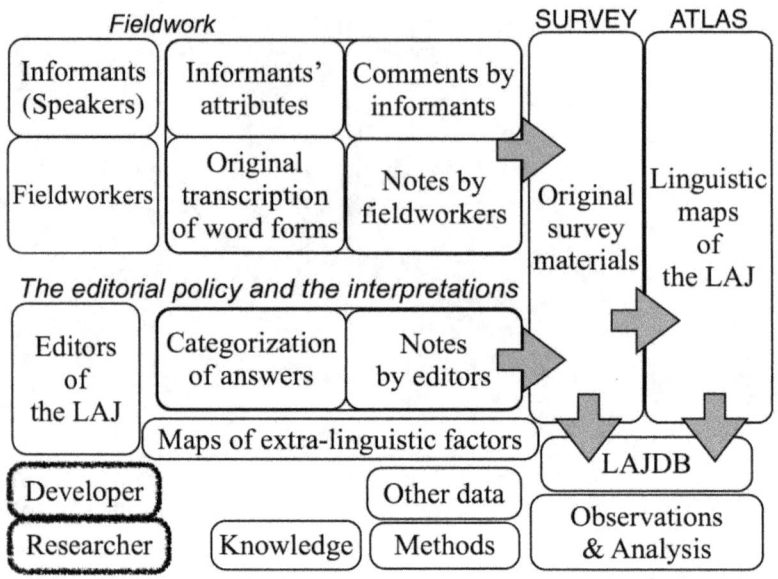

Figure 25: Factors related to the development and utilization of the LAJDB.

Figure 25 illustrates the factors that play an important role in the development and utilization of the LAJDB. All factors relate to developing the LAJDB and advancing the analysis of the geographical distribution of dialects. The digitized data of the LAJ and related information as well as the new methods and perspectives will contribute to advancing the analysis of the geographical distribution of dialects. The LAJDB[18] is expected to be a good tool for utilizing the LAJ and to contribute to advancing the study of the geographical distribution of dialects.

Abbreviations

LAJ   Linguistic Atlas of Japan
LAJDB   Linguistic Atlas of Japan Database
LAJDB42   a subset of LAJDB55
LAJDB55   a subset of LAJDB
NLRI   National Language Research Institute
NINJAL   National Institute for Japanese Language and Linguistics

---

[18] The LAJDB website is under development (http://www.lajdb.org). This website is currently a work-in-progress, and the LAJDB is only partially open. The site will be updated in accordance with LAJDB progress.

NORM   non-mobile, older, rural males
GDF   geographical distributions of frequency
NC   number of common linguistic features (number of common word forms)
GIS   geographic information system
NT-1(r)n   a method of network representation of linguistic similarities
Lcond   level conditioned (threshold condition)

Acknowledgements

The Linguistic Atlas of Japan Database (LAJDB) was supported by a Grant-in-Aid for Publication of Scientific Research Results (database) in 2001, 2002, 2003, 2004, 2005, and 2008 (Project Leader: Yasuo Kumagai). This paper includes some outcomes of the collaborative research projects "Analyzing large-scale dialectal survey data from multiple perspectives" (2009–2012, Project Leader: Yasuo Kumagai), "General Research for the Study and Conservation of Endangered Dialects in Japan" (2013–, Project Leader: Nobuko Kibe) at the National Institute for Japanese Language and Linguistics, and "Development of quantitative methods of analyzing large-scale dialectal distribution data" (Grants-in-aid for scientific research (c), JSPS KAKENHI Grant Number 26370555, 2014–, Project Leader: Yasuo Kumagai). I thank the anonymous reviewers and the editors for their valuable comments and suggestions.

References

Chambers, J. K. & Peter Trudgill. 1998. *Dialectology.* 2nd edn. Cambridge, New York: Cambridge University Press.

Hondô, Hiroshi. 1980. Gendai hyôjun nihongo no bunpu: Nihon gengo chizu de mite [Distribution of modern standard Japanese: An observation by using the LAJ]. In Shigeru Satô (ed.), *Sato shigeru Kyoju taikan kinen ronshu kokugogaku.* 479–498. Tokyo: Ohfusha.

Ichii, Tokiko. 1993. *Hôgen to keiryô bunseki [Dialect and quantitative analysis].* Tokyo: Shintensha.

Inagaki, Shigeko. 1980. Hôgen sesshoku to gokei heiyô: "Nihon gengo chizu" no bunpu kara [Dialect contact and doublets: Some examples from the distributions in the LAJ]. *Tôkyô toritsu daigaku hôgen kenkyûkai kaihô* 92. 1–10.

Inoue, Fumio. 2001. *Keiryôteki hôgen kukaku [Quantitative dialect division].* Tokyo: Meiji shoin.

Inoue, Fumio. 2004. Heiyô genshô to gengo genshô no chûkan dankai: Kasai data 3 kurasutâ no hukyû katê [Joint usage of forms and intermediate stages of linguistic change: Process of diffusion of 3 clusters of Kasai data]. *Gogaku kenkyûjo ronshû (Journal of the Institute of Language Research)* 9. 1–19.

Kasai, Hisako. 1981. Hyôjun gokei no zenkoku bunpu [Nationwide distribution of standard forms]. *Gengo seikatsu* 354. 52–54.

Kobayashi, Takashi. 2004. *Hôgengakuteki nihongoshi no hôhô [Method of dialectological study of Japanese language history]*. Tokyo: Hituzi Syobo.

Kokuritsu Kokugo Kenkyûjo (NLRI). 1966. Nihon gengo chizu kaisetsu: Hôhô [Introduction to the linguistic atlas of Japan: Methodology]. In Kokuritsu Kokugo Kenkyûjo (NLRI) (ed.), *Nihon gengo chizu (Linguistic atlas of Japan)*. Tokyo: Printing bureau, Ministry of Finance.

Kokuritsu Kokugo Kenkyûjo (NLRI). 1966–1974. *Nihon gengo chizu (Linguistic atlas of Japan)*. Tokyo: Printing bureau, Ministry of Finance.

Kumagai, Yasuo (ed.). 2013a. *Daikibo hôgen dêta no takakuteki bunseki seika hôkokusho: Gengo chizu to hôgen danwa shiryo [Analyzing large-scale dialectal survey data from multiple perspectives]*. Tokyo: Kokuritsu Kokugo Kenkyûjo (NINJAL).

Kumagai, Yasuo. 2013b. Development of a way to visualize and observe linguistic similarities on a linguistic atlas. *Working papers from NWAV Asia-Pacific* 2.

Kumagai, Yasuo. 2013c. Nihon gengo chizu no dêtabêsuka to keiryôteki bunseki: Heiyô genshô, hyôjungokei no bunpu to kôtsûmô, hôgenruijido [Development of database of Linguistic atlas of Japan and quantitative analysis]. In Yasuo Kumagai (ed.), *Daikibo hôgen dêta no takakuteki bunseki seika hôkokusho: Gengo chizu to hôgen danwa shiryo [Analyzing large-scale dialectal survey data from multiple perspectives]*, 111–128. Tokyo: Kokuritsu Kokugo Kenkyûjo (NINJAL).

Satô, Ryôichi. 1986. Chiikishakai no kyôtsûgoka [Standardization in regional society]. In Kiichi Iitoyo (ed.), *Hôgenkenkyû no mondai*, vol. Kôza hôgengaku, 145–178. Tokyo: Kokusyokankôkai.

Sibata, Takesi & Yasuo Kumagai. 1993. The S&K Network method: Processing procedures for dividing dialect areas. *Zeitschrift für Dialectologie und Linguistik* 74. 458–495.

Takada, Makoto. 1969. Kotoba no chiri: Nihon gengo chizu kara [Geography of words, Kyûshû district: An observation by using the LAJ]. *Gengo seikatsu* 216. 30–38.

Tanaka, Akio. 1991. *Hyôjungo: Kotoba no komichi [Standard language: A lane of speech]*. Tokyo: Seibundô Shinkôsha.

Tokugawa, Munemasa. 1993. *Hôgenchirigaku no tenkai [Development of dialect geography]*. Tokyo: Hituzi Syobo.

Chapter 21

Tracing real and apparent time language changes by comparing linguistic maps

Chitsuko Fukushima

University of Niigata Prefecture, Faculty of International Studies and Regional Development

Geographical distributions on linguistic maps show what language changes have occurred in a surveyed area. In Japan, two national geolinguistic surveys have been conducted in the past: the Linguistic Atlas of Japan (National Language Research Institute 1966, LAJ) and the Grammar Atlas of Japanese Dialects (National Language Research Institute 1989, GAJ). Recently, a third nation-wide geolinguistic survey, the Field-Research Project for Analyzing the Formation Process of Japanese Dialects (FPJD) was conducted to analyze the current geographical distributions of the phonological, lexical, and grammatical items. The informants in the surveys were elderly people. The data from the surveys conducted in different periods was compared, and real-time language changes occurring over the generations were traced. The regional geolinguistic data of the younger generation was also used for comparison to examine apparent-time changes. Thus linguistic maps from different surveys have been redrawn using the same symbols for comparison and then superimposed. The results of the study show two patterns of language change for completed changes and changes in progress.

1 Introduction

Geographical distributions on linguistic maps indicate what language changes have occurred in a surveyed area. To examine real-time changes, a survey is repeated after a period of time, and, to observe apparent-time changes, different generations are surveyed. Fukushima (2013) reported results of a comparison between two geolinguistic surveys of Tokunoshima dialects of Japanese. The two surveys were conducted 30 years apart with a focus on real-time changes. Although it is difficult to repeat a geolinguistic survey with the same scope, especially on a national level, a nation-wide geolinguistic survey, the Field-Research Project for Analyzing the Formation Process of Japanese Dialects (FPJD), was

Chitsuko Fukushima. 2016. Tracing real and apparent time language changes by comparing linguistic maps. In Marie-Hélène Côté, Remco Knooihuizen & John Nerbonne (eds.), *The future of dialects*, 363–376. Berlin: Language Science Press. DOI:10.17169/langsci.b81.160

conducted in Japan. The aim of this real-time interval research is to compare the dialectal distributions from different surveys and to examine the interpretation of linguistic maps from the older surveys (Onishi 2014). In this paper, data from the national surveys and the recent regional survey of the young generation is compared to trace real- and apparent-time language changes.

2 Data and Methods

Three nation-wide geolinguistic surveys targeted at the elderly have been conducted in Japan to examine linguistic variation and change: (i) the Linguistic Atlas of Japan (LAJ), which mainly focused on lexical items and was conducted around 1960; (ii) the Grammar Atlas of Japanese Dialects (GAJ), which was exclusively concerned with grammatical items and was conducted around 1980; and (iii) the FPJD, which has recently been completed and which focuses on phonological, lexical, and grammatical items. A recent regional survey targeted at the younger generation, which includes phonological, lexical, and grammatical items, is the Survey of College Students in Niigata (CS) (see Table 1).

Table 1: A comparison of characteristics of four surveys

Title	Type	Informants	Time of survey	# of all-Japan localities	# of localities in Niigata	Mean birth year of informants
LAJ	National	elderly	1957–1965	2400	91	1887
GAJ	National	elderly	1979–1982	807	29	1916
FPJD	National	elderly	2010–2014	554	22	1937
CS	Regional	youth	1994–2002	-	103 max.	1980 approx.

The data from the national surveys LAJ and GAJ was compared with that from FPJD to trace real-time changes, while the FPJD data was compared with that from CS to examine apparent-time changes. The CS informants were 631 college students from various localities in Niigata prefecture. To construct the CS maps such as Figure 8, Figure 11 and Figure 14 below, symbols were plotted at the location of each student's town of origin.

The data examined here illustrate the dialectal variation in Niigata prefecture, where the border between Western and Eastern Japanese dialects is situated. Figure 1 shows a linguistic map for *iru* '(a person) to be or exist' from LAJ.[1]. The

---

[1] LAJ Maps Download: http://www.ninjal.ac.jp/publication/catalogue/laj_map/

21 Tracing real and apparent time language changes

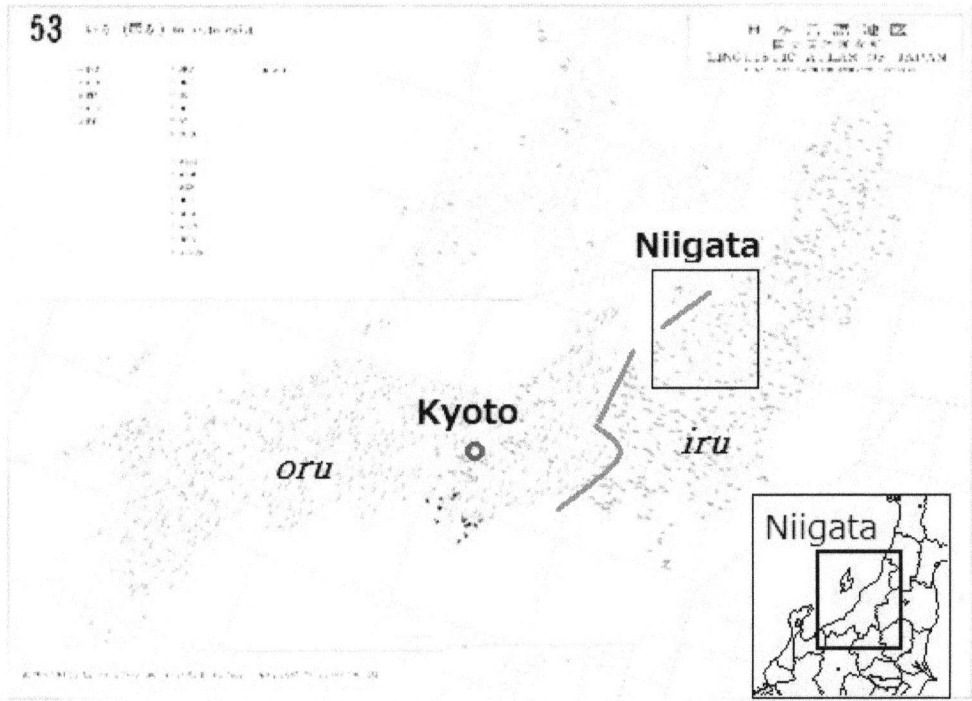

Figure 1: LAJ 53 *iru* 'to be or exist' and Niigata (Original map downloaded from LAJ Maps Download).

lexical variation shown here is a contrastive East-West distribution pattern with a clear isogloss drawn just within Niigata prefecture. The geographical distribution shows that the Western form has diffused from the central part of Japan where the old capital Kyoto is located. A bundle of such isoglosses is found in Niigata prefecture, which shows the division between Western and Eastern dialects.

Fukushima (2007) compared geolinguistic survey results for Niigata dialects from two different surveys in order to examine linguistic variation and change. Either GAJ or LAN — the Linguistic Atlas of Niigata, a regional survey conducted by Katsuo Ohashi in 1980–1985 (Ohashi 1998) — was used as the data from the older generation, and CS was adopted as the data from the younger generation. Two linguistic maps were superimposed by using the SEAL 7.0J system developed by the author. This paper compares geolinguistic survey results for Niigata dialects from three different surveys: LAJ or GAJ, FPJD, and CS. The GIS software SIS 7.1 was used to make comparable linguistic maps by adopting the same symbols and superimposing the distribution of relevant words from different surveys. The results of the comparison are discussed in the following sections.

3 Completed changes

Figures 2–4 show changes that were completed in the past. All three maps show East-West contrastive patterns with isoglosses in Niigata but do not show much difference over time.

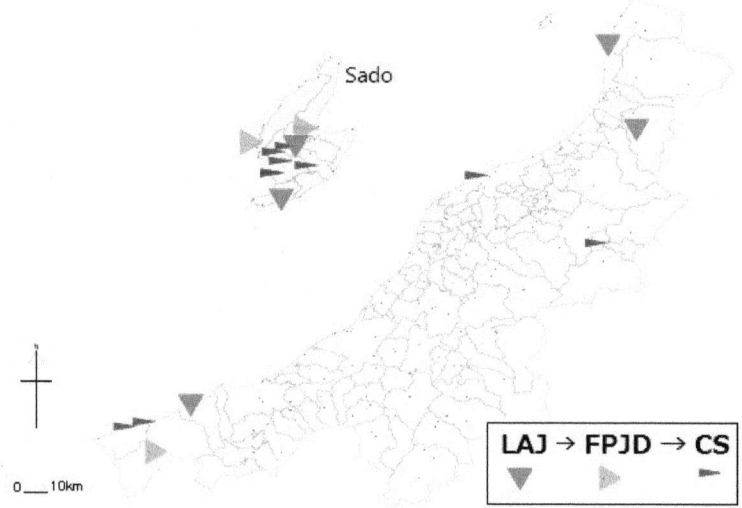

Figure 2: Diffusion of the Western form *oru* for *iru* '[a person] to be or exist'.

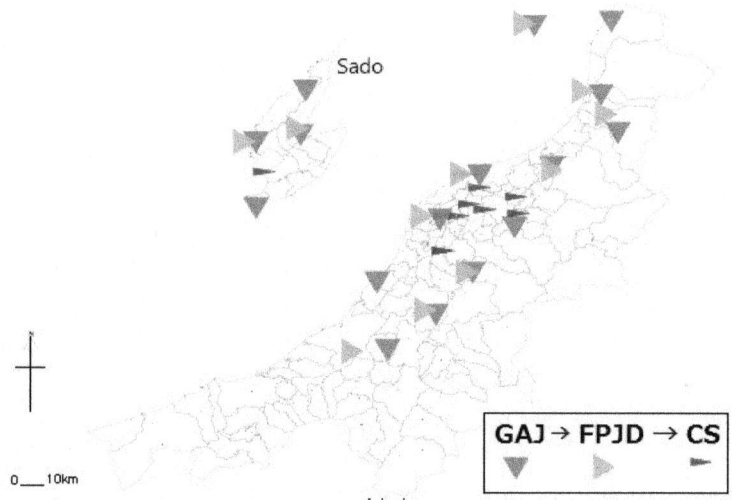

Figure 3: Diffusion of the Western form *kô ta* for *katta* 'bought [past tense]'.

21 Tracing real and apparent time language changes

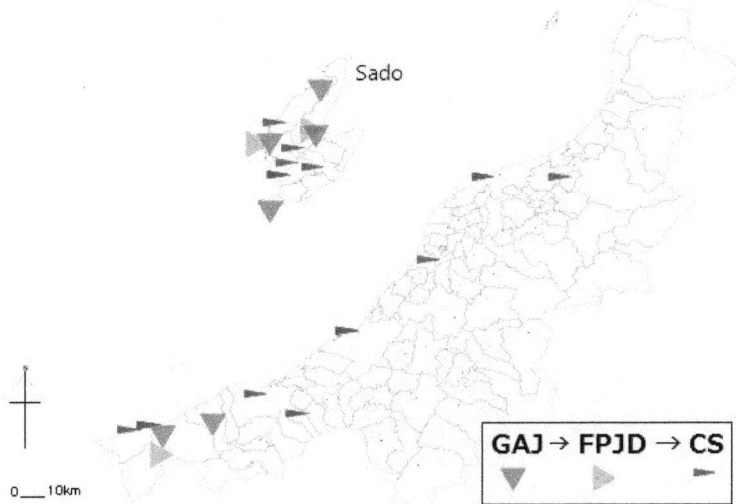

Figure 4: Diffusion of the Western forms *sen, sin* for *sinai* 'do not perform or act [a negative form]'.

Each map shows the distribution of Western form(s) in LAJ/GAJ (red symbols), FPJD (green symbols), and CS (blue symbols). Figure 2 maps the lexical variation of *iru* '(of a person) to be or exist'. In LAJ, the Western form *oru* is found on Sado Island, and in the westernmost and northernmost parts of mainland Niigata. In FPJD and CS, the Western form is still found on Sado Island and in the westernmost part of mainland Niigata. Thus the distributions do not vary much between LAJ, FPJD and CS. Figure 3 maps the morphological variation of *katta* 'bought [a past tense form of the verb 'buy'].' The Western form *ko:ta* is found in GAJ on Sado Island and also in the central and northern parts of mainland Niigata (this area almost coincides with the Kambara Plains). The distributions in FPJD are the same as those in GAJ, but those in CS, although located in the same area, are more restricted. Figure 4 maps the morphological variation of *sinai* "do not perform [a negative form of the verb 'perform']." The Western forms *sen* and *sin* are distributed in GAJ on Sado Island and in the westernmost part of mainland Niigata. The distributions in FPJD are the same, but the distribution of the Western forms has expanded slightly in mainland Niigata in CS.

These linguistic maps show the contrastive distributions between Eastern dialect forms and Western dialect forms. From the maps, we can conclude that Western dialect forms expanded to Sado Island and part of mainland Niigata in the past, but that they later lost their influence due to the spread of Eastern dialect

367

forms, which happened to be the standard forms. The Eastern forms were maintained as the linguistic repertoire of the younger generation as a result of language standardization. Figure 4 shows a slight expansion of the Western forms on the coast of mainland Niigata probably due to competition from localized variants *sine* and *sinê:* as well as a standard form *sinai*.

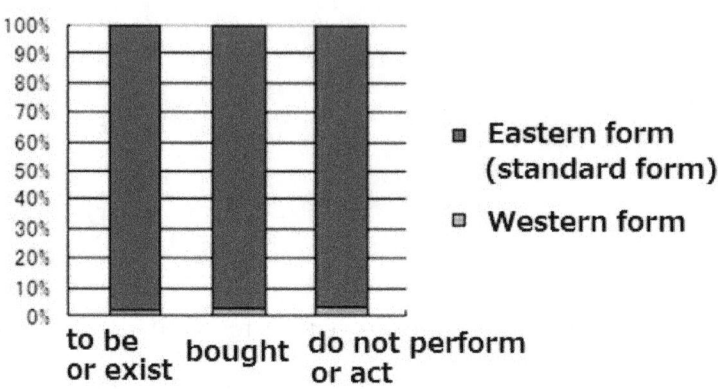

Figure 5: Percentage of actual users of Western forms in the CS data.

Figure 5 confirms this interpretation, as users of Western dialect forms make up less than 5 percent of all CS informants.

4 Changes in Progress

The next group of maps shows changes in progress. Here, the linguistic distributions in different surveys show conspicuous differences.

Figure 6, Figure 7, and Figure 8 map the lexical variation of *kara* 'because' in GAJ, FPJD, and CS respectively. Unlike the maps shown in the previous section, these maps show different distributions for the different surveys. The traditional dialectal form *suke* and its variants occupy most localities in GAJ. The map for FPJD shows two new words, *kke* and *si*, both of which have increased their distribution as shown in the map for CS: the form *kke* is a phonological derivation from *suke*, and the form *si* is a Western dialect form. The FPJD map thus clearly indicates the beginning of lexical innovation, which was expanded later.

Figures 9–14 map the lexical changes in *siasatte* 'two days after tomorrow' and *yanoasatte* 'three days after tomorrow'. For each lexical item, maps are shown from LAJ, FPJD, and CS. This pair of lexical items shows some interesting changes. In LAJ, Figure 9 and Figure 12 show contrastive distributions between Eastern

21 *Tracing real and apparent time language changes*

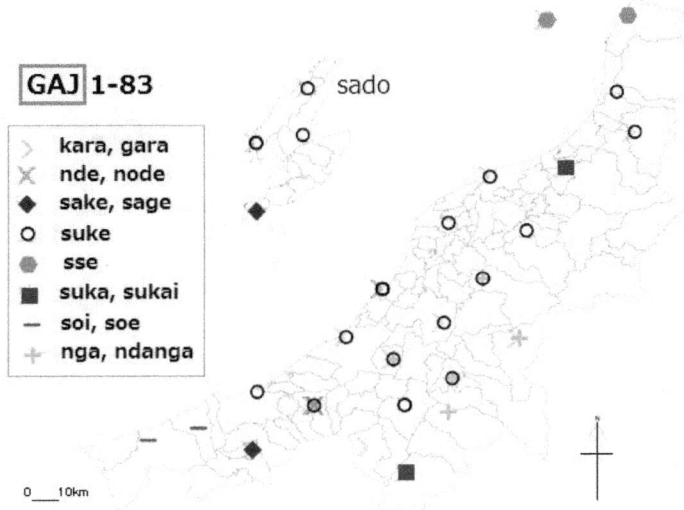

Figure 6: *kara* 'because' from GAJ

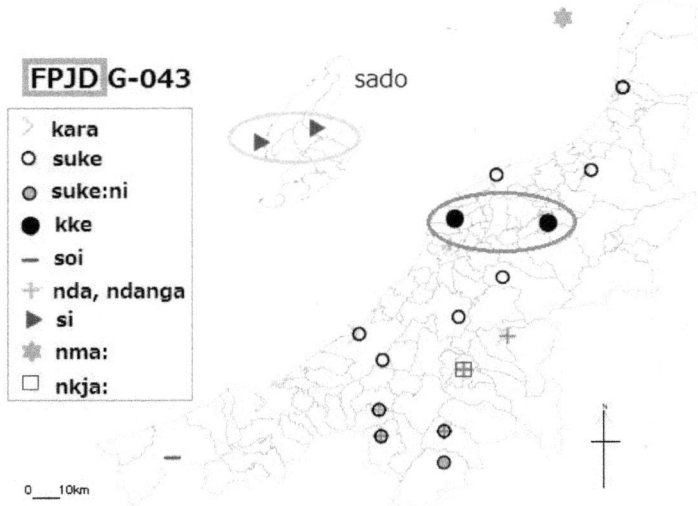

Figure 7: *kara* 'because' from FPJD

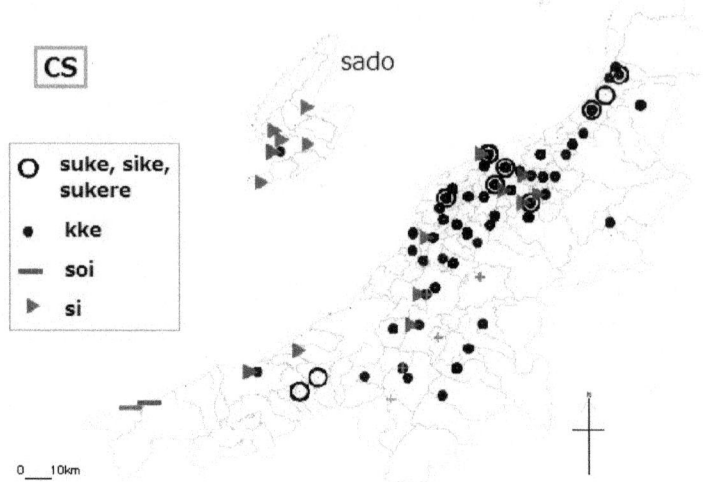

Figure 8: *kara* 'because' from CS

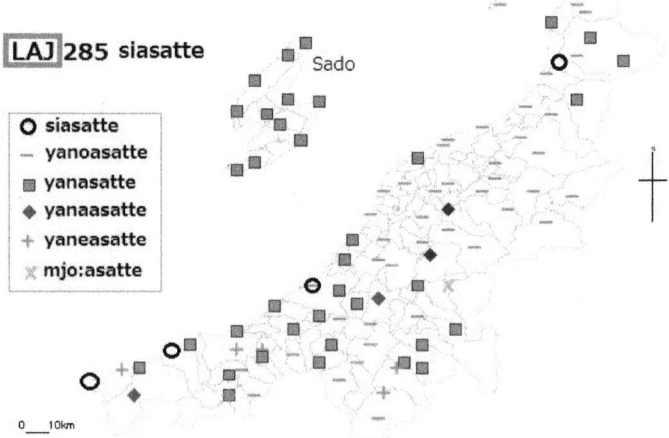

Figure 9: 'two days after tomorrow' from LAJ

21 *Tracing real and apparent time language changes*

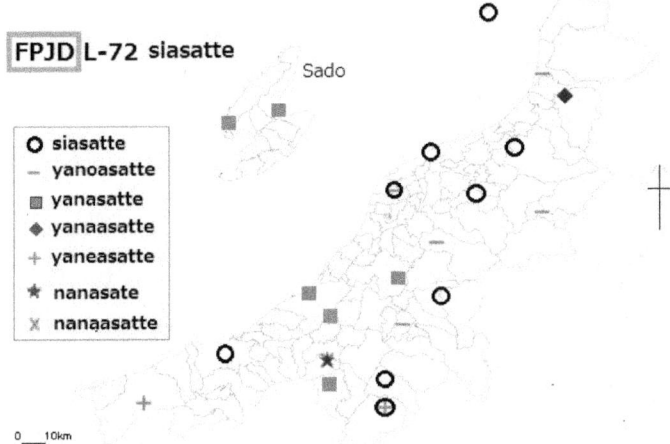

Figure 10: 'two days after tomorrow' from FPJD

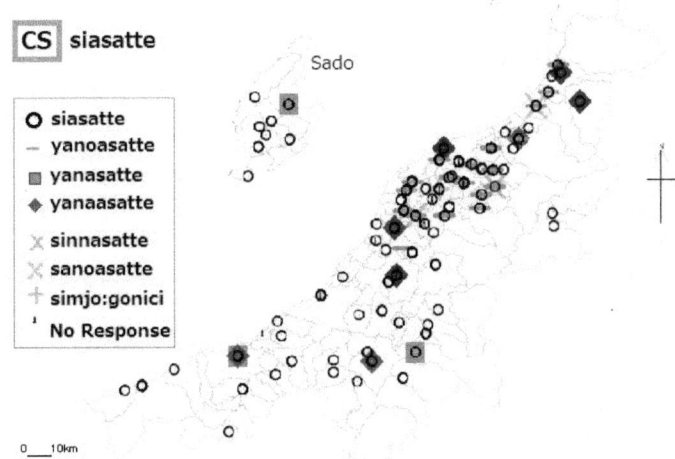

Figure 11: 'two days after tomorrow' from CS

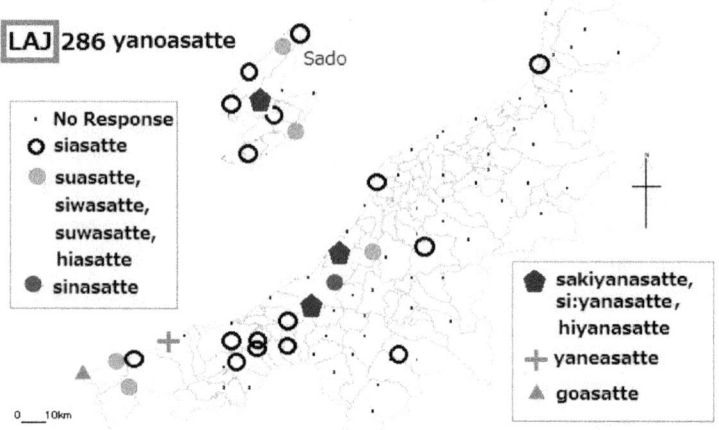

Figure 12: 'three days after tomorrow' from LAJ

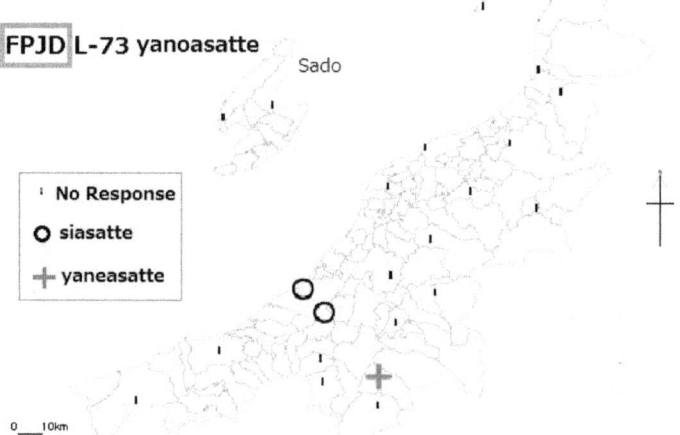

Figure 13: 'three days after tomorrow' from FPJD

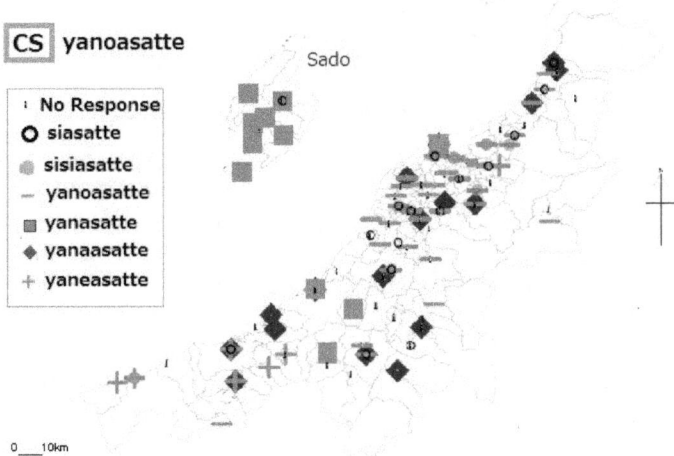

Figure 14: 'three days after tomorrow' from CS

Niigata and Western Niigata (including Sado). In Eastern Niigata, the traditional dialect had a localized form *yanoasatte* which means 'two days after tomorrow' but there was no equivalent word for 'three days after tomorrow'; on the other hand, in Western Niigata, there were localized words, *yanasatte, yanaasatte,* and *yaneasatte* with the meaning of 'two days after tomorrow', but *siasatte* meant 'three days after tomorrow', unlike in the standard system. In FPJD, influenced by the system of standard Japanese, the standard word *siasatte* was introduced with the meaning of 'two days after tomorrow', but this resulted in a conflict with the localized system especially in Western Niigata (see Figure 10 and Figure 13). In CS, some of the young generation adopted the standard system but others used localized dialectal forms *yanasatte, yanaasatte,* and *yaneassatte* with the meaning of 'three days after tomorrow' (see Figure 11 and Figure 14). This has resulted in a new system, shown in Figure 15.

In both cases, the FPJD data shows the transitional stage of dialectal changes between the LAJ/GAJ data and the CS data. If the changes have occurred in the local area recently, they will be captured by the FPJD maps.

5 Conclusion

Regional language changes are traced back using data from three different geolinguistic surveys. Two patterns of results are reported. In the first case, the expansion of Western dialect forms is weakened due to language standardiza-

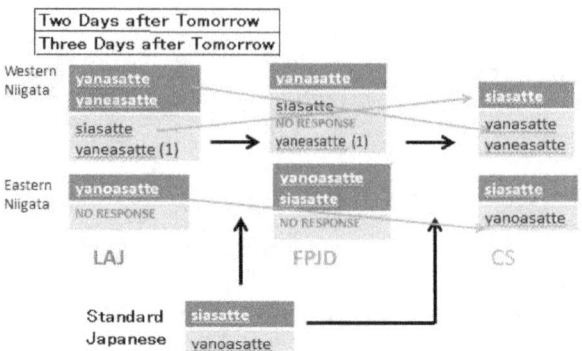

Figure 15: Changes of usage in "two days after tomorrow" and "three days after tomorrow"

tion. Changes were observed in the past but no additional advancement was reported in the linguistic maps. In the second case, local dialectal change is still on-going. The recent nation-wide survey of elderly speakers has captured the transition in progress. The results of the study show "a shift in focus from studying the spread of older linguistic features to studying the spread of innovative features" as observed by Gordon (2000: 412). Geographical Information Systems (GIS) are useful in statistical and quantitative analysis as stated by Lee & Kretzschmar (1993), while the georeferencing function of GIS is used to compare and superimpose linguistic maps from different surveys as reported in this paper. The author has been involved in integrating or comparing the distribution patterns of linguistic features found in individual linguistic maps with an objective to "describe" and "explain" or "adduce reasons for the distributions" (Trudgill 1974: 216). Only a few common items from different surveys were compared in this paper, but the patterns reported should be seen as representative. When more data from the younger generation is available for comparison, this opens the way to quantitative analysis.

Acknowledgment

This paper is part of the outcomes of the collaborative research project "Field-Research Project for Analyzing the Formation Process of Japanese Dialects", carried out at the National Institute for Japanese Language and Linguistics, and was supported by Grant-in-Aid for Scientific Research (A) 23242024 and (C) 25370487.

References

Fukushima, Chitsuko. 2007. Superimposing linguistic maps to trace linguistic changes. *Linguistica Atlantica* 27–28. 40–45.

Fukushima, Chitsuko. 2013. Revisiting regional variation on an island after thirty years. In Alena Barysevich, Alexandra D'Arcy & David Heap (eds.), *Proceedings of Methods XIV: Papers from the Fourteenth International Conference on Methods in Dialectology*, 305–314. Frankfurt am Main: Peter Lang.

Gordon, Matthew J. 2000. Changes in progress: Tales of the Northern cities. *American Speech* 75(4). 412–414.

Lee, Jay & William A. Kretzschmar. 1993. Spatial analysis of linguistic data with GIS functions. *International Journal of Geographical Information Systems* 7(6). 541–560.

National Language Research Institute (ed.). 1966. *Linguistic atlas of Japan*. Tokyo: National Printing Bureau.

National Language Research Institute (ed.). 1989. *Grammar Atlas of Japanese Dialects*. Tokyo: National Printing Bureau.

Ohashi, Katsuo. 1998. *Linguistic atlas of Niigata (LAN)*. Niigata: Koshi Shoin.

Onishi, Takuichiro. 2014. *Timespan comparison of dialectal distributions*. University of Groningen.

Trudgill, Peter. 1974. Linguistic change and diffusion: Description and explanation in sociolinguistic dialect geography. *Language in Society* 3(2). 215–246.

Chapter 22

Timespan comparison of dialectal distributions

Takuichiro Onishi

National Institute for Japanese Language and Linguistics

Traditional Japanese dialectology has held that dialectal distributions are caused by the diffusion of language changes from a central area, as in the dialect radiation theory. If this is true, then we can capture the radial spread of changes in dialectal distributions by surveying an area over a period of time. Since Japanese dialectology has published many dialect maps, we have at least half a century's excellent geolinguistic data. We have researched the same area with the same methodology of past geolinguistic surveys to compare the dialectal distributions over a timespan of 30 to 50 years. This study shows two main results. The first is that changes in dialectal distributions are neither continual nor gradual. Diffusions are completed in one breath, and the new forms cover each area quickly. The second result is that dialectal distributions do not change easily. Many features have retained their past distributions. These results inform our knowledge of language change and dialect formation. Dialect is a means for people to communicate with one other; once a language change occurs, the change should spread throughout the community to maintain communication. Language change is the unpreferred option, since linguistic variation introduced by language change can impede smooth communication.

1 Introduction

How do time and space relate in dialects, especially in dialectal distributions? According to traditional Japanese dialectology, dialectal distributions are caused by the diffusion of linguistic changes from a central area to surrounding areas. This idea has been known as the dialect radiation theory since Yanagita (1930). If this is correct, we should be able to capture radial changes in dialectal distributions when we survey an area over a period of, for example, 30 to 50 years.

Since Japanese dialectologists have published over 400 dialectal atlases over the last 50 years, including 30,000 maps of dialectal distributions, we have at

Takuichiro Onishi. 2016. Timespan comparison of dialectal distributions. In Marie-Hélène Côté, Remco Knooihuizen & John Nerbonne (eds.), *The future of dialects*, 377–388. Berlin: Language Science Press. DOI:10.17169/langsci.b81.161

least half a century's excellent geolinguistic data both for Japan as a whole and for specific regions. We have investigated the same areas with the same methods as in past geolinguistic surveys to compare the distributions we find over the timespan of 30 to 50 years with the distributions predicted by traditional Japanese dialectology.

We have reached two main results in this study. The first result is that changes of dialectal distributions are neither continual nor gradual. The pattern of diffusion seems not to be expansion but rather filling. The diffusions we studied were completed in one breath, and the new forms covered each area quickly. The second result is that dialectal distributions do not change often. We expected that more changes of dialectal distributions would easily be captured through the investigation, since traditional Japanese geolinguistics interprets dialectal distributions as expanding diffusions of continual linguistic changes from the center. However, many of the distributions have kept their past conditions.

These results suggest that linguistic changes and spatial formations (including geographical boundaries) of dialects are related. The purpose of dialect, and indeed that of any language variety, is communication; once a linguistic change has occurred, it should diffuse quickly to support communication. On the other hand, it is better for a language not to change, since variation caused by linguistic change can block smooth communication. Therefore, after finishing a linguistic change, dialectal distributions become stable once again.

The examples presented in this paper include that of a grammatical item in a large area and those of lexical items in a smaller area.

2 Real-time research on dialectal distributions

We are conducting three projects comparing modern dialectal distributions to past dialectal distributions. Within each project, data has been acquired over a 30- to 50-year period. One project treats a wide area (all of Japan), the others treat smaller areas (separate regions). The informants in each project were around 70 years old at the time of the investigation.

The projects use data from three linguistic surveys. The Field Research Project to Analyze the Formation Process of Japanese Dialects (FPJD) has conducted research in 500 places across Japan between 2010 and 2014. The Linguistic Atlas of Japan (LAJ) project mainly investigated lexical items in 2,400 places around 50 years ago (1957–1965). The Grammar Atlas of Japanese Dialects (GAJ) project investigated grammatical items in 800 locations about 30 years ago (1979–1982). In this paper, I compare data from FPJD to data from GAJ, a real-time interval of 30 years.

In collaboration with Professor Seiichi Nakai of Toyama University, I investigated around 200 locations in the Shogawa River basin in the Toyama prefecture between 2009 and 2012, and compared the results to the data from Sanada (1976). Sanada investigated the upper regions of Shogawa River basin between 1967 and 1969. The timespan between Sanada's and the present study is 40 years.

In an ongoing collaboration with Professor Motoei Sawaki of Shinshuu University, we investigated some 200 locations in the Ina and Suwa regions in the Nagano prefecture between 2010 and 2013 for a comparison with the data from Mase (1980). Mase investigated this area between 1968 and 1973, so real-time data is available for a 40-year interval.

3 Language change and dialectal distributions

In this section, I present my hypothesis of how linguistic changes proceed in dialectal distributions, and I suggest a concrete verification.

In the event of a linguistic change, dialectal distributions are expected to change as in Figure 1. Initially, features x and y are distributed as in the left-hand panel (a). The feature x changes to z in some locations; as a result, the dialectal distribution changes as indicated in the right-hand panel (b).

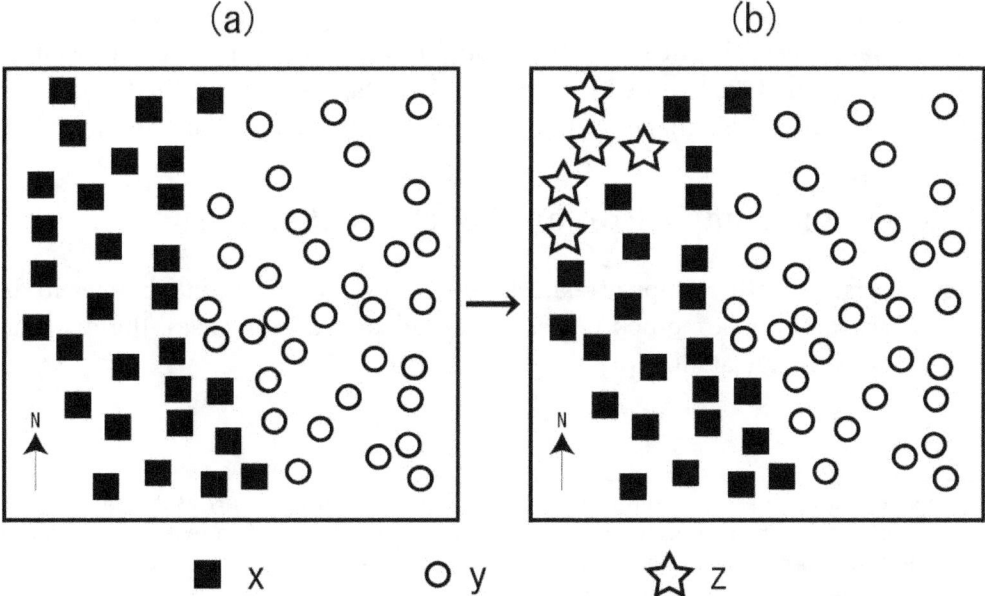

Figure 1: Linguistic change and change in dialectal distributions.

Evidence comes from change in the past-tense negative verb suffix. The form *-nanda* was the standard form and was used in official written language in the early modern period; for example, *nom-u* 'drink', *nom-a=N*[1] 'do not drink', *nom-a=nanda* 'did not drink'. However, *-nanda* is not a well-segmented form. It is not clear which segment in *-nanda* expresses negation, and the form has an unclear etymology (Onishi 1999). In terms of grammar, verbs are dynamic (+activity, -condition), but negative verbs become static (or stative) (-activity, +condition) and similar to adjectives, which are also static rather than dynamic. *-Nkatta* is a newly occurring form of the past-tense negative verb suffix in some dialects, the final element *-katta* coming from the past-tense form of adjectives; for example, *taka-i* 'be high', *taka-katta* 'was high', so also *nom-a=N* 'do not drink', *nom-a=Nkatta* 'did not drink'. *-Nkatta* is a dialectal form and is used in spoken but not written language. Modern standard Japanese uses *–nakatta*, which is different from the dialectal form *-Nkatta*.

Figure 2 shows that *-nanda* was used almost everywhere in Osaka[2] in the GAJ data from around 1980. Few places in the area used *-Nkatta* as the past-tense negative verb suffix. Sanada (1992) reported a change from *-nanda* to *-Nkatta* in Osaka[3]. Sanada's data is shown in Figure 3. Speaker age in this graph is at the time of investigation (1988–1989); the informants in FPJD correspond to the 50-year-old age group in Sanada (1992). The FPJD data (Figure 4) clearly shows an expanded distribution for *-Nkatta*. When we compare Figure 2 and Figure 4, we see that parts of the area of distribution for *-nanda* show a change to *-Nkatta*, similar to the model presented in Figure 1. This example verifies the hypothesis of the link between language change and a change in dialectal distribution.

4 Real-time comparison of dialectal distributions

A comparison of other maps of dialectal distributions shows that changes in dialectal distributions are quick rather than gradual; in some cases, the distributions do not change at all.

---

[1] The present-tense negative suffix of verbs *-n* is written *-N* in this paper as it is pronounced as one syllable. The present-tense negative suffix is a well-known feature dividing Japanese dialects into east and west: *-N* is used in the western area and *-nai* in the eastern area. *-nai* is the standard Japanese form, since the capital city Tokyo is in the eastern area.

[2] The Osaka dialect is representative of western dialects of Japanese; the Osaka prefecture is a core area in western Japan with a population of 8 million.

[3] Sanada's (1992) interpretation of the change is that *-Nkatta* was formed under the influence of standard Japanese *-nakatta*.

22 Timespan comparison of dialectal distributions

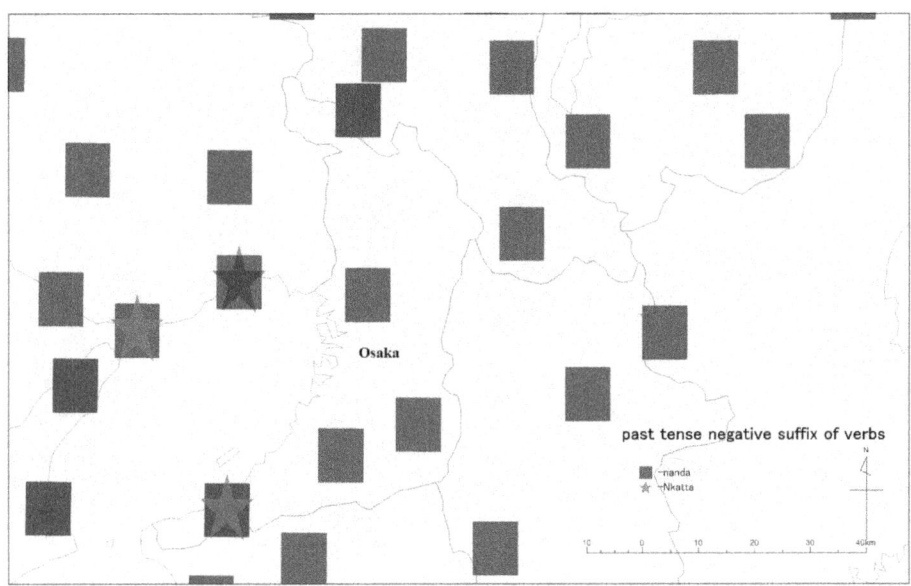

Figure 2: Dialectal distributions of the past-tense negative verb suffixes in Osaka in the GAJ (around 1980).

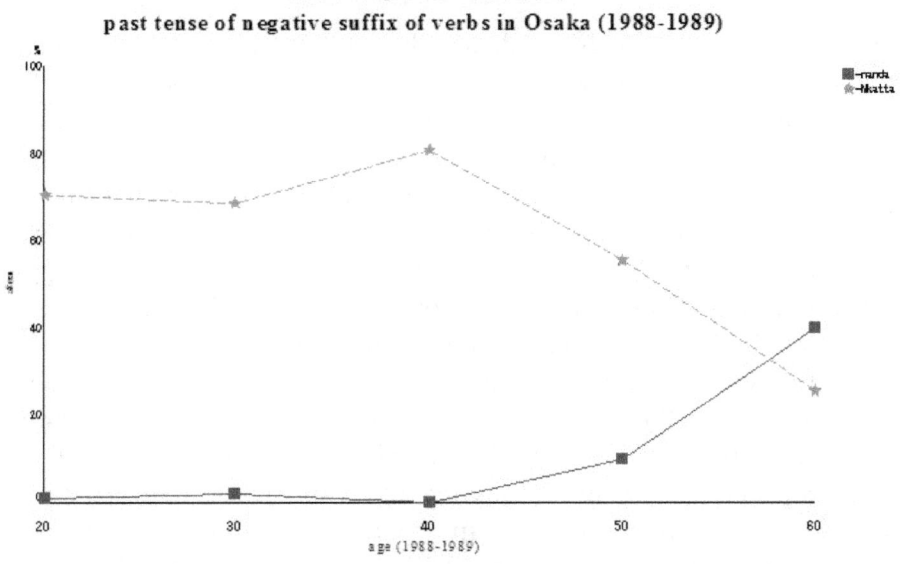

Figure 3: Linguistic change of -*nanda* to -*Nkatta* in Osaka. Based on data from Sanada (1992).

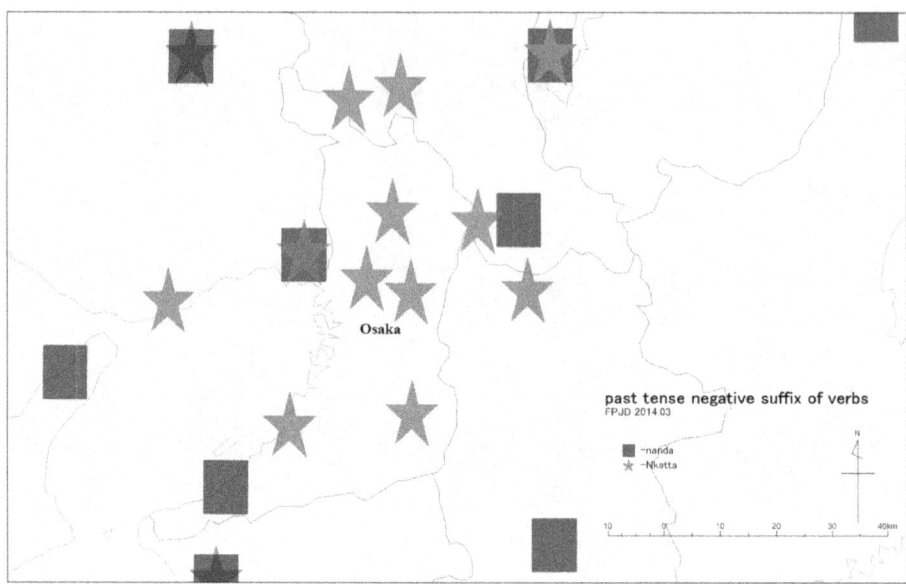

Figure 4: Dialectal distributions of past-tense negative verb suffixes in Osaka according in FPJD (around 2010).

4.1 Rapid change

Since our comparison of real-time data of dialectal distributions is limited to two generations, it is difficult to see the precise stages in which change has occurred. However, when changes do occur, they seem to spread through the area in 30 to 50 years, which is more rapid than we expected.

Figure 5 shows the change in distribution of BEBE[4] forms of the name for the tick-trefoil plant in the Chino area in the Ina-Suwa region.[5] The BEBE- in BEBE-BASAMI and BEBEKKUSA is related to the word for 'clothes'; BASAMI is 'putting', and KUSA is 'grasses'. The names come from the nature of this plant: seeds of the plant stick to the clothes of those walking in the fields or mountains.

BEBE forms were used in the Chino area 40 years ago, as the blue symbols in Figure 5 show. In the data 40 years later, new words occur: ZIZIBASAMI and CHINKOROBASAMI. ZIZI- is related to the word for 'old man, grandfather' and occurs under folk etymology and paronymic attraction to BABA 'old woman, grandmother', cf. the original form BEBE. CHINKORO- refers to the male genital organ, and is associated in folk etymology to a homonym of BEBE 'female genital organ'.

---

[4] Small capitals denote umbrella terms for some of the variants in Figure 5 and Figure 7.
[5] The dialect in this area is representative of Tokai-Tosan dialects and is classified as an eastern Japanese dialect.

22 Timespan comparison of dialectal distributions

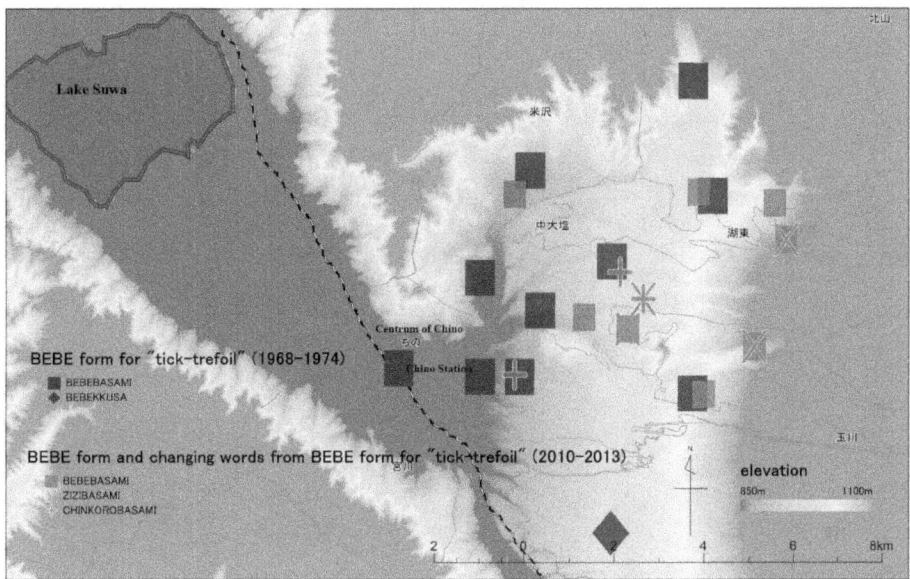

Figure 5: The distribution of BEBE forms and the spread of alternative names for the tick-trefoil plant in the Chino area in the Ina-Suwa region.

ZIZIBASAMI appears to have diffused in the area of high elevation, and CHINKO-ROBASAMI in areas of mid-high elevation. People at the same elevation in these two areas are said to form communities; for example, they have traditionally established marital relations within the contour lines depicting elevation on maps of the area. The diffusing areas of new words for the tick-trefoil plant match these small community areas.

As shown in Section 3, the area of distribution of the past-tense negative verb suffix -*Nkatta* formed rapidly in Osaka. The same change is seen in Aichi, on the border between eastern and western dialect areas of Japanese. The GAJ data (Figure 6) shows that -*Nkatta* was used in a small part of the Aichi area 30 years ago, but since then it has spread to the entire area.

In these cases of language change – the past-tense negative verb suffix in Osaka and Aichi, and the name of the tick-trefoil plant in Chino – the new forms seem to diffuse as if to fill the community areas, i.e., the prefecture areas of Osaka and Aichi, and areas with the same elevation in Chino. Diffusion of features does not happen in a radiating pattern from the center, since the new forms -*Nkatta*, ZIZIBASAMI and CHINKOROBASAMI originate in the area surrounding Osaka rather than in Osaka itself (Figure 2), in the rural area of Aichi rather than in its capi-

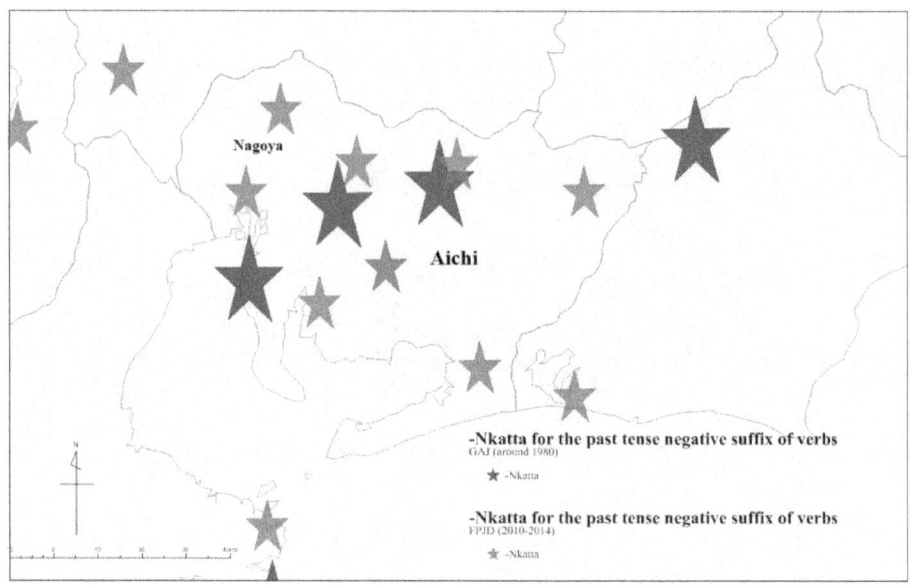

Figure 6: The spread of the past-tense negative verb suffix -*Nkatta* over a 30-year period in the Aichi region.

tal city Nagoya (Figure 6),[6] and in the more elevated agricultural area in Chino (Figure 5).

4.2 Standstills

Figure 7 shows the distribution of names for a fruit-like potato, growing from the branches of Japanese yam roots (Standard Japanese *mukago*) in the Shogawa River basin.[7] The map overlays data from 40 years ago with the current distribution of names.

In the older data, words ending in -zyo (GAGOZYO, GONGOZYO) were found in lower areas in the north, whereas words without -zyo (GAGO, GONGO) were found in higher areas in the south. Comparing this data to the present-day distribution, we make two important observations. Firstly, the basic distribution has been maintained, with lower regions using the -zyo ending and higher regions using forms without -zyo. The isogloss has not changed significantly. Secondly, within this stable pattern, more detailed distributions have been maintained. For

---

[6] Nagoya is the largest city in this area with a population of approx. 2 million.

[7] The Shogawa River flows from south to north. The southern, upper reaches form an agricultural area; the northern, lower reaches are an urban area.

22 Timespan comparison of dialectal distributions

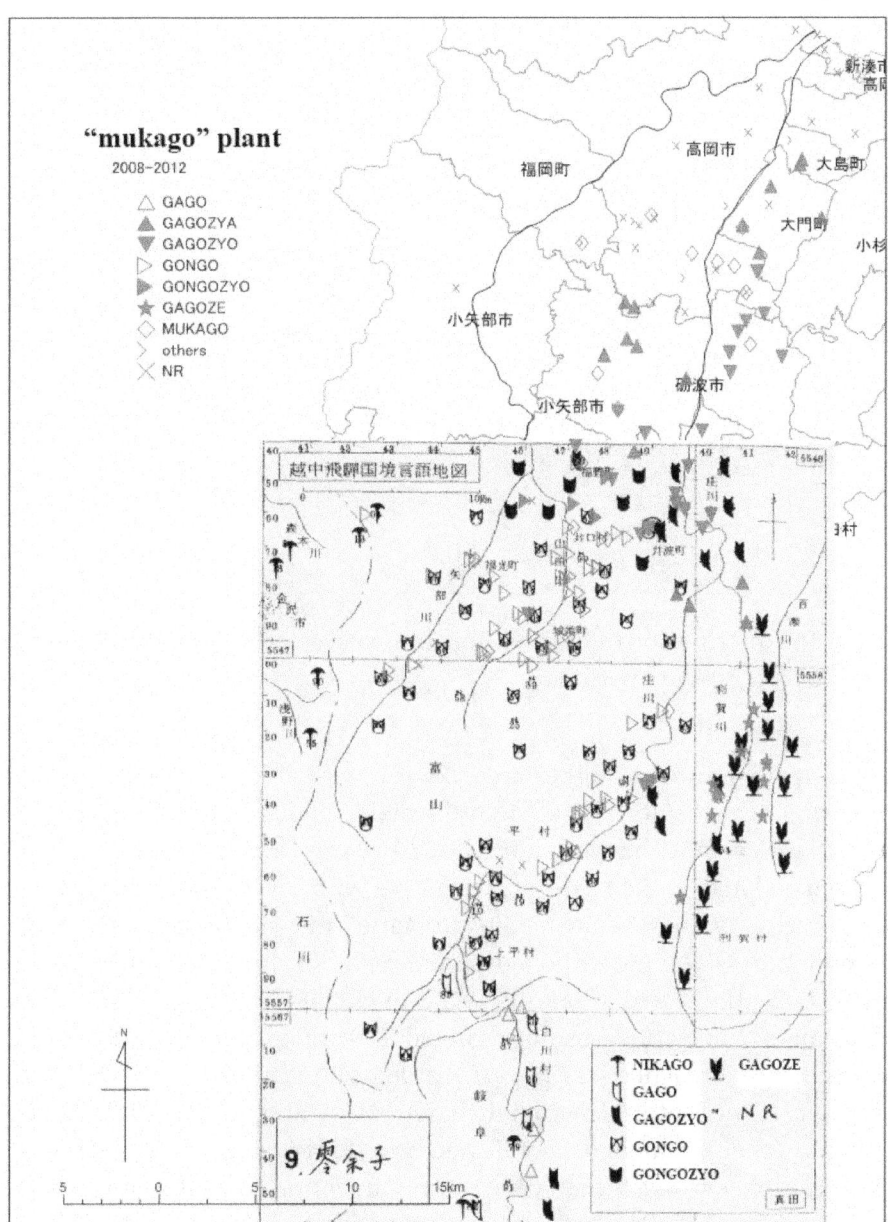

Figure 7: Distribution of names for the *mukago* plant in the Shogawa River basin over a 40-year period. The older map, in black and white, is taken from Sanada (1976).

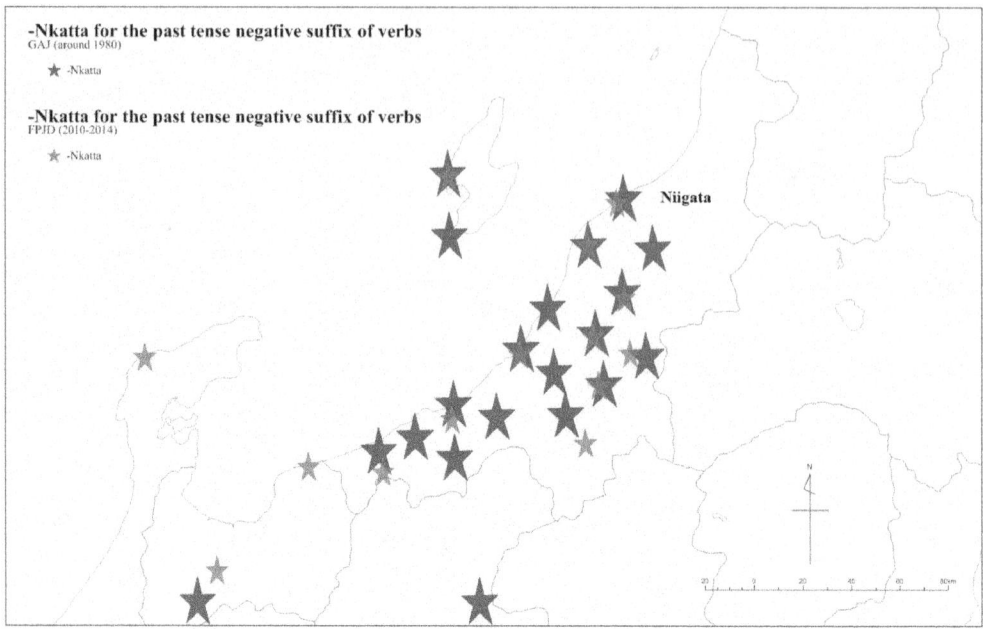

Figure 8: The distribution of the past-tense negative verb suffix -*Nkatta* in Niigata over a 30-year period.

instance, in the southern, higher area, a word with -zyo exists on the east bank of the river. These results indicate that the dialectal distribution of names for the *mukago* plant has not changed in the last 40 years (Onishi in print).

As discussed above, the past-tense negative verb suffix -*Nkatta* has diffused in the Osaka and Aichi areas in the 30-year time interval studied. When we turn our attention to Niigata, we find a different result of this real-time comparison.[8] Figure 8 shows the distribution of -*Nkatta* in Niigata over a 30-year period. The distribution of this feature has not changed. It is thought that the distribution of -*Nkatta* in Niigata reached its final form at least 30 years ago; it does not diffuse any further, as the feature covered the community area 30 years ago already.

Once a language change occurs, it needs to diffuse so the language or dialect can continue to serve its function as a communication tool. The change needs to diffuse and cover the whole area where communication occurs in the language or dialect in question. After this spread has completed, the change stops to diffuse. The distribution of -*Nkatta* in Niigata has been in this state of completion for the last 30 years.

---

[8] The Niigata dialect is classified as an eastern dialect of Japanese, but as Niigata is located on the border between west and east, it uses the western present-tense negative verb suffix -*N*.

5 Conclusions

The examples presented in this paper confirm the hypothesis about how linguistic changes in dialectal distribution spread. A real-time interval comparison shows that new areas of dialectal distributions of linguistic change are formed abruptly and quickly, and neither continually nor gradually. Rather than expanding from a center in a radial fashion, linguistic changes within dialects appear to start in areas that are not necessarily central, and expand until they fill the area where the people communicate in the relevant dialect. Stability in dialectal distributions is not rare. After the formation of a new distribution area, some dialectal distributions do not change any further.

The reason for this stability can be related to the function of language as a means of communication. Once a linguistic change has started, its use needs to become widespread enough so the language can continue to fulfil this role. This causes new forms to diffuse quickly, but only to fill the community area. On the other hand, since linguistic changes obstruct smooth communication, they do not continue to easily expand once the area of dialectal distribution is filled.

The examples suggest that the hypothesis is verified. Future work on additional examples aims to further test the hypothesis.

References

Mase, Yoshio. 1980. *Kami-ina-no Hougen. [Dialects in Kami-Ina.]* Kamiinashikankoukai: Ina.

Onishi, Takuichiro. 1999. Atarashii hougen-to furui hougen-no zenkoku-bunpu. [New and old dialectal distributions.] *Nihongogaku* 18(13). 97–110.

Onishi, Takuichiro. in print. *The relationship between area and human lives in dialect formation. Proceedings of 7th SIDG.* Vienna: Praesens Verlag.

Sanada, Shinji. 1976. *Ecchū-Hida Kokkyō Gengochizu. [Language atlas of the Ecchū-Hida border area.]* Toyama: private print.

Sanada, Shinji. 1992. Kansaihougen-no genzai. [The Kansai dialect in the present day.] *Nihongogaku* 11(7). 117–126.

Yanagita, Kunio. 1930. *Kagyuukoo. [On snail.]* Tokyo: TookooShoin.

Chapter 23

Tonal variation in Kagoshima Japanese and factors of language change

Ichiro Ota
Kagoshima University

Hitoshi Nikaido
Fukuoka Jo Gakuin University

Akira Utsugi
Nagoya University

> According to Kubozono (2007), tonal changes are in progress among young native speakers of Kagoshima Japanese due to the influence of Standard Japanese through mass media broadcasting. This report presents the results of statistical analyses which demonstrate that variables related to mass media broadcasting (media content viewing habits) seem to have positive effects on the tonal changes. In addition, we suggest a tentative theory that the asymmetrical progress of the tonal changes are reflections of de-dialectization and de-standardization taking place in this variety.

1 Theoretical background and the research aim

In many dialects of Japanese, two types of word tone are recognized in terms of the accentuation. One is the tone called 'accented', which has an abrupt pitch fall within the prosodic boundary of a word. The other is 'unaccented', which has no pitch fall. In Standard Japanese (henceforth SJ), for example, the tone of *na'mida-ga* 'eyedrop-NOM', with a pitch fall on the first syllable, is accented, and that of *sakana-ga* 'fish-NOM', with no pitch fall, is unaccented. In addition, SJ is considered to have 'n(= number of moras) + 1' tonal patterns. Thus, for three-

Ichiro Ota, Hitoshi Nikaido & Akira Utsugi. 2016. Tonal variation in Kagoshima Japanese and factors of language change. In Marie-Hélène Côté, Remco Knooihuizen & John Nerbonne (eds.), *The future of dialects*, 389–398. Berlin: Language Science Press. DOI:10.17169/langsci.b81.162

syllable words, there are four possible tonal patterns in the surface forms. (See the 'Tokyo' section of Table 1).[1]

Kagoshima Japanese (henceforth KJ), which is one of the provincial dialects of Japanese, has the same accentuation system as SJ. However, KJ allows only two types of tone, Tone A (with a pitch fall on the penultimate syllable) and Tone B (with no pitch fall), no matter how many syllables a word has within its prosodic boundary.[2] Thus, for the three-syllable words in Table 1, only either Tone A (... HL) or Tone B (... LH) is assigned.[3]

Table 1: Tonal correspondence between SJ and KJ, adapted from Kubozono (2007: 329) with the authors' modification.

		word gloss	namida (ga) eyedrop-(NOM)	kokora (ga) heart-(NOM)	otoko (ga) man-(NOM)	sakana (ga) fish-(NOM)
SJ	surface tone		na'mida- (ga) HLL-(L)	koko'ro- (ga) LHL-(L)	otoko'- (ga) LHH-(L)	sakana- (ga) LHH-(H)
	accentuation		initially accented	medially accented	finally accented	unaccented
KJ	surface tone		namida-(ga) LLL-(H)	kokoro-(ga) LLL-(H)	otoko-(ga) LLL-(H)	sakana'-(ga) LLH-(L)
	accentuation			unaccented (...LH) [Tone B]		accented (...HL) [Tone A]

In addition, there is a sharp discrepancy between SJ and KJ in auditory impression. This is caused by a disagreement in accentuation pattern. For example, for the words in Table 2, the SJ tone of *mo'miji* is accented (HLL), while the KJ counterpart is unaccented (LLH). This is also the case for *kaede* (LHH), although their accentuations are the opposite.

However, presumably to resolve this discrepancy, tonal changes are in progress in KJ (Kubozono 2007). Young native speakers of KJ tend to pronounce words with the same accentuation pattern as that of SJ, although the two-type tone system is still sufficiently preserved. Thus, a traditionally unaccented word like *momiji* is likely to be produced with the accented tone (LHL), whereas *kaede*, a

---

[1] The prime " ' " attached to words indicates the location of pitch fall.

[2] The prosodic structure of nouns consists of the word itself and a case-marking particle, such as -*ga* 'NOM' and -*o* 'OBJ'.

[3] In fact, there is another interpretation for these tonal patterns (Kubozono 2007). For example, Hirayama (1957) considers that the difference of tones is due to "the location of high tone" (Kubozono 2007: 327). However, following Kubozono, we adopt the analysis based on the accentuation proposed by Haraguchi (1977) and Shibatani (1990) as our theoretical presupposition, because the tonal change of KJ seems to involve the presence/absence of pitch fall.

traditionally accented word, can be realized as unaccented (LLH), as shown in the column 'Kagoshima innovative' of Table 2. Their surface forms are not perfectly identical to the SJ counterparts (HLL and LHH, respectively), but their accentuation patterns (i.e., the presence/absence of pitch fall) correspond to those of SJ. Kubozono (2007: 348) claims that this tonal change is "the result of interaction of a phonetic (or perceptual) factor" (i.e., speakers' sensitivity to the pitch accentuation) and "a phonological factor" (i.e., the native prosodic system), and suggests a relation with the bilingualism of KJ speakers which results from the exposure "to standard Tokyo Japanese through TV, radio and other mass media", with social dominance of SJ as the backdrop of this innovation (Kubozono 2007: 323).

Table 2: Surface tone and accentuation in SJ, Traditional KJ and Innovative KJ.

		SJ	KJ	Kagoshima Innovative
momiji	**surface tone**	*mo'miji* HLL	*momiji* LLH	*momi'ji* LHL
'autumn leaves'	**accentuation**	accented	unaccented	accented
kaede	**surface tone**	*kaede* LHH	*kae'de* LHL	*kaede* LLH
'maple'	**accentuation**	unaccented	accented	unaccented

In this report, following Kubozono's reasoning, we will attempt to present additional statistical results which can specify relevant factors to this change, and consider their implications for this tonal change in terms of variation theory.

2 Research design

2.1 Data collection

[Speakers and social variables] The speech data was collected in 2011 and 2012 from 20 college students (10 males and 10 females), who were raised in the 'Satsuma area' of Kagoshima Prefecture. Their parents were also native KJ speakers, except for one female speaker's parents. So it is likely that the speakers were raised in linguistic conditions where they could pick up the traditional prosodic features. The information about speakers' variables such as gender, hometown, and social network were obtained by employing a structured questionnaire.[4]

---

[4] This questionnaire was made up by adopting the basic structure of the questionnaire created by the Glasgow Media Project team led by Jane Stuart-Smith. We would like to express our deepest gratitude for their cooperation.

[Speech data] The results presented here are parts of a research project investigating prosodic innovations called Prosodic Subordination (PS) of multiple accentual phrases (MAP) (cf. Stuart-Smith & Ota 2014). Since Kubozono's results are based on the analysis of mono-stylistic productions (only in word list style), we attempted to collect more data in two other stylistic contexts. One is the task of reading sentences (RS), and the other is playing roles in scripted conversations (SC). Only eight target words with higher sonority were selected to obtain clear pictures of pitch movement. The target words consist of four place names and four general nouns as shown in Table 3. Each group has two 4-syllable words and two 3-syllable words. Both tasks were recorded in both SJ and KJ. In this paper, we will discuss the results of the latter variety only.

Table 3: Target words in two tasks (RS and SC) and their tones in SJ and KJ.

syllables	word	gloss	tone and accentuation of traditional KJ	tone and accentuation of SJ
		1st noun of MAP		
3	*Nagano*		LLH unaccented	HLL accented
	Ueno	(place names)	LHL accented	LHH unaccented
4	*Aomori*		LLLH unaccented	LHLL accented
	Miyajima		LLHL accented	LHHH unaccented
		2nd noun of MAP		
3	*nomiya*	'bar'	LLH unaccented	HLL accented
	nimono	'stewed food'	LHL accented	LHH unaccented
4	*omiyage*	'souvenir'	LLLH unaccented	LHHH unaccented
	nizakana	'fish cooked in broth'	LLHL accented	LHLL accented

(1) Miyajima-no/de   omiyage-o   takusan moratta
    Miyajima-GEN/LOC souvenirs-ACC a lot   receive-PST
    'I received a lot of souvenirs from/in Miyajima.'

The target phrases in both tasks were formed with the combination of two phonological words. There are three components for each phrase: the first word + the case marking particle (genitive –*no* or locative –*de*) + the second word as shown in (1). In RS, we obtained 16 MAP phrases in KJ. For the 3-syllable version, there are eight phrases (two for the first word by two for the particle by two for the second word), and the 4-syllable version also has eight phrases. For SC, only 8 MAP phrases with the genitive particle were recorded. In total 24 MAP phrases for each speaker were recorded. The recordings contained 48 tokens for

23 Tonal variation in Kagoshima Japanese and factors of language change

each speaker, since each MAP phrase comprises two target words, word 1 and word 2 as exemplified in (1).

2.2 Data coding

[Dependent variables] According to Kubozono (2007), two tonal changes show an asymmetry; the change from tone B to A, from the unaccented to the accented, goes farther than the other. This is also attested in our overall results. The number of tokens for the change from Tone B to A is 322 out of 480 (67.0%), whereas the the number in the other direction is 244 out of 480 tokens (50.8%), including the words *omiyage* and *nizakana*, whose traditional accentuations are identical to that of SJ. This fact led us to speculate that each change has its own orientation. Thus, we set up two different dependent variables in terms of accentuation: One is the change from the unaccented tone (Tone B) to the accented one (Tone A); the other is the opposite, i.e., from the accented one (Tone A) to the unaccented one (Tone B). We call the former 'accentual correspondence to the accented words of SJ (in short, 'correspondence to accented')' and the latter 'accentual correspondence to the unaccented words of SJ (in short, 'correspondence to unaccented')'. For the multivariate analysis (Logistic Regression), dependent variables were coded with one of the binary values, 1 or 0; when the target variant occurs, the token was coded as '1', otherwise '0' was given.

[Independent variables] Categorical variables include the number of syllables of target words (3 or 4), style (RS or SC), gender (male or female), and hometown (city or rural). Since they are all binary variables, the first category in the parentheses was set as a reference category in regression analyses. The case marking particles, *-no* and *–de*, mentioned in (1), were not included in multivariate analyses, because they had no effect on tonal changes in the preliminary analyses.

Quantitative variables are classified into three categories. The first indicates the possibility of taking in variation from other varieties, the other two are 'density of current social network' and 'dialect contact within current social network'. Speakers were asked to list five people who they usually hang out with. The density of social network was measured by checking the degree of mutual acquaintance of the five people: A score from 1 'don't know each other' to 3 'know very well' was given to each relationship. There were 10 combinations for each network, so the range of the score is from 10 to 30. Dialect contact was measured by examining the regional varieties which the five people usually used. If they use a variety other than KJ of the Satsuma area, one point was added. The total score for the five people ranged from 0 to 5.

The next category, the most significant in this report, is media content viewing habits. This is for investigating whether the broadcast media has any effect on language variation and change, which has been a long-standing controversy in sociolinguistics. This category is divided into two parts. One is watching habit of anime in the past. Twenty anime programs for children were listed and speakers were asked to give scores to each program on a five-point scale, 1 (never watched) to 5 (watched very often). Since anime is a single category of broadcasting content, we set the total score of all programs as the value of this variable. The other category is current TV programs viewing habits. Since dramas and anime for teenagers and young adults are generally broadcast only three months, it is difficult to define a specific program like *East Enders* for checking speakers' viewing habits. So we listed ten categories of TV programs, such as news, variety shows, anime, etc., and asked the speakers to score them on a five-point scale, 1 (never watched) to 5 (watched vary often). At first, we attempted to set all the categories as an individual variable, but there were correlations between them. Then, we created three new variables by Principal Component Analysis (the contribution ratio is 56.23%): 'watching information programs' (news, information shows, etc.), 'watching entertainment programs' (variety shows, local area shows, etc.), and 'watching pop culture programs' (anime, music shows, etc.).

The last variable is the one indicating speakers' competence of SJ. As Kubozono (2007: 324) refers to the bilingualism of native speakers of KJ as a bilingual listener, it would be presumable that the ongoing tonal change is deeply related to speakers' bilingual competence of using both KJ and SJ. Thus, we set up a variable, 'standard style score', which consists of the total number of successful tokens in the tasks of RS and SC in SJ. The range of the value is from 19 to 48 (its maximum).

In fact, there were other social variables included in the questionnaire, such as dialect contact beyond the Kagoshima area, and speakers' daily social practice. However, we decided to adopt the variables mentioned above by considering their theoretical relevance.

3 Statistical results

Due to the asymmetry of ongoing tonal changes, we carried out two Logistic Regressions with two dependent variables; one is for the variation 'accentual correspondence to the accented words of SJ', the other for 'accentual correspondence to the unaccented words of SJ'. The results are shown in Table 4. The statistical values for the categorical variables are indicated only for the parenthesized category. The most important value is Exp(B) indicating the probability of the target variant. When the value is greater than one, the variable has a positive effect on the occurrence of the target variant, while a value between zero and one means that the effect is negative.

For 'correspondence with accented words' (the left half of Table 4), the variables having a positive effect are only '4 syllables' and 'TV1: news and information shows'. The variables with negative significance (p < .05) are 'female', 'watching anime in childhood', and 'TV3: pop culture'. Only 'rural' (positive) and 'style' (negative) are marginally effective, and the other variables are not statistically significant. The variables concerning dialect contact do not have a clear effect on this variation.

The results of 'correspondence with unaccented words' (the right half of Table 4) obtained more positive variables. The variables with a positive effect are '4 syllables', 'scripted conversation style', 'density of social network', 'watching anime in childhood', 'TV3: pop culture programs', and 'standard style score'. The only negative effect variable is 'rural'. There are no marginal ones.

4 Discussion

A more elaborate theoretical discussion is needed, both in phonology and variation theory, to present a more conclusive and persuasive analysis. We will only suggest here a possible reasoning about the asymmetry of tonal change by considering the social meaning of this tonal variation (cf. Eckert 2008).

Why is there a difference in the progress of change between 'correspondence with accented' and 'correspondence with unaccented'? It may be ascribed to the difference of social meaning attached to each tone. It is possible that the accented tone sounds more like SJ, because the variable 'information programs' associated with the standard variety has a positive effect on the accented tone. Thus, we can assume that this tone indexes 'normative SJ'. Its normativeness would be also supported by the negative correlation with the variable 'pop culture programs' containing novelty or deviation from the standard social norm. On the other hand, considering the positive effect of the variable 'pop culture programs', the unaccented tone seems to be associated with 'youth culture' with a flavor of reduced normativeness. Another piece of supportive (but only speculative) evidence is the spread of the flat pitch (or unaccented) tone pattern for some traditionally accented words, such as *kareshi* (LHH) 'boyfriend' and *baiku* (LHH) 'motorbike', since the 1990s. This innovative tone pattern seems to have spread nationwide largely through mass media broadcasting, implying a certain indexical meaning

Table 4: Logistic Regression for accentual correspondence with SJ words. 'SN' refers to the social network in 'density of ... SN'.

Factors	Accentual correspondence to accented words of SJ[a]				Accentual correspondence to unaccented words of SJ[b]			
	B	Wald	Sig.	Exp(B)	B	Wald	Sig.	Exp(B)
gender (female)	−1.38	26.84	0.000	0.252	−0.16	0.37	0.541	0.856
hometown (rural)	0.52	3.03	0.082	1.680	−1.19	18.43	0.000	0.305
syllable (4)	1.19	29.18	0.000	3.292	1.52	50.77	0.000	4.557
style (SC)	−0.38	2.89	0.089	0.682	0.48	4.74	0.029	1.618
density of current SN	−0.02	0.37	0.545	0.985	0.09	10.99	0.001	1.088
density of contact within current SN	−0.04	0.10	0.754	0.960	0.09	0.50	0.478	1.089
watching anime during childhood	−0.03	5.31	0.021	0.971	0.04	10.49	0.001	1.038
TV1: information programs	0.39	9.93	0.002	1.472	−0.14	1.49	0.222	0.869
TV2: entertainment programs	0.18	1.77	0.183	1.193	−0.18	2.16	0.142	0.837
TV3: pop culture programs	−0.30	7.53	0.006	0.739	0.27	6.22	0.013	1.310
standard style score	−0.01	0.52	0.469	0.989	0.07	17.12	0.000	1.069
Constant	3.70	11.83	0.001	40.329	−7.38	47.41	0.000	0.001

[a] N = 480, df=1, Nagelkerke R Square: .240.
[b] N = 480, df=1, Nagelkerke R Square: .283.

associated with the youth culture of the Tokyo metropolitan area. Considering these facts, it is assumable that these two ongoing tonal changes in KJ have different orientations; the orientation towards the accented tone is de-dialectization, whereas the other towards the unaccented tone is de-standardization. The other factors with a positive/negative effect could be incorporated into this line of reasoning, although we do not discuss their theoretical significance here.

Finally, we make a brief comment on the variables of media content viewing habits. These variables should not be regarded as a direct stimulus which can cause a speaker's language to change. Rather, they seem to work not only as a linguistic model for exhibiting socially dominant or counter norms, but also as a circumstantial or cultural factor to provide language resources for, e.g., a speaker's styling as well as the input for children's language acquisition.

References

Eckert, Penelope. 2008. Variation and the indexical field. *Journal of Sociolinguistics* 12. 453–476.

Kubozono, Haruo. 2007. Tonal change in language contact: Evidence from Kagoshima Japanese. In Tomas Riad & Carlos Gussenhoven (eds.), *Tones and tunes. Volume 1: Typological studies in word and sentence prosody*, 323–351. Berlin: Mouton de Gruyter.

Stuart-Smith, J. & Ichiro Ota. 2014. Media models, 'the shelf', and stylistic variation in East and West. Rethinking the influence of the media on language variation. In Jannis K Androutsopoulos (ed.), *Mediatization and sociolinguistic change*, 127–170. Berlin: De Gruyter.

Name index

Abadía de Quant, Inés, 264
Abercrombie, David, 156
Adank, Patti, 246
Alber, Birgit, 322
Aldenderfer, Mark S., 230
Allbritten, Rachael, 176
Anders, Christina Ada, 78
Anderwald, Lieselotte, 225
Andres, Marie-Christine, 198
Androutsopoulos, Jannis, 246
Angkititrakul, Pongtep, 157
Archangeli, Diana, 314
Ash, Sharon, 84, 121, 158, 175–177, 182, 183, 188, 189, 313
Assmann, P. F., 313
Auer, Peter, 3, 16, 17, 23, 35, 36, 39, 40, 54, 57, 80, 114, 291, 300
Azuma, Shoji, 306

Babel, Molly, 246
Bailey, Guy, 27, 55
Baker, Adam, 314
Barbiers, Sjef, 42, 43
Barthes, Roland, 282, 295
Baur, Siegfried, 321
Becker, K., 313
Bekkering, Harold, 246
Bell, Allan, 39
Belletti, Adriana, 66
Bellmann, Günter, 101, 195, 196
Berns, J. B., 64
Berruto, Gaetano, 79

Berthele, Raphael, 78
Bertolotti, V., 264
Biber, Douglas, 82
Bielenstein, August Johann Gottfried, 77
Bivand, Robert, 183
Blake, Barry J, 278
Blashfield, Roger K., 230
Boberg, Charles, 80, 84, 121, 158, 175, 177, 182, 183, 188, 189, 313, 317
Boersma, Paul, 41
Bouchard, Chantal, 17
Bourdieu, Pierre, 276
Bright, Elizabeth, 189
Brockman, Irene M., 5, 216
Brun-Trigaud, Guylaine, 137, 143
Bucheli Berger, Claudia, 196–198, 208, 211
Budzhak-Jones, Svitlana, 24
Bybee, Joan L., 216, 225

Cacoullos, Rena, 23
Cano Aguilar, Rafael, 262, 277
Carignan, C., 314
Carpenter, Malinda, 245
Carver, Craig M, 175, 215
Catalán Menéndez-Pidal, Diego, 262, 277
Cattell, Raymond Bernard, 85
Chambers, J. K., 1, 23, 76, 124, 174, 227, 265, 276, 292, 335

Name index

Chelliah, Shobhana L., 268
Cheshire, Jenny, 35, 308
Childs, Becky, 268
Chomsky, Noam, 245
Christen, Helen, 78
Chumak-Horbatsch, Roma, 24
Ciccolone, Simone, 321
Clark, Wilma, 282, 295
Clopper, Cynthia, 83, 175, 176, 179
Coco, Alessandra, 21
Coll, M., 264
Çöltekin, Çağri, 4, 156, 158, 159
Corbett, Greville G, 263
Cornips, Leonie, 42, 43, 64, 65, 197
Corrigan, Karen P., 197
Costa, Patrício Soares, 43
Costaouec, Denis, 136, 139
Council of Local Authorities for International Relations [CLAIR], 307, 308
Coupland, Nikolas, 38
Coursen, Charlotte, 17
Cucurullo, Nella, 119
Čuka, Anica, 284, 285
Cummins, James, 16
Cysouw, Michael, 250

Danesi, Marcel, 16, 18, 21, 22
Davidson, Lisa, 323
De Caluwe, Johan, 35–37, 40
De Decker, P. M., 29, 313
de Reuse, Willem J., 268
De Schutter, Georges, 42, 43
De Sutter, Gert, 43, 48
De Vogelaer, Gunther, 36, 42, 43, 47
De Wulf, Chris, 42, 43
Delaere, Isabelle, 43, 48
Delarue, Steven, 38
Detges, Ulrich, 65

Devos, Magda, 42, 43
Dhillon, Inderjit S., 118
Di Franco, Giovanni, 50
Dossey, Ellen E., 246
Drager, Katie, 176

Echenique Elizondo, Maria Teresa, 262, 277
Eckert, Penelope, 308, 311, 395
Elspaß, Stephan, 252
Espinal, Maria Teresa, 67, 68
Evans, Betsy, 175
Evans, Bronwen, 176

Falc'hun, François, 138–140
Farrington, Charlie, 174
Fidell, Linda S., 82
Filipi, Goran, 283, 284, 288
Fitch, William Tecumseh Sherman, 245
Fleischer, Jürg, 212, 251
Flynn, Patrick J., 230
Foley, W., 20
Fontanella de Weinberg, Beatriz, 264
Fox, R. A., 313
Frey, Natascha, 198
Fridland, Valerie, 173, 174, 177–182
Fruehwald, Josef, 313
Fuchs, Susanne, 322
Fukushima, Chitsuko, 363, 365

Gabel, Heidi, 37, 40
Gao, Lili, 157
Garside, Roger, 227
Geeraerts, Dirk, 5, 43, 48, 49, 51, 83, 118, 173, 174, 183, 184
German, Gary, 136, 138
Getis, Arthur, 183, 184, 206
Ghyselen, Anne-Sophie, 36, 37, 39, 43

Name index

Giacomelli, Gabriella, 118, 123, 128, 216
Giannelli, Luciano, 123, 125
Giles, Howard, 39
Giovanardi, Claudio, 21
Girard, Dennis, 77
Glaser, Elvira, 196–198, 208, 212
Glück, Helmut, 99
Goebl, Hans, 5, 81, 139, 199, 215, 226, 230
Goeman, Ton, 42, 43
Gooskens, Charlotte, 175, 232
Goossens, Jan, 42, 43
Gordon, Matthew J., 374
Gries, Stefan Thomas, 49
Grieve, Jack, 5, 80, 83, 118, 173, 174, 178, 183, 184, 206, 225, 234
Grishakova, Marina, 282, 295
Grondelaers, Stefan, 36–38, 48, 49
Grosjean, François, 323
Gu, Chong, 315
Gualdo, Riccardo, 21
Guiter, Henri, 136
Gynan, Shaw Nicholas, 157

Haas, Walter, 210, 211
Haeseryn, Walter, 42
Hagoort, Peter, 246
Hansen, John HL, 157
Hauser, Marc D., 245
Hawkes, Terence, 294
Hay, Jennifer, 176
Heap, David, 264
Heemskerk, Josée S, 42
Heeringa, Wilbert, 35, 37, 41, 136, 226, 230
Henry, Alison, 197
Herk, Gerard van, 268
Hernández, Nuria, 227

Herrgen, Joachim, 101, 195
Hickey, Raymond, 3
Hinskens, Frans, 3, 16, 17, 23, 35–37, 41, 54, 57, 291, 300
Hirano, Keiko, 308, 309
Hondô, Hiroshi, 334
Horn, Laurence R., 68
Hotzenköcherle, Rudolf, 100, 104, 114, 196
Hudyma, Khrystyna, 22
Hueber, T., 314
Hundt, Markus, 78
Hyvönen, Saara, 82, 83

Iannozzi, Michael, 19
Ichii, Tokiko, 334
Inagaki, Shigeko, 346, 349
Inoue, Fumio, 334, 338, 339, 346
Iverson, Paul, 176

Jacewicz, E., 313
Jackson, Kenneth Hurlstone, 140
Jain, Anil K., 230
Jarvis, E. D., 245
Jekosch, Ute, 157
Jespersen, Otto, 65
Jutronić, Dunja, 291

Kambhamettu, C., 314
Kang, Yoonjung, 19
Kasai, Hisako, 334
Kasper, Simon, 212
Katz, W. F., 313
Kaufman, Terrence, 27
Kayne, Richard, 196
Kehrein, Roland, 41
Kendall, Tyler, 173, 174, 177–182
Kerswill, Paul, 3, 16, 17, 21, 23, 101, 106, 114, 291, 300

401

Name index

Kilgarriff, Adam, 235
Kleiner, Stefan, 1, 246
Kleiweg, Peter, 5, 215, 220, 226, 234
Klepsch, Alfred, 104, 106
Kobayashi, Takashi, 333
Koch, G. G., 42
Kochetov, Alexei, 19
Kokuritsu Kokugo Kenkyûjo (NLRI), 335, 336, 347
Kokuritsu Kokugo Kenkyûjo (NLRI), 333–335, 337, 348
Kretzschmar, Brendan A., 5, 216
Kretzschmar, William A., 5, 78, 174, 216, 374
Kristiansen, Gitte, 78
Kristiansen, Tore, 36, 38
Kroch, Anthony, 197
Kubozono, Haruo, 389–391, 393, 394
Kulušić, Sven, 284
Kumagai, Yasuo, 337, 354–357
Kunath, Stephen A, 158, 160
König, Werner, 83, 101, 104

Labov, William, 27, 28, 39, 78, 84, 121, 158, 175–177, 182, 183, 188, 189, 263, 308, 313
Lakoff, George, 78
Lameli, Alfred, 255
Landis, J. R., 42
Language Factory, 22
Lanthaler, Franz, 322
Lapesa, Rafael, 262, 277
Lara, Víctor, 262, 266, 268
Larmouth, Donald, 77
Lasch, Alexander, 78
Lauttamus, Timo, 236
Lebart, L., 49
Lee, Jay, 174, 374
Leino, Antti, 82, 83

Leinonen, Therese Nanette, 83
Lenz, Alexandra N., 3, 41, 80, 212
Leser, Stephanie, 252
Le Dû, Jean, 135, 136
Le Roux, Pierre, 138
Li, M., 314
Liberman, M., 314
Lijffijt, Jefrey, 236
Llop, Ares, 68, 69
Lončar, Nina, 284, 285
Loporcaro, Michele, 117
Lotman, Juri, 6, 282, 295, 299
Löffler, Heinrich, 196
Lötscher, Andreas, 198

Macaulay, Ronald K. S., 276
Mallinson, Christine, 268
Manning, Christopher D, 215, 216
Markham, Duncan, 245
Marradi, Alberto, 50
Martinet, André, 145
Mase, Yoshio, 379
Mathussek, Andrea, 4, 100, 107–110, 112, 113
Mayer, Benedikt, 246
Mayer, Thomas, 250
McDermott, Richard A, 312
Menéndez Pidal, Ramón, 262, 277
Medda, Roberta, 321
Meltzoff, Andrew, 245
Meyerhoff, Miriam, 16, 25, 28
Mielke, Jeff, 314
Milroy, Lesley, 308
Mioni, Alberto, 321
Mirkin, B. G., 49
Moles, Abraham A., 295
Mondéjar, Jose, 262, 277
Montemagni, Simonetta, 118, 122, 216, 218

Name index

Montgomery, Chris, 199
Möller, Robert, 252
Moore, M. Keith, 245
Moran, P. A. P., 183
Moseley, Chris, 135
Munske, Horst Haider, 4, 100
Murty, M. Narasimha, 230
Myers-Scotton, Carol, 6

Nagy, Naomi, 16, 19, 25, 28
Nerbonne, John, 2, 4, 5, 77, 81, 83, 107, 109, 117–121, 136, 156, 158–160, 170, 174, 199, 215, 217, 220, 226, 230, 232, 234–236
Neuhauser, Sara, 246
Niedzielski, Nancy, 5, 67, 175, 176
Nycz, J. R., 313, 314
Nádasdy, Ádám, 164, 169
Nübling, Eduard, 85

Ogura, Mieko, 106
Ohashi, Katsuo, 365
Onishi, Takuichiro, 364, 380, 386
Ord, J. Keith, 183, 184, 206
Ota, Ichiro, 392

Paolillo, John C., 83
Pellegrini, Giovanni Battista, 123, 125
Penny, R., 262, 277
Petkov, C. I., 245
Petrova, Olga, 165
Pickl, Simon, 83, 84, 91, 117
Pisoni, David, 175, 176, 179
Plevoets, Koen, 38, 43, 48, 49
Plichta, Bartek, 176, 313
Poggi Salani, Teresa, 128
Poletto, Cecilia, 64, 65
Powesland, Peter Francis, 39
Preston, Dennis, 67, 78, 175, 176

Prinz, Wolfgang, 245
Prokić, Jelena, 4, 81, 156, 158, 159
Pröll, Simon, 83, 84, 117
Purschke, Christoph, 6, 246
Pustka, Elissa, 78

Recasens, Daniel, 326
Reed, Carroll E., 189
Reed, David W., 189
Reichel, Sibylle, 107
Richter, Matthias, 254
Riemann, Andreas, 246
Rifkin, Benjamin, 157
Rigau, Gemma, 65, 70
Roberts, Ian G., 65, 67
Rosch, Eleanor, 78
Rosenfelder, Ingrid, 313
Rumpf, Jonas, 234
Ryan, Ellen Bouchard, 156
Ryckeboer, Hugo, 47
Rys, Kathy, 40

Salmenkivi, Marko, 82
Samuel, Arthur G., 176, 177
Sanada, Shinji, 379–381, 385
Sanchís Guarner, M., 264
Sanders, Nathan C., 236
Satô, Ryôichi, 333, 349
Sayers, Dave, 9
Schaden, Stefan, 157
Scherrer, Yves, 235
Schilling-Estes, Natalie, 39, 265, 274
Schmidt, Jürgen Erich, 101, 195
Schmidt, Tanja, 41
Schneider, Edgar W., 16, 117
Schwegler, Armin, 65
Schwenter, Scott, 66
Schütze, Hinrich, 215, 216
Seara, I. C., 276

Name index

Sebregts, Koen, 167
Segerup, My, 246
Séguy, Jean, 117, 136, 215
Seiler, Guido, 197, 203
Shackleton, Robert, 81–83, 118
Sibata, Takesi, 357
Sibler, Pius, 206, 207
Siedle, Christine, 230
Siegel, Jeff, 246
Škevin, Ivana, 282, 283, 285, 291, 292
Smith, Nicholas, 227
Snyder, William, 312
Soete, Nel, 55
Solliec, Tanguy, 136
Speelman, Dirk, 5, 48, 49, 83, 118, 173, 174, 183, 184
Spettl, Aaron, 83, 117
Spiekermann, Helmut, 36
Spruit, Marco René, 5
Stellmacher, Dieter, 41
Stoeckle, Philipp, 199
Stone, Maureen, 314, 323
Story, Brad H., 314
Strand, Elizabeth A., 176
Strange, Winifred, 178
Strassel, S., 313
Struk, Danylo, 20–22
Stuart-Smith, J., 392
Sumner, Megan, 176, 177
Szmrecsanyi, Benedikt, 82, 174, 216, 225–227, 229–232, 239

Tabachnick, Barbara G, 82
Taeldeman, Johan, 35, 38, 40, 42, 43, 51
Tagliamonte, Sali, 27, 234
Takada, Makoto, 334
Tanaka, Akio, 343
Thieberger, Nick, 268

Thomas, Erik R., 178
Thomason, Sarah Grey, 27
Thompson, Ann, 119, 158, 216–218
Thorburn, Jennifer, 29
Toda, Martine, 322
Tokugawa, Munemasa, 333
Tomasello, Michael, 225, 245
Travis, Catherine, 23
Trevelyan, G. D, 276
Trudgill, Peter, 1, 3, 4, 16, 21, 23, 64, 70, 76, 124, 174, 227, 233, 265, 276, 292, 306, 335, 374
Tse, Holman, 28

Upton, Clive, 119, 158, 216–218
Užgiris, Ina Čepėnaitė, 245, 248

van Bezooijen, Renée, 175
Van de Velde, Hans, 51
van den Doel, Rias, 156, 157, 162, 166–170
Van Herk, Gerard, 29
van Hout, Roeland, 36–38
Van Keymeulen, Jacques, 37
van Marle, Jaap, 64
Vandekerckhove, Reinhild, 35–38
Vandenberghe, Roxanne, 42, 43
Vandenbussche, Wim, 40
Verleyen, Geert, 42, 43

Walker, Douglas C, 164, 169
Walker, James A, 27
Waltereit, Richard, 65
Wang, W. S.-Y., 106
Waniek-Klimczak, Ewa, 156
Warren, P., 176
Weenink, David, 41
Weinberger, Steven H, 158, 160
Wells, John C, 156

Wenger, Etienne, 312
Wieling, Martijn, 4, 81, 83, 117–122, 158–160, 170, 215–218, 234
Wiersma, Wybo, 235, 236
Wiesinger, Peter, 76, 321
Wikipedia, 21
Willemyns, Roland, 35, 36, 38, 40
Wmffre, Iwan, 145
Wolfram, Walter, 265, 274
Wolk, Christoph, 6, 82, 226, 229, 234, 237
Wong, A. W., 313
Woolhiser, Curt, 117
Worner, K., 41
Wright, Susan, 101, 106, 114
Wälchli, Bernhard, 225

Yanagita, Kunio, 377
Yonekawa, Akihiko, 311
Yuan, J., 314

Zadeh, Lotfi A., 77
Zimmerer, Peter, 246
Zonneveld, Wim, 42

Language index

Breton, 135–154

Catalan, 63–72

Chinese, 20n3, 20, 29, 157
    Cantonese, 15, 17, 20–22, 24

Croatian, 281–305

Dutch, 35, 37, 38, 41, 42n9, 43–45, 48, 50, 51, 53–56, 118, 155–158, 161, 162, 164, 166–169
    Flemish, 37n1, 35–63, 169, 248, 251, 257

English
    American English, 164, 166–168, 173–194
    British English, 166–168, 225–240

Faetar, 15, 19, 20, 24, 25, 27

French, 161–164

German, 75–116
    Alemannic, 211, 248, 251
    Hessian, 248, 250, 252, 253, 256
    Low German, 248, 250, 251, 257
    Swiss German, 198, 210
    Tyrolean, 320–330
    Upper German, 248, 258

Hungarian, 27, 155, 158, 161, 162, 164–166, 170

Italian, 116–135

Tuscan, 118, 119, 122, 123, 125–130, 215, 216, 219, 221

Tyrolean, 320–330

Venetian, 282, 283n2, 283, 292, 299

Japanese, 305–313, 333–398

Korean, 15, 19, 20, 24, 27

Spanish, 261–281

Yiddish
    Eastern Yiddish, 248, 254, 255
    Western Yiddish, 254

Subject index

19th century, 254–255

accent classification, 157
accent perception, 156, 166
accent transcription, 158
accentuation pattern, 390, 391
age differences, 234, 271–274
aggregated Levenshtein distance, 160
alignment, 250
animation, 350, 352n14, 353, 355n15
ANOVA, 181, 182
apparent-time changes, 363, 364
articulatory phonetics, 327
Atlas of North American English, 177, 189
audiovisual stimuli, 264

bilingualism, 321, 322, 391, 394
bipartite spectral graph partitioning, 80–81
bootstrap clustering, 77, 81
broadcasting media, 394, 395
buffer, 353
bundle of isoglosses, 124, 131

California vowel shift, 188
category, 76–77
changes in progress, 368
characteristic accent feature, 157–158, 168–170
chi-squared, 271, 274
cluster analysis, 49, 80, 81, 85, 91, 255

clustering, 217–219
code-switching, 305–307, 309, 311, 312
community of practice, 311, 312
comparative variationist linguistics, 23
completed changes, 366
concept-lexicalization pair, 119, 131
condensation, 82
conservative vs. innovative dialect areas, 210–211
continuum, 76, 81
convergence, 285, 291, 293, 302, 303
core linguistic, 245
corpus-based dialectometry, 226–239
correlation, 232, 233, 236n7, 237
correspondence analysis, 48, 49
cross-over points, 180
cue validity, 79

data elicitation, 264
de-dialectization, 397
de-standardization, 397
Delaunay triangulation, 354
demotisation, 38
density, 309
dental fricative, 162, 164
destandardisation, 38
diachrony, 247
diaglossia, 36
dialect area, 3, 80–82, 86, 91, 135
dialect areas, 152
dialect awareness, 67

Subject index

dialect border, 125
dialect classification, 91, 92
dialect clustering, 118, 120, 125–127, 129, 132
dialect continuum, 254
dialect divergence, 15
dialect geography, 99
dialect levelling, 6, 7, 286, 291, 295, 302, 303
dialect loss, 36
dialect perception, 246
dialect radiation theory, 377
dialect syntax, 196, 212
dialect type, 77–91
dialectal border, 364
dialectometry, 81, 83, 100–106, 135–152, 156, 173–175, 178, 189, 226, 230, 239
diffusion, 366, 367
diffusion route, 334, 339, 340, 346, 351
diglossia, 36
distance matrix, 355
distinctiveness, 120–121, 123, 125, 128, 131, 158–159, 218
divergence, 294, 302, 303
dynamism, 197, 210, 211

edit distance, 135–152, 160
educational level differences, 271, 275
emic, 78, 93
emphatic negation, 65–68
emphatic particles, 69
English teacher, 306–311
ethnic orientation, 18, 27
etic, 78, 93

factor analysis, 77–93
feature validity, 79, 85
fiction, 254

fictional language, 247
flap, 309, 310
foreign accent, 156–161
formation process of Japanese dialects (FPJD), 378
forms of address, 279
fortis/lenis neutralization, 167
Freiburg Corpus of English Dialects, 227
fricatives, 326, 327
fundamental dialectological postulate, 234, 235
fuzzy clustering, 80
fuzzy set, 77–78

Gabmap, 107–113, 160
gender differences, 234
generalized additive model, 234
geographic information system (GIS), 174, 199, 206, 338
geographical information systems (GIS), 365, 374
geolinguistics, 363
georeferencing, 374
geospatial autocorrelation, 174, 178–184, 189
Getis-Ord Gi, 183–188, 190n3, 206n16, 206, 207
granularity of dialectal areas, 125, 128, 131
gravity model, 274
group phraseology, 311

heritage language, 15–30
hierarchical bipartite spectral graph partitioning, 118, 119, 217
hierarchical clustering, 230, 231, 238
hot spot analysis, 206, 208n19

I-language, 246

Subject index

image database, 336
importance, 121, 123, 128, 130, 218
indexical meaning, 395
informant's comment, 347–349
integrated research and teaching, 28, 30
interactive speaker-sample map, 30
internet survey, 249
interpersonal variation, 197
intrasystemic qualitative variation, 301
intrasystemic quantitative variation, 295, 297, 302
isogloss, 77, 99, 124, 125, 127, 128, 131

Jespersen's Cycle, 65

k-means clustering, 120, 217
koinéization, 23

language acquisition, 245
language change, 196, 197, 212
language contact, 16, 27, 305–307, 311
language perception, 251
lay concepts, 251
layer, 77–82
layer model, 79
leveling, 23
Levenshtein distance, 135–152
lexical area, 121, 128, 130, 131
lexical change, 118, 128, 129, 132
lexical features, 117–119, 123–125, 127–129, 131
lexical innovation, 368
lexical variable, 84
lexical variation, 84, 118, 131, 365, 367, 368
lexicon, 83
lexis, 246
linear regression, 314, 315

linguistic accommodation, 291, 295, 303
linguistic change, 307
linguistic geography, 135–152
linguistic maps, 364, 365, 367, 374
localized system, 373
logistic regression, 271, 274, 393, 394, 396

mass media broadcasting, 395
Matlab, 314n1
matrix language frame model, 246
metacorpus, 67
micro-syntax, 63, 65
microvariation, 196
minimiser, 65
morphological variable, 83
morphological variation, 83, 84, 367
morphology, 83, 85, 246
multi-dimensional scaling, 81
multiple answers, 333, 336, 346, 347, 349
multiple regression, 309, 310
multiplexity, 309

n-grams, 236n7, 236, 237, 239
natural stimuli, 246
nested isoglosses, 127, 128, 131
network representation, 354–356
network structure, 308
new dialect, 16–18
noisy clustering, 77, 81
non-native speakers of English, 309

optionality in grammar, 197
orality, 251

participant observation, 67
parts-of-speech, 236, 239

Subject index

past-tense negative verb suffix, 380–384, 386
Pearson correlation, 310
perceptual dialectology, 175
permutation, 236, 237, 239
person disagreement, 279
phonetic variable, 83
phonetic variation, 84, 135–152
phonetics, 83, 85
phonology, 246
pop culture program, 394, 395
primary modeling system, 299
principal components analysis, 82, 182, 184, 314
pronoun doubling, 251
pronunciation error hierarchy, 162
pronunciation teaching, 164, 169
prototype theory, 78, 93

qualitative analysis, 135–152
qualitative methodology, 278
quantitative analysis, 135–152
quantitative methodology, 268, 278
quantitative methods, 156, 166

rapid change, 382
reading sentence, 392
real-time, 378, 379, 382, 386
real-time changes, 363
real-time comparison of dialectal distributions, 380
real-time interval comparison, 387
real-time interval research, 364
real-time research, 378
regiolect, 3
regression modeling, 234
regressive assimilation, 165
representativeness, 119–121, 123, 125, 128, 131, 158–159, 218

road network, 340n8, 340, 346n9, 356
RuG/L04, 240

s-retraction, 322, 327
saliency, 290–292, 302, 303
Satzklammer, 254
schema theory, 78
scripted conversation, 392, 395
secondary modeling system, 281, 299
segment, 158
self-assessment, 250
semiological sign, 282, 296
semiosis, 296
semiosphere, 282, 299
semiotic space, 283, 285, 286, 290, 294–296, 299, 300, 302, 303
semiotic triangle, 296
shibboleths, 156
Short-a, 313
similarity, 352–355
singular value decomposition, 120
smoothing-spline ANOVA, 315
social meaning, 395
social network, 305–311
sociolinguistic interview, 28
sociophonetics, 322, 327
Southern vowel shift, 177, 188
spatial autocorrelation, 206
spatial distance matrix, 183
spatial pattern, 82
spatial weighting function, 183
Speech Accent Archive, 158
speech atlas, 100–113
speech errors, 169
standard form, 333, 338–342, 352
standard system, 373
standardisation, 279
standardization, 368, 373
standstills, 384

Subject index

style-shifting, 39
superimposing maps, 365, 374
synchrony, 247
syntactic hierarchy, 266, 277, 278
syntactic theory, 197
syntactic variation, 196, 204, 206, 208, 210, 211
syntax, 246

tensing, 315–317
time-aligned transcription and integrated coding, 28, 30
tonal change, 390, 391, 393, 394
transcription, 99–113
transition area, 79
transportation, 340, 343, 351, 357
tussentaal, 37
typicality, 78

ultrasound, 314–315, 317
ultrasound tongue imaging, 323
ultraspeech, 314
usage data, 226, 240

variability, 247
variation index, 203–211
variationist sociolinguistics, 24, 25n5, 27
variety, 79–89
verb doubling, 198
vowel reduction, 163
VRT-Dutch, 51, 53

word frequency, 216

www.ingramcontent.com/pod-product-compliance
Lightning Source LLC
Chambersburg PA
CBHW060417300426
44111CB00018B/2883